Instructional-Design Theories and Models
Volume III

Instructional-Design Theories and Models
Volume III
Building a Common Knowledge Base

Edited by

Charles M. Reigeluth
Alison A. Carr-Chellman

Routledge
Taylor & Francis Group
2009

TAYLOR AND FRANCIS, PUBLISHERS
New York and London

First published 2009
by Routledge
270 Madison Ave, New York, NY 10016

Simultaneously published in the UK
by Routledge
2 Park Square, Milton Park, Abingdon, Oxon OX14 4RN

Routledge is an imprint of the Taylor & Francis Group, an informa business

© 2009 Taylor & Francis

Typeset in Minion by EvS Communication Networx, Inc.
Printed and bound in the United States of America on acid-free paper by Sheridan Books, Inc.

Library of Congress Cataloging in Publication Data

Reigeluth, Charles M.
Instructional-design theories and models / Charles M. Reigeluth.
p. cm.
Includes bibliographies and indexes.
1. Lesson planning. 2. Curriculum planning. 3. Learning, Psychology of. I. Charles M. Reigeluth.
II. Title: Instructional-Deisgn theories and models.
LB1025.2 .I646 1983
371.3 19
83014185

ISBN 10: 0-8058-6456-3 (hbk)
ISBN 10: 1-4106-1884-6 (ebk)

ISBN 13: 978-0-8058-6456-4 (hbk)
ISBN 13: 978-1-4106-1884-9 (ebk)

Dedication

This book is dedicated to future generations of learners, to the teachers who will inspire and guide them, to the instructional designers who will provide exciting and effective learning resources for them, and to the instructional theorists who will inspire and guide the teachers and instructional designers.

— CMR & ACC

This book is also dedicated to my mentor, M. David Merrill, whose brilliant thinking, open mind, and intellectual curiosity have inspired me greatly.

— CMR

This book is also dedicated to my mentor, Charles Morgan Reigeluth, who has given me the intellectual capacities to follow him, and mostly to keep up. I am grateful for his continuing to open doors for me and continuing to invite me to work with him. It is among my greatest intellectual joys.

— ACC

Contents

List of Figures and Tables

Figures

Tables

Preface

How to help people learn better. That is what instructional theory is all about. It describes a variety of methods of instruction (different ways of facilitating human learning and development) and when to use—and not use—each of those methods.

Volume I of *Instructional-Design Theories and Models* (1983) provides a "snapshot in time" of the status of instructional theory in the early 1980s. Its main purpose was to raise awareness of instructional theories. Volume II (1999) provides a concise summary of a broad sampling of work in the late 1990s on a new paradigm of instructional theories for the Information Age. Its main purpose was to raise awareness of the diversity of theories that provide a customized or learner-centered learning experience in all different domains of human learning and development. It also raised awareness of the importance of values in instructional theory.

However, after the appearance of Volume II, we became increasingly concerned about the extent to which instructional theorists seemed to be working in relative isolation from each other, building their own view of instruction with little regard to building on what knowledge already exists and what terminology has already been used for constructs they also describe. We recognized that every area of knowledge goes through an initial developmental phase in which these differences predominate. We also saw that, as an area of knowledge matures, it enters a second phase of development in which work focuses more on contributing to a common knowledge base with a consistent terminology. While it would be a mistake to push an area of knowledge into phase 2 too soon, we believe that instructional theory is now ready to begin such a transition.

Therefore, the purpose of this Volume III is to take some early steps in building a common knowledge base about instruction with a common use of terms. The primary audience for this volume, like that of the previous two volumes, is instructional theorists, researchers, and graduate students. An additional audience is instructional designers, teachers, and trainers who are interested in guidance about how to design instruction of high quality.

Unit 1 offers some organizational schemes for understanding and developing a common knowledge base about instruction. We strongly urge you to read the four chapters in this unit before reading any of the theories that follow. Unit 2 offers a chapter on each of five major *approaches* to instruction: the direct-instruction, discussion, experiential, problem-based, and simulation approaches. Each of these chapters synthesizes the current knowledge about that approach as a step toward building a common knowledge base. Unit 3 offers a chapter on instruction for each of four major *outcomes* of instruction: skill development, understanding, affective development, and integrated learning outcomes. Each of these chapters also synthesizes the current knowledge about that kind of instruction. Finally, Unit 4 offers ideas that may prove useful for building a common knowledge base about instruction.

Because this volume contains many ideas that may be difficult for all but the most experienced to digest, we have tried to make it easier for the reader by preparing the same kind of unconventional **foreword** for each chapter as was done for Volume II. Each chapter foreword outlines the major ideas presented in the chapter. This offers something akin to a hypertext capability for you to get a quick overview of a chapter and then flip to parts of it that particularly interest you. It can also serve preview and review functions and make it easier to compare different theories. Furthermore, we have inserted **editors' notes** in most chapters to help you relate elements in a chapter to fundamental ideas presented in other chapters. Finally, each unit has a foreword that introduces the chapters in that unit.

It is our sincere hope that this book will help to move instructional theory to the next stage of development—creating a truly common knowledge base with a consistent terminology. We hope it will help instructional theorists and researchers to contribute to the growing knowledge base about instruction in a way that acknowledges and builds on prior work, and that it will help instructional designers and graduate students to understand and utilize the full range of accumulated knowledge about how to help people learn.

— CMR & ACC

Unit 1
Frameworks for Understanding Instructional Theory

Unit Foreword

This unit lays the groundwork for a shared language and a set of common understandings in instructional theory. This unit foreword provides brief descriptions of the primary ideas in each of the chapters in this unit, which offer some organizational schemes for understanding and developing a common knowledge base about instruction. We strongly recommend reading this unit before reading any of the other chapters in this book.

In chapter 1 we (Reigeluth & Carr-Chellman) look at the constructs and terminology used to describe and understand instructional theory. First, we define instruction as anything that is done purposely to facilitate learning. Based on this definition and understanding of the entire field of instructional design, we make the case for the need for a common knowledge base and then relate design theory, instructional design theory, student-assessment design theory, curriculum design theory, learning theory, and the learning sciences to instruction. We identify several aspects of instructional design theory, including event, analysis, planning, building, implementation, and evaluation design theory within instructional design theory. These aspects are then related to the concept of layers of design (Gibbons & Rogers, chapter 14). We identify the need for a significantly new paradigm for future change efforts and describe the need for learner-centeredness in that paradigm. We share the results of a small Delphi study to help build consensus on common terms, which lays a foundation for a common language in our field.

Chapter 2 takes up the issue of what we mean by instruction itself (as opposed to instructional theory, which we deal with in chapter 1). Here Reigeluth and Keller take up the issues associated with major constructs that make up instructional theories. They settle on instructional situations, methods, approaches, components, and content sequencing as the categories of constructs concerned with instruction. Built on an analogy to rules of English grammar, these constructs are linked and designers are advised to carefully consider the relationships among the categories.

In chapter 3 Merrill discusses the principles of good instruction that may be common to all instruction. Calling these "First Principles," Merrill lays out the qualifications for inclusion in this list, along with the principles in brief and in more detail. The principles include the demonstration principle, application principle, task-centered principle, activation principle, and integration principle. The chapter takes up the difficult task of elaborating on these principles and relating them to one another to create a defensible set of principles that Merrill asserts will create effective and efficient instruction.

Chapter 4 (Reigeluth & Carr-Chellman) focuses on the situational principles of instruction—ones that vary from one situation to another. This chapter describes what situational principles are and links them to the notion of universal principles through an analogy of the universe and galaxies. In an effort to increase precision in our language and knowledge base, we elaborate on kinds, parts, and criteria as ways to make methods more precise. Principles as heuristics, or rules of thumb, are particularly important for precise descriptions of methods. A review of learning taxonomies leads us to a description of the instructional theories we have included in units 2 and 3.

—CMR & ACC

1
Understanding Instructional Theory

CHARLES M. REIGELUTH
Indiana University

ALISON A. CARR-CHELLMAN
Pennsylvania State University

Charles M. Reigeluth received a BA in economics from Harvard University. He was a high school teacher for three years before earning his doctorate in instructional psychology at Brigham Young University. He has been a professor in the Instructional Systems Technology Department at Indiana University's School of Education in Bloomington since 1988, and served as chairman of the department from 1990 to 1992. His major area for service, teaching, and research is the process for facilitating district-wide paradigm change in public school systems. His major research goal is to advance knowledge to help school districts successfully navigate transformation to the learner-centered paradigm of education. He has published nine books and over 120 journal articles and chapters. Two of his books received an "outstanding book of the year" award from the Association for Educational Communications and Technology (AECT). He also received AECT's Distinguished Service Award and Brigham Young University's Distinguished Alumnus Award.

Alison A. Carr-Chellman is a professor of instructional systems at Pennsylvania State University in the Department of Learning and Performance Systems. She received a B.S. and an M.S. from Syracuse University. She taught elementary school, community education, and worked as an interactional designer for McDonnell Douglas before returning to Indiana University to earn her doctorate. She is the author of more than 100 publications including two books, many book chapters, and a wide variety of refereed and nonrefereed journal articles. Her research interests are diffusion of innovations, systemic school change, e-learning, systems theory, and design theory.

EDITORS' FOREWORD

Vision

- *To build a common knowledge base and a common language about instruction*

Definition of Instruction

- *Instruction is anything that is done purposely to facilitate learning.*

The Nature of Theories Related to Instruction

- *Design theory is goal oriented and normative.*
- *Instructional design theory is a set of design theories that pertain to various aspects of instruction and include:*
  1. *Instructional-event design theory (DT)*
  2. *Instructional-analysis DT*
  3. *Instructional-planning DT*
  4. *Instructional-building DT*
  5. *Instructional-implementation DT*
  6. *Instructional-evaluation DT*
- *Related theories include:*
  1. *Student-assessment design theory*
  2. *Curriculum design theory*
  3. *Learning theory*
  4. *Learning sciences*
- *Interrelationships among all these kinds of theories are powerful, and it is often beneficial to integrate them.*
- *Instructional design theories and layers of design*
  1. *Content layer*
  2. *Strategy layer*
  3. *Message layer*
  4. *Control layer*
  5. *Representation layer*
  6. *Media logic layer*
  7. *Data management layer*

The Role of Instructional Theory in Educational Reform

- *Why a new paradigm of education is needed and possible*
- *Relation to paradigm change in education*
- *Relation to Learner-Centered Instruction*
- *Learner-centered psychological principles*
- *The science of learning*
- *New paradigm of instructional theory (volume 2)*
- *Cognitive flexibility theory, personalized learning, brain-based learning, and differentiated instruction*

The Nature of Instructional Theories: Constructs and Terms

- *Results of a Delphi study*
- *Recommended constructs and terms*
  1. *Instructional method*
     1.1. *Scope (micro-meso-macro)*
     1.2. *Generality (universal-local)*
     1.3. *Precision (imprecise-precise) based on parts, kinds, or criteria*
     1.4. *Power (low-high)*
     1.5. *Consistency (low-high)*
  2. *Instructional situation*
     2.1. *Values*
        2.1.1. *About learning goals*
        2.1.2. *About priorities (effectiveness, efficiency, appeal)*
        2.1.3. *About methods*
        2.1.4. *About power (learner, teacher, institution)*
     2.2. *Conditions*
        2.2.1. *Content*
        2.2.2. *Learner*
        2.2.3. *Learning environment*
        2.2.4. *Instructional development constraints*

—CMR & ACC

UNDERSTANDING INSTRUCTIONAL THEORY

Instructional theory may sound, at first, like a dense and difficult topic, but it is easier to understand than you might think. Furthermore, this knowledge is central to helping you improve the quality of your teaching and training. Taking the time to understand the nature of instructional theory will help you to understand individual instructional theories and even help you make contributions to this growing knowledge base. Therefore, an understanding of the nature of instructional theory is important to both your growth and the growth of our field.

Vague and inconsistent language is impeding such growth. Different theorists use the same term to refer to different things and different terms to refer to the same things. This is confusing for all of us, from beginning graduate students to expert designers and researchers. When a discipline is young, it is natural for there to be such inconsistent language. We propose that instructional theory has now reached a level of development where a common knowledge base with a consistent terminology would greatly facilitate the future development of knowledge in this important area.

This chapter begins by defining *instruction*. We then discuss the need for building a common knowledge base about instruction. We describe several different kinds of theories related to instruction and contrast them with other related kinds of theories, such as student-assessment theories, curriculum theories, and learning theories. Then we discuss Gibbons and Rogers's concept of "layers of design" (see chapter 14) and their implications for instructional theory. Next, we turn our attention to the role of instructional theory in educational reform, and specifically discuss the relationship of learner-centered instruction to this book. Finally, we offer particular constructs and terms for a common knowledge base about instruction. These terms may be useful as a foundation upon which instructional theorists and researchers can build, and they should help you, whether a practitioner, a researcher, or a graduate student, to understand the knowledge available to you about fostering learning more effectively.

A Definition of Instruction

A distinction has been made in the literature recently between "instruction" and "construction," with the implication that instruction is necessarily done *to* learners (i.e., learners are passive), whereas construction is done *by* learners (i.e., learners are active). However, a principal tenet of constructivism is that people can only learn by constructing their own knowledge—that learning requires active manipulation of the material to be learned and cannot occur passively. Our concern is with how to help learners learn, which means identifying ways to help learners construct knowledge. Therefore, if instruction is to foster any learning at all, it must foster construction. Instruction is not instruction if it does not foster construction. Furthermore, if construction is what the *learner* does, then we need a different term for what a *teacher* (or other agent) does to foster construction, and "instruction" has commonly been used more than any other term to convey that meaning. Therefore, we define *instruction* as *anything that is done purposely to facilitate learning*. It includes constructivist methods and self-instruction, as well as more traditional views of instruction, such as lecture and direct instruction.

The Need

Volume 2 of *Instructional-Design Theories and Models* (Reigeluth, 1999) was a small sample of the wide variety of information-age instructional-design theories that had been created by 1998. That book made it evident that many instructional theories were constructed with little regard for prior theories. Until theorists begin to build upon each other's contributions, the field will remain in its infancy. The main purpose of this volume, then, is to help instructional theorists and researchers to build a common knowledge base about instruction.

The Nature of Theories Related to Instruction

To build (or to understand) a common knowledge base about instruction, it is helpful to understand the nature of such a knowledge base. However, there are many important things to know about instruction, including what an instructional product itself should be like, the process by which it should be designed and built, how it should be implemented, how it should be evaluated, how its effects (e.g., learning) should be assessed, what content should be instructed, how people learn, and the interrelationships among all these kinds of knowledge about instruction. It is also helpful to distinguish between design theory and descriptive theory. Each of these is discussed next.

Design Theory

Design theory is different from descriptive theory in that it is goal oriented and normative—it identifies good methods for accomplishing goals—whereas descriptive theory describes cause–effect relationships, which are usually probabilistic (meaning that the cause does not always result in the effect), especially in the social sciences. Design theory is aimed at facilitating generative outcomes; that is, it assists in the *creation* of something, while descriptive theory seeks to describe what already exists. We very much agree with Nelson and Stolterman's (2003) notions of design expertise. They recognize that there are different fields of design expertise, such as instructional design or engineering or architecture. But they also indicate that all designers share some similar field experiences:

> It is even more important to emphasize that every informally recognized designer has a similar field of expertise. It goes without saying that every designer needs knowledge and skills concerning materials, tools, methods, languages, traditions, styles, etc., in his or her specific field. (p. 25)

Their book, *The Design Way*, is not about the particular knowledge and skills, but is indeed about those areas that are relevant for all designers, including instructional designers.

Some people do not like the term *theory* for such goal-oriented or instrumental knowledge. Some of the terms that they prefer include: *method, model, technology, technique, strategy, guidance,* and *heuristic*. However, none of these terms captures the full scope of this kind of knowledge, which includes not only methods (or models, techniques, strategies, and heuristics), but also when and when not to use each method. We have found no other term that fits as well as *design theory* for capturing methods *and* when to use them. Second, these two types of knowledge (descriptive and instrumental) are widely recognized as the two major kinds (e.g., the famous distinction by Simon, 1996, between the natural sciences and the sciences of the artificial), and hence are "coordinate" (subordinate to, or kinds of, the same concept—theory). Third, the term *theory* has been used for decades to characterize the instrumental knowledge base in several fields, and in instruction its use goes back at least to Bruner (1966) and Gagné (1985). For these three reasons, we find it appropriate to refer to each of the two basic kinds of knowledge as theory, and to the instrumental kind of knowledge as design theory. Consequently, we offer the following definitions.

Instructional Design Theory

Instructional design theory is a set of design theories that pertain to various aspects of instruction. One perspective is that those aspects include:

- what the instruction should be like, which could be called instructional-event design theory (DT), or instructional-program DT, or instructional-product DT;
- what the process of gathering information for making decisions about instruction should be like, which could be called *instructional-analysis* DT;
- what the process of creating the instructional plans should be like, which could be called *instructional-planning* DT;[1]
- what the process of creating the instructional resources should be like, which could be called *instructional-building* DT;[2]
- what the process of preparing for implementation of the instruction should be like, which could be called *instructional-implementation* DT;[3]
- what the process for evaluating the instruction should be like (summative and formative), which could be called instructional-evaluation DT.

While these six terms represent a largely new way of referring to the various design theories that inform our practice, we hope they are sufficiently more intuitive and less ambiguous that they are worth adopting. We welcome dialogue about these six terms and any changes that might make them more intuitive and less ambiguous. Since they are all design theories, we could drop "design" from the labels. A graphic is perhaps a valuable way to represent this new language (see Figure 1.1).

Note that instructional-event theory is the only one that offers guidance about the nature of the instruction itself. The other five all offer guidance about what is commonly called the *instructional systems design* (or development) process (ISD). Also, please note that there are many interrelationships among these six kinds of instructional-design theory. Obviously, they have input–output relationships with each other. However, analysis and evaluation each play a far more integrated

---

1. Sometimes the term *instructional design* is used with this meaning, and it is one part of the ISD process.
2. Sometimes the term *instructional development* is used with this meaning, and it is another part of the ISD process.
3. Sometimes the terms *change* or *adoption and diffusion of innovations* is used with this meaning, and it is another part of the ISD process. Please note that instructional implementation is not the same as the instructional event. Rather, it is about the process of preparing for the implementation, rather than the implementation itself. It includes procuring and installing necessary resources and providing necessary training for teachers and support personnel.

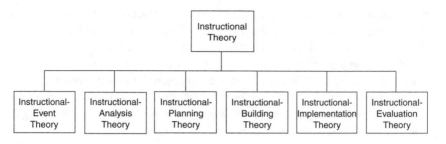

Figure 1.1 Six Major Kinds of Instructional Design-Theory

role in the other kinds of theory. For example, analysis should be used to provide useful information in the application of all the other five kinds of instructional–design theory and should be integrated with each. For example, there is a series of decisions that need to be made for planning an instructional event, including decisions about scope and sequence, instructional approach, instructional tactics, media selection, media utilization, and so forth. Each of these kinds of decisions requires a different kind of analysis at a different point in time during the planning process. So instructional-analysis theory must be integrated with instructional-planning theory. Similarly, different kinds of decisions are made during the instructional-building process, and different kinds of information are needed for making those decisions. Therefore, instructional-analysis theory must be integrated with instructional-building theory. The same applies to instructional-implementation theory and instructional-evaluation theory.

In a parallel manner, evaluation should be conducted on each major decision that is made during the instructional-planning process, so instructional-evaluation theory must be integrated with instructional-planning theory. Similarly, it must also be integrated with each of the other four kinds of instructional theory.

So while it is conceptually helpful to understand that all these different kinds of instructional design-theory exist, it is essential to understand that useful guidance for practitioners must integrate *all* of them.

An Analogy

We feel that a good analogy here would be that of the building process that results in homes, offices, skyscrapers, hospitals, and other buildings. First, there is a body of theory about architecture. These theories are about the buildings themselves, about the products. They study Gaudí and his use of art in the form of everyday structures, for example. This is most akin to instructional-event theory. Then there is a body of literature that looks at theories of architectural process; that is, what architects *do*, how they go about the business of creating and producing a blueprint. This is most akin to instructional-planning theory. Now the architect produces a blueprint, which is given to a builder, and the builder translates that blueprint into a physical manifestation in the form of a final home, or townhouse, or shopping mall. This process is guided by design theories as well, which are most akin to instructional-building theory. Next, people are prepared to use the building. A homeowner may be shown how to use and provide light maintenance on the furnace, water heater, oven, electrical panel, and so forth. And the utilities will be connected. These kinds of activities are similar to instructional-implementation theory. Finally, as a building is lived in, worked in, or shopped in, we and others draw some conclusions about it. Do the air systems work well, or are some rooms always too hot or too cold? If this can be fixed, we might see this as formative evaluation. If not, it might be considered, unfortunately, a summative evaluation of the effectiveness of the building. This, of course, is most like instructional-evaluation theory.

Now we turn to a discussion of several other kinds of theory that are not kinds of instructional-design theory. They include student-assessment theory, curriculum theory, learning theory, learning sciences, and instructional science.

Student-Assessment Design Theory

Student-assessment design theory is guidance for assessing student learning. To the extent that student assessment is integrated with instruction, it would make sense to combine student assessment theory with all six kinds of instructional theories: integrating guidance about the nature of assessment with guidance about the nature of instruction, integrating guidance for the process of analysis for assessments with guidance for the process of analysis for instruction, and so forth for planning, building, implementing, and evaluating assessments and instruction.

Curriculum-Design Theory

Curriculum-design theory concerns *what* should be learned, the content of instruction, including higher-order thinking skills and metacognitive skills, in contrast to instructional-event theory, which concerns *how* it should be learned (Snelbecker, 1974; see also Reigeluth, 1999, chapter 1—volume 2 of this series). For example, a curriculum-design theory may address the inclusion of more racial and gender diversity in American history. To the extent that "what to teach" is interdependent with "how to teach it," it would make sense to combine curriculum theory with all six kinds of instructional theories. It is no wonder that many departments in schools of education are called "Curriculum and Instruction."

Learning Theory

Learning theory is descriptive theory rather than design (or instrumental) theory, for it describes the learning process. For example, schema theory and information-processing theory describe processes that are believed to occur within learners' heads. If they identified methods for helping those processes to occur, they would be instructional-event design theories. Learning theory may provide an understanding of why a certain method of instruction (in an instructional-event theory) works so well, and hence a rationale for using it, but an instructional-event theory can as easily lead to the development of learning theory (to explain that instructional-event theory) as a learning theory can lead to the development of an instructional-event theory (to apply the learning theory).

Learning Sciences

Learning Sciences is a term that has become popular recently. The term *instructional science* has also been used, and there is a journal by that name. Based on those labels, one would expect that the learning sciences are dedicated to the development of learning theory, and that instructional science is dedicated to the development of instructional theory. However, in practice most learning scientists are interested in developing knowledge about both learning (descriptive theory) and instructional events (design theory). An operational definition of learning sciences would perhaps be a hybrid discipline that includes learning theory and instructional-event theory. It also seems that most learning scientists are not interested in instructional-planning theory, instructional-building theory, instructional-implementation theory, instructional-evaluation theory, or curriculum theory. There is some interest in student-assessment theory. The field of learning sciences is akin to cognitive science in that it is purposely multidisciplinary and not so interested in goals as in the use of certain kinds of instructional methods to shed light on certain kinds of learning processes.

Interrelationships

The interrelationships among all the kinds of theories related to instruction are powerful and systemic. In many cases, it is most helpful for a theory to be a hybrid of several of these kinds of theories, as we have already mentioned. Such hybrids have been common from the early pioneers in instructional theory (e.g., Dewey, Skinner, Gagné, and Ausubel) to recent theorists (e.g., Bransford, Brown, & Cocking, 2000; McCombs & Whisler, 1997).

In spite of the importance of *all* these kinds of theories and the relationships among them, this book focuses on instructional-event theory, not just because it would be too large an undertaking to do justice to all of the above theories and their interrelationships, but more importantly because instructional-event theory is in dire need of a common knowledge base. Since the term *instructional theory* is commonly used to refer to what we have called "instructional-event design theory," we often use this simpler term in the remainder of this book.

Instructional Design Theories and Layers of Design

One additional aspect of the nature of theories related to instruction is the notion of "layers of design" discussed by Gibbons and Rogers in chapter 14. Their chapter helps us to understand that designing an instructional system requires considerable attention to the ways in which its parts will interact, wear out, progress, and be utilized at different rates and in different ways. A good example of this, given by Gibbons at a recent conference, was that, while many classrooms did not have overhead fixed video projectors in their ceilings when they were built, the "ceiling layer" of the room was created in such a way as to afford that change in the delivery system by putting in a drop ceiling with tiles that were easily removed. This is an example of one layer wearing out or becoming obsolete sooner than others, and ways that a layer can shift around others without an entire building having to be gutted each time new wires need to be run, for instance.

In chapter 14 Gibbons and Rogers identify seven layers of design that they believe are important in designing instruction: content, strategy, message, control, representation, media logic, and data management layers. Each of these is briefly described next.

Within the *content layer* a designer specifies the structure of the subject-matter elements. This layer is most concerned with the many ways content can be structured. For example, instructional theories related to the content layer of designs might identify subject matter elements divided into sets of tasks, sets of propositions, sets of if/then rules, or sets of discrete semantic (meaning) elements.

Within the *strategy layer* a designer specifies the organization and properties of learning events, including participant roles and responsibilities, goals and times afforded to goals, and instructional strategies. Theories pertaining to the design at the strategy layer therefore pertain to the setting, the social organization, the "siting," and the strategies of instructional interactions.

Within the *message layer* a designer describes the ways that individual messages are used to communicate content and other information to the learner. In essence, if the strategy layer describes a general strategic plan, then the message layer describes the tactical messaging plan for carrying out that strategy. For example, a designer might define in a messaging plan the elements to be used to construct feedback messages in terms of individual message units (right/wrong judgment, error explanation, remedy explanation, etc.) that will generally comprise feedback messages. There are many classes of messages used during most typical instructional interactions.

Within the *control layer* a designer specifies how learners express messages back to the source of learning. Theories related to control-layer designs describe ways that learners can take actions, ask questions, make responses, and generally carry out their side of the instructional conversation. An example might be a theory that specifies ways that the learner can take action during practice in an interactive medium, such as a computer.

Within the *representation layer* a designer describes the way or ways in which messages will be delivered to the learners' senses, including the media channels that will be used, how messages will be assigned to those channels, and how individual messages that use multiple channels are synchronized. Thus, theories used within the design of the representation layer might describe how to visualize certain kinds of messages, how to maximize the coordination of different media channels, and how to synchronize the messages within their different channels for best effect.

Within the *media logic layer* a designer specifies how media mechanisms will be made to deliver representations, how to carry out communications (through messaging and control operation), how to implement strategies in a dynamic, unpredictable interaction, how to compute current knowledge model states, and how to gather and analyze data in ways useful during the instruction. This is the part of the design that tells us how media will be used to carry out instructional event plans. For example, a theory related to media logic design might specify ways in which a multimedia computer could be made to deliver a dynamic visual representation simultaneously with an audio description while teaching how to prepare a fine soup.

Within the *data management layer* a designer specifies what we do with data in the system in terms of capture, archiving, analysis, interpretation, and reporting. An instructional theory related to the design of the data management layer might specify that the result of each step of the process of adding a fraction be captured and analyzed for correctness or incorrectness so that errors can be debugged, or might specify that certain response patterns should be noted as a student executes a tricky procedure so that later analysis can identify possible sources of errors.[4]

We believe that there is an interaction between Gibbons and Rogers's concept of layers (chapter 14) and the application of the six types of instructional theory (event, analysis, planning, building, implementation, and evaluation) that we have defined. For example, to be comprehensive, instructional-event theory should provide guidance for what all seven layers should be like, given the nature of the situation. Similarly, instructional-planning theory should offer guidance for a process in which all seven layers will be designed, and instructional building theory should offer guidance for a process in which all seven layers will be developed, and so forth.

The Role of Instructional Theory in Educational Reform

The major purpose of most instructional theories is to improve learning in P-12 schools (from preschool through 12th grade), though instructional theories are

---

4. The authors thank Andrew Gibbons for his contribution to writing the previous seven paragraphs. For more information about these layers, see chapter 14.

also valuable in many other contexts. Chapter 1 in volume 2 proposed that the industrial-age paradigm (or factory model) of schooling is obsolete—inadequate to meet learning needs today—and that a new paradigm of education is needed.

Why Is a New Paradigm Needed?

We know that students learn at different rates, yet the current industrial-age paradigm of education requires all students to learn the same thing at the same time and rate. This means that slow learners are forced on before mastering the content, and they accumulate learning deficits that make future learning more difficult, while fast learners are forced to wait and lose both motivation and the opportunity to learn more. The alternative to holding time "constant" for all students and thereby forcing achievement to vary, is to hold achievement constant (at the level specified by the standards), which requires time to vary— to allow each student the time needed to attain each standard, and allow each student to move on as soon as the standard is attained (Reigeluth, 1994). Without this change in paradigm, we will inevitably continue to leave many children behind no matter what reforms we implement, and we will continue to waste much of our top talent in schools.

Is a New Paradigm Possible?

Two developments allow such a customized, attainment-based paradigm of education to replace the current standardized, time-based paradigm: (1) the development of advanced technologies and (2) the advancement of learner-centered psychological principles and methods of instruction, such as active learning and collaborative problem-based learning. These developments allow a true paradigm shift in instruction that has the potential for a quantum improvement in learning (Banathy, 1991; Branson, 1987; Covington, 1996; Duffy, Rogerson, & Blick, 2000; Egol, 2003; Jenlink, Reigeluth, Carr, & Nelson, 1996; Reigeluth, 1994), not just the 5 or 10% improvement found in typical piecemeal educational reform efforts, including most Comprehensive School Reform programs (American Institutes for Research, 1999; Franceschini, 2002; Holdzkom, 2002; Ross et al., 1997; Wong, Nicotera, & Manning, 2003).

What Areas of Knowledge Need to Be Developed to Make It Possible?

Much remains to be learned about the learner-centered paradigm of instruction (Bransford et al., 2000; McCombs & Whisler, 1997). However, the major gap in our knowledge for dramatic improvements in learning is how to help schools transform themselves from the standardized, industrial-age paradigm to a learner-centered, information-age paradigm of education. The history of fundamental educational reform has been dominated by classroom-based and school-based efforts to change to a learner-centered paradigm; but those changes have been incompatible with the larger school systems, communities, and social systems within which they existed and consequently were gradually forced by those encompassing systems to transform back into the industrial-age model (Sarason, 1990, 1995; Tyack & Cuban, 1995). While fundamental changes are needed in the ways teachers and students interact to foster learning, those changes require changes at the classroom level, which in turn require changes on the school level, which in turn require changes on the district level. In other words, to be successful, fundamental transformation of education must occur on the school district level, as well as the school and classroom levels (Duffy et al., 2000; Squire & Reigeluth, 2000). There is also evidence that related changes are helpful, if not essential, on the state level (Fullan, 2003).

Therefore, large improvements in learning in public schools require advances in two kinds of knowledge: knowledge about learner-centered methods of instruction (e.g., Watson & Reigeluth, 2008, for an overview) and knowledge about how to help school districts transform themselves to an information-age paradigm of education (e.g., Duffy & Reigeluth, 2008; Reigeluth & Duffy, 2008). This book focuses on advancing the former: knowledge about the learner-centered paradigm of instruction. We see this as pivotal to the advancement of the larger agenda of school reform as well as reform of all organizations in which intentional human learning occurs.

Relation to Learner-Centered Instruction

To make the most valuable contribution to knowledge, this book attempts to synthesize the current knowledge about effective instruction to formulate a common knowledge base about instruction and a common terminology about instruction. Toward this end, it may be helpful to briefly summarize current knowledge about learner-centered instruction (see also Watson & Reigeluth, 2008).

Learner-Centered Psychological Principles

The present knowledge about the learner-centered paradigm of instruction is widely dispersed, but several noted attempts to synthesize or summarize that knowledge have been published. First, the American Psychological Association conducted an extensive project to identify research-based, learner-centered, psychological principles (American Psychological Association Presidential Task Force on Psychology in Education, 1993). Its report identifies 12 such principles and presents the research evidence that supports each. McCombs and colleagues (Lambert & McCombs, 1998; McCombs & Whisler, 1997) summarize that work and describe specific features and characteristics of learner-centered classrooms and schools, along with descriptions of their experiences with learner-centered teachers and schools. They describe the nature of the shift in focus from teaching to learning, including ways to customize learning to student differences, how to motivate students to put more effort into learning, how to help students assume increasing responsibility for directing their own learning (to prepare them better to be lifelong learners), how to manage the learning process so that faster students can move on as soon as they reach a standard and slower students are not forced to move on before they have reached a standard, and much more. Technology plays a central role in all of these aspects of the learner-centered paradigm. Methods such as these have been proven to significantly advance the ability of students to reach high standards (American Psychological Association Presidential Task Force on Psychology in Education, 1993; Lambert & McCombs, 1998; McCombs & Whisler, 1997). However, McCombs and Whisler caution that "learner-centered teaching is as much a way of being, a disposition, as it is doing one thing or another" (p. 100), and they discuss the qualities that learner-centered teachers need to have, along with ways to help develop those qualities. These are all important elements of a comprehensive design theory for learner-centered instruction.

The Science of Learning

A second line of work was undertaken by the National Research Council to synthesize present knowledge about how people learn (Bransford et al., 2000). This two-year study resulted in a comprehensive synthesis of research findings that suggest there are new approaches to instruction that "make it possible for the majority of individuals to develop a deep understanding of important subject matter" (p. 6). This growing body of knowledge, which the authors called the science of learning, emphasizes the importance of customizing the instruction to the preexisting knowledge of each individual learner, helping learners take control of their own learning, and developing deep understandings of the subject matter. Both design theory and descriptive theory are offered regarding the design of learning environments that are learner centered, knowledge centered, assessment centered, and learning-community centered. Technology also plays a central role in such learning environments and in design theory to guide creation of such environments. There is much overlap between this line of work and the APA learner-centered psychological principles in terms of the research-based design theory offered by each.

New Paradigm of Instructional Theory

A third line of work was undertaken by Reigeluth in volume 2 to summarize and compare a broad range of instructional design theories that fit the learner-centered paradigm of instruction (Reigeluth, 1999). This included design theories for fostering a wide range of kinds of human learning and development, namely cognitive, physical, affective, and integrated learning of all those types. It also included a wide range of methods, such as problem-based, collaborative, self-directed, individualized, discussion-based, and much more. Again, there is great overlap between this line of work and the first two.

Other Work

We are particularly impressed with Rand Spiro's cognitive flexibility theory (Spiro et al., 1992) and his observation that information-age (or "post-Gutenberg") technologies both require and facilitate a different worldview (or frame of mind) and a different style of thinking, through prefigurative schemas (schemas for the development of schemas). This has important implications for dramatic changes in the goals of education, as well as the means, as we evolve deeper into the information age. Other lines of work include personalized learning (Clarke, 2003; Keefe, 2007), brain-based learning (Caine, 2005; Caine & Caine, 1997), and differentiated instruction (Tomlinson, 1999, 2001, 2003). Of course, there is much additional work that has been done by researchers that contributes valuable elements of a comprehensive design theory for learner-centered instruction that is frequently made possible only by advanced technologies. This book attempts to identify and synthesize new work as knowledge that educators can utilize to improve learning for all students.

The Nature of Instructional Theories: Constructs and Terms

Instructional theorists often use different terms to refer to the same constructs and the same term to refer to different constructs. This is confusing for researchers, practitioners, and graduate students, and it is the most obvious indicator of the lack of a common knowledge base. Therefore, as a first step to building a common knowledge base for instructional theory, it would be helpful to reach some consensus on constructs about the nature of instructional theory and terms for those constructs.

To initiate this first step, we engaged in several rounds of a Delphi process (Adler & Ziglio, 1996) in which we sent out a list of constructs and terms to a sample of leading instructional theorists to try to build some consensus. A total of 53 e-mail invitations to participate in the Delphi were sent to authors of chapters in all three volumes of *Instructional-Design Theories and Models*, and to other well-known instructional theorists. The e-mail asked them to read a preliminary version of the terms and definitions that we felt might be best and to click on a link to answer four questions online about the constructs and terms *they* felt were best for the discipline of instructional theory. The Internet was used to ensure anonymity for their responses, thereby encouraging complete frankness. The response rate on the first round was low (16%), which we believe was, in part, due to our attaching a 3-page preliminary version of terms and definitions to the e-mail. We suspect that participants felt it would take too much time to open and read and review a document prior to taking the survey.

Delphi Results: Round 1

The results of the first round of the Delphi were varied, though most (6 of 9) respondents saw *instructional theory* as the best term to represent the knowledge base about ways to facilitate human learning and development. However, *learning and performance technology* and *instructional model* were also supported. There was a certain amount of criticism of the terms *instructional-design theory* and *instructional-development design theory* as being "unwieldy," though clearly descriptive. An alternative term, *instructional design principles,* was offered during round 1. Suggesting that we link with other design disciplines was another idea offered by three of the nine participants in round 1. In some cases, participants felt that the definitions needed to remain somewhat fuzzy and not get too specific. In other cases, the participants really wanted to narrow the definitions that were seen as too broad, such as for "instructional situation." One participant felt uncomfortable about the entire survey, indicating, "I do not believe in instructional theories of any kind...." There was also a sense that stronger contrasts were needed among the definitions that were provided for the terms. Finally, respondents to round 1 generally did not find any additional new terms they thought should be added, but did caution us about being too ambitious in terms of the possibilities of this Delphi leading to consensus. As one respondent wrote,

> What you are hoping to achieve is consensus. That won't happen.... Learning is such a complex phenomenon that shares little common variance with instruction. Micro-macro is overly simplistic (even if we include meso). They are too arbitrary. Learning aggregates in many ways, depending on activity, interests, needs. You can use those terms to describe aggregates, but unfortunately, such categories have a tendency to become self-fulfilling prophecies.

Two respondents were concerned that we were not sufficiently tuned in to the need for, and power of, localized and flexible definitions.

> In general, it is useful to have definitions, but I would add some caution with regard to this task. Definitions should be regarded with some degree of fuzziness and not held too rigidly. When definitions prove useful and enlightening, great—when they become burdensome and are used to badger people, then they have outlived their usefulness.

Delphi Results: Round 2

The second round Delphi took the responses from the first round and carefully represented them to the same 53 participants, whether or not they had participated in round 1, for further refinement of the terms and definitions of importance in instructional theory. We sent no attachments, and we achieved a higher response rate (39%).

A few reasons were given by some of the people who did not participate in either round of the study. A few challenged the very notion that we, as a field, really need to have further clarification of terms and constructs. Several stated that they were no longer active in the field and felt that the opportunity to help define the terms should be reserved for those who are currently engaged in the field. In addition, some felt that, during the second round, the choices were too narrowly defined or circumscribed. One respondent who did participate sent feedback indicating that he felt the answers were "predetermined and restrained" and suggesting that it was impossible to "define an enterprise as complex and dynamic as ours."

Despite these few criticisms, we found that a considerable degree of consensus was reached among those who participated, and therefore we believe that the results are an important step in the process of reaching some consensus on constructs and terms for a common knowledge base in instructional theory.

In Round 2 the largest number of respondents (n = 10 or 45%) again felt that *instruction* is the proper term to refer broadly to all ways of facilitating human learning and development (see Table 1.1). However, the term *education* also enjoyed some support (n = 5 or 22%). Most of the respondents felt that the term *design theory* (n = 12 or 54%) was the appropriate term to characterize sets of goal-oriented, normative, artificial-science principles. However, the term *instructional theory* only enjoyed 18% (n = 4) support, while there was strong support for *learning sciences* as a more appropriate alternative to instructional theory (n = 7 or 32%). During the initial round of the Delphi there was a suggestion that there was no need for "design theories" to be part of the label for different kinds of instructional theory (e.g., instructional-development design theories), but rather to make things less awkward by simply saying "instructional development theories." There was mild support for this by the broader round 2 Delphi respondents, with an average of 3.1 (meaning "neutral") on a Likert scale of 1–7 (with 1 being strongly agree). There was broad support for greater recognition of the ways the word *design* has been used in related fields (average 2.5 agreement on the Likert scale). Similarly, there was support for explicit recognition of the evolutionary nature of definitions themselves as changes in technology and context accompany definitional refinement (average 2.3) (see Table 1.1).

Thus, while this Delphi study did not enjoy as high a response rate as we might like, there was consensus among respondents around some terms for use in our field. There was also clear support for flexible definitions and giving greater importance to design theories in the field.

Recommended Constructs and Terms

Following is the description of constructs and terms that resulted from this process, though we hasten to add that these are offered as a suggestion to theorists, and we encourage those who believe they have a better term or definition to propose it to the community of instructional theorists. Furthermore, we expect that some of these constructs and terms, even if accepted now, will evolve over time. Examples of the following constructs are identified with editors' notes in the theory chapters that follow (chapters 5–9 and 10–13).

Perhaps the most important construct is defined as "all things that are done

Table 1.1 Delphi Round 2 Results

Question	Responses	Comments/Interpretation
What term should be used to refer broadly to "all ways of facilitating human learning and development? (Selecting more than one option was permissible.)	10 - Instruction 5 - Education 1 - Education engineering or learning design 1 - Training 1 - Facilitating learning and development 3 - Numerous terms 1 - Learning opportunities 1 - Not sure	These terms were provided by round-I respondents
What term should be used for the knowledge base associated with human learning and development?	7 - Learning sciences 5 - Education 4 - Instructional theory 4 - Other 2 - Instructional design principles 2 - Instructional design theory 1 - Learning and performance technology 0 - Instructional model 0 - Learning environments 0 - Instructional science	It is interesting that the group felt that "learning sciences" was a better term than "learning theory" for the descriptive knowledge base.
Given Simon's distinction between the natural sciences and the sciences of the artificial, if "descriptive theory" is the term used to characterize sets of natural-science principles, what term should be used to characterize goal-oriented, normative, artificial-science principles?	12 - Design theory 2 - Design 2 - Prescriptive theory 1 - Technological theory 1 - Read Stokes, Pasteur's Quadrant 1 - Not sure	Design theory is clearly the most preferred term for this construct; there is considerable agreement here.
It is not useful to have "design-theories" as part of the label for the different kinds of instructional theory—just say "theories" (e.g. in "instructional development design-theories" just say "instructional development theories."	Average of 3.1 on a 7-point Likert scale (n=20)	This seems, on the face of it, very middle of the road, but when compared with the neutral rating of 4, it does represent some small level of agreement.
We need further recognition and acknowledgement of the contributions and the ways "design" has been used in other related fields.	Average of 2.5 on a 7 point Likert scale (n=20)	Respondents generally agreed with this finding from round I.
We need, as a field, to explicitly recognize the evolutionary nature of definitions (that they change as technologies, goals, and our context change).	Average of 2.3 on a 7 point Likert scale (n=20)	Consensus for flexible definitions over time

to facilitate learning," for those are the tools that an instructional theory offers to accomplish its goals. The next most important construct is defined as "all factors that help one to decide when each of those tools should and should not be used." All elements of any instructional theory can be categorized as one or the other of these two constructs.

1. *Instructional method*: Anything that is done purposely to facilitate learning or human development.

    Other terms often used for part or all of this construct include strategy, technique, tactic, and approach.
2. *Instructional situation*: All aspects of an instructional context that are useful for deciding when and when not to use a particular instructional method. Each individual aspect of the context is referred to as a "situationality." Collectively, they are the "situation."[5]

    Other terms often used include context and condition.

Instructional methods can vary in several ways, each of which is an important construct for instructional theories. They are as follows.

1.1 *Scope* of a method: The amount of instruction with which a method deals.

    While this is really a continuum, it is often divided into three major levels (van Merriënboer, 1997):

    1.1.1. Micro: Instruction on an individual skill or understanding, such as a sequence of examples and practice.

    1.1.2. Meso: Instruction on a single unit (or cluster of related skills and understandings), such as a sequence of types of cases for a complex cognitive task.

    1.1.3. Macro: Instruction on a course (or even a curriculum), such as a sequence of different types of complex tasks.

1.2. *Generality of a method*: The breadth of instructional situations in which a method should be used.

    This is a continuum that ranges from high to low or universal to local. Other descriptors include pervasive, common, restricted, rare, narrow, and local.

1.3. Precision of a method: The level of detail of the description of a method. Precision is a reflection of the componential nature of methods. A description of a method typically can be broken down or elaborated into more precise descriptions of the method for facilitating learning. While this characteristic is commonly referred to as a general-versus-

---

5. The situations in which a whole instructional theory should be used are referred to as "preconditions" (see Reigeluth, 1999, chapter 1).

detailed distinction among descriptions of a method (or a general-to-detailed continuum of descriptions of a method), "general" can be confused with the generality of a method itself (versus its description; see 1.2), so we prefer the term precision of a description of a method (imprecise-to-precise continuum). The level of precision is influenced by three constructs:

1.3.1. *Parts: More precise descriptions that describe pieces that, when combined, make up the method.*

1.3.2. *Kinds: More precise descriptions that describe alternatives from which one must choose in using the method.*

1.3.3. *Criteria: More precise descriptions that provide criteria for making a decision regarding the method.*

1.4. *Power of a method*: The amount a method contributes toward the attainment of the learning goal for which it was selected.

Using any particular instructional method does not ensure that the learning goal will be attained, for there are many factors that influence whether or not learning occurs. Some methods are more powerful than others in fostering learning. Every method contributes a certain amount to the probability that learning will occur. The power contribution of any given method can vary from very low (or even zero) to very high (though never reaching a probability of 1.0).

1.5. *Consistency of a method*: The reliability with which a method contributes its power toward the attainment of the learning goal for which it was selected within the situations for which it is appropriate.

Whereas power is similar to the concept of between-group variance in statistics, consistency is related to the concept of within-group variance. A method may be highly consistent in contributing a given amount of power toward the attainment of a learning goal within the situations for which it is appropriate, or it may be highly inconsistent in the amount of power (or probability) it contributes. In other words, the probability that the method contributes toward learning may be very high in some situations, but only moderately high in other situations for which it is still appropriate to use. The consistency of a method (or the variability of its power) within appropriate situations may range from low to high. Regarding generality and precision, it is helpful to note that the more precise (or detailed) a method, the less general (or more situational) it is.

Instructional situations, like instructional methods, can vary in several ways, each of which is an important construct for instructional theories. They are as follows.

2.1. *Values*: The elements of instruction that are deemed important by an instructional theory but are a matter of opinion rather than a matter that can be empirically verified.

The complete set of values underlying a theory of instruction represents a philosophy of instruction. It is helpful to ensure alignment of values about instruction across all stakeholders. Therefore, values about instruction should be made explicit for every instructional theory, to aid in selection of an appropriate instructional theory. The values of the designer are less important than the values of the "owners" of the instruction, the teachers, the learners, and the other beneficiaries (e.g., employers and communities). We have identified four major kinds of instructional values.

2.1.1. *Values about learning goals:* Statements about which learning outcomes are valued philosophically (opinion). These stand in contrast to identifying goals empirically through a needs analysis.

2.1.2. *Values about priorities:* Statements about which priorities should be used to judge the success of the instruction. These were formerly called "instructional outcomes" in volumes 1 and 2 (Reigeluth, 1983, 1999), but that term led to a misunderstanding of the construct. Values about priorities address the relative importance of the effectiveness, efficiency, and appeal of the instruction as criteria for judging how good the instructional methods and guidelines are.

2.1.3. *Values about methods:* Statements about which instructional methods are valued from a philosophical point of view (opinion). These stand in contrast to selecting methods empirically based on research results.

2.1.4. *Values about power:* Statements about who is given the power to make decisions about goals, priorities, and methods.

While values about power could be viewed as subcategories of the three other kinds of instructional values, we believe power is such an important issue that it deserves a category of its own. Learner empowerment is an integral part of the whole concept of an information-age, learner-centered paradigm of instruction (see Reigeluth, 1999), but different amounts of empowerment are often appropriate for different situations, making empowerment a method variable (that spans goals, priorities, and methods), as well as a value.

2.2. *Conditions:* All other factors that influence the selection or effects of methods.

The word *context* has a similar meaning, but not all aspects of context influence when a method of instruction should and should not be used. For example, one could find oneself in a context of low socioeconomic standing (SES) and find that this situation has a major impact on what instructional method should be used, or it may not have such an impact, as many things are taught in similar ways regardless of student SES or community poverty. On the other hand, there are times when context is very important and should affect our instructional choices. We have identified four major kinds of instructional conditions.

2.2.1. *Content:* The nature of what is to be learned, defined comprehensively to include not only knowledge, skills, and understandings, but also higher-order thinking skills, metacognitive skills, attitudes, values, and so forth.

2.2.2. *Learner:* The nature of the learner, including prior knowledge, learning styles, learning strategies, motivations, interests, and so forth.

2.2.3. *Learning environment:* The nature of the learning environment, which includes human resources, material resources, organizational arrangements, and so forth.

2.2.4. *Instructional development constraints:* The resources available for designing, developing, and implementing the instruction, including money, calendar time, and person hours.

Figure 1.2 shows a summary of these constructs. While each of these constructs can and should be further broken down into additional constructs, if instructional theorists would use these constructs and terms in describing their instructional theories, that would represent an important step in building a foundation, or common knowledge base, to which instructional theorists and researchers could add, and it would help practitioners and graduate students understand the knowledge available to them. Yet, as our Delphi study pointed

```
Instructional method
        Scope of a method (a continuum from micro through meso to macro)
        Generality of a method (a continuum from universal to local)
        Precision of a method (a continuum from highly precise to highly imprecise)
                Parts of a method (categories that are more precise)
                Kinds of a method (categories that are more precise)
                Criteria for a method (categories that are more precise)
        Power of a method (a continuum from low to high)
        Consistency of a method (a continuum from low to high)
Instructional situation
        Values (categories)
                Values about learning goals
                Values about priorities
                Values about methods
                Values about who has power
        Conditions (categories)
                Content
                Learner
                Learning environment
                Instructional development constraints
```

Figure 1.2 Constructs about the Nature of Instructional Theory

out, it is important to always keep in mind that an evolving field must have evolving constructs and evolving terminology. These terms and constructs are offered as a beginning point for building an ever-evolving consensus on terms and constructs.

In this chapter we offered a definition of *instruction and have started the significant task of creating a common knowledge base and language about instruction*. We described six different kinds of theories related to instruction (event, analysis, planning, building, implementing, and evaluation theories) and contrasted them with other related kinds of theories (student-assessment, curriculum, and learning theories, as well as learning science and instructional science). Then we discussed Gibbons and Rogers's concept of "layers of design" (see chapter 14) and their implications for instructional theory. Next, we turned our attention to the role of instructional theory in educational reform, and discussed the relationship of learner-centered instruction to this book. Finally, we presented the results of a Delphi study and offered particular constructs and terms for a common knowledge base about instruction. These terms may be useful as a foundation upon which instructional theorists and researchers can build, and they should help you, whether you are a practitioner, a researcher, or a graduate student, to understand the knowledge available to you about fostering learning more effectively.

References

Adler, M., & Ziglio, E. (1996). *Gazing into the oracle: The Delphi method and its application to social policy and public health.* London: Kingsley.

American Institutes for Research. (1999). *An educator's guide to schoolwide reform.* Washington, D.C.: Author. (ED460429)

American Psychological Association Presidential Task Force on Psychology in Education. (1993). *Learner-centered psychological principles: Guidelines for school redesign and reform.* Washington, D.C.: American Psychological Association and the Mid-Continent Regional Educational Laboratory.

Banathy, B. H. (1991). *Systems design of education: A journey to create the future.* Englewood Cliffs, NJ: Educational Technology.

Bransford, J. D., Brown, A. L., & Cocking, R. R. (Eds.). (2000). *How people learn.* Washington, D.C.: National Academy.

Branson, R. K. (1987). Why the schools can't improve: The upper limit hypothesis. *Journal of Instructional Development, 10*(4), 15–26.

Bruner, J. (1966). *Toward a theory of instruction.* Cambridge, MA: Belknap.

Caine, R. N. (2005). *12 brain/mind learning principles in action: The fieldbook for making connections, teaching, and the human brain.* Thousand Oaks, CA: Corwin Press.

Caine, R. N., & Caine, G. (1997). *Education on the edge of possibility.* Alexandria, VA: ASCD.

Clarke, J. (2003). Personalized learning and personalized teaching. In J. DiMartino, J. Clarke, & D. Wolk (Eds.), *Personalized learning: Preparing high school students to create their futures.* Lanham, MD: Scarecrow Press.

Covington, M. V. (1996). The myth of intensification. *Educational Researcher, 25*(8), 24–27.

Duffy, F. M., & Reigeluth, C. M. (2008). The school system transformation (SST) protocol. *Educational Technology, 48*(4), 41–49.

Duffy, F. M., Rogerson, L. G., & Blick, C. (2000). *Redesigning America's schools: A systems approach to improvement.* Norwood, MA: Christopher-Gordon.

Egol, M. (2003). *The education revolution: Spectacular learning at lower cost.* Tenafly, NJ: Wisdom Dynamics.

Franceschini, L. A., III. (2002). *Memphis, what happened? Notes on the decline and fall of comprehen-*

sive school reform models in a flagship district. Paper presented at the Annual Meeting of the American Educational Research Association, New Orleans, LA, April 1–5, 2002.

Fullan, M. (2003). *Change forces with a vengeance*. New York: Routledge.

Gagné, R. M. (1985). *The conditions of learning and theory of instruction*. New York: Holt, Rinehart & Winston.

Holdzkom, D. (2002). *Effects of comprehensive school reform in 12 schools: Results of a three-year study*. Charleston, WV: AEL. (ED473723)

Jenlink, P. M., Reigeluth, C. M., Carr, A. A., & Nelson, L. M. (1996). An expedition for change. *Tech Trends*, 21–30.

Keefe, J. (2007). What is personalization? *Phi Delta Kappan, 89*(3), 217–223.

Lambert, N. M., & McCombs, B. (Eds.). (1998). *How students learn: Reforming schools through learner-centered education*. Washington, D.C.: American Psychological Association.

McCombs, B., & Whisler, J. S. (1997). *The learner-centered classroom and school: Strategies for increasing student motivation and achievement*. San Francisco: Jossey-Bass.

Nelson, H. G., & Stolerterman, E. (2003). *The design way*. Englewood Cliffs, NJ: Educational Technology.

Reigeluth, C. M. (1983). *Instructional-design theories and models: Vol. 1. An overview of their current status*. Hillsdale, NJ: Lawrence Erlbaum.

Reigeluth, C. M. (1994). The imperative for systemic change. In C. M. Reigeluth & R. J. Garfinkle (Eds.), *Systemic change in education* (pp. 3–11). Englewood Cliffs, NJ: Educational Technology.

Reigeluth, C. M. (Ed.). (1999). *Instructional-design theories and models: Vol. 2. A new paradigm of instructional theory*. Mahwah, NJ: Erlbaum.

Reigeluth, C. M., & Duffy, F. M. (2008). The AECT FutureMinds initiative: Transforming America's school systems. *Educational Technology, 48*(3), 45–49.

Ross, S. M., Henry, D., Phillipsen, L., Evans, K., Smith, L., & Buggey, T. (1997). Matching restructuring programs to schools: Selection, negotiation, and preparation. *School Effectiveness and School Improvement, 8*(1), 45–71.

Sarason, S. B. (1990). *The predictable failure of educational reform: Can we change course before it's too late?*. San Francisco: Jossey-Bass.

Sarason, S. B. (1995). *Parental involvement and the political principle: Why the existing governance structure of schools should be abolished*. San Francisco: Jossey-Bass.

Simon, H. A. (1996). *The sciences of the artificial* (3rd ed.). Cambridge, MA: MIT Press.

Snelbecker, G. E. (1974). *Learning theory, instructional theory, and psychoeducational design*. New York: McGraw-Hill.

Spiro, R. J., Feltovich, P. J., Jacobson, M. J., & Coulson, R. L. (1992). Cognitive flexibility, constructivism and hypertext: Random access instruction for advanced knowledge acquisition in ill-structured domains. In T. M. Duffy & D. H. Jonassen (Eds.), *Constructivism and the technology of instruction: A conversation* (pp. 57–74). Hillsdale, NJ: Erlbaum.

Squire, K. D., & Reigeluth, C. M. (2000). The many faces of systemic change. *Educational Horizons, 78*(3), 145-154.

Tomlinson, C. A. (1999). *The differentiated classroom: Responding to the needs of all learners*. Alexandria, VA: Association for Supervision and Curriculum Development.

Tomlinson, C. A. (2001). *How to differentiate instruction in mixed-ability classrooms* (2nd ed.) Alexandria, VA: Association for Supervision and Curriculum Development.

Tomlinson, C. A. (2003). *Fulfilling the promise of the differentiated classroom: Strategies and tools for responsive teaching*. Alexandria, VA: Association for Supervision and Curriculum Development.

Tyack, D. B., & Cuban, L. (1995). *Tinkering toward utopia: A century of public school reform*. Cambridge, MA.: Harvard University Press.

Van Merrienboer, J. (1997). *Training Complex Cognitive Skills; a four-compenent instructional design model for technical training*. Englewood Cliffs, NJ: Educational Technology Publications.

Watson, S .L., & Reigeluth, C .M. (2008). The learner-centered paradigm of education. *Educational Technology, 48*(5), 42–48.

Wong, K., Nicotera, A., & Manning, J. (2003). *Synthesis of the research conducted in the first three years of the comprehensive school reform demonstration program*. Washington, DC: Institute of Education Science. (ED483041)

2

Understanding Instruction

CHARLES M. REIGELUTH

Indiana University

JOHN B. KELLER

Indiana Department of Education

Charles M. Reigeluth received a B.A. in economics from Harvard University. He was a high school teacher for three years before earning his doctorate in instructional psychology at Brigham Young University. He has been a professor in the Instructional Systems Technology Department at Indiana University's School of Education in Bloomington since 1988, and served as chairman of the department from 1990 to 1992. His major area for service, teaching, and research is the process for facilitating district-wide paradigm change in public school systems. His major research goal is to advance knowledge to help school districts successfully navigate transformation to the learner-centered paradigm of education. He has published nine books and over 120 journal articles and chapters. Two of his books received an "outstanding book of the year" award from Association for Educational Communications and Technology (AECT). He also received AECT's Distinguished Service Award and Brigham Young University's Distinguished Alumnus Award.

John B. Keller is currently serving the Indiana Department of Education in the Center for Information Systems where he collaborates on the development of teacher productivity software and contributes to the creation of longitudinal data systems. John has also worked in the nonprofit sector on grants for designing, developing, and implementing a teacher productivity portal. Teaching endeavors have included six years of elementary school and a variety of courses as an adjunct professor for several Indiana teacher preparation institutions. John completed his doctoral work at Indiana University in the Instructional Systems Technology Department in the School of Education.

EDITORS' FOREWORD

Vision

- *To help build a common knowledge base by offering a flexible framework for organizing constructs about instruction (in contrast to constructs about instructional theory, discussed in chapter 1).*

Instructional Approaches (macrostrategies)

- *They are bundles of instructional methods (components).*
- *Each has some required components and some optional components.*
- *Each can be broken down into (eventually) elements of instruction.*

Instructional Components (meso- and microstrategies)

- *They are more "atomic" than "molecular."*
- *They can be selected individually or in bundles with other component methods.*
- *Variable components should be chosen after an approach has been chosen.*

Content Sequencing

- *Sequencing can be done with chunks of content that are very small or very large.*
- *It can be used with many different approaches to instruction.*
- *Some sequencing strategies can be large enough to be considered approaches.*

Grammar Rules and Rules of Thumb

- *Just as a subject and a verb are needed in every sentence, so an approach, components, and sequences are needed in all instruction.*
- *The careful analysis of situational constructs aids in selecting and combining instructional methods.*
- *The priority of highly appealing instruction is particularly important for the information-age paradigm of education*

—CMR & ACC

UNDERSTANDING INSTRUCTION

Chapter 1 described the nature and importance of instructional theory and presented the results of a Delphi study to reach consensus among many instructional theorists about terminology for the major constructs that make up all instructional theories. However, in addition to those constructs about theory, there are also constructs about instruction—the particular instructional methods and situations that may be used in any given theory. Examples of constructs about instruction include: practice, demonstration, collaboration, analogy, problem-based instruction, simple-to-complex sequencing, and many more. The major difference between constructs about instructional theory and constructs about instruction is that the former apply to all instructional theories, whereas the latter may or may not be used in any given theory. This chapter focuses on constructs about instruction.

There have been numerous attempts to prescriptively arrange a set of constructs about instruction (e.g., Gagné's Nine Events) but few efforts to develop a descriptive schema to accommodate the numerous constructs of instruction. Prescriptive arrangements such as Gagné's (1985) Nine Events of Instruction provided a useful framework for selecting instructional constructs for use in an archetypal instructional sequence. As part of building a common knowledge base about instruction, we believe that a flexible framework is needed to organize the constructs about instruction and to illustrate their relationships. We think of this framework as a "grammar of instruction." Just as the grammar of the English language is based on eight parts of speech, so it is possible to trace the many constructs of instruction to a discrete number of sufficiently flexible categories and descriptions. It is our hope that this categorization scheme will sharpen communication about instruction and instructional design. The remainder of the chapter will lay out a set of categories for organizing constructs about instruction with example constructs to illustrate each.

Categories of Constructs about Instruction

Chapter 1 proposed that all constructs of importance to instruction fall into two major categories: instructional methods (what the instruction should be like) and instructional situations (when it should be like that). This chapter will focus on methods, but first we will briefly review what chapter 1 said about situations.

Categories of Instructional Situations

Chapter 1 proposed that instructional situations fall into two main categories: values about instruction and conditions of instruction. Values are about learning goals, criteria, methods, or who has power. Conditions are about the nature of the content, the learner, the learning environment, or the instructional development constraints. Table 2.1 provides an overview of these categories.

Categories of Instructional Methods

Methods of instruction are more difficult to organize into a single conceptual scheme, partly due to their rich variety. This is good news and bad news. The major benefit of the variety of instructional methods is that they can be combined in a nearly infinite number of permutations as appropriate for the instructional situation. The major challenge with this variety is in organizing the profusion of methods in a scheme that is powerful and useful for practitioners.

Table 2.1 Categories of Constructs about Instructional Situations

Values (about):	Examples
Learning goals	The topic should be one about which the students are enthusiastic
Criteria	The instruction should be fun for the learner
Methods	Project-based learning should be used because it affords the most relevance to students
Who has power	Student should generate the learning goals
Conditions:	**Examples**
Content	Understanding causes of the Civil War
Learner	High ability sixth graders with low motivation for the subject
Learning environment	A multi-media computer lab, the classroom, the school library, and a classroom visit by a Civil War survivor
Instructional development constraints	Lesson is due tomorrow

Many classifications of instructional methods are possible, such as the classifications explicated in volume 1 (Reigeluth, 1983, chapter 1):

- Organizational strategies (micro to macro)
- Delivery strategies (media selection and utilization)
- Management strategies

Other ways of classifying methods include those presented in volume 2 (Reigeluth & Moore, 1999, chapter 3):

- The type of learning they promote (memorize information, understand relationships, apply skills, apply generic skills, affective development, or so forth; see volume 2, Reigeluth & Moore, 1999, Table 3.2),
- who controls the learning (the learner, teacher, or instructional designer),
- the focus of the learning (a topic or a problem; a single domain or interdisciplinary),
- the grouping for the learning (individuals, pairs, small groups, or large groups),
- the interactions for the learning (with humans: student-teacher, student-student, or student-other; with nonhumans: student-tool, student-information, student-environment/manipulatives, or student-other),
- the support for the learning (cognitive support or emotional support).

Still other potentially useful categorizations for methods include:

- the authenticity of the instructional tasks (a continuum from artificial or fantasy to authentic),
- the instructional approach used (drill-and-practice, tutorial, simulation, experiential learning, direct instruction, problem-based instruction, discussion, and so forth),
- the purpose of the method (to motivate, to provide information, to build linkages, to empower the learner, to generalize skills, to automatize performance of skills or recall of information, and so forth),
- the role that technology can play in supporting the method (offering interactivity, showing motion, providing sound, facilitating communications, and so forth).

Each of the categorizations above applies in some contexts and may be useful in helping instructional designers think about the alternatives available to them. However, we would like to propose three categories that could be useful across contexts and help in classifying most instructional methods: instructional approaches, instructional components, and content sequencing. These are discussed next.

Instructional Approaches

Instructional methods that fit this category are macrostrategies. Instructional approaches set a general direction or trajectory for the instruction and are comprised of more precise or detailed components. Consider the terms, *problem-based learning, experiential learning, direct instruction*, and *instructional simulation*. These terms refer to general instructional approaches in which other instructional methods (components) are bundled. This notion of bundling is related to the precision of a method, which is the level of detail of description of a method (a construct introduced in chapter 1). For example, problem-based learning is comprised of many smaller methods, and describing each of those smaller methods provides a practitioner with more detail (precision) about the larger (less precise) method.

For any given approach, some components are required and some are optional. When optional components are bundled, they comprise a major "flavor" of the approach. For example, there are several flavors of problem-based learning (PBL), each of which is often referred to as a different strategy for PBL, and the component methods that make up each strategy are often called instructional tactics. One can envision bundles within bundles within bundles, and so forth until one reaches what might be considered the "elements" of instruction.

Instructional Components

As implied above, instructional components are more atomic than molecular. Such methods can be selected individually, depending on the instructional situation, but are often selected in concert with other methods as parts of an instructional approach. For example, practice is a method that is included in nearly every instructional approach because of its importance in helping learners grasp the knowledge, skills, or attitudes that are the focus of instruction.

These categories, approach and component, are useful to instructional designers in that a designer should choose an approach first, and then choose variable components for the approach, depending on the situation.

Content Sequencing

This third category of instructional methods deserves particular attention, because such methods are used with both approaches and components, because the chunks of content that are sequenced can range from very large to fairly small. As an example, a procedural elaboration sequence (the simplifying conditions method; see volume 2, Reigeluth & Moore, 1999, chapter 18) entails starting the instruction with the simplest real-world version of a complex task and progressing to ever more complex versions until all important versions have been learned. The task on which this sequencing method is used could range from very large to quite small. Also, this kind of sequence can be used with many different approaches to instruction, including problem-based instruction, direct instruction, simulation-based instruction, discussion-based instruction, and so forth. At the component level, examples of content sequencing methods include an easy-to-difficult sequence to present examples of a concept and a concrete-to-abstract sequence in mathematics instruction when the instructor utilizes manipulatives to portray an abstract concept in the first steps of learning the symbolic representations of numbers and mathematical operations. To further complicate matters, some sequencing strategies are broad enough to be considered "approaches" to sequencing, while others are components of larger sequencing methods.

To summarize this section about the organization of instructional methods, we have shown that there are many ways to classify methods. We proposed three general categories for classifying most instructional methods (see Table 2.2). While the categories are not mutually exclusive, we believe they are sufficiently broad that most instructional methods fit into at lease one of these categories, and we believe they provide a useful organizing scheme for instructional designers.

Table 2.2 Categories of Constructs about Instructional Methods

Instructional Methods	Examples
Instructional approach	Discovery-based learning; Direct Instruction; Problem-based Learning
Instructional component	Advance Organizer; Coaching; Guided Practice
Content sequence	Concrete-Abstract Sequencing

Grammar Rules and Rules of Thumb

Chapter 1 presented a set of constructs related to instructional situations:

Values

- about learning goals
- about priorities
- about methods
- about power

Conditions

- the content
- the learner
- the learning environment
- the instructional development constraints

When combined with the constructs about methods just presented (Table 2.2), these constructs might prove useful to practitioners by implying a set of questions for analyzing an instructional situation and selecting appropriate methods.

Questions about Instructional Situations

- What are the valued learning goals or outcomes from the instruction?
- What are the priorities in the instruction?
- Which methods are most valued in the instructional context?
- How should power be distributed among those in the instructional interaction?
- How is the nature of the content likely to influence the selection of instructional methods?
- How is the nature of the learner likely to influence the selection of instructional methods?
- How is the instructional environmental likely to influence the selection of instructional methods?
- How are instructional development constraints or limitations likely to influence the selection of instructional methods?

Questions about Instructional Methods

- What instructional approach should be used?
- What variable instructional components are most appropriate within that approach?
- How should instruction be sequenced?

These questions can act as a preliminary guide to analysis and design efforts of the instructional designer. They also serve as issues for instructional theorists to address in their theories.

Returning to the analogy of English grammar presented at the beginning of this chapter, the eight parts of speech are combined according to rules of grammar on which we depend for effective communication. The various categories we have proposed for organizing constructs about instruction are analogous to the parts of speech. Guidelines for combining these constructs to achieve effective instructional design depend largely on a set of heuristics that are learned as expertise develops.

The categories above do suggest a few rules of thumb for thinking through instructional design. Just as a sentence requires a subject and a verb, so instruction requires an approach, components, and sequences. Few English sentences employ all parts of speech. Similarly, designing effective instruction is not as easy as using all the categories described earlier as a checklist of considerations.

There is an understanding about the internal relationships among the categories that is critical to effective instructional design. Specifically, a thorough understanding of the instructional situation helps a theorist (or designer) to select and combine instructional methods to the best effect. These constructs about instruction are not meant to be so many ingredients in whole-grain instruction. Rather, the careful analysis of situational constructs aids in selecting and combining instructional methods. The selection heuristics may be offered by specific instructional theories, but they may also be developed by each instructional designer as insights about the instructional utility of methods in varying instructional situations accrue from experience. While the categorization of instructional methods is descriptively useful, it offers little in the way of prescription, since the selection depends on the grasp that an instructional theorist (or designer) has developed regarding the utility of each instructional method, including its advantages and disadvantages in particular instructional situations.

A final rule of thumb for designing instruction is to pay close attention to the priorities for selecting instructional methods that were described in chapter 1. They strongly influence a method's desirability.

One of the most important priorities for the information-age paradigm of education in both K-12 and higher education contexts is how motivating the method is for learners, since learning is a constructive process that requires considerable student effort. As Schlechty (2002) puts it, the challenge for a teacher is to design engaging work for students. Student engagement and the relevance of learning are key factors in designing instruction for information-age learners.

Effectiveness and efficiency are additional priorities for selecting instructional methods. For example, to learn a skill, demonstrations of the performance of the skill and practice in performing the skill (with immediate feedback) have been well proven to make the instruction more effective and efficient. Recent policy at the federal level spotlights the importance of instructional programs that are evidence-based; that is programs shown to be effective through research (Slavin, 2008). Instructional theorists and designers should continually cultivate their knowledge of the effectiveness and efficiency of instructional methods.

Conclusion

To conclude, we have described categories of constructs about instructional situations and instructional methods. We hope that these categories provide designers with useful tools for classifying instructional constructs as well as a framework for analyzing and designing instruction. We believe that the use of this grammar will help to build a common language and knowledge base if these basic notions are applied. To this end, the appendix to this chapter provides a list of common instructional methods organized in these categories.

Utilizing an instructional method from each category will not lead to elegant and effective instructional designs. Insight into the relationships among the categories is still required, along with knowledge of key characteristics of instructional methods, including their motivational potential and situation-dependent effectiveness and efficiency. The value of this organizational scheme is its broad embrace of all constructs of instruction and its small number of generally useful categories that can be used to order the rich array of terms important to the field.

References

Engelmann, S., Becker, W .C., Carnine, D., & Gersten, R. (1988). The direct instruction follow through model: Design and outcomes. *Education and Treatment of Children, 11*(4), 303-317.

Gagné, R. M. (1985). *The conditions of learning and theory of instruction.* New York: Holt, Rinehart & Winston.

Reigeluth, C. M. (1983). *Instructional-design theories and models: Vol. 1. An overview of their current status.* Hillsdale, NJ: Erlbaum.

Reigeluth, C. M., & Moore, J. (1999). Cognitive education and the cognitive domain. In C. M. Reigeluth (Ed.), *Instructional-design theories and models: Vol. 2. A new paradigm of instructional theory* (pp. 51–68). Mahwah, NJ: Erlbaum.

Schlechty, P. (2002). *Working on the work.* New York: Wiley.

Slavin, R. (2008). Perspectives on evidence-based research in education what works? Issues in synthesizing educational program evaluations. *Educational Researcher, 37*, 5–14.

Appendix Sample List of Instructional Methods

Term	Instructional Approaches
Anchored instruction	One kind of authentic learning environment that is organized so that all learning originates from the learner's attempts to solve a real problem. [Synonyms: Situated learning]
Authentic learning environments	When in the control of the instructional designer, authentic learning environments are approaches that focus on providing some degree of authenticity to the instructional event. In this context, authenticity is synonymous with real world. (Syn: Constructivist learning environments, situated learning)
Case-based learning	A broad method which organizes instruction around consideration of and interaction with a real-world scenario.
Cognitive apprenticeship	A method in which instruction is organized around the interactions of novice and expert, much as with an expert artisan and an apprentice. In this case, the work to be mastered is thought processes.(Syn: Apprenticeship learning)
Direct instruction	An instructional method that draws on carefully scripted instruction intended to promote efficient learning. The method was developed by Sigfried Engelmann.
Discovery-based learning	A broad method in which instruction is organized around a process of helping learners to discover a pre determined model, concept, or proposition.
Drill and practice	A method focused on rote learning and automatization through the repeated presentation of prompts and corrective feedback.
Expository teaching	Instruction depending primarily on teacher lecture. (Syn: Didactic, teacher-centered)
Hands-on learning	A method focused on learner involvement in discovery of principles and the mastery of skills or ideas through activity and direct experience—learning by doing.
Individualized instruction	A method that is responsive to the needs of individual students.
Inquiry-based instruction	A method in which instruction is organized by the interests of the students. Students are encouraged to ask questions and the learning is centered upon answering those questions.
Instructional game	A method in which the knowledge, skills, and abilities that are the focus of the instruction are acquired through a game devised for that purpose.
Instructional simulation	Instruction that simulates the critical elements of a real-life context to approximate the complexity surrounding the skill to be learned or the understanding to be gained.
Learner-centered instruction	A method that focuses on individual learners (e.g., their backgrounds, interests, capabilities, and needs) and on learning (e.g., knowledge about methods to promote the highest levels of motivation and learning for all kinds of learners).
Problem-based learning/ instruction	Instruction that is organized around helping students to achieve or arrive at the solution to a problem.
Project-based Learning/ instruction	Instruction organized around making a product, task, or service.

Term	Instructional Approaches
Role play	A method in which key ideas and skills are illustrated or practiced by learners assuming roles and contexts in which the ideas and skills would typically be applied.
Teacher-centered instruction	An instructional approach in which the teacher is the primary delivery channel for instructional content—often through presentation and lecture. (Syn: Expository, didactic, transmission-oriented)
Tutorial	A broad method that involves a high level of adaptation or instructional events to cater to the individual needs of the student.

	Instructional Components
Advance organizer	A component method, by all accounts attributed to David Ausubel, that is used at beginning of an instructional sequence to help "bridge" the gap between what the learner knows and what she will be learning or doing.
Analogies	A component method that draws comparisons between something familiar and something unfamiliar for the purpose of learning or understanding the latter.
Authentic tasks	A component method that is used for its similarity to the real-world and for its motivational appeal to the learner.
Coaching	A method that centers on a more accomplished learner providing guidance and encouragement to a more novice learner in the context of instruction or a learning exercise. (Syn: Facilitating, mentoring)
Collaborative work	A method that capitalizes on the learning advantages that come from learners working together to solve a problem or accomplish a task. (Syn: Cooperative work)
Cooperative work	This method provides structures for completing work or products by dividing work among group members. Cooperative work is chosen because bigger projects can be tackled and completed by groups working collectively. (Syn: Collaborative work)
Demonstration	A basic component method in which an instructor demonstrates to learners how to do or make something. This method is often followed by student trial of the same skill. [Syn: Model]
Elaboration	Expanding from a simple instance of a concept or skill to a more complex or nuanced instance to aid the learner's full grasp of the content.
Examples/Nonexamples	The use of instances of a concept that illustrate key attributes of the concept in contrast with instances that do not illustrate the key attributes of the concept, to aid the learner in discrimination regarding salient characteristics or dimensions of the concept.
Feedback	A component method that provides the student with information about the quality of the performance and specific guidance about the correct and incorrect aspects of the performance.
Guided practice	A method involving the learner's practice of a skill, with supervision and assistance from the teacher as needed.

(continued)

Appendix Sample List of Instructional Methods (Continued)

Term	Instructional Approaches
Independent practice	A method involving the learner's practice of a skill without supervision or assistance from the teacher.
Peer tutoring	A technique in which a peer of the learner helps him or her to grasp ideas and concepts through close monitoring and feedback.
Personalization	Instruction that focuses on tailoring methods to target the particular learning needs of each student. Depending on the scope of this method, it could be an approach or a component. (Syn: Customization, individualized instruction)
Practice	A component method involving repetitive interaction of learner with content.
Preview	A technique often used at the onset of instruction to establish instructional targets and raise the interest of the learner by some technique that allows the learner to glimpse what the instructional experience will be like.
Reciprocal teaching	Instruction that utilizes a pair of students or a small group to act as teachers for each other, thus requiring each student to bear some responsibility for helping the others to learn the content.
Reflection	A metacognitive method that helps a learner to derive deeper and broader understandings of an experience or that promotes self-evaluation through the comparison of one's work to a standard or through an analysis of individual change as a result of the learning experience.
Review	A summarizing method that draws together the main points of a learning experience to reinforce the grasp of key concepts.
Self-assessment	A component that guides students to reflect upon and compare their work to a standard.
Team work	A collaborative method that promotes learning through the accomplishment of an activity, project, or task as a group of learners.
Content Sequencing	
Concrete-abstract sequencing	A microlevel sequencing method that organizes content from concrete, physical, being there experiences to abstract, symbolic experiences. (Syn: Inductive sequencing)
Deductive sequencing	A microlevel sequencing method that organizes content from general to specific.
Easy-to-difficult sequence	A microlevel sequencing method that organizes content from the easiest examples to the most difficult examples.
Elaboration sequencing: Conceptual	A sequencing method that proceeds from general concepts to detailed concepts. (Syn: Progressive differentiation sequence)
Elaboration sequencing: Procedural	A sequencing method that proceeds from simpler versions of a complex procedure to more complex versions. (Syn: Shortest path sequence)
Elaboration sequencing: Theoretical	A sequencing method that proceeds from broader, more inclusive principles to narrower, more restricted principles. (Syn: Spiral curriculum)

Term	Instructional Approaches
Hierarchical sequencing	A sequencing method that teaches simpler component skills before the more complex skills of which they are a part. (Syn: Learning prerequisite sequence)
Procedural sequencing	A sequencing method that teaches the steps of a simple procedure in the order in which they are performed. (Syn: Forward chaining sequence)
Scaffolding	A variety of methods that include a sequence that gradually reduces and removes supports of various kinds (fading) and a sequence that gradually increases the acceptable standards of performance (shaping). (Syn: Fading, shaping)

3

First Principles of Instruction

M. DAVID MERRILL

Consultant

M. David Merrill makes his home in St. George, Utah. He is an instructional effectiveness consultant, a visiting professor at Florida State University, Brigham Young University—Hawaii, and professor emeritus at Utah State University. Since receiving his PhD from the University of Illinois in 1964 he has served on the faculty of George Peabody College, Brigham Young University—Provo, Stanford University, the University of Southern California, and Utah State University. He is internationally recognized as a major contributor to the field of instructional technology, has published many books and articles in the field, and has lectured internationally. Among his principle contributions: TIC-CIT authoring system (1970s), component display theory and elaboration theory (1980s), instructional transaction theory, automated instructional design, and ID based on knowledge objects (1990s), and currently first principles of instruction. He was honored to receive the AECT Life Time Achievement Award. He and his wife Kate together have nine children and 37 + 4 (by marriage) grandchildren which he claims as his most important accomplishment.

EDITORS' FOREWORD

Vision

- *To distill a set of interrelated prescriptive instructional design principles*

Demonstration Principle

- *Instruction should provide a demonstration of the skill consistent with the type of component skill: kinds-of, how-to, and what-happens.*
- *Instruction should provide guidance that relates the demonstration to generalities.*
- *Instruction should engage learners in peer discussion and peer demonstration.*
- *Instruction should allow learners to observe the demonstration through media that are appropriate to the content.*

Application Principle

- *Instruction should have the learner apply learning consistent with the type of component skill: kinds-of, how-to, and what-happens.*
- *Instruction should provide intrinsic or corrective feedback.*
- *Instruction should provide coaching, which should be gradually withdrawn to enhance application.*
- *Instruction should engage learners in peer collaboration.*

Task-Centered Principle

- *Instruction should use a task-centered instructional strategy.*
- *Instruction should use a progression of increasingly complex whole tasks.*

Activation Principle

- *Instruction should activate relevant cognitive structures in learners by having them recall, describe, or demonstrate relevant prior knowledge or experience.*
- *Instruction should have learners share previous experiences with each other.*
- *Instruction should have learners recall or acquire a structure for organizing new knowledge.*

Integration Principle

- *Instruction should integrate new knowledge into learners' cognitive structures by having them reflect on, discuss, or defend new knowledge or skills.*
- *Instruction should engage learners in peer critique.*
- *Instruction should have learners create, invent, or explore personal ways to use their new knowledge or skill.*
- *Instruction should have learners publicly demonstrate their new knowledge or skill.*

Four-Phase Cycle of Instruction

- *The four principles of activation, demonstration, application, and integration form a four-phase cycle of instruction.*
- *At a deeper level there is within this cycle a more subtle cycle consisting of structure-guidance-coaching-reflection.*

A Scale for Rating Instructional Strategies

- *The quality of the instruction will improve with each principle that is added: demonstration, application, task-centered, activation, and integration.*

—CMR & ACC

FIRST PRINCIPLES OF INSTRUCTION

I systematically reviewed instructional design theories, models, and research. From these sources I abstracted a set of interrelated prescriptive instructional design principles (Merrill, 2002). A subsequent paper (Merrill, 2007) quoted similar principles that have been identified by other authors and supported by research.

For purposes of this work a principle is defined as a relationship that is always true under appropriate conditions[1] regardless of the methods or models which implement this principle. Principles are not in and of themselves a model or method of instruction, but rather relationships that may underlie any model or method. These principles can be implemented in a variety of ways by different models and methods of instruction. However, the effectiveness, efficiency, and engagement of a particular model or method of instruction is a function of the degree to which these principles are implemented.

To be included in this list, the principle had to be included in most of the instructional design theories that the author reviewed. The principle had to promote more effective, efficient, or engaging learning. The principle had to be supported by research. The principle had to be general so that it applies to any delivery system or any instructional architecture (Clark, 2003). Instructional architecture refers to the instructional approach, including direct methods, tutorial methods, experiential methods, and exploratory methods. The principles had to be design-oriented; that is, they are principles about instruction that have direct relevance for how the instruction is designed to promote learning activities, rather than activities that learners may use on their own while learning.

From this effort five principles were identified. Following is an abbreviated statement of these principles:

- The *demonstration* principle: Learning is promoted when learners observe a demonstration.

---

[1] Editors' note: The "always true" part of this statement implies universality, whereas the "under appropriate conditions" part implies situationality. This issue is discussed in some depth in chapter 4.

- The *application* principle: Learning is promoted when learners apply the new knowledge.
- The *task-centered* principle: Learning is promoted when learners engage in a task-centered instructional strategy.
- The *activation* principle: Learning is promoted when learners activate relevant prior knowledge or experience.
- The *integration* principle: Learning is promoted when learners integrate their new knowledge into their everyday world.

In this chapter I elaborate these five principles and their interrelationships. Please refer to previous papers for a brief identification of some of the theories and research that supports these principles (Merrill 2002, 2007).

Demonstration Principle

- Learning is promoted when learners observe a demonstration of the skills to be learned that is *consistent* with the type of content being taught.
- Learning from demonstrations is enhanced when learners are *guided* to relate general information or an organizing structure to specific instances.
- Learning from demonstrations is enhanced when learners observe *media* that is relevant to the content.
- Learning from demonstrations is enhanced by *peer discussion* and *peer demonstration*.

Demonstration Consistency

First principles are most appropriate for generalizable skills. A generalizable skill is one that can be applied to two or more different specific situations. Remembering the name of a specific object or naming the parts of a specific device is not a generalizable skill. The demonstration principle is most appropriate for three types of generalizable skill: concept classification (or *kinds-of*); carrying out a procedure (or *how-to*); and predicting consequences or finding faulted conditions in the execution of a process (or *what-happens*). A generalizable skill is represented by both information and portrayal. *Information* is general, inclusive, and applicable to many specific situations. *Portrayal* is specific, limited, and applicable to one case or a single situation.[2] Information can be presented (tell) and recalled (ask). A portrayal can be demonstrated (show) and submitted to application (do). The demonstration principle emphasizes the use of specific cases (portrayal). Failure to provide sufficient demonstration is a common problem in much instruction. While the demonstration principle emphasizes portrayal, effective and efficient instruction involves both presentation of information[3] and

---

2 Editors' note: Information and portrayal correspond to Merrill's earlier distinction between generality and instance.

3 Editors' note: Presentation of information is universal, for it is useful for fostering other kinds of learning, such as remembering, naming, and understanding, as well as for generalizable skills.

Table 3.1 Consistent Information and Portrayal for Categories of Component Skill

	Information		Portrayal	
	Present (Tell)	**Recall (Ask)**	**Demonstrate (Show)**	**Apply (Do)**
Kinds-of	Tell the definition.	Recall the definition.	Show several specific examples.	Classify new examples.
How-to	Tell the steps and their sequence.	Recall the steps and their sequence.	Show the procedure in several different situations.	Carry out the procedure in new situations.
What-happens	Tell the conditions and consequence involved in the process.	Recall the conditions and consequence involved in the process.	Show the process in several different situations.	Predict a consequence or find faulted conditions in new situations.

*Editors' note: This table and the related discussion identify situationalities (the three different kinds of generalizable skills) that call for variation in the methods. Hence, while present, recall, demonstrate, and apply are—at a very imprecise level of description—universal methods for generalizable skills, if you want to provide more precise (detailed) guidance about how to use each of those methods, you must offer variations in the description of the method based on a situational variable (situationality), in this case, the kind of generalizable skill. For more about this, see chapter 1.

demonstration with portrayal.[4] Table 3.1 indicates information and portrayal that are consistent for each category of generalizable skill. A presentation and demonstration must be consistent if they are to promote effective, efficient, and engaging learning.

Learner Guidance

Learner guidance helps focus the learner's attention on critical elements of the information and relate these critical elements to the portrayal. The following paragraphs list steps for presenting and demonstrating each kind of generalizable skill (Merrill, 1997). The learner guidance that enhances the demonstration is indicated by hollow bullets.

Kinds-of Kinds-of or concept classification occurs when learners must discriminate among members of two or more related categories of objects or events. An effective presentation/demonstration for concept classification (kinds-of) requires the following instructional activities.

- Tell learners the name of each category or alternative procedure.
- Show learners an example of each category.
- Provide learners with a definition for each category. (A definition is a list of discriminating properties that determine class membership.)

---

4 *Editors' note: In contrast, demonstration with portrayal is not universal, for it applies primarily to generalizable skills.*

- Emphasize the discriminating properties for each category.
- Show learners additional examples of each category. (Portrayals for examples must illustrate the discriminating properties.)
- Call attention to the portrayal of each discriminating property for each example.
- Show matched examples among categories—examples which have similar nondiscriminating properties.
- Show divergent examples within a category for which nondiscriminating properties are different.
- Show increasingly difficult-to-discriminate examples among categories.

How-to How-to or procedure learning occurs when learners must carry out a series of steps. A presentation/demonstration for a procedure (how-to) involves the following instructional activities.

- Show learners a specific instance of the whole task.
- Demonstrate each of the steps required to complete the whole task.
- Clearly identify and label each step as it is executed.
- Show the consequence of each step.
- Focus the learner's attention on the portrayal of the consequence, especially if the consequence is hidden from view or not obvious.
- Summarize the steps in the procedure and their sequence.

What-happens What-happens or process learning occurs when learners understand how some device works or the process underlying some phenomenon. A presentation/demonstration for a process (what-happens) involves the following instructional activities.

- Demonstrate the process in a specific, real or simulated situation.
- During the demonstration tell the name and show the portrayal for each necessary condition for each event in the process.
- Focus the learner's attention on the consequence of each event and the consequence of the process as a whole.
- Repeat the demonstration for several increasingly complex scenarios.

Relevant Media

Mayer (2001; Clark & Mayer, 2003) identifies a number of principles for the effective use of media. Demonstrations are enhanced as these media-use principles are implemented. These principles are summarized without elaboration as follows:

- Include both words and graphics as long as the graphics convey information that is being taught and are not merely decorative.

- Place corresponding words and graphics near each other.
- Present words as audio narration rather than onscreen text.
- Presenting words as both text and simultaneous audio narration can interfere with learning.
- Adding interesting, but unnecessary, material can interfere with learning.

Peer-demonstration and Peer-discussion

Learning from demonstrations is enhanced when learners actively engage in interaction with one another rather than passively observing the demonstration. When learners are required to find a new portrayal of the information that has been presented, they are required to process the information at a deeper level in order to identify and demonstrate this new portrayal. When they are required to demonstrate their new portrayals to one another, this provides additional portrayals of the information being taught, thus increasing the richness of the instruction.

Peer discussion promotes opportunities for learners to discuss a given portrayal with one another to determine whether or not it is a good representation of the information; that is, is this example really an example of a kind of x? Does this specific execution of a procedure really involve each of the steps in the statement of the procedure? Does this consequence really follow from the conditions that have been identified for a specific process?

Application Principle

- Learning is promoted when learners engage in application of their newly acquired knowledge or skill that is *consistent* with the type of content being taught.
- Learning from an application is effective only when learners receive intrinsic or corrective *feedback*.
- Learning from an application is enhanced when learners are *coached* and when this coaching is gradually withdrawn for each subsequent task.
- Learning from an application is enhanced by *peer-collaboration*.

This paper uses the word *practice* to refer to those instructional interactions for which learners are required to recall information. This means to recall a definition of a concept, recall and order the steps in a procedure, or recall the conditions and consequences for a process. The word *application* refers to those instructional interactions in which learners are required to use the knowledge and skill they are in the process of acquiring. Using the knowledge or skill means to classify a new example, carry out a new procedure, predict a consequence, or find faulted conditions in a new specific situation. As indicated earlier in this paper, first principles are most appropriate for generalizable knowledge and skills. Generalizable knowledge and skills are applied when learners use them to solve a new problem or complete a different task from the one that was used for demonstration.

Application Consistency

Table 3.1 indicates consistent practice and application for each of the three types of generalizable skill: kinds-of, how-to, and what-happens. Application for kinds-of occurs when learners are required to classify new examples of each category by labeling, sorting, or ranking the examples. Application for how-to occurs when learners are required to carry out each step in the task in a new real or simulated situation. Application for what-happens occurs when learners are required to predict the outcome from a given set of conditions in a new specific situation or when learners are required to find faulted conditions when an unexpected consequence occurs as a result of a process.

Feedback

Intrinsic feedback for application of *kinds-of* allows learners to see the consequence of their classification decision. Corrective feedback focuses learners' attention on the discriminating properties that determine class membership.[5]

Intrinsic feedback for application of *how-to* enables learners to see the consequences of their actions. Corrective feedback informs learners of the quality of their performance and shows them how they did or should have performed the step.

Intrinsic feedback for *what-happens* executes the process to enable learners to see if the consequence is consistent with their prediction. Intrinsic feedback also occurs when, after correcting faulted conditions, learners can see if the expected consequence occurs. Corrective feedback focuses learners' attention on the consequence and helps them see that the expected consequence is consistent with their prediction.

Enhancing Application Performance

Application for *kinds-of* is enhanced when learners are asked to explain their classification by pointing out the presence or absence of discriminating properties. Application of *how-to* is enhanced when learners are required to carry out a progression of increasingly complex tasks. *What-happens* application is enhanced when learners are required to make predictions or correct faulted conditions for an increasingly complex progression of specific situations.

---

5 *Editors' note: Here is another example of universal methods (within the domain of generalizable skills) becoming variable methods when we seek to provide more detailed guidance. Here, the same situationality (kind of generalizable skill) is used to indicate when to use each variation of the method. Try to identify other cases of variations with situationalities as you read on.*

Coaching

Application is also enhanced when learners are given considerable help or coaching with their performance on early component skills and this help is gradually withdrawn with each succeeding application of this component skill.[6]

Peer Collaboration

Learning from an application is enhanced when learners collaborate with each other on the application. Collaboration requires more active learning. The most effective use of peer collaboration is when learners must first come to some solution on their own and then interact with fellow learners to describe, discuss, and defend their solution in an attempt to come to some agreed solution.

Task-Centered Principle

- Learning is promoted when learners engage in a *task-centered* instructional strategy.
- Learning from a task-centered instructional strategy is enhanced when learners undertake a simple-to-complex *progression of whole tasks.*

Task-Centered versus Problem-Based Instructional Strategies

While there are many different variations of problem-based instructional strategies, a typical problem-based instructional strategy gives a small group of learners a complex problem to solve, identifies resources that can be used to solve this problem, and expects learners to acquire the necessary skills by searching the resources and struggling with the problem solution.[7] Learners are expected to learn from each other and to seek other sources when the identified resources are insufficient to solve the problem. A large body of research during the past several decades has demonstrated that this type of open problem solving is frequently not only inefficient but often ineffective in teaching the desired skills (Kirschner, Sweller, et al., 2006). A task-centered instructional strategy is not the same as problem-based learning. A task-centered instructional strategy is a form of direct instruction but in the context of authentic, real-world problems or tasks. Van Merriënboer (1997) has described such a task-centered instructional strategy in some detail.

Topic-centered instructional strategies typically teach the component skills for the task in a hierarchical fashion by teaching all the related skills of one type and then the related skills of another type, chapter by chapter, until all of the component skills have been taught. Learners are then given a task to which they

---

6 Editors' note: *This may not be a universal method within the domain of generalizable skills. If the task is relatively easy to learn, the coaching may not be necessary or beneficial.*

7 Editors' note: *For more details, see chapter 8.*

can apply their skills as a final project in a course. A topic-centered approach is often characterized as the "you won't understand this now, but later it will be very important to you" approach to skill development.

Figure 3.1 illustrates an example of a task-centered instructional strategy. The *Ts* in the diagram indicate a progression of whole complex tasks from the same class of tasks. The increase in size of the *Ts* indicates an increase in task complexity with each subsequent task in the progression. (1) Rather than teaching topics out of context, a simple whole task of the type they are learning to do is demonstrated right up front. (2) Learners are then given instruction—presentation, demonstration, application—of the skills required to do this task. This instruction does not teach all there is to know about a given topic or component skill, but only what learners need to know to complete the task. (3) The whole task is revisited at this point, and learners are shown how these component skills were applied to complete the task or solve the problem. This constitutes one cycle of instruction. (4) A new, slightly more complex task is then given to the learners.[8] Learners are asked to apply their newly acquired skills to this task. (5) In addition they are taught additional skills or more detail for the initial skills that are required for this new task. (6) Again learners are shown or asked to recognize how the previous and new skills are used to complete the task. This constitutes a second cycle of instruction.

This cyclical procedure is repeated for each new task in the progression, with the learners required to do more and more of the task as they acquire skill, while the instructional system demonstrates less and less. Eventually learners are expected to complete the next task in the progression on their own. If the progression of tasks is carefully chosen and sequenced, then when learners have demonstrated their ability to satisfactorily complete one or more whole tasks without coaching or additional demonstration, they have acquired the skill intended by the goals of the instruction.

A minimal task-centered instructional strategy is a single worked task. However, a truly effective task-centered strategy involves a progression of increasingly complex tasks and a corresponding decreasing amount of learner guidance and coaching.

Activation Principle

- Learning is promoted when learners activate relevant cognitive structures by being directed to recall, describe or demonstrate relevant *prior knowledge or experience*.

---

8 *Editors' note: For more information about how to identify and sequence tasks in order of increasing complexity, see Reigeluth's Elaboration Theory chapter in Volume II. However, please note that Merrill uses "version" to refer to a single performance of a task, whereas Reigeluth uses it to refer to a class of similar performances of a task. Merrill refers to the latter as "tasks." He also refers to what Reigeluth calls a "task" as a "class of tasks". Examples are: driving a car (Merrill – "class of tasks"; Reigeluth – "task"), driving a particular type of car in a particular type of situation (Merrill – "task"; Reigeluth – "version of a task"), and driving my car last Sunday afternoon (Merrill – "version of a task"; Reigeluth – "instance of a task").*

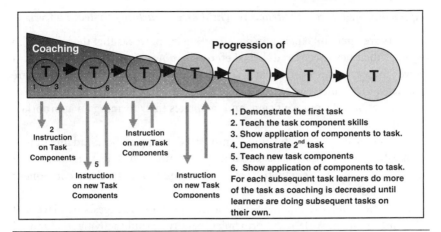

Figure 3.1 An Example of a Task-Centered Instructional Strategy

- Learning from activation is enhanced when learners *share* previous experience with one another.
- Learning from activation is enhanced when learners recall or acquire a *structure for organizing* the new knowledge, when the structure is the basis for guidance during demonstration, is the basis for coaching during application, and is the basis for reflection during integration.

Prior Knowledge or Experience

Associative memory is insufficient for performing complex tasks. Complex tasks require learners to use some form of mental model that organizes the diverse skills required into some interrelated whole. When left on their own, learners often activate an inappropriate mental model, thus increasing the mental effort required to acquire the integrated set of skills necessary for doing the task. Building on an inappropriate mental model often results in misconceptions that show up as errors when learners attempt to complete the new task. Directing learners to recall past relevant experience and checking this recollection for relevance to the task under consideration are more likely to activate an appropriate mental model that facilitates the acquisition of the new set of interrelated skills (Mayer, 1992).

Sharing Previous Experience

Peer sharing of previous experience is a way not only to have the learner who is sharing activate their related mental model for the experience, but also to provide vicarious experience to their fellow students and to stimulate similar recollection on the part of those hearing the shared experience.

Supporting Structure and Structure–Guidance–Coaching–Reflection Cycle

Learners are often not efficient in constructing frameworks that they can use to organize their newly acquired skills. Left on their own, they often use inefficient or even inappropriate organizational schemes. Providing learners with a structure that helps them interrelate the required skills often makes their acquisition of the new set of skills more efficient and facilitates their forming an appropriate mental model.

The four principles of activation, demonstration, application, and integration form a four-phase cycle of instruction (see Figure 3.2). Effective instruction involves all four of these activities repeated as required for teaching component skills or whole tasks.

The cycle of instruction identified for first principles suggests two layers of relationship. On the surface first principles identify learning activities that should be included in effective instruction as described in this paper. At a deeper level there is within this cycle a more subtle cycle consisting of *structure–guidance–coaching–reflection.*

> In general, research has demonstrated that making students aware of specific structure in information helps them summarize that information [and subsequently be able to remember and use this information more effectively]. (Marzano, Pickering, et al., 2001, p. 32)

Rosenshine (1997) describes the importance of well-connected knowledge structures. He says that asking students to organize information, summarize information, and compare new material with prior material are all activities that require processing and should help students develop and strengthen their cognitive structures.

During the activation phase first principles prescribe that the instruction should provide an organizing *structure* based on what students already know. This structure should then be used to facilitate the acquisition of the new knowledge during the remaining phases of the instructional cycle. During the demonstration phase not only should *guidance* help learners relate general information to

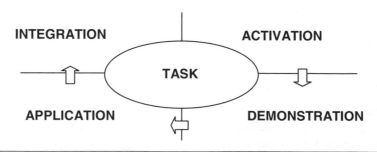

Figure 3.2 The Four-Phase Cycle of Instruction

specific portrayals, but guidance should also help learners relate new material to the structure provided during the activation phase. During the application phase *coaching* should help students use this structure to facilitate their use of the newly acquired skill to complete new tasks. During the integration phase *reflection* should encourage learners to summarize what they have learned and again examine how the new knowledge is related to what they previously knew via the structure that was recalled or provided.

It is interesting to note that many of the courses we have critiqued on the basis of first principles fail to include activation or integration in any form, so the use of guidance or coaching to relate new material to previously learned material via some structure is therefore not included. This deeper cycle, *structure–guidance–coaching–reflection*, deserves more study and research.

Integration Principle

- Learning is promoted when learners integrate their new knowledge into their everyday life by being directed to *reflect-on*, discuss, or defend their new knowledge or skill.
- Learning from integration is enhanced by *peer critique*.
- Learning from integration is enhanced when learners create, invent, or explore *personal ways to use* their new knowledge or skill.
- Learning from integration is enhanced when learners *publicly demonstrate* their new knowledge or skill.

Reflection

"Think about it" is an admonition often given by effective teachers. But merely admonishing learners to think is usually not sufficient. It is often said that the teacher learns more than the student. When instruction provides an opportunity for learners to discuss what they have learned with other students or to defend what they have learned when challenged, then they are put in the role of teacher. Meaningful discussion and the need to defend one's skills requires the kind of deep reflection that enables learners to refine their mental models, to eliminate misconceptions, and to increase the flexibility with which they use their new skill. An opportunity for meaningful reflection increases the probability that the skill will be retained and used in the everyday lives of the learners.

Peer-Critique

Evaluating the work of other learners requires learners to once again reflect on what they have done and how it compares to what others have done. They must revisit the information involved to see if the portrayal they are critiquing does indeed implement this information. When done by a group of two or more students, peer critique can also involve peer discussion where learners must defend their own interpretation and application of the material in their attempt to critique another application.

Personal Use

When instruction is remember-information-only, it is stored in associative memory. Except for traumatic events or significant amounts of rehearsal, associative memory has a steep forgetting curve, and large amounts of the information are difficult or impossible to recall after only a short time. On the other hand, integrated skills that can be used to complete real-world tasks are stored in schematic memory as mental models. If a mental model is used over a progression of whole tasks, then, except for the information-only components of the task, forgetting is much less pronounced, and learners retain their ability to perform complex tasks over much longer periods of time. Even when learners do not use their skill for a period of time, their relearning time is much less.

When learners can immediately use their newly acquired skills to do necessary or desired tasks in their everyday lives, then the learning is even more stable and likely to survive for much longer periods of time. Effective integration finds ways to extend the instruction beyond the classroom or on-line course into the everyday life of the student.

Public Demonstration

Graphics, animation, and other presentation enhancements are often used with the intent of increasing learner motivation. While these devices can attract a learner's attention, they are usually insufficient for sustaining attention over an extended period of time. Too often such devices become tiring and actually interfere with effective learning. Perhaps the greatest motivator of all is learning itself. Human beings are wired to learn. When learners perceive that they have acquired real skill, that is, the ability to solve real-world problems or complete real-world tasks, they are usually anxious to demonstrate this skill to significant others in their lives. When learners know that they will have an opportunity to demonstrate their newly acquired skill to significant others in their world, then their motivation to perform in an effective way is significantly increased.

Instructional Strategy Scaling

Even though these first principles of instruction are well known, it is obvious even to the casual observer of current instructional products that much instruction fails to adequately implement these principles. It is hypothesized that there is a scale of instructional strategy that will correlate with levels of performance on complex tasks. The reader is familiar with the prevalence of information-only instruction with "remember-what-I-told-you" questions tacked onto the end, which might be identified as a level-0 instructional strategy.

The author hypothesizes that performance on complex, real-world tasks will be incremented (successively improved) when an instructional strategy implements each of the first principles in turn (Merrill, 2006a, 2006b). Adding consistent demonstration to information promotes the first increment (level 1) in learning effectiveness, efficiency, and engagement. Adding consistent application with corrective feedback to information with demonstration adds a second increment (level 2). Using a task-centered instructional strategy adds the third increment (level 3). Activation will add an additional learning increment, especially if the structure-guidance-coaching-reflection cycle is also implemented. Personal-use and going-public integration will also add an additional learning increment. Much research remains to be done to support this hypothesized scale of instructional strategy efficacy.

Conclusion

The quest for first principles of instruction was launched with the publication of the second "green book" (Reigeluth, 1999). The author argued that in spite of the diversity represented by the various instructional theories and models represented in that volume that, in fact, the underlying principles for all of those theories are fundamentally the same. Reigeluth questioned this hypothesis and challenged the author to identify these underlying principles, if, in fact, they do exist. This paper and those cited are a result of that challenge.

The above litany of principles may not be complete. Many of the theories and models reviewed do not include all of these principles. However, to date the author has not identified any theory or model that includes contrary principles. Anecdotal evidence from a number of development projects has demonstrated that, when instructional design incorporates these principles, the resulting instruction is more effective. A major study by a large corporation found that, when their flagship instructional product was compared to a new product that incorporated these first principles, the new product was significantly more effective and efficient than their existing product (Thompson Inc., 2002).

Being involved in application of their new skills early in the instruction provides significant motivation to students. Learning is the greatest motivator when learners can see that they have acquired a new skill. Merely remembering concepts, terminology, principles, and facts for recall on a multiple choice test in a testing center is not motivating. However, being able to do something that they could not do before is very motivating. Students who have engaged in problem-centered courses that implement first principles of instruction express greater satisfaction and interest in the course and actually perform better than students in more traditional courses (Frick, Chadha, Watson, Wang, & Green, 2008; in press; Frick, Chadha, Watson, Green, & Zlatkovska, 2008).

As all dissertations end with "more research is needed," so, true to his academic roots, the author also acknowledges that much remains to be done to verify these principles in a wide variety of settings, for a wide variety of different audiences, in other cultures, and across subject-matter domains. It is the author's hope that perhaps these principles might form a starting point for developing a common knowledge base about instructional models, methods, and theory, and for encouraging future research on instructional design.

References

Clark, R. C. (2003). *Building expertise: Cognitive methods for training and performance improvement.* Washington D.C.: International Society for Performance Improvement.

Clark, R. C., & Mayer, R. E. (2003). *e-Learning and the science of instruction.* San Francisco: Jossey-Bass Pfeiffer.

Frick, T., Chadha, R., Watson, C., Green, P., & Zlatkovska, E. (2008). *Improving course evaluations to improve teaching in higher education.* Paper presented at the Summer Research Symposium, Association for Educational Communications and Technology, Bloomington, IN.

Frick, T., Chadha, R., Watson, C., Wang, Y., & Green, P. (in press). College student perceptions of teaching and learning quality. *Educational Technology Research and Development.*

Frick, T., Chadha, R., Watson, C., Wang, Y., & Green, P. (2008). *Theory-based course evaluation: Implications for improving student success in postsecondary education.* Paper presented at the annual conference of the American Educational Research Association, New York.

Kirschner, P. A., Sweller, J. ,et al. (2006). Why minimal guidance during instruction does not work: An analysis of the failure of constructivist, discovery, problem-based, experiential, and inquiry-based teaching. *Educational Psychologist, 41*(2), 75–86.

Marzano, R. J., Pickering, D. J., et al. (2001*). Classroom instruction that works: Research-based strategies for increasing student achievement.* Alexandria, VA: Association for Supervision and Curriculum Development.

Mayer, R. E. (1992). *Thinking, problem solving, cognition* (2nd ed.). New York: Freeman.

Mayer, R. E. (2001). *Multimedia learning.* Cambridge, UK: Cambridge University Press.

Merrill, M. D. (1997, November–December). Instructional strategies that teach. *CBT Solutions,* 1–11.

Merrill, M. D. (2002). First principles of instruction. *Educational Technology Research and Development, 50*(3), 43–59.

Merrill, M. D. (2006a). Hypothesized performance on complex tasks as a function of scaled instructional strategies. In J. Enen & R. E. Clark (Eds.), *Handling complexity in learning environments: Theory and research* (pp. 265–281). Amsterdam: Elsevier.

Merrill, M. D. (2006b). Levels of instructional strategy. *Educational Technology, 46*(4), 5–10.

Merrill, M. D. (2007). First principles of instruction: A synthesis. In R. A. Reiser & J. V. Dempsey (Eds.), *Trends and issues in instructional design and technology* (2nd ed., pp. 62–71). Upper Saddle River, NJ: Merrill/Prentice-Hall.

Reigeluth, C. M. (Ed.). (1999). *Instructional-design theories and models: Vol. 2. A new paradigm of instructional theory.* Mahwah, NJ: Erlbaum.

Rosenshine, B. (1997). Advances in research on instruction. In E. J. Lloyd, E. J. Kame'enui, & D. Chard (Eds.), *Issues in educating students with disabilities* (pp. 197–221). Mahwah, NJ: Erlbaum.

Thompson, Inc. (2002). *Thompson job impact study.* Naperville, IL: Thompson NETg.

van Merriënboer, J. J. G. (1997). *Training complex cognitive skills: A four-component instructional design model for technical training.* Englewood Cliffs, NJ: Educational Technology.

4
Situational Principles of Instruction

CHARLES M. REIGELUTH
Indiana University

ALISON A. CARR-CHELLMAN
Pennsylvania State University

Charles M. Reigeluth received a BA in economics from Harvard University. He was a high school teacher for three years before earning his doctorate in instructional psychology at Brigham Young University. He has been a professor in the Instructional Systems Technology Department at Indiana University's School of Education in Bloomington since 1988, and served as chairman of the department from 1990 to 1992. His major area for service, teaching, and research is the process for facilitating district-wide paradigm change in public school systems. His major research goal is to advance knowledge to help school districts successfully navigate transformation to the learner-centered paradigm of education. He has published nine books and over 120 journal articles and chapters. Two of his books received an "outstanding book of the year" award from Association for Educational Communications and Technology (AECT). He also received AECT's Distinguished Service Award and Brigham Young University's Distinguished Alumnus Award.

Alison A. Carr-Chellman is a professor of instructional systems at Pennsylvania State University in the Department of Learning and Performance Systems. She received a B.S. and an M.S. from Syracuse University. She taught elementary school, community education, and worked as an interactional designer for McDonnell Douglas before returning to Indiana University to earn her doctorate. She is the author of more than 100 publications including two books, many book chapters, and a wide variety of refereed and nonrefereed journal articles. Her research interests are diffusion of innovations, systemic school change, e-learning, systems theory, and design theory.

EDITORS' FOREWORD

Vision

- *To increase the precision of universal principles such that we can create higher quality instruction*

Defining Situational Principles

- *Situational principles only apply in some situations. They range from being close to universal to being very rare.*
- *Some situational principles are sequential, but most are heuristic in nature, due to the complexity of the task of designing instruction.*

Important Situations

- *Analogy: A universe with galaxies and solar systems*
- *Two types of situationalities that call for fundamentally different methods:*
  1. *Situationalities based on different approaches to instruction (means), such as:*
     1.1. *Role play*
     1.2. *Synectics*
     1.3. *Mastery learning*
     1.4. *Direct instruction (see unit 2)*
     1.5. *Discussion (see unit 2)*
     1.6. *Conflict resolution*
     1.7. *Peer learning*
     1.8. *Experiential learning (see unit 2)*
     1.9. *Problem-based learning (see unit 2)*
     1.10. *Simulation-based learning (see unit 2)*
  2. *Situationalities based on different learning outcomes (ends), such as:*
     2.1. *Knowledge*
     2.2. *Comprehension (see unit 3)*
     2.3. *Application (see unit 3)*
     2.4. *Analysis*
     2.5. *Synthesis*
     2.6. *Evaluation*
     2.7. *Affective development*
     2.8. *Integrated learning*

—CMR & ACC

SITUATIONAL PRINCIPLES OF INSTRUCTION

In chapter 3 Merrill identified five "first principles" that he characterized as "general," meaning that they apply to "any…instructional approach, including direct methods, tutorial methods, experiential methods, and exploratory methods" (see p. 43). But clearly, to be of high quality, instruction must be different in different situations, as was discussed in chapter 1. This does not necessarily mean that there are no general (universal) principles of instruction, just that they are not sufficiently precise (or detailed) for practitioners to create high quality instruction. Instructional designers and teachers need more precise guidance about how to implement such general principles, and the more precise the guidance we offer, the less it generalizes to all situations—in other words, the more situational the principles become. One could envision a vertical continuum that ranges from a few highly general (or universal) yet imprecise principles (or methods) on the top, to many highly precise yet extremely local (situational) principles (or methods) on the bottom.

In this chapter we first explain what situational principles are and how they can serve to increase the precision of guidance for instruction. We then turn our attention to understanding which situations are important; that is, which situations are likely to have the greatest influence on the selection of methods. After defining both values and conditions as situations that are important, in our view, we link situationalities with universalities through the metaphor of a universe with galaxies and solar systems, to illustrate the relationships among various methods and approaches. We believe that there are clusters of methods tied to clusters of situationalities, and that one way to move toward a common knowledge base in instructional theory is to identify where those clusters may best serve one another. We conclude with some thoughts about these clusters of situationalities and methods.

Situational Principles

Situational principles are ones that are not universal—they only apply in some situations. They exist on a continuum from situations that are very common (close to universal) to ones that are highly local (apply very rarely). They become necessary when we attempt to offer precision in our instructional principles or guidelines.[1] For example, practice (or learner activity of some kind) is called for at some point during instruction—this is a universality for good instruction. But what should the practice be like? When we address this question, we are moving from a universal, "Use practice," to a situational form of guidance. Practicing a skill, for instance, is far different from practicing an understanding or an emotional disposition. So the directive, "Use practice," is highly imprecise, yet in its imprecision it maintains a universal quality. In contrast, "Students should practice this concept-classification skill by distinguishing between examples and nonexamples of apples" is much more precise and necessarily situational.

---

1 *Instructional guideline* is defined as having two major components: an instructional method and an instructional situation (when to use the method). A *prescriptive instructional principle* is synonymous with "instructional guideline," whereas a *descriptive instructional principle* has the following two major components: an instructional method and its probable effects or influence on learning (see volume I, chapter 1).

Increased precision is important for helping practitioners to design and enact quality instruction, as well as for helping researchers to design useful research for building a common knowledge base. Therefore, instructional theorists seek to increase precision, and we have found three ways to make methods more precise: kinds, parts, and criteria (see chapter 1).

Kinds

If we continue with our example of practice as a largely universal method offered by instructional theories, we might add precision by asking, what are the different *kinds* of practice? They might include concept-classification practice (which asks the learner to select examples of the concept) and procedure-using practice (which asks the learner to use a set of steps to accomplish a goal). Descriptions of each of these kinds of practice increase the precision of the method (the amount of guidance it offers). But the more precise descriptions are each less broadly applicable—each should only be used in some situations (in this case, for fostering the development of concept-classification skills or for fostering mastery of a procedure). Therefore, it is a situational method, and the method combined with its situationality (when to use the method) is called a guideline or a situational principle of instruction.

Parts

An instructional theory may alternatively provide additional precision for a method by describing parts of the method. For example, for practice on a procedural skill, the theory might identify the following parts: first present a particular case (including the goal and inputs), then ask the learner to achieve the goal for that particular case and provide coaching or scaffolding for the learner's performance. One critical difference between parts and kinds is that with kinds you will use only one for any given use of the method, whereas with parts, you typically use all the parts that are recommended (though some of those parts could be situational, such as only using coaching or scaffolding in the early stages of the development of the skill). In essence, all the parts are needed to make up a whole method, whereas each kind *is* a whole method.

Criteria

Often more precise guidance doesn't take the form of either a kind or a part, but instead may specify some standard or criterion. For example, "Practice should be short" is neither a part nor a kind. An instructional theory may specify criteria or standards that a given method should meet in order to be considered "good."

While it is possible that a practitioner may look at a recommendation and see that it is parts of a method or a kind of a method or a criterion for a method, these distinctions are typically more useful for theorists and researchers to consider. When developing instructional-event theory, it is important to utilize all three of these when each is appropriate for giving more precise guidance. In some cases guidance will entail all three, whereas in other cases any of the three might be inappropriate.

Heuristics

To oversimplify the world, experts think in terms of steps when they perform some tasks, but not for other tasks—they think instead of heuristics; that is principles, rules of thumb, guidelines, causal models, and so forth. For example, a complex heuristic task, such as instructional design or psychological counseling, is not performed by experts as a step-by-step procedure. Rather, experts use heuristics of various kinds to guide their performance.

Now, most tasks have a combination of heuristic and procedural elements and may be normally distributed along a continuum from simple, procedural tasks on one extreme to complex, heuristically based ones on the other, with the majority of tasks in the middle somewhere. Such "combination" tasks often have a procedure on the highest (most imprecise) level of description. For example, when we *describe* the instructional systems design (ISD) process, we often list the steps in analysis, design, development, implementation, evaluation (ADDIE), but as we attempt to provide more precise guidance, we find we must resort mostly to heuristics and nonlinear thinking. As another example, in psychological counseling, first the counselor welcomes the patient and helps him or her to feel comfortable, then tries to diagnose the nature of the patient's problem, determines some possible solutions, selects the most appropriate one, develops a plan, and so forth. We can describe these steps at a very high level, but, when we try to offer more precision on *how* to accomplish each of those steps (to provide more detailed guidance for that performance), there are many, many factors that experts must consider, so substeps are inadequate for capturing the way an expert thinks and the kind of knowledge an expert uses. For example, what are the steps involved in welcoming the patient and helping him or her to feel comfortable? Experts' performances of this step vary tremendously from one situation to another (a friendly patient, an angry patient, a despondent patient, and so forth), so it is impractical for the expert to think in terms of steps.

Instruction is a combination task but is predominantly heuristic. Therefore, the kinds of knowledge that may be most helpful in an instructional theory include some sequential elements, but mostly heuristic elements. And the sequential elements are likely to be on the less precise levels of description, while the heuristics are likely to be on the more precise levels of description. Of course, both steps and heuristics can be situational. But when a method or guideline is elaborated to a more precise level of description, heuristics are more likely to be used.

Important Situations

Which situations are important? Since their only purpose is to tell us when and when not to use a particular method, important situations are the ones that are most useful for deciding what the instruction should be like.

In chapter 1 we identified two broad kinds of situational variables:

- Values (about goals, about methods, and about priorities) and
- Conditions (content, learner, learning constraints, and ISD process constraints).

But which situationalities have the broadest *impact*—which ones lead us to choose fundamentally different methods?

A Metaphor

To address this question, we can use a metaphor based on Merrill's first principles (chapter 3) as potentially "universal" principles:[2] some of the principles might apply to the entire universe of instructional-event theory. However, there are galaxies in the universe, and some principles and methods of instruction may only apply within one galaxy. Also, within each galaxy there are both "universal" principles (that apply throughout the galaxy) and situational principles (that may apply only in one solar system). This assumes that there are some sets of methods that work together as a *system* to promote optimal learning (as opposed to thinking of methods as a kind of smorgasbord in which one can pick and choose any methods to go with each other).

If we assume there are such "systems" of methods, this gives rise to the question, "What are the 'galaxies' that represent significantly different systems of methods from other galaxies?" Do Gagné's five domains of learning outcomes (Reigeluth, 1983, chapter 4) constitute five different galaxies? If so, his different kinds of intellectual skills could represent different solar systems in that galaxy. Or could the major levels in Bloom's (1956) taxonomy be considered galaxies, with his sublevels as solar systems? Or could problem-based instruction and direct instruction be considered galaxies? The answer to these questions is critical to building (and understanding) a common knowledge base about instruction.

Methods of instruction may not fit so neatly into this universe-galaxy-solar system view of instructional theory as we might hope. The same type of solar system may exist in many galaxies. Similar suns may exist in many solar systems. And instructional situations are so complex that there may be a need for some smorgasbord-type selections of methods in addition to those methods that are "universal" within a galaxy or a solar system. Furthermore, there is an important

---

2 Merrill makes some claim that his First Principles are universal. Certainly, the concept of "universal" principles (that apply to all instruction) is a tantalizing one and useful for this discussion.

creative element that may strongly influence the quality of instruction, and it may be difficult to address this in instructional-event theories.

However, this does not make the concept of galaxies and solar systems of instructional methods and principles useless, any more than it makes Merrill's first principles useless. They still have much value. There is considerable economy in having a class of instructional situations that calls for the use of a system of methods that can be used as a "package deal," even if there are additional situationalities to further tailor that package to a particular instructional situation.

The challenge is to figure out what are the galaxies (and solar systems)—what are the systems of methods that are frequently used together in high quality instruction, and what are the situations in which they work so well together. We recognize that there may be many methods that do not cluster at all, and so they may be more like a smorgasbord, where you pick and choose depending on your situation, and these will also need to be addressed by a common knowledge base on instruction.

Common Systems of Methods

We have attempted to identify the most common systems of methods, but these are certainly not exhaustive. We believe some of these systems will prove very useful, while others may not, depending on your particular situation.

Our first observation was that methods for developing skills are quite different from methods for helping students to memorize information, which in turn are quite different from methods for fostering deep understandings. The situationalities for selecting these systems of methods are clearly based on the kind of *learning outcome* they promote. Gagné and Merrill based their instructional theories primarily on this kind of situationality.

Our second observation was that methods in problem-based instruction tend to be very different from methods in direct instruction, both of which are quite different from experiential instruction. Furthermore, they are not tied to kinds of learning outcomes; they represent different *approaches* one could use for teaching the same learning outcome. Yet they are clearly systems of methods that are interrelated and interdependent with each other.

Therefore, we have found two major kinds of situationalities that influence the selection of different systems of methods: those based on different approaches to instruction, and those based on different learning outcomes. Approaches are *means-centric*, for they are focused on the methods, whereas learning outcomes are *ends-centric* for they are focused on the nature of what is learned. While means and ends seem to cover much territory, these two may not be the only categories or even necessarily the most useful categories of systems of methods, but they are the most useful categories that we have found to date.

Our next challenge was to identify the systems of methods within each category.

Approaches to Instruction

Approaches to instruction vary widely, and the most common confusion here tends to be confusing approaches with learning outcomes (which are addressed following this section). Joyce, Weil, and Calhoun (2000) are among the leaders in instructional approaches with their seminal text, *Models of Teaching*. Some of the models are oriented toward approaches, others toward outcomes. Among the more clearly approach-oriented models that they describe are role playing, synectics, mastery learning, and direct instruction. Similarly, Gunter, Estes, and Schwab (2003) describe several models of teaching that are clearly approaches— direct instruction, synectics, and classroom discussion—while others are more clearly outcomes related.

McKeachie (2002) offers the following teaching methods: (1) learning through journaling, writing, papers, reports; (2) reading as active learning; (3) cooperative, collaborative, and peer learning; (4) problem-based learning (PBL) (cases, games, simulations); (5) laboratory instruction; (6) experiential learning (service learning, fieldwork, collaborative research); and (7) project methods (independent study, one-on-one teaching). Fenstermacher and Soltis (2004) break approaches to teaching into three broad classroom approaches: *executive, facilitator, and liberationist*.

However, these differ from what we typically think of as approaches in that they are primarily management and classroom-attitude approaches rather than specific methods of teaching/learning.

We have included five instructional approaches in unit 2 of this text—*direct instruction, discussion, experiential, problem-based*, and *simulation*. In our view, these are among the most well-grounded and well-researched methods in instructional theory today, although these clearly do not constitute an exhaustive list of the most current or influential approaches to instruction. Based on our current understandings of human learning and advanced theories of instruction, we suspect that these are among the most useful approaches, but there are clearly many others that could and should be added to develop a common knowledge base.

Learning Outcomes

For the learning outcomes category, there has been a long tradition of learning taxonomies. Bloom, for example, has taxonomies in three broad domains: cognitive (head), affective (heart), and psychomotor (hand). Bloom's cognitive taxonomy (1956) breaks cognitive learning into knowledge, comprehension, application, analysis, synthesis, and evaluation. *Knowledge* is typically understood to be recall tasks such as list, define, tell, and so on. *Comprehension* is a higher-level learning outcome asking for students to grasp meanings such as distinguish, describe, predict, and so forth. *Application* asks learners to use, in novel situations, the information gained from knowledge and comprehension tasks. In this taxonomy, we may ask the learner to demonstrate, calculate, show, relate, or classify. *Analysis* asks the learner to understand patterns or parts. Here we might see if the learner can separate, order, connect, explain, infer, and classify. In *synthesis*, new ideas are created by using prior learning and knowledge. So we might ask learners to integrate, plan, create, design, invent, and so forth. Finally, *evaluation* is considered the highest level of thinking (though this is switched with synthesis in Anderson and Krathwohl's (2001) update of Bloom's cognitive taxonomy), and here students are using lower levels of learning in order to discriminate and assess value. We might ask the learner to decide, grade, measure, select, or judge. While Bloom's taxonomy is well known and thoroughly describes a number of naturally cohesive learning outcomes, we feel that Bloom's taxonomy was primarily designed to describe and assess learning outcomes rather than to select different sets of methods.

Anderson and Krathwohl's (2001) update of Bloom's classic taxonomy incorporated types of knowledge as well as processes for learning; creating the knowledge dimension (fact, concept, procedure, metacognitive), as well as the cognitive process dimension (remember, understand, apply, analyze, evaluate, create).

Perhaps the next best known taxonomy in the instructional arena is Gagné's (1965, 1984) learning outcomes. Gagné's taxonomy accounts for the cognitive domain (in the form of intellectual skills, cognitive strategies, and verbal information), as well as motor skills and attitudes, much like Bloom's cognitive, psychomotor, and affective domains, respectively (though attitudes are but one aspect of the affective domain). Within the *intellectual skills* part of the cognitive domain, Gagné breaks down learning outcomes into discriminations, concrete concepts, defined concepts, rules, and problem solving (higher-order rules). Intellectual skills of the *discrimination* type ask learners to respond differently to different stimuli. Those of the *concrete concept* type ask learners to classify instances of concepts that cannot be verbally defined. Intellectual skills of the *defined concept* type typically ask learners to label or classify instances based on a definition. Those of the *rule* type ask learners to apply rules and demonstrate principles. Those of the *problem solving* type ask learners to generate solutions requiring sets of rules. *Cognitive strategies* are complex sets of rules that tend to generalize across subject domains, such as strategies for learning (e.g., use of mnemonics or reflection). *Verbal information* is typically understood as recall and typically asks students to state some information, but it does include understanding as well. Gagné's taxonomy was more specifically intended for guiding the selection of methods of instruction, so his categories could serve well as galaxies and solar systems in the universe of instructional methods.

Ausubel (1963; Ausubel, Novak, & Hanesian, 1978) has distinguished between rote and meaningful learning. Rote learning is relatively isolated bits of information that a learner is able to relate to other bits of information only in arbitrary ways. Meaningful learning, however, entails making nonarbitrary and substantive connections among ideas. Anderson (1983) dichotomizes learning as either declarative or procedural knowledge: declarative knowledge is chunked into not more than five elements in which the learner is asked to describe facts, things, tasks, or methods, while procedural knowledge is knowledge of how to do things, including both motor and mental skills. This is more of a say vs. do dichotomy, compared to Ausubel's rote vs. meaningful learning dichotomy.

Merrill (Merrill, Reigeluth, & Faust, 1978) expanded Gagné's taxonomy into a two-dimensional taxonomy of learning outcomes based on the type of content being learned and the level on which it is learned (which was subsequently used in the revision of Bloom's taxonomy of the cognitive domain). The types of content include facts, concepts, procedures, and principles, while the levels of learning include remember (verbatim or paraphrased), use (identify or produce), and find. With the exception of facts, all the types of content can be learned at any of the levels of learning. Facts can only be learned at the remember level.

Reigeluth has carefully analyzed these taxonomies in terms of their usefulness for selecting different systems of instructional methods and has developed a synthesis of them (see Table 4.1). In his analysis, he found that "verbal information" requires very different methods of instruction, depending on whether it entails Ausubel's rote learning (memorizing) or meaningful learning (understanding). He also found that analysis, synthesis, and evaluation require very similar methods of instruction. This left four types of learning outcomes that have a significant impact on selecting methods of instruction in the cognitive domain: memorize information, understand relationships, apply skills, and apply generic skills (see Table 4.1). There is certainly more overlap in methods between apply skills and apply generic skills than between any of the other kinds of learning outcomes, so one could make an argument for combining them, and then having variations for concept classification, procedure using, principle using, and generic skills (or cognitive strategies), somewhat similar to Gagné's intellectual skills.

Based on these various taxonomies, we believe that each of the following learning outcomes calls for a unique system of methods:

Table 4.1 A Comparison of Taxonomies of Learning Outcomes

Bloom	Gagné	Ausubel	Merrill	Reigeluth
Knowledge	Verbal information	Rote	Remember verbatim	Memorize information
Comprehension	Verbal information	Meaningful	Remember paraphrased	Understand relationships
Application	Intellectual skill		Use	Apply skills
Analysis Synthesis Evaluation	Cognitive strategy		Find	Apply generic skills

- Memorization
- Understanding
- Skills (including generic skills)
- Emotional development
- Integrated learning (across types of learning outcomes and subject domains)

Again, this is not a comprehensive list. We have added a kind of learning from the affective domain, but there are many other kinds of learning in this domain (e.g., the taxonomy in Reigeluth, 1999, chapter 20). We have also added integrated learning, because authentic tasks require learning many kinds of outcomes simultaneously, and there are unique methods for addressing this type of learning. An argument could be made that integrated learning is an approach to instruction rather than a learning outcome, but we believe it results in a qualitatively different way of thinking. In fact, we believe it is some of both but have chosen to include it in the learning outcomes section of this volume. Unit 3 includes chapters that describe elements of a common knowledge base for each of the last four of these five kinds of learning outcomes. We are not including a chapter for memorization outcomes because we believe that a common knowledge base has already been well established in this area (see e.g., Anderson, 1976; Cooke & Guzaukas, 1993; Merrill & Salisbury, 1984; Salisbury, 1990; Woodward, 2006).

Organization of Units 2 and 3 of this Book

The next two units of this book are dedicated to capturing the common knowledge base within systems of methods that fall within our two major categories: instructional approaches and learning outcomes. Unit 2 describes five different approaches, and Unit 3 describes systems of methods for four different kinds of learning outcomes. It should be clear by now that these are not mutually exclusive categories, rather these are two different perspectives about how to organize instructional theories and methods. We hope this will encourage other theorists to identify other categories that are useful for selecting systems of instructional methods.

References

Anderson, J. (1983). *The architecture of cognition.* Cambridge, MA: Harvard University Press,.
Anderson, J. R. (1976). *Language, memory, and thought.* Hillsdale, NJ: Erlbaum.
Anderson, L. W., & Krathwohl, D. R. (Eds.). (2001). *A taxonomy for learning, teaching, and assessing: A revision of Bloom's taxonomy of educational objectives.* New York: Longman.
Ausubel, D. (1963). *The psychology of meaningful verbal learning.* New York: Grune & Stratton.
Ausubel, D., Novak, J., & Hanesian, H. (1978). *Educational psychology: A cognitive view* (2nd ed.). New York: Holt, Rinehart & Winston.
Biggs, J. B., & Collin, K. F. (1982). *Evaluating the quality of learning: The SOLO taxonomy.* New York: Academic.
Bloom, B. S. (1956). *Taxonomy of educational objectives: Handbook 1. The cognitive domain.* New York: McKay.

Cooke, N. L., & Guzaukas, R. (1993). Effects of using a ratio of new items to review items during drill and practice: Three experiments. *Education and Treatment of Children, 16*(3), 213–234.

Fenstermacher, G. D., & Soltis, J. F. (2004). *Approaches to teaching.* New York: Teachers College Press.

Gagné, R. M. (1965). *The conditions of learning.* New York: Holt, Rinehart & Winston.

Gagné, R. M. (1984). Learning outcomes and their effects: Useful categories of human performance. *American Psychologist, 39*(4), 377–385

Gunter, M. A., Estes, T. H., & Schwab, J. (2003). *Instruction: A models approach.* Boston: Allyn & Bacon.

Hauenstein, A. D. (1984). *A conceptual framework for educational objectives: A holistic approach to traditional taxonomies.* New York: University Press of America.

Joyce, B., Weil, M., & Calhoun, E. (2000). *Models of teaching* (6th ed.). Boston: Allyn & Bacon.

Martin, B. L., & Reigeluth, C. M. (1999). Affective education and the affective domain: Implications for instructional design theories and models. In C. M. Reigeluth (Ed.), *Instructional design theories and models: A new paradigm of instructional theory* (Vol. II). Hillsdale, NJ: Erlbaum.

McKeachie, W. J. (2002). *Teaching tips: Strategies, research, and theory for college and university teaching.* Boston: Houghton Mifflin.

Merrill, M. D., Reigeluth, C. M., & Faust, G. W. (1979). The instructional quality profile: A curriculum evaluation and design tool. In H. F. O'Neil, Jr. (Ed.), *Procedures for instructional systems development.* New York: Academic Press.

Merrill, P. F., & Salisbury, D. F. (1984). Research on drill and practice strategies. *Journal of Computer-Based Instruction, 11*(1), 19–21.

Piaget, J. (1963). *The origins of intelligence in children.* New York: W.W. Norton.

Reigeluth, C. M. (1983). *Instructional-design theories and models: Vol. 1. An overview of their current status.* Hillsdale, NJ: Erlbaum.

Salisbury, D. F. (1990). Cognitive psychology and Its implications for designing drill and practice programs for computers. *Journal of Computer-Based Instruction, 17*(1), 23–30.

Woodward, J. (2006). Developing automaticity in multiplication facts: Integrating strategy instruction with timed practice drills. *Learning Disability Quarterly, 29*(4), 269–289.

Unit 2
Theories for Different Approaches to Instruction

Unit Foreword

In chapter 4 we identified means and ends as two major ways to define different galaxies in the universe of instruction. This unit addresses the means—the different kinds of approaches that represent different systems of methods to use. This introduction provides a bit more detail on the approaches that are described in this unit.

In chapter 5, William Huitt, David Monetti, and John Hummel describe elements of a common knowledge base about the direct approach to instruction, or just direct instruction (DI). It is a method that accounts for student differences, groups students based on pretests, and presents information in an active format. DI focuses on student–teacher interaction and heavy use of examples, as well as constant assessment of student learning prior to moving on. We believe that DI, while perhaps not in vogue among scholars currently, likely has a useful place within an information-age paradigm of education. While DI can be used as a separate approach in its own right, it can also be used as a component within other approaches, such as problem-based instruction or experiential instruction to build lower-level skills and knowledge. Huitt, Monetti, and Hummel point out that DI has been shown through empirical research to increase standardized test scores—a common measure of instructional effectiveness in an increasingly accountable education system. Chapter 5 describes what the authors propose as the common knowledge base for this approach.

In chapter 6 Joyce Gibson describes elements of a common knowledge base about the discussion approach to instruction. It is a method for incorporating student experiences into the learning process rather than relying strictly on content presentation. There are kinds of learning that seem to particularly benefit from deep discussions, such as understanding. We also appreciate the ways in which this method tends to alter established power relations between learners and instructors. The emphasis on valuing learner experiences and learner empowerment are important for an information-age society. The effectiveness of the discussion approach depends to some extent on discussion-leading and participation skills. Just as direct instruction is often called for by other approaches, discussion is also often called for by other approaches, such as problem-based instruction. Discussion is used by other methods as a primary tool for reflection.

In chapter 7 experiential instruction is defined by Lee Lindsey and Nancy Berger as learning from our experiences. They go on to differentiate this type of learning as learner-centered, authentic, and self-directed with expectation failure. Experiential instruction is a very common and well-researched approach that is particularly powerful for learning transfer to real-world environments and values authenticity, which we see as important in the information age. The primary strength of this approach is its grounding in reality, which can result in better transfer. The first three approaches (direct instruction, discussion, and experiential instruction) are quite different from one another. In contrast experiential instruction has more overlap with, and similarity to problem-based instruction.

In chapter 8 John Savery defines the problem-based approach to instruction (PBI) as an experientially oriented approach in which students learn from solving problems. PBI has a great deal of coherence as an approach, in that all its component methods fit systemically together. It also has a fairly distinct identity as compared to other types of instruction. PBI is a powerful and effective approach to instruction that is consistent with the information-age paradigm of education. In addition, as Savery points out, the use of PBI has been increasing in recent years and now serves thousands of teachers and students in a wide variety of content areas.

In chapter 9 Andrew Gibbons, Mark McConkie, Kay Kyeongju Seo, and David Wiley define the simulation approach to instruction as including dynamic system models, student ability to change those models, nonlinear logic, augmenting instructional functions, and a specific instructional goal. Simulation-based instruction is similar to experiential instruction, but it provides affordances that are not available in experiential instruction. It also has much in common with PBI. Direct instruction and discussion can both be used in the service of simulation-based instruction. In a simulation there could be points where the learners can hop out into some direct instruction that prepares them for something they need to accomplish in the simulation environment. Discussion, on the other hand, serves more as a reflective tool at the end of a performance in the simulation. Simulations are now more affordable and easier to develop, so they are more feasible for classroom application. Also, simulations are safer and can be done more quickly, easily, and affordably than many real experiences; and it is much easier to add other elements, such as direct instruction, reflection, guidance, scaffolding, and mentoring, through avatars and puppets.

These are but a few of the approaches identified in chapter 4, and it should be apparent that many approaches overlap with each other. We have not included others here because:

- They have considerable overlap with approaches we have already included.
- Some are less in alignment with the information-age paradigm of education.
- Some are linked to out-of-date technologies.
- There are obvious space limitations.

We focused on approaches that we felt were most important for the information-age paradigm of education. But we strongly believe that others are important for a common knowledge base on instruction, and we encourage you to work on synthesizing and advancing the current knowledge about those additional approaches.

In conclusion this unit contains chapters on the following five approaches:

- Direct approach to instruction
- Discussion approach to instruction
- Experiential approach to instruction
- Problem-based approach to instruction
- Simulation approach to instruction

The following unit addresses learning outcomes (the ends of instruction) in a similar fashion.

—CMR & ACC

5
Direct Approach to Instruction

WILLIAM G. HUITT, DAVID M. MONETTI, AND JOHN H. HUMMEL

Valdosta State University

William G. Huitt is a professor in the Department of Psychology and Counseling at Valdosta State University. His research interests include holistic human development, educational reform, problem solving and decision making, and moral character development. He completed his undergraduate degree at the University of South Alabama and his graduate degrees at the University of Florida. He has teaching experience at the middle grades, high school, technical school, community college, and university levels. His Web site, Educational Psychology Interactive (http://teach.valdosta.edu/whuitt/), is one of the largest, most active Web sites in educational psychology.

David M. Monetti is an associate professor in the Department of Psychology and Counseling at Valdosta State University. He teaches courses in educational psychology, learning theory, and measurement and evaluation. He earned his PhD in educational psychology at Florida State University; and bachelor's and master's degrees from the University of South Florida. David completed his teaching internship in English and worked for Leon County Schools' Student Assessment Department. He remains actively involved with the public schools as a researcher and evaluator of school improvement practices. His research interests include service learning, psychometrics, psychological effects of Internet usage, formative assessment, epistemology of learning, and he is currently working on a text through Cengage Learning with Bruce Tuckman entitled *The Theory and Practice of Educational Psychology*.

John H. Hummel is a professor of educational psychology. His specialty areas included applied behavior analysis, direct instruction, and positive behavior supports. He is a certified coach and teacher for Direct Instruction programs, and has recently completed four years as Principal Investigator for a School Improvement Grant for Georgia's Department of Education to help schools across Georgia develop and implement PBS programs.

EDITORS' FOREWORD

Preconditions *(when to use the theory)*

Content
- *Information, skills, understandings, higher-order thinking*

Learners
- *All K-12 students*

Learning environments
- *K-12 classrooms*
- *Trained teachers*

Instructional development constraints
- *Minimal, given the large amount of instruction already developed*

Values *(opinions about what is important)*

about ends *(learning goals)*
- *The importance of mastery of information, skills, understandings, and higher-order thinking*

about criteria *(for successful instruction)*
- *Efficiency: To maximize academic learning time (ALT) as measured by student success, coverage of content objectives, and time-on-task*

about means *(instructional methods)*
- *Variations in students' prerequisite skill levels may require variable time to allow all learners to achieve mastery or different goals/objectives for different learners. Learners may need to be grouped accordingly.*
- *Presentation of essential content should be active, generally as a step-by-step progression*

about power *(to make decisions about the previous three)*
- *The teacher should be in control*

Universal Methods

1. *Presentation phase involves five events: (a) review prior learning/skills; (b) state knowledge or skill to be learned; (c) state importance/relevance; (d) clearly explain knowledge or skill to be learned; and (e) provide multiple opportunities to demonstrate learners' initial understandings.*
2. *Practice phase involves three events: (a) practice under the guidance and supervision of a teacher; (b) practice under independent conditions; and (c) periodically review in order for learners to use their new knowledge and skills.*
3. *The assessment and evaluation phase involves two events: (a) collect daily data to judge student success; and (b) collect longitudinal data (weekly, bi-weekly, monthly).*
4. *The monitoring and feedback phase involves two events: (a) provide cues and prompts; and (b) provide corrective feedback and reinforcement.*

Situational Principles

- Scripted lessons, colloquially thought of as DI, is a variation of direct instruction.
- Scripted lessons follow all the same basic phases and events in the general (universal) model, but differ in the specificity of the teacher statements and student responses.
- Scripted lessons do not provide as much new information in each lesson; instead, the new information is distributed among several lessons so that it represents only about 10 to 15% of a lesson.
- Concepts to be learned in scripted lessons are broken into logically arranged small pieces and follow a "question → answer" format.
- After scripted demonstration of initial understandings, students complete a workbook assignment individually or in small groups.
- Scripted instruction is fast-paced and repetitive, but can be tiresome to instructors and learners alike if continued for longer than about 20 minutes.
- Chained behaviors (math word problems, step-by-step procedures) are excellent candidates for scripted lessons.

—CMR & ACC

DIRECT APPROACH TO INSTRUCTION

Defining quality instruction has been a goal of researchers from the beginning of formal schooling. Since the late 1960s, data have accumulated showing that students who receive high quality instruction demonstrate more successful school learning as measured on standardized tests of basic skills than students who do not (Joyce, Weil, & Calhoun, 2003). While there is a consensus that student learning is important, as well as a recognition that a teacher's classroom behavior is related to that learning (Darling-Hammond, 2000), a major problem arises when the quality of instruction (the "how" of teaching) is discussed outside the context of specific educational objectives or desired educational outcomes and the processes and instruments used to measure learning (the "what" of teaching). That is, decisions regarding curriculum objectives, the form and instrumentation of assessment, and the standards used for evaluation come first; decisions about processes and methods defining quality instruction should follow, for they depend to some extent on the former.

There is currently a national discussion regarding desired outcomes for successful adulthood in the 21st century[1] (e.g., Huitt, 1997; Partnership for 21st Century Skills, 2003; Secretary's Commission on Achieving Necessary Skills, 1991). However, at this time the most widely used measures of student learning are standardized tests of basic skills (Bolon, 2000). When these outcome measures are used, direct or explicit instruction models most often produce the highest

---

1. *Editors' note: Desired outcomes would constitute curriculum theory, and they are addressed in the content layer of instructional design.*

student scores (Rosenshine, 1995) and, therefore, educators should give them consideration when designing instruction.

This chapter provides an overview of the direct instruction approach and is divided into three sections: (1) an introduction to general research-based design attributes of quality instruction; (2) a general model of direct instruction a teacher could utilize to create direct instruction lessons; and (3) an explanation of the design attributes used for the development of scripted lesson plans. Thus, the chapter describes a number of methods or principles, both general and specific, for the application of direct instruction in different instructional situations.

General Design Attributes

Given the importance of student learning and achievement, instructional-event theory requires serious analysis, consideration, and reflection. In volume 2 of this book, Reigeluth (1999) took the position that instructional-event theories (1) should improve learning and development; (2) should inform the practitioner which methods of instruction (and there may be competing or complementary ones) to employ to achieve specific outcomes in specific situations (i.e., an instructional method *designed* to prepare students to score high on an achievement test may not be the best method to help them learn to run and evaluate an experiment); and (3) only increase the likelihood (though to high levels) that the desired outcomes will occur rather than guaranteeing them for all learners and situations.

Reigeluth (1999; chapter 1 this volume) identified three criteria to evaluate how well a method works in achieving instructional outcomes: effectiveness, efficiency, and appeal.[2] Effectiveness requires that appropriate indicators of learning (such as specific levels of achievement and fluency) be identified to objectively measure the learning outcomes. Efficiency requires an optimal use of resources, such as time and money, to obtain a desired result. Appeal is the degree to which learners enjoy the instruction, and it can be especially effective in motivating students to stay engaged and on task (Perkins, 1992). Some educators, especially those espousing a child-centered approach, suggest this last criterion should take precedence over the other two. However, this is problematic in that the academically relevant content public schools must cover as part of their charge can require copious time and effort on the part of many students. As a result, *immediate* satisfaction and enjoyment of the instruction may be difficult to attain. However, if several methods produce equally effective and efficient results, one should employ the approach learners like most. For example, Martin (1999) found that individual written exercises produced similar levels of effectiveness and efficiency as did analogous cooperative learning activities, but the latter were overwhelmingly preferred by the students. In such cases one should opt to use the instructional methods that students prefer.

---

2. *Editors' note: These are now called "values about priorities" (see chapter 1).*

The design attributes of a direct instruction model described in the following section have their roots in classroom research in the 1950s and 1960s. This research, supported by newly developed techniques for applying systematic observation to classroom practices (Flanders, 1970) and reviewed by Carroll (1963), led to the development of new ideas about school learning. The types of studies using this approach came to be known as process-product studies (Gage, 1978, 1994) because they directly connected classroom and school process variables with measures of student learning. Findings from these studies were summarized in a number of models of effective classroom practice (Cruickshank, 1985; Proctor, 1984; Squires, Huitt, & Segars, 1983).

Logically, a primary purpose of providing quality instruction is for students to successfully complete both classroom academic tasks assigned by the teacher and external audits of classroom learning completed through standardized testing (Darling-Hammond, 2000). However, it should be emphasized that most models of quality instruction do not purport that quality instruction, by itself, always leads to student success. Rather, in addition to the specification of how instructional lessons should be planned and implemented, most approaches to instruction advocate additional activities such as curriculum alignment, correct placement of the student within the curriculum, and classroom management.

A basic principle of curriculum alignment[3] is that lesson planning must be directed toward objectives measured on an appropriate achievement instrument (Cohen, 1995). Brady, Clinton, Sweeney, Peterson, and Poynor (1977), as well as Cooley and Leinhart (1980), reported that, on average, objectives covered in textbooks and objectives covered by standardized tests overlap between 40% and 60%. Taking the time to make sure that content overlap occurs is vital, because alignment of a school district's curriculum with objectives assessed by standardized tests can explain up to two-thirds of variance among scores (Wishnick, as cited in Cohen, 1995). Additionally, the curriculum should be constructed using task analyses that identify the prerequisites for all learning objectives (Gagné, Briggs, & Wager, 1992) and should provide opportunities for students to revisit previously covered objectives as they move through the curriculum (called a spiral curriculum, Bruner, 1990).

The principle of student placement[4] emphasizes that students must be properly placed within the curriculum. Quite often this means that students have been grouped based on a pretest of prerequisite skills. The grouping of students is typically accomplished by either a between-classes or within-class procedure. The between-classes grouping would be made prior to beginning the instruction process with the goal of having the students in a classroom be fairly homogeneous with regards to their prerequisite skills in an area. The within-class grouping would permit the teacher to adjust instruction to best address students' current

---

3. *Editors' note: This principle lies at the interrelationship between Curriculum, Assessment, and Instruction.*

4. *Editors' note: This principle is a part of curriculum theory, for it determines what content the student is taught, and it is addressed in the content layer of instructional design.*

knowledge and skills without stigmatizing them or placing students in permanent groups that are not adjusted as the students' knowledge and skills change.

Planning and implementing a long-term, solution-oriented, classroom management program is another effective classroom practice and one of the most effective means of increasing students' time-on-task or engaged time, an important predictor of students' academic achievement (Berliner, 1990; Brophy, 1983; Brophy & Good, 1986).

Combined, these three measures of student classroom behavior (student success on classroom assignments, student coverage of content objectives that will be tested, and student time-on-task) result in the measure called academic learning time (ALT) (Berliner, 1990; Squires et al., 1983). Academic learning time is defined as the amount of time students are successfully involved with important and meaningful content, especially content that will be tested through external audits of the schooling process, such as standardized achievement tests. It is a combined measure of both the quantity of time (time-on-task) as well as the quality of time (success and content overlap) that students accumulate in the classroom. It is the acquisition of ALT (that is, large quantities of quality time) that should be the central focus of teachers and students during the relatively short period they spend in the formal learning environment.

A General Model of Direct Instruction

Several popular models of instruction were developed using the process-product research findings discussed above (e.g., Gagné et al., 1992; Good & Grouws, 1979; Hunter, 1982; Rosenshine & Stevens, 1986; Slavin, 1986). Rosenshine (1995) provided an updated version of this approach and showed how the latest research from cognitive psychology could be incorporated in a direct instruction model.

One general condition included in all these models, identified by Carroll (1963) and elaborated by Bloom (1976), is that students come to the learning task with different levels of prerequisite skills and varying capacities for learning academic material. Therefore, selection of academic objectives[5] and methods of instruction must be adapted to the background and skills of students (Walberg, 1999), and additional learning time must be provided to slower students for all students to attain mastery on curriculum objectives[6] (Guskey & Gates, 1986; Guskey & Pigott, 1988). As much as possible, student attainment of prerequisites should be assured and instruction provided only for those students who have demonstrated mastery on them.

Another general attribute included in all direct instruction models is that essential content should be taught to students via an active presentation of in-

---

5. *Editors' note: Deciding what to teach is a matter of Curriculum Theory and is addressed in the content layer of instructional design.*

6. *Editors' note: Mastery of objectives or standards is incompatible with the industrial-age paradigm of education, which is designed to sort students (see chapter 1).*

formation[7] (Rosenshine, 1995). Fisher et al. (1978) stated that teacher-directed instruction should occur for more than 50% of a lesson and seatwork should occur less than 50%. Bloom (1981) stated that teachers should provide a clear organization of the presentation with a step-by-step progression from subtopic to subtopic based on prerequisite knowledge and skills. This is discussed in more detail in the presentation phase below.

Additional research-based attributes of direct instruction include: (1) pretesting or prompting of relevant knowledge (Block, 1971); (2) more student-teacher interaction (Walberg, 1991); (3) the use of many examples, visual prompts, and demonstrations to mediate between concrete and abstract concepts[8] (Gage & Berliner, 1998); and (4) a constant assessment of student understanding before, during, and after the lesson (Brophy & Good, 1986).[9] Each of these suggestions is included in the description below.

The following is a description of the specific methods of instruction advocated in the general model of direct instruction. It is labeled a transactional model because it emphasizes teacher/student interaction at each point in the lesson (Huitt, 1996). This model proposes four categories of methods of instruction: (A) a presentation phase; (B) a practice phase; (C) a summative assessment and evaluation phase; and (D) methods dealing with monitoring students and giving them feedback.[10] The presentation, practice, and assessment/evaluation phases are done in a somewhat linear fashion, with monitoring (which might be considered formative assessments) and feedback occurring throughout the three phases (see Figure 5.1). Within each of the four major categories there are important instructional methods that increase the likelihood that the learner will successfully learn new concepts and skills.

A. The Presentation Phase

There are five important instructional methods that should be used during the presentation phase of direct instruction: (1) review of previous material or prerequisite skills;[11] (2) a statement of the specific knowledge or skills to be learned; (3) a statement or experience that provides students with a reason or explanation of why these particular objectives are important; (4) a clear, active explanation of the knowledge or skills to be learned; and (5) multiple opportunities for students to demonstrate their initial understandings in response to teacher probes.[11]

---

7. *Editors' note: This is an instructional method, and hence a part of instructional-event theory and is addressed in the strategy layer of instructional design. This method (like the others in this general model) is on the universal end of generality within this galaxy of methods, and it is therefore a relatively imprecise part of the model.*

8. *Editors' note: This fits Merrill's Demonstration Principle.*

9. *Editors' note: (a), (b), and (d) are parts of instructional-event theory, and (c) is part of instructional-evaluation theory.*

10. *Editors' note: These are parts of the instructional theory that provide more precision to the description of the theory.*

11 *Editors' note: These are parts of the first part. They are all in the strategy layer of instructional design. The fifth one could be used for assessment purposes, as well as for instructional purposes, represent-*

Transactional Model of Direct Instruction

A. Presentation

    Overview

        1. Review

        2. What

        3. Why

        4. Explanation

        5. Probe & Respond

D. Monitoring and Feedback

    11. Cues & Prompts

    12. Corrective Feedback

B. Practice

      6. Guided Practice

      7. Independent Practice

      8. Periodic Review

C. Assessment & Evaluation

Figure 5.1 Transactional Model of Direct Instruction

An important instructional implication from cognitive psychology is that learning is made more meaningful if the presentation is preceded by an advance organizer (Ausubel, 1960). While Ausubel referred to an advance organizer as information at a higher level of abstraction than the material to be learned, the term has come to refer to activities that link or bridge new information to existing cognitive structures (Mayer, 2002). The first three universal methods of the general model of direct instruction discussed in this chapter provide this orientation to the lesson in that they provide a rich structure or framework within which instruction will take place.[12] While the three methods are listed in an order, there is no logical or empirical evidence that suggests this particular order. Rather there are legitimate reasons why an instructional designer or teacher might want to switch the order. However, it is vital that these three methods occur before the explanation of new concepts begins.

1. Review. In the first method, teachers and students go over previously learned knowledge or skills that are relevant or prerequisite to the new learning that is to take place. Teachers could have students check homework or discuss difficult material from the previous day's lesson (Walberg, 1999). Teachers could also create an activity that has students utilize concepts and skills that have been previously learned. It is important that students activate prior knowledge so that

---

ing the kind of integration of teaching and testing that is an integral part of the Information-Age paradigm of education. The fifth one also fits Merrill's Application Principle.

12. Editors' note: Merrill's Activation Principle.

they can more easily establish links to new information (called elaboration by information processing theorists such as Craik & Lockhart, 1972).

2. What. In the second method, teachers describe what is to be learned in the lesson. Teachers state the objectives and how the student is to be held accountable for the learning activity (Gronlund, 2003; Mager, 1997). Perkins (1992) maintains that clarity of content is one of the most important conditions for quality instruction. This clarity should include what is to be learned and the standards for mastery. For more performance-based outcomes, Gibbons, Bunderson, Olsen, and Robertson (1995) suggest that "work models" demonstrating the expected processes or operations provide additional clarity as to what the student should be able to do at the end of the learning process.[13] The lesson plans utilizing the design principles of direct instruction (for which URLs are provided later in the chapter) might be considered more in the nature of work models described by these authors. A similar approach, advocated by McCarthy (2000) in her 4MAT model, has the teacher first provide students with direct experiences and then help them organize those experiences into concepts.

The most important aspect of the "what" method is that students should be informed as explicitly as possible what they should be able to do at the end of the learning process. There are two types of objectives[14] teachers can include in this method. The first are activity objectives: These state what the teacher and students will be doing in the present lesson and serve as an organizer for the lesson's or unit's activities. They are also statements about how the teacher will monitor student performance for formative evaluation purposes. For example, the teacher might say, "Today we are going to begin reading Shakespeare's *Taming of the Shrew*." The second are terminal objectives stating what the student will be able to demonstrate at the end of instruction on summative assessments. These will generally be written and will specify what the student will know or be able to do, as well as how learning will be assessed and the standards that must be met. There may be several lessons that will prepare students for the knowledge or skills that will be summatively evaluated, and students should be informed of how multiple lessons tie together.

3. Why. In the third method, teachers describe why a particular objective is important for students to master. The teacher might have students engage in an activity that could be done more efficiently once the new content or skills have been mastered. The teacher might also lead a discussion of tasks[15] performed in other classes or subject areas that are relevant to the new learning. Ultimately, it is important that students have a personal reason to be engaged in the learning process. McCarthy (2000) stated that as many as 40% of students in normal K-12

---

13. *Editors' note: Merrill's Demonstration Principle.*
14. *Editors' note: These provide more precision in the description of the methods by identifying kinds. However, it is possible that both kinds may be recommended by the theory, in which case they are also parts. So there is an area where the difference between parts and kinds blurs. If they were just kinds, it would be important to provide guidance as to when each kind should be used in preference over the other, which is a situationality.*
15. *Editors' note: This begins to address Merrill's Task-Centered Principle.*

classrooms have a learning style that demands a satisfactory answer to "Why should I be involved," before they will engage in a learning task. These students are overrepresented in remedial and special education classes, perhaps because traditional instruction does not successfully address this issue in a personally meaningful way.

4. Explanation. The fourth method is the active, careful explanation to students of the content or skill to be learned. An important principle guiding this method is that the teacher should move from subtopic to subtopic in an efficient manner, introducing new material in small portions and connecting each new subtopic to the previous one (Bloom, 1981; Walberg, 1999). One of the most important considerations is to sequence the presentation such that the organization is clear and obvious to students. Researchers have identified a number of organizations that might be used:

a. Component relationships—the lesson could be organized from parts to whole (inductive) or from whole to parts (deductive).[16] For example, this current discussion of direct instruction could be organized inductively from a discussion of specific activities that should be incorporated into a lesson to an overall description of the lesson, or by using a more deductive approach through a description of the lesson followed by ever-increasing detail regarding the parts. Other K-12 content examples where a teacher could organize lessons either inductively or deductively include presentations on the major systems of the human body or instruction on the different categories of literature. In general, while there are no definitive rules as to when a teacher should opt for one organization over the other, research does suggest a rule-example-rule approach is an effective means to teach concepts to students (Van Patten, Chao, & Reigeluth, 1986).

b. Relevance relationships—Quite often this type of organization is based on a logical or empirical relationship among factors or categories within the lesson that are not hierarchically organized. For example, in a middle school language arts classroom, the teacher could explain the different types of writing (i.e., expository, narrative, and persuasive) based on the associations between the writing methods and the appropriateness of the usage of different types of writing for a given situation. A teacher or curriculum designer may opt to use relevance as a means to organize lessons when the content that is being learned is organized in categories that are not hierarchical.[17]

c. Sequential relationships—the lesson could be organized in terms of a step-by-step sequence. For example, how to repair an appliance or how

---

16. *Editors' note: These are kinds of sequences—alternatives to choose from.*
17. *Editors' note: Here is a situationality for deciding when to use this type of relationship to sequence the instruction.*

to administer an injection could be organized in terms of the actions that would be made in a specific order.

d. Transitional relationships—the lesson could be organized in terms of the movement or transformation from one phase or stage to another in the content being taught; oftentimes these changes go beyond a simple sequence of steps and imply a qualitative change. Presentations on Piaget's stages of cognitive development, biological evolution, or historical sociocultural trends would be examples of this type of qualitative change.

Additionally, teachers should use many examples, visual aids (e.g., concept maps and flow charts), and demonstrations in their presentation to enhance the effectiveness and efficiency of instruction (Gage & Berliner, 1998; Walberg, 1999).

5. Probe and respond. In the fifth method, teachers probe the students regarding their initial understandings.[18] These are formative assessment activities and should be quick, short explorations of student knowledge or skills that inform the teacher if students are acquiring the concepts being presented. Two important issues related to questioning should be considered. First, Gage and Berliner (1998) suggested that teachers should ask more lower-level (knowledge and comprehension) questions (80 to 90%) in elementary grades. Teachers in the middle and upper grades should ask relatively higher-level questions that require students to actively process information (Walberg, 1986). Second, teachers need to make instructionally effective use of wait-time, defined as the interval between a teacher probe and student response (Wait-time I) or the interval between the student response and the teacher response (Wait-time II). Rowe (1974a, 1974b) found that increasing either led to increased achievement, with increases in both having a compound effect. Moreover, Fagan, Hassler, and Szabo (1981) found that using both higher-order questions and increased wait-time had greater impact than using either separately.

B. The Practice Phase

As shown in Figure 5.1, there are three methods of instruction in the practice phase of the direct instruction model: (6) guided practice under the teacher's direct and immediate supervision, (7) independent practice where the student is working on his or her own, and (8) periodic review (often incorporated daily in guided and independent practice) whereby students are utilizing previously learned content or skills.[19] Perkins (1992) suggested that providing learners with

---

18. *Editors' note: This fits Merrill's Application Principle, but with integration of teaching and testing (assessment).*

19. *Editors' note: These also all fit Merrill's Application Principle. While these are all kinds of practice, they are also parts of the instructional theory because they should all be used. If you had to choose just one of them for any given piece of instruction, they would just be kinds (not parts).*

numerous opportunities to practice the skills being learned is a critical activity for student learning.

6. Guided practice. In the sixth method, students practice the newly learned knowledge or skills under the teacher's direct supervision (Walberg, 1999). Students could engage in such activities as practicing reading to each other in small groups, solving a few math problems, writing a short outline of important points covered in the teacher's presentation, or comparing and contrasting two historical events or two species of animals. Students could work by themselves, in pairs, or in small groups. At this point in the lesson, the teacher must actively monitor student activity while providing immediate feedback. At the end of this method, teachers should have rather precise information regarding each student's knowledge or skill with respect to the lesson objective(s).

7. Independent practice. In the seventh method, students practice the new concepts independently. This may be done in the classroom or at home. While there has been some research that homework is relatively less important for elementary students (Cooper, Jackson, Nye, & Lindsay, 2001), the vast majority of research supports the positive effects of homework for middle grade and high school students (Walberg, 2003; Walberg, Paschal, & Weinstein, 1985). Most importantly, homework must be completed and graded if it is to be effective (Cooper, Lindsay, Nye, & Greathouse, 1998; Walberg, 1999). It seems obvious that if the instructional day can be increased, thereby giving students more en-gaged time (Berliner, 1990), then student achievement will increase. However, if students do not have the supportive home environment that leads to successful homework completion, the school needs to provide additional time after school to complete homework in a supervised environment.

8. Periodic review. In the eighth method, which can be incorporated into teacher probes, guided practice, and independent practice, students connect with and practice material they have already learned. Research done more than 60 years ago detailed the benefits of distributed practice (Hull, 1943). In fact, Saxon (1982) made this principle one of the hallmarks of his successful approach to mathematics instruction (Klingele & Reed, 1984). Based on classroom obser-vations of practicing teachers, this method and providing an overview before beginning an explanation are two of the most often omitted. Teachers would be well served, when designing instruction, to make sure students have opportunities to revisit material learned a week, a month, or even a year previously.[20] While cognitive research has shown that once material is in long-term memory it is there permanently (Atkinson & Shiffrin, 1968), students need practice retriev-ing that information and using it appropriately. This is an excellent place in the lesson to use cooperative learning techniques (Johnson & Johnson, 1998; Slavin, 1994). Students can be assigned tasks or problems that incorporate both recently and previously covered content and skills. Students should have to remember previous material and make decisions as to its appropriate use for a particular problem or situation.

---

20. *Editors' note: This may partially address Merrill's Integration Principle.*

C. The Assessment and Evaluation Phase

There are two instructional methods in the assessment and evaluation phase of the transactional direct instruction model (see Figure 5.1): (9) daily reflection on formative data collected during and at the end of the lesson, and (10) collecting summative data over longer intervals such as weekly, biweekly, and monthly. It is important to clarify that phase C (assessment and evaluation) involves collecting data and making decisions about end-of-lesson or end-of-unit assessments, whereas phase D (monitoring and feedback) occurs throughout the lesson and involves collecting data and making necessary clarifications or providing additional instruction.

9. Formative assessment. In the ninth method, teachers make formative evaluation decisions about students on a daily basis to determine if they are making progress. Data from the previous methods of probing and responding, guided and independent practice, and periodic review activities might be used. Alternately, teachers may decide to give quizzes to gather additional information if they are uncertain about the learning of the group or of particular individuals.[21] The primary function of this evaluation process is to make plans for additional teaching on the topic, if necessary. Walberg (1999) asserts that additional teaching should occur when students perform at less than a 90% level during guided and independent practice exercises.

10. Summative assessment. In the 10th method, teachers gather summative assessment data to see if students have mastered the required concepts and skills. This usually is in the form of unit tests or projects covering material from a week or two of instruction. Other types of summative evaluation may include semester or annual exams. It is important that summative evaluations match the content, form, and standards of external audits of classroom learning. Teachers should know the expectations of standardized tests, the requirements of any related courses students might take in the future, expectations of learning requirements at the next level of schooling, and requirements for future employment. Not every summative evaluation must take all of these into consideration, but students and parents have every right to expect that teachers' summative evaluations of students' classroom performance are related to judgments that will be made by others.

D. Monitoring and Feedback

There are two important instructional methods that should occur throughout the lesson on an "as needed" basis (see Figure 5.1): (11) providing cues and prompts, and (12) providing corrective feedback and reinforcement.

11. Cues and prompts. Method 11, providing cues and prompts, is often used when teachers review previous material, ask questions or probes, or have students

---

21. *Editors' note: Here we see alternatives to choose from, so this is elaboration through identifying kinds of a method. Of course, situationalities should be offered to help a practitioner decide when to use each kind.*

engage in guided practice. The use of cues to hint at important information or indicate lesson transitions and the use of prompts when having students demonstrate the initial understandings or during guided practice are important instructional activities (Doenau, 1987). When a student is in what Vygotsky (1978) called the Zone of Proximal Development, the student will sometimes need a cue or prompt in order to be able to recall the required information or demonstrate the desired skill. However, when no amount of prompting evokes the desired response,[22] further instruction is indicated. This assistance or further instruction should take place through a process of scaffolding whereby the teacher models the learning task or activity and then carefully and systematically relinquishes more and more responsibility to the student to perform it (Moll, 1992).

12. Corrective feedback. Finally, the 12th method, providing corrective feedback and reinforcement, is done whenever the teacher has made an assessment of student learning at any point in the lesson. Perkins (1992) suggested that corrective feedback is one of the most important instructional activities provided during instruction. Walberg (1986), in his meta-analysis of research on teaching, found that providing corrective feedback and reinforcement showed the strongest relationship to student achievement of any of the single teacher action studied. Feedback should be provided for both correct and incorrect responses. An important principle is that students should not only hear or see the correct answers; they should also know why a particular answer is correct or incorrect. For example, when conducting probes, the teacher could ask a student a question and then ask another student if the first student's answer was correct or incorrect and why. The teacher could do the same type of activity when reviewing homework or other independent practice activities. Additionally, when going over a multiple choice test, the teacher could select questions with which many students have difficulty and go over each of the possible answers, having students tell her whether that answer is correct or incorrect and why.[23] Dihoff, Brosvic, Epstein, and Cook (2004) showed that immediate feedback is superior to delayed feedback and the teacher should strive to provide feedback as quickly as possible.

The relationship of reinforcement during instruction to academic achievement has been one of the most consistent findings in process-product research (Brophy & Good, 1986; Rosenshine, 1995; Walberg & Paik, 2000). The most common form of such reinforcement is teacher attention: a nod, a smile, or a quick comment. Cheery notes on the assignment or stickers can also be used effectively. Making a practice of sending a positive note home to parents or caregivers for at least one student in each subject area or class period is an excellent way to provide reinforcement for quality work.

In summary, a general model of direct instruction has teachers actively present new content or skills to students, covering small amounts of material

---

22. *Editors' note: This is a situationality.*
23. *Editors' note: Here we see that "examples" of a principle often represent "kinds" of a method that provide more precision about the method (or principle).*

in an organized, step-by-step manner, having them practice that, and providing corrective feedback and reinforcement continuously throughout the lesson. Summative evaluations match the content, form, and standards of those who will audit classroom learning, thereby facilitating the student's movement from the classroom to successful adulthood.

Direct Instruction and Scripted Lessons

In the previous section of this chapter, the universal methods of the general model of direct instruction were presented. This section describes a scripted lesson approach to designing instruction that utilizes the term *Direct Instruction* as a proper noun and is often referred to in the literature as DI (e.g., K. Engelmann, 2004). The methods of instruction for scripted lessons are the same as in the general model, but differ in terms of the specificity of teacher statements and student responses. Scripted lessons present smaller amounts of new information and skill training in each lesson, often accounting for only 10 to 15% of the total lesson (S. Engelmann, 1999). The remainder of the lesson firms and reviews content presented in earlier lessons. As in the general model, a scripted lesson approach assumes that nothing is completely taught in a single lesson. Instead, new content is presented in parts of two or three consecutive lessons to provide students with enough exposure so they are able to use it in applications. Each lesson presents content that is new today; content that is being firmed, having been presented in the last two or three lessons; and content that was presented even earlier in the sequence and is assumed to be thoroughly mastered.[24] This content often takes the form of problems or applications that require earlier-taught content (S. Engelmann, 1999). Thus, scripted lesson approaches could potentially utilize more allocated class time than other approaches to address learning objectives.

While a scripted lesson approach was originally developed as a method to help predominately impoverished children who were not academically successful in traditional public school programs, it has been shown to be effective and efficient with both low and high performing students (Adams & Engelmann, 1996). In Project Follow Through, this scripted-lesson approach was compared to eight other models of instruction (including traditional and constructivist approaches and a home-based model) on outcome measures of three dimensions: academic basic skills, cognition, and affect (Stallings & Kaskowitz, 1974). The scripted-lesson approach produced the highest average performance of any program in all three dimensions (Watkins, 1988). In an analysis of Project Follow Through, Watkins (1988) found that there was an increased emphasis on mastery of content and skill prerequisites for additional lessons for *all* students. The analysis also indicated that a high degree of student success helped raise students' self-efficacy and, indirectly, improved the students' satisfaction with their schooling.

---

24. *Editors' note: This is part of the content layer of instructional design.*

Even though scripting is an effective form of instruction that efficiently increases achievement and helps lower-performing students to catch up with their peers, it is not a panacea for eliminating low achievement. Comparison studies (Rosenshine, 2002) showed that, when implemented with fidelity, programs using scripted lessons produced achievement gains, but these gains were not always sustained when the use of scripted lessons was discontinued. To help sustain achievement gains, many schools combine scripting with other methods, especially in the areas of reading and math.

One explanation for the achievement gains made when teachers used a scripted lesson approach is that there is an explicitness in scripted lessons that reduces the guesswork required on the part of the student as to what is expected to demonstrate mastery. Too often traditional curricular materials and instruction require the student to *figure out* what is important (Hummel, Venn, & Gunter, 2004). Even well designed lessons might present too much material or require students to make connections for which they are ill prepared. Gersten, Taylor, and Graves (1999) assert that an emphasis on detail sets a scripted lesson approach apart from the general model.

The scripted lesson approach shares many similarities with the general model of direct instruction. Scripted lessons begin with outcome behaviors being identified and then aligned with national and state curricular standards. The responsibility for this identification and alignment rests with the party (the individual teacher, a group of teachers, or a commercially available program) who generated the scripted lesson(s). These identified and aligned outcomes are then thoroughly "task analyzed." This involves breaking the complex skill or concept specified in the outcome into its component parts so that every student in a particular track has the background skills and knowledge to learn the new skills and content. The scripted lesson approach differs from the general model in that: (1) the scripted lesson approach often involves a more detailed analysis, producing smaller steps in the task analysis than might be used in the general model; and (2) in scripted lessons, the exact wording the teacher and student use is written down.

There are several additional design elements that tend to be associated with successful use of scripted lessons. Scripted content follows an "answer→question→response" format. A piece of content is presented to the students. The teacher then asks a question about the piece of content just presented. Immediately after the question, a signal (a visual hand drop or an auditory prompt such as a thumb snap) is given, and the students chorally respond to the question. The vast majority of scripted lessons use chorally answered questions rather than questions directed toward individuals. The ratio of choral to individual questions is about 10:1.

If at least 95% of the students answer the question correctly and at the same time, the teacher will usually do a "firm-up" by saying yes, good, etc., followed by the answer to the question. (Repeating the answer the students gave is favored over just using general verbal praise (i.e., "Good job"), because such praise is often, by itself, ineffective.) The teacher follows with a correction procedure when (1) fewer than 95% respond; (2) the students do not respond together as a group; or (3) when the answer given is incorrect.[25]

Corrections are never punitive. If fewer than 95% respond, the teacher simply says, "I need everyone to participate," then restates the question and gives the signal again. If the students do not answer together, the teacher would say something like: "I need everyone to answer together immediately after the signal. Let's try it again." The teacher would then restate the question and give the signal. When an incorrect answer is made, the teacher, in most cases, simply states the correct answer and says, "Let's do it again. My turn." The teacher would then present the same piece of information followed by the same question and signal.

Immediately following the delivery of a script, students complete assignments over the lesson, though these assignments also review related content from previous lessons. Such practice is critical to students mastering the content, and includes work done both individually and in small groups.

Many teachers initially have difficulty with scripting because of their previous experiences. Too often in teacher-made scripts, as in other methods of instruction, the teacher covers the content only one time. This is usually insufficient for any type of lesson. In and across lessons the teacher must give students frequent opportunities to be actively engaged with new content and reviews of previously covered material. The pace of the teacher-delivered script is fast, therefore tiring to both instructor and students. The actual presentation of the script itself should take no more than 20 minutes. The remainder of the class period is spent on practice activities designed to help students master content, or assessment activities to determine what they have learned. Students can do practice or assessment activities individually or in cooperative learning groups. Once students demonstrate proficiency on these activities, they should immediately have a graded individual assessment. Independent practice work, especially work done outside the classroom, should be similar in structure to these classroom-based activities. Each completed lesson (i.e., after covering all the objectives) should be followed by a summative quiz or test.

An example of a scripted lesson covering the four types of sentences (i.e., declarative, exclamatory, imperative, and interrogative) is available at http://chiron.valdosta.edu/whuitt/edpsyc/DI_lp_sentences.doc.

Notice that it begins with an advance organizer (Ausubel, 1978; Walberg, 1999), and the day's objectives are communicated and explained. Next, a few minutes are spent reviewing the prerequisites to the day's lesson (often, checking homework is part of the review). Then the day's script is delivered. The script is followed by the informal activity (a written exercise usually). Based on how well the students perform, the teacher may do another such activity, or a formal assessment (seatwork, a quiz, or homework if it is close to the end of the period).

---

25. *Editors' note: These are three situationalities for using the correction procedure.*

http://chiron.valdosta.edu/whuitt/edpsyc/lpexam3.html shows the same lesson using the methods of instruction for the general model of direct instruction discussed above.

A significant advantage in training teachers to use the design elements of scripted lessons is that there are commercially available materials that teachers can use in the training process. When teachers are properly trained and coached using these materials, many teachers state that they begin using more of the scripted-lesson principles (small pieces, signaled choral responding) in their classes and begin to develop and use their own scripted lessons (Hummel et al., 2004).

Deciding when and if a scripted-lesson approach is appropriate is as important as deciding when to use direct instruction itself. Content and skills that represent chained behaviors, such as the steps one follows to solve a math word problem or any other academic activity that has specific steps, are likely candidates for scripted lessons.[26] Another factor that helps a teacher determine whether scripting might be useful is the attributes of students. If the content or skill is so fundamental to future academic learning that it must be mastered by all students, when students are not keeping pace with grade-level requirements, or if there is a concern that a significant number of students has not mastered the prerequisites for a new lesson, a scripted-lesson approach should be employed. Because these circumstances occur in every classroom, all teachers should, as part of their teaching repertoire, possess expertise in scripting.

Scripted lessons, like any lesson, do not have to be limited to only those skills requiring students to perform at the lower levels of the Bloom, Engelhart, Furst, Hill, and Krathwohl (1956) taxonomy of cognitive objectives. Through careful planning, scripts can be developed that also teach students how to analyze and evaluate, skills typically associated with problem solving. Scripted lessons have been developed in all subjects to reflect *big* ideas, defined as:

> …highly selected concepts, principles, rules, strategies, or heuristics that facilitate the most efficient and broadest acquisition of knowledge. Big ideas serve to link several different little ideas together within a domain such as science, reading, math, or social studies. They are the keys that unlock a content area for a broad range of diverse learners and are best demonstrated through examples instead of definitions. (Kame'enui, Carnine, Dixon, Simmons, & Coyne, 2002, p. 9)

Summary and Conclusions

While there has been some criticism of the research methodology on which direct instruction is based (Garrison & MacMillan, 1994), especially the atheoretical nature of the results from process-product research, the general guidelines,

---

26. *Editors' note. Here is a situationality for use of the Scripted Lessons variation of Direct Instruction. Another one follows.*

the general model, and the scripted lesson approach to direct instruction have demonstrated their effectiveness in today's classrooms. And rather than an atheoretical approach to instruction, direct instruction is actually an eclectic approach using principles from four of the major learning theories associated with the study of classroom learning. The influence of operant conditioning and behavior analysis, we think, is obvious, based on the advocacy of stating explicit, observable objectives, breaking down learning into small steps, and correcting and reinforcing mastery of each step. The influence of information processing and cognitive learning theory is seen in the use of advance organizers, the connection of new learning to prior learning, use of higher-order questioning, and the advocacy of having students engage in elaboration activities. Other theories of learning have also contributed principles that can be easily implemented in direct instruction. For example, principles advocated in facilitative teaching (a humanistic approach to education), such as responding to students' feelings and smiling at students, can be implemented throughout a lesson (Asby & Roebuck, 1977). Components of a social cognitive approach, such as cooperative learning (Johnson & Johnson, 1998; Slavin, 1994), can be readily implemented in the guided practice method of instruction.

S. Engelmann (1999) views effective instruction within a specified curriculum as a stairway. Each step of the stairway presents new content and skills for which the student already has the prerequisites. The teacher directs the learning activities associated with that level, and students acquire mastery of those skills. Each new step or lesson takes the student about the same amount of time and effort to master the associated content. While higher steps (i.e., later lessons) represent more complex content, from the student's perspective they are not viewed as more difficult because they have already acquired the lesson's prerequisites.

Today, academic achievement is primarily evaluated through standardized tests of basic skills. Critics of standardized testing object that explicitly teaching the objectives measured by the standardized test narrows the curriculum (Kohn, 2001). Yet that is exactly what must be done if we expect all students to cover and demonstrate mastery on an explicit body of knowledge in a specified amount of time. If our society changes the measures of school learning so that assessments are made of a student's ability to inquire (Minstrell & van Zee, 2000) or demonstrate higher-level or critical thinking (Kuhn, 1999; Oxman, 1992) or produce products that would demonstrate their disciplined minds (Gardner, 1999a, 1999b), then it is entirely appropriate to suggest approaches to instruction that will accomplish those tasks. However, direct or explicit instruction is most often the selected approach to designing and implementing quality instruction when students are expected to master a broad spectrum of knowledge and skills as advocated by Hirsch (1996) or evaluated by standardized tests, as it is a very efficient way to manage the scarce resources of teacher expertise and classroom time.

Even though this chapter has focused on the design attributes of direct instruction, it should not be assumed that all students will demonstrate mastery of academic content if quality instruction is provided. Carroll (1963) made it clear that because students differ in their capability to learn academic material, educators have two choices. Either all students can be expected to attain an explicitly stated level of mastery, which means educators must allow time-to-learn to vary, or students can all be provided the same time-to-learn, in which case students will attain different levels of mastery. The reality of current education practice is that time-to-learn is held constant for most students (i.e., 180 days, 5 to 6 hours per day). The efficiency of coverage of a breadth of objectives appears to be more highly valued than effectiveness (i.e., having all students demonstrate mastery of core content). This is a major critique of traditional practice leveled by Bloom (1976). Even in schools or districts where students are provided with after-school or Saturday tutoring or opportunities for summer school, these are seldom mandatory, providing the impression that time-in-the-classroom is the important factor, rather than mastery of required content and skills.

In an era of accountability, classroom teachers should be expected to deliver high quality teaching (i.e., planning, management, and instruction). However, students are nested within a family, a school, a neighborhood and community, a culture. People and institutions whose actions contribute to school learning should also be held accountable (Berliner, 2005). Principals need to provide effective leadership (Huitt, 1997), schools need to be sized appropriately (Howley & Howley, 2004; McMillen, 2004), schools and districts need to provide adequate time for all students to master required content and skills (Berliner, 1990; Caldwell, Huitt, & Graeber, 1982), families need to provide a home atmosphere that facilitates school learning (Evan, 2004; Walberg, 1999), state departments need to provide adequate instructional materials for the objectives that will be tested on mandated criterion- and norm-referenced tests (Bracey, 1987), and the federal government needs to adequately fund its mandates for school improvement (Fratt, 2005). These issues should receive an equally high priority to that of encouraging and training classroom teachers to deliver the highest possible quality instruction.

References

Adams, G. L., & Engelmann, S. (1996). *Research on direct instruction: 25 years beyond DISTAR.* Seattle, WA: Educational Achievement Systems.

Aspy, D., & Roebuck, F. (1977). *Kid's don't learn from people they don't like.* Amherst, MA: Human Resources Development Press.

Atkinson, R., & Shiffrin, R. (1968). Human memory: A proposed system and its control processes. In K. Spence & J. Spence (Eds.), *The psychology of learning and motivation: Vol. 2. Advances in research and theory* (pp. 742–775). New York: Academic Press.

Ausubel, D. (1960). The use of advance organizers in the learning and retention of meaningful verbal material. *Journal of Educational Psychology, 51,* 267–272.

Ausubel, D. (1978). In defense of advance organizers: A reply to the critics. *Review of Educational Research, 48,* 251–258.

Berliner, D. (1990). What's all this fuss about instructional time? In M. Ben-Peretz & R. Bromme (Eds.), *The nature of time in schools* (pp. 3–35). New York: Teachers College Press. Retrieved December 2006, from http://courses.ed.asu.edu/berliner/readings/fuss/fuss.htm

Berliner, D. (2005, August 2). Our impoverished view of educational reform. *Teachers College Record.* Retrieved December 2006, from http://www.tcrecord.org/Content.asp?ContentID=12106

Block, J. (1971). *Mastery learning: Theory and practice.* New York: Holt, Rinehart, & Winston.

Bloom, B. (1976). *Human characteristics and school learning.* New York: McGraw-Hill.

Bloom, B. (1981). *All our children learning: A primer for parents, teachers, and other educators.* New York: McGraw-Hill.

Bloom, B. S., Engelhart, M. D., Furst, E. J., Hill, W. H., & Krathwohl, D. R. (1956). *Taxonomy of education objectives: Handbook 1. Cognitive domain.* New York: McKay.

Bolon, C. (2000). School-based standard testing. *Education Policy Analysis Archives, 8*(23). Retrieved December 2006, from http://epaa.asu.edu/epaa/v8n23/

Bracey, G. (1987). Texts, tests don't match—But does it matter? *Phi Delta Kappan, 68*(5), 397–401.

Brady, M., Clinton, D., Sweeney, J., Peterson, M., & Poynor, H. (1977). *Instructional dimensions study.* Washington, D.C.: Kirschner.

Brophy, J. (1983). Effective classroom management. *The School Administrator, 40*(7), 33–36.

Brophy, J., & Good, T. L. (1986). Teacher behavior and student achievement. In M. C. Wittrock (Ed.), *Handbook for research on teaching* (pp. 328–375). New York: Macmillan.

Bruner, J. (1990). *Acts of meaning.* Cambridge, MA: Harvard University Press.

Caldwell, J., Huitt, W., & Graeber, A. (1982). Time spent in learning: Implications from research. *Elementary School Journal, 82*(5), 471–480.

Carnine, D. (1988). Breaking the failure cycle in the elementary school. *Youth Policy, 10*(7), 22–25.

Carroll, J. (1963). A model of school learning. *Teachers College Record, 64,* 723–733.

Cohen, S. A. (1995). Instructional alignment. In J. Block, S. Evason, & T. Guskey (Eds.), *School improvement programs: A handbook for educational leaders* (pp. 153–180). New York: Scholastic.

Cooley, W. W., & Leinhardt, G. (1980). The instructional dimensions study. *Educational Evaluation and Policy Analysis, 2,* 7–26.

Cooper, H. M., Jackson, K., Nye, B., & Lindsay, J. J. (2001). A model of homework's influence on the performance evaluation of elementary school students. *The Journal of Experimental Education, 69*(2), 181–202.

Cooper, H., Lindsay, J. J., Nye, B., & Greathouse, S. (1998). Relationships among attitudes about homework, amount of homework assigned and completed, and student achievement. *Journal of Educational Psychology, 90,* 70–83.

Craik, F., & Lockhart, R. (1972). Levels of processing: A framework for memory research. *Journal of Verbal Thinking and Verbal Behavior, 11,* 671–684.

Cruickshank, D. (1986). Profile of an effective teacher. *Educational Horizons, 64*(2), 80–86.

Darling-Hammond, L. (2000). Teacher quality and student achievement: A review of state policy evidence. *Education Policy Analysis Archives, 8*(1). Retrieved December 2006, from http://epaa.asu.edu/epaa/v8n1/

Dihoff, R., Brosvic, G., Epstein, M., & Cook, M. (2004). Provision of feedback during preparation for academic testing: Learning is enhanced by immediate but not delayed feedback. *The Psychological Record, 54,* 207–231.

Doenau. S. (1987). Structuring. In M. J. Dunkin (Ed.), *International encyclopedia of teaching and teacher education* (pp. 398–407). Oxford: Pergamon.

Engelmann, K. (2004). Direct instruction model (K-8). In J. Raphael (Ed.), *The catalog of school reform models* . Portland, OR: Northwest Regional Educational Laboratory. Retrieved December 2006, from http://www.nwrel.org/scpd/catalog/ModelDetails.asp?modelID=13

Engelmann, S. (1999, July). *Student-program alignment and teaching to mastery.* Paper presented at the 25th National Direct Instruction Conference, Eugene, OR.

Engelmann, S., Osborn, S., & Hanner, S. (1999). *Corrective reading.* New York: SRA/McGraw-Hill. Retrieved December 2006, from https://www.sraonline.com/di_family.html?PHPSESSID=ae 957ab994e1a34fe5e7a21aae5e7855&section=1&family=2713

Evan, R. (2004). *Family matters: How schools can cope with the crisis in childrearing.* San Francisco: Jossey Bass.

Fagan, E., Hassler, D., & Szabo, M. (1981). Evaluation of questioning strategies in language arts instruction. *Research in the Teaching of English, 15,* 267–273.

Fisher, C., Filby, N., Marliave, R., Cahen, L., Dishaw, M., Moore, J., et al. (1978). *Teaching behaviors: Academic learning time and student achievement: Final report of Phase III-B, Beginning Teacher Evaluation Study.* San Francisco: Far West Laboratory for Educational Research and Development.

Flanders, N. (1970). *Analyzing teacher behavior.* Reading, MA: Addison-Wesley.

Fratt, L. (2005, February). Education budget rises but falls short of needs. *District Administration, 12* .

Gage, N. (1978). *The scientific basis of the art of teaching.* New York: Teachers College Press.

Gage, N. (1994). The scientific status of research on teaching. *Educational Theory, 44*(4), 371–383.

Gage, N., & Berliner, D. (1998). *Educational psychology* (6th ed.). Boston: Houghton Mifflin.

Gagné, R., Briggs, L. & Wager, W. (1992). *Principles of instructional design* (4th ed.). Fort Worth, TX: Harcourt, Brace & World College.

Gardner, H. (1999a). Multiple approaches to understanding. In C. Reigeluth (Ed.), *Instructional-design theories and models: Vol 2. A new paradigm of instructional theory* (pp. 69–89). Mahwah, NJ: Erlbaum.

Gardner, H. (1999b). *The disciplined mind: Beyond facts and standardized tests, the K-12 education that every child deserves.* New York: Penguin.

Garrison, J., & MacMillan, C. (1994). Process-product research on teaching: Ten years later. *Educational Theory, 44*(4), 385–397.

Gersten, R., Taylor, R., & Graves, A. (1999). Direct instruction and diversity. In R. Stevens (Ed.), *Teaching in American schools* (pp. 81–102). Upper Saddle River, NJ: Merrill.

Gibbons, A., Bunderson, C., Olsen, J., & Robertson, J. (1995) Work models: Still beyond instructional objectives. *Machine-Mediated Learning, 5*(3&4), 221–236.

Good, T., & Grouws, D. (1979). The Missouri Mathematics Effectiveness Project: An experimental study in fourth-grade classrooms. *Journal of Educational Psychology, 71*, 355–362.

Gronlund, N. (2003). *Writing instructional objectives for teaching and assessment* (7th ed.). Upper Saddle River, NJ: Prentice-Hall.

Guskey, T., & Gates, S. (1986). Synthesis of research on the effects of mastery learning in elementary and secondary classrooms. *Educational Leadership, 43*(8), 73–80.

Guskey, T., & Pigott, T. (1988). Research on group-based mastery learning programs: A meta-analysis. *Journal of Educational Research, 81*(4), 197–216.

Hirsch, E. D. (1996). *The schools we need: And why we don't have them.* New York: Doubleday.

Howley, C., & Howley, A. (2004). School size and the influence of socioeconomic status on student achievement: Confronting the threat of size bias in national data sets. *Education Policy Analysis Archives, 12*(52). Retrieved December 2006, from http://epaa.asu.edu/epaa/v12n52/v12n52.pdf

Huitt, W. (1997). *The SCANS report revisited.* Paper delivered at the Fifth Annual Gulf South Business and Vocational Education Conference, Valdosta State University, Valdosta, GA, April 18. Retrieved December 2006, from http://chiron.valdosta.edu/whuitt/col/student/scanspap.html

Huitt, W. (2001). Direct instruction: A transactional model. *Educational Psychology Interactive.* Valdosta, GA: Valdosta State University. Retrieved December 2006, from http://chiron.valdosta.edu/whuitt/col/instruct/instevnt.html

Hull, C. L. (1943). *Principles of behavior: An introduction to behavior theory.* New York: Appleton-Century.

Hummel, J., Venn, M., & Gunter, P. (2004). Teacher-made scripted lessons. In D. J. Moran & R. W. Malott (Eds.), *Empirically supported education methods: Advances from the behavioral sciences* (pp. 95–108). San Diego, CA: Elsevier/Academic Press.

Hummel, J., Wiley, L., Huitt, W., Roesch, M., & Richardson, J. (2004). *Implementing corrective reading: Coaching issues.* Retrieved February 4, 2007, from http://coefaculty.valdosta.edu/lschmert/gera/current_issue.htm

Hunter, M. (1982). *Mastery teaching.* El Sequndo, CA: TIP.

Johnson, D., & Johnson, R. (1998). *Learning together and alone: Cooperative, competitive, and individualistic learning* (5th ed.). Boston: Allyn & Bacon.

Joyce, B., Weil, M., & Calhoun, E. (2003). *Models of teaching* (7th ed.). Boston: Allyn & Bacon.

Kame'enui, E. J., Carnine, D. W., Dixon, R. C., Simmons, D. C., & Coyne, M. D. (2002). *Effective teaching strategies that accommodate diverse learners* (2nd ed.). Upper Saddle River, NJ: Merrill Prentice-Hall.

Klingele, W., & Reed, B. (1984). An examination of an incremental approach to mathematics. *Phi Delta Kappan, 65*(10), 712–713.

Kohn, A. (2001). Fighting the tests: A practical guide to rescuing our schools. *Phi Delta Kappan, 82*(5), 348–358. Retrieved December 2006, from http://www.alfiekohn.org/teaching/ftt.htm

Kozloff, M. A. (2003). Seeing is believing versus believing is seeing: The fundamental problem in education. *Direct Instruction News, 3*(1), 15–19.

Kuhn, D. (1999). A developmental model of critical thinking. *Educational Researcher, 28,* 16–25, 46.

Mager, R. (1997). *Preparing instructional objectives: A critical tool in the development of effective instruction* (3rd ed.). Atlanta, GA: CEP Press.

Martin, J. A. (1999). *Effects of cooperative learning on the achievement of secondary students.* Unpublished educational specialist's thesis, Valdosta State University, Valdosta, Georgia.

Mayer, R. (2002). *Learning and instruction.* Upper Saddle River, NJ: Prentice Hall.

McCarthy, B. (1996). *About learning.* Wauconda, IL: Excel.

McCarthy, B. (2000). *About learning.* Wauconda, IL: Excel.

McMillen, B. J. (2004, October 22). School size, achievement, and achievement gaps. *Education Policy Analysis Archives, 12*(58). Retrieved December 2006, from http://epaa.asu.edu/epaa/v12n58/v12n58.pdf

Minstrell, J., & van Zee, E. (Eds.). (2000). *Inquiring into inquiry learning and teaching in science.* Washington, D.C.: American Association for the Advancement of Science.

Moll, L. (Ed.). (1992). *Vygotsky and education: Instructional implications and applications of sociohistorical psychology.* New York: Cambridge University Press.

Partnership for 21st Century Skills. (2003). *Learning for the 21st century.* Washington, D.C.: Author. Retrieved December 2006, from http://www.21stcenturyskills.org/downloads/P21_Report.pdf

Perkins, D. N. (1992). *Smart schools: Better thinking and learning for every child.* New York: The Free Press.

Proctor, C. D. (1984). Teacher expectations: A model for school improvement. *The Elementary School Journal, 84*(4), 469–481.

Oxman, W. (Ed.). (1992). *Critical thinking: Implications for teaching and teachers.* Upper Montclair, NJ: Montclair State College.

Reigeluth, C. M. (1999). What is instructional-design theory and how is it changing? In *Instructional-design theories and models: Vol. 2. A new paradigm of instructional theory* (pp. 5–29). Mahwah, NJ: Erlbaum.

Rosenshine, B. (1986). Synthesis of research on explicit teaching. *Educational Leadership, 43*(7), 60–69.

Rosenshine, B. (1995). Advances in research on instruction. *The Journal of Educational Research, 88*(5), 262–268.

Rosenshine, B. (2002). Helping students from low-income homes read at grade level. *Journal of Education for Students Placed At Risk, 7*(2), 273–283.

Rosenshine, B., & Stevens, R. (1986). Teaching functions. In M. Wittrock (Ed.), *Handbook of research on teaching* (3rd ed., pp. 376–391). New York: Macmillan.

Rowe, M. (1974a). Wait-time and rewards as instructional variables, their influence on language, logic and fate control: Part I, Fate Control. *Journal of Research in Science Teaching, 11,* 81–94.

Rowe, M. (1974b). Relation of wait-time and rewards to the development of language, logic, and fate control: Part II, Rewards. *Journal of Research in Science Teaching, 11,* 291–308.

Saxon, J. (1982). Incremental development: A breakthrough in mathematics. *Phi Delta Kappan, 63,* 482–484.

Secretary's Commission on Achieving Necessary Skills, The (SCANS). (1991). *What work requires of schools.* (A SCANS Report for America 2000). Washington, D.C.: U.S. Department of Labor. Retrieved December 2006, from http://wdr.doleta.gov/SCANS/whatwork/whatwork.pdf

Slavin, R. (1986). *Educational psychology.* Boston: Allyn & Bacon.

Slavin, R. (1994). *Cooperative learning: Theory, research, and practice.* Upper Saddle River, NJ: Prentice-Hall.

Slavin, R. (1997). *Educational psychology, theory and practice* (5th ed.). Boston: Allyn & Bacon.

Squires, D., Huitt, W., & Segars, J. (1983). *Effective classrooms and schools: A research-based perspective.* Washington, D.C.: Association for Supervision and Curriculum Development.

Stallings, J., & Kaskowitz, D. (1974). *Follow through classroom observation evaluation, 1972–1973.* Menlo Park, CA: Stanford Research Institute.

Van Patten, J., Chao, C., & Reigeluth, C. (1986). A review of strategies for sequencing and synthesizing instruction. *Review of Educational Research, 56,* 437–471.

Vygotsky, L. (1978). *Mind in society.* Cambridge, MA: Harvard University Press.

Walberg, H. (1986). Synthesis of research on teaching. In M. Wittrock (Ed.), *Handbook of research on teaching* (3rd ed., pp. 214–229). New York: Macmillan.

Walberg, H. (1991). Productive teaching and instruction: Assessing the knowledge base. In H.

Waxman & H. Walberg (Eds.), *Effective teaching: Current research* (pp. 33–62). Berkeley, CA: McCutchan.

Walberg, H. (1999). Generic practices. In G. Cawelti (Ed.), *Handbook of research on improving student achievement* (pp. 9–21). Arlington, VA: Educational Research Services.

Walberg, H. (2003). *Improving educational productivity*. Philadelphia: Laboratory for School Success. Retrieved December 2006, from http://www.temple.edu/lss/pdf/publications/pubs2003-1. pdf

Walberg, H., & Paik, S. (2000). *Effective educational practices*. Paris: International Bureau of Education, UNESCO. Retrieved December 2006, from http://www.ibe.unesco.org/publications/EducationalPracticesSeriesPdf/prac03e.pdf

Walberg, H., Paschal, R., & Weinstein, T. (1985). Homework's powerful effects on learning. *Educational Leadership, 42*(7), 76–79.

Watkins, C. L. (1988). Project Follow Through: A story of the identification and neglect of effective instruction. *Youth Policy, 10*(7), 7–11.

6
Discussion Approach to Instruction

JOYCE TAYLOR GIBSON
University of Massachusetts, Lowell

Joyce Taylor Gibson, an Associate Professor in the Graduate School of Education at University of Massachusetts Lowell (UML), has been an educator for over thirty years, with her research, teaching and publications focused on leadership, diversity and systemic change. Dr. Gibson has served as Co-Director of the Center for Family, Work and Community, where she helped initiate a long-term project to address college readiness of poor and minority students in the Merrimack Valley along with many local, federal and private sponsors. She recently returned to the faculty after serving as Associate Vice Chancellor for Academic Services at her home institution, and is currently the UML coordinator of two undergraduate retention projects funded respectively by NSF and the College Board. Joyce has been a student of discussion teaching for many years, participating in seminars and case study conferences through AERA, Harvard's Derek Bok Center for Teaching and Learning, and Pace University's Case Study Institutes.

EDITORS' FOREWORD

Preconditions (when to use the theory)

Content
- *In-depth exploration of topics, not presentation of large amounts of information*
- *Critical thinking and problem-solving skills*

Learners
- *All students*

Learning environments
- *All classrooms*
- *As part or whole of lesson*

Instructional development constraints
- *Minimal, given that few resources need to be developed*

Values (opinions about what is important)

about ends (learning goals)
- *Emphasizes learning, not teaching*
- *The importance of deep thinking, sharp analytical skills, and empowerment of learners*

about priorities (criteria for successful instruction)
- *Effectiveness and appeal are highly valued*
- *Efficiency is not highly valued, for this method takes more time for interactions and processing*

about means (instructional methods)
- *Values active student learning (participation)*
- *Values respecting different perspectives*
- *Values collaboration and democratic processes*
- *Values questioning, critical thinking, and problem-solving skills*
- *Values creating a community of learners*
- *Life experiences should be inseparable from learning*

about power (to make decisions about the previous three)
- *Values empowering learners*
- *Should be very inclusive and participatory*

Universal Methods

related to Merrill's first principles
- *Engage learners in real-life problems, connected to their own diverse backgrounds.*
- *Activate prior learning on which to build new knowledge.*
- *Demonstrate critical thinking and problem-solving skills during the discussion*

- *Apply new knowledge through exercises done by individuals or small groups, with the help of advance organizers and group feedback or reflection.*
- *Integrate new knowledge through future interactions with others, changes in respect for others.*

related to principles of discussion teaching

- *Share the responsibility for learning between instructor and learner.*
- *Create a climate of collaboration and respect for diverse world views.*
- *Ensure that instructors using the discussion approach have clear mastery of a discipline as well as strong facilitation skills.*
- *Acknowledge and utilize the life experiences of learners.*
- *Include opportunities for higher-order learning, such as listening, reflection, and synthesis.*
- *Promote a more democratic learning community.*
- *Ensure that the physical set up in the classroom allows for interactions among learners as well as instructor(s).*

related to the process of discussion teaching

- *Develop a plan.*
- *Develop a concept outline.*
- *Add a question outline.*
- *Create a visible outline.*
- *Model the discussion process through demonstration.*
- *State clear expectations.*
- *Set ground rules for interaction.*
- *Design practice session.*
- *Anticipate obstacles and problems.*

Situational Principles

- *Very young learners, special needs learners, or others who have lack of facility with language and expression may require some changes in the principle of shared responsibility for learning.*
- *Online discussions present special requirements for change in flow of conversation, but also exciting new opportunities for communication.*
- *If you have resistant students, who can rob the discussion approach of its power, allow for more time practicing or more small-group discussions to overcome resistance.*

—CMR & ACC

DISCUSSION APPROACH TO INSTRUCTION

The discussion approach to instruction, commonly known as discussion teaching, is a pedagogical method that has active learning of students and instructors at its core (Christensen, Garvin, & Sweet, 1991). Discussion teaching is organized to (1) create shared responsibility for teaching and learning; (2) honor the voices, experiences, and worldviews of students; (3) promote democratic participation in the teaching/learning dynamic; (4) develop critical thinking and problem-solving skills;[1] and (5) create a community of learners who work together in the pursuit of knowledge (Brookfield & Preskill, 2005; Dillon, 1994; Freire & Shor, 1987).[2] Discussion teaching, by its nature, is inclusive and participatory, thus changing the teaching methodology from an instructor-centered approach to a shared responsibility approach that can be both invigorating and challenging, for the same reasons. Whenever responsibility is shared, and the instructor does not have total control, the risk-taking and unpredictability of the instructional process can be threatening and exciting as it evolves into a partnership for learning that can be life changing, especially for students. Christensen et al. (1991) relate the differences of this teaching methodology: "Discussion teaching demands a milieu of freedom, an openness that encourages students to share power over, and responsibility for leadership and conduct of a class" (p. 106)

Brookfield and Preskill (2005), who believe that the discussion teaching method is necessarily a democratic way of learning, view the methodology as one that demonstrates a high level of learning activity: "Our understanding of discussion incorporates reciprocity and movement, exchange and inquiry, co-operation and collaboration, formality and informality" (p. 6). Whether used as a major approach to instruction or one of several methods, discussion teaching requires greater interaction among all participants in a quest for higher learning. Learning as a cooperative act is the major premise of this type of instruction. To fully appreciate the power in discussion teaching, one must understand that it reverses the focus of the industrial-age paradigm of education by emphasizing learning as the priority, not teaching.[3] This approach entails students and instructors learning from each other, as well as students learning from each other. This unique learning exchange promotes deeper thinking, sharpens analytical skills, and empowers participants to become social actors in society (Brookfield & Preskill, 2005).

The values that are reflective of this instructional methodology include:

- Believing that individuals should participate in their own learning;
- Respecting different perspectives of concepts and problems;
- Promoting collaboration and a democratic process for learning;
- Emphasizing questioning, critical thinking, and problem-solving skills;
- Creating a community of learners;
- Accepting that life experiences should be inseparable from learning.

---

1. *Editors' note: Addressing what to learn is a part of curriculum theory, which is often integrated with instructional theory, and it is in the content layer of instructional design.*
2. *Editors' note: These are the goals of the theory, some of which are learning goals and some of which are not.*
3. *Editors' note: This is an important feature of the customized, Information-Age paradigm of education and stands in contrast with the standardized, one-size-fits-all, Industrial-Age paradigm of education.*

Though there are many structures and activities that embrace discussions of many types in teaching, the pedagogy should reflect the values cited above. Berquist and Phillips (1975) list a number of these structures in a faculty development handbook for small-college teaching.

The discussion teaching approach is best suited for learning situations where in-depth exploration of topics, interactions of ideas and people from multiple perspectives are valued, or in settings where developing strengths in analysis and critical thinking within a community are important.[4] Circumstances not well suited for discussion teaching include those where building a specific knowledge-base or broadening a base of knowledge through presenting material or sharing information is the primary focus. In addition, when a vast amount of material must be presented in a defined timeframe, discussion teaching is not the optimal approach, as it takes more time for process and interactions.

Universal Principles of Discussion Teaching

The universal principles of discussion teaching embrace all of Merrill's (chapter 3) first principles of instruction.[5] I will comment briefly on the relationship between the two sets of principles, then describe the discussion principles in more detail. Later in this section, I will present guidelines on getting started with this approach, noting suggestions for the instructor and for students.

Engagement of learners in real-life problems is the first of Merrill's principles that promote learning. Active learning necessarily involves inquiry and problem solving for growth of learners. Relating the problems of everyday issues of life with more formal schooling has been an important component of education expressed over the decades by Dewey (1938) connecting experience and education, and is supported by contemporary theorists such as Bruner (1966) in his work on constructionist theory, in which a learner connects new ideas with concepts already known in the past and constructs new meaning for problem solving. Questioning, the most basic tool of discussion teaching, and the participatory nature of the approach draw on the differences among the students as they respond from their unique backgrounds that reflect their respective cultures and experiences.

Activation, the next of Merrill's principles, refers to building on existing knowledge as a foundation for new learning. As participants in discussion teaching respond to the ever-increasing complexity of questions, structured and modeled by the instructor early in the process, they necessarily draw on their own current knowledge, as well as prior information that is awakened through critical thinking and reflection, two activities critical to this approach. A concept called linking, or bridging, is also employed by the instructor to connect existing knowledge and new information.

---

4. *Editors' note: These are preconditions for use of the theory.*
5. *Editors' note: These are all related to instructional methods, and hence are part of instructional-event theory and are addressed in the strategy layer of instructional design.*

Demonstration of new learning is the third principle that promotes learning in Merrill's set of instructional principles. This principle is evident in discussion teaching through instructors providing a type of guidance that Merrill references as instructional consistency, that is, offering information, as well as directing students to relevant sources that are consistent with learning goals. Modeling types of questioning and presenting multiple ways to be involved in discussions—even through bringing in colleagues to role play the variety of ways to participate in discussion teaching (Brookfield & Preskill, 2005)—are ways to teach the higher-order skills involved in productive discussions. As students' learning progresses, the instructor does less directing, sharing of information, and offering of examples about the process and structure of discussion teaching, signaling a shift to more focus on teaching the content than on demonstrating the higher-order skills involved in discussion.

Application of new knowledge, a fourth Merrill principle is incorporated in the discussion teaching approach, usually through the freedom of small-group teaching exercises, and through use of advance organizers, to aid students in applying the new concepts. Exercises to apply new knowledge can be built into each class or session by individuals or small groups, and then analyzed by others through listening and reflecting on ideas presented; this type of rotation can occur from class to class to ensure practice for each person. Presenting case studies with explanations of learning concepts intended, critiquing each other's work and debating perspectives using course materials can illustrate new knowledge. Written assignments are another means for participants to show application of new knowledge.

Integration of new knowledge into the learner's world, Merrill's fifth principle, can be found through the discussion teaching approach in several ways. Reflections in conversations on new insights uncovered because of new learning can be revealed through changes evident in a person's interactions with others, such as language, tone, and type of questions, over a period of time. End of term individual capstone projects and group field projects[6] designed to address challenges relevant to the content are two ways for students to demonstrate integration of knowledge. One colleague of mine requires students to create a book of tips with explanations reflective of new knowledge and changed personal perspectives for an external jury to review on the usefulness and the realistic nature of the tips. Brookfield and Preskill (2005) offer a very appealing activity called a discussion log in which students are asked to keep notes on what they have learned, and to describe what they can now teach or do with others that they could not do earlier.

Clearly, Merrill's first principles are reflected in discussion pedagogy, and many are aligned directly with the universal principles of discussion teaching described below.[7]

---

6. *Editors' note: Clearly there is some overlap with problem-based instruction here (see chapter 8).*

7. *Editors' note: These are also all related to instructional methods, and hence are part of instructional-event theory and are addressed in the strategy layer of instructional design. Note the extent to which*

1. **Shared responsibility.** *Discussion teaching should shift the instructor-centered approach to one of shared responsibility for learning between instructors and students.* This shift to shared responsibility is a major and often unexpected change for students, in particular, who are accustomed to the instructor assuming authority for teaching and learning outcomes. This sharing of roles does not signify that the instructor abdicates responsibility for managing the direction of the course or for how students interact with instructors and other students. This partnership does not magically happen and must be orchestrated by the instructor, who must take practical steps to help create the partnership. Creating clear ground rules on communication with students, for example, is one step; others include developing a contract about roles and responsibilities to demonstrate seriousness about sharing responsibility; listening carefully and responding consistently to students' contributions; and showing vulnerability—through not having all the answers and allowing silences—to foster understanding that there is risk for all members in the learning community. Greater details on this unique partnership can be found in Christiansen et al. (1991).

2. **Collaboration and multiple perspectives.** *Discussion teaching should create a climate for collaboration and respect for multiple perspectives and worldviews to be heard.* Introducing discussion teaching to students may be more difficult than it seems, as most students are used to playing passive roles in the classroom. Students can be introduced to this approach through the syllabus, introductory remarks, modeling what is expected in a discussion, and direct coaching on the process until they understand their roles in the learning community. Learning from each other while in class will take on a whole new meaning as the discussion process unfolds and reveals the treasures that arise from hearing and exploring various perspectives on themes and ideas with each other, not in competition with others. Wilkinson and Dubrow (1991) related the reticence of students to venture into discussion and become independent thinkers: "...powerful forces inhibit the spontaneous display and development of independent thought.... Only when students stop deferring to others' opinions can they learn to identify and assess problems, form reasoned, defensible interpretations, and reach and test conclusions unaided" (p. 249). Students need to feel safe in the classroom to take this leap to independent thought.

Creating and managing such a climate of collaboration requires a sensitivity to societal issues often not addressed in more teacher-directed teaching, such as social class, race, and gender; they will surface sooner or later and need to enrich the dialogue, not arrest it (Friere, 1970; Rogers & Freiberg, 1994).

3. **Instructor competencies.** *The discussion teaching instructor should have competency in a discipline[8] and skills in facilitation of groups.* Discussion teaching is hard work for instructors who choose this method, as it demands greater skills

---

these principles reflect the learner-centered, Information-Age paradigm of education (see chapter 1).

8. *Editor's note: You may have noticed that this does not deal with a method of instruction. Therefore, it is not in the strategy layer of instructional design. Which layer is it in?*

and knowledge than didactic forms of teaching. Not only does the instructor have to prepare for sharing knowledge, she or he must also manage the discussion, in part by planning for what might occur, knowing that the plan might have to be abandoned! Those who have to stay in control should not venture into using this methodology, since there is no guarantee that a planned-for outcome will be realized. Yet the excitement for many educators is the "unknown" and how to generate and sustain lively, intellectual intercourse. Christensen et al. (1991) reassure those who take this path that skillful discussion leaders do not really "wing it" when spontaneous, unplanned discussions or new discoveries arise that are not in our plans. If instructors are following the discussion method, they have planned for the unexpected to occur, and they can handle those moments by honing their listening and facilitation skills, along with their own freedom to let the argument lead the way.

This dual role, when practiced well, is a form of professional artistry in the sense that Schön (1987) defined: "the kinds of competence practitioners display in unique, uncertain and conflicted situations of practice" (p. 22). In responding to what evolves in discussion, in spite of planning, instructors of the method must draw not only on their tacit knowledge, but also on what Schön refers to as reflection-in-action, a type of critical thinking in the moment, to create a new or different way to respond to the situation at hand. Careful listening to the flow of the dialogue is a key to practicing this type of artistry, along with letting go and following one's instincts in the moment.

4. Life experiences. *In discussion teaching the life experiences of the students should be acknowledged and utilized in the learning process.* This recognition of students' worldviews and experiences is often the trigger that spurs the students on to participate in this type of teaching/learning dynamic. This principle goes beyond learning names and faces and requires that participants learn more about each other's lives and the experiences they bring to the class. Autobiographical pieces can be requested, for example, through an introductory exercise that requests the students' personal goals for the class. Friere (1970) and others support capitalizing on what the student already knows, and using that information to serve the current educational setting. When instructors broaden their knowledge of students to include their personality, speaking and leadership styles, and other aspects of communicating, they learn much about how to include student's lives in the learning process. Such details are addressed by Christensen et al. (1991) and Brookfield and Preskill (2005).

This inclusion of the life experiences of the students also requires relationship building, the cornerstone of establishing learning communities in discussion teaching. Thus, creating an environment for the flow of discussions, questioning, and even debate is initially the responsibility of the instructor, but readily becomes another shared role as students learn to participate as partners in this approach.[9] The behaviors of participants in the community impact the function

---

9. *Editors' note: Is the culture of the learning community an instructional method? What layer of design is it in?*

of that community. How people speak to each other, what they say, the type of questions asked of each other, the frequency of interaction, the amount of time spent together, the way people respond—all have to do with how people regard each other and build relationships. What happens in this learning community has an impact on how people learn, what they learn, and how they use the knowledge that emanates from the discussions.

5. Activities for higher learning. *Discussion teaching should include listening, reflecting, responding and linking as essential activities in promoting higher learning.* One could call these activities the "tools of the method" as communication with one another through logical progression of thought is at the heart of the instructional process in this method. It is through this principle that both instructors and students have the opportunity to bring forth new knowledge, either through presentation or discovery. The advantage here is that everyone learns in discussion teaching, although instructors retain their role of imparting new knowledge through facilitation or coaching, engineering discovery, and learning. Students, on the other hand, are now free in this model to question each other or the instructor, and can become the catalyst for sharing new knowledge based on their own experiences. Boehrer (1995), Christensen et al. (1991), and Welty (1989) all have useful guidance on how to make this happen, and emphasize the instructor's responsibility in setting the stage for building trust for students to participate and ultimately demonstrate their skills in the same way. These communication skills require ample practice for instructors and students so that all may be fully engaged in learning.

6. Democratic learning community. *Discussion teaching should promote a more democratic learning community.*[10] When the discussion teaching approach functions well, each party should be able to describe a climate where she or he believed that each person could speak freely without worrying about asking permission or feeling anxious about the content of what is expressed. This freedom to participate results from building a climate of trust over the course of spending time together, examining values, and working through common ground rules for discussion by participating parties. No one can declare that the process is democratic for another; it must be felt and sensed by each member of a group. Creating a contract that addresses explicit and implicit behaviors and activity is one strategy to employ in building such a community. This includes setting clear ground rules together to ensure that everyone understands how to proceed in class, setting up rules of accountability that are modeled by the instructor, and using herself whenever possible to teach students that it is ok to make her accountable. Asking students to become partners in accountability with the instructor can be a delicate, challenging task and may be included in the contract to legitimize use by the students. This can often be done through periodic, brief, and anonymous written evaluations of discussion sessions that ask participants to critique any aspect of the process. It can be instructive for all participants to

---

10. *Editor's note: Is this a method? A value? Which layer of design does it belong in?*

summarize these evaluations in class as feedback, and can be part of regular debriefing sessions at the end of each class or at designated times. An instructor can also coach students in class during debriefings or during individual office meetings by describing examples where she could have been challenged or made accountable. Hansen (1991) and Dillon (1994) offer more specific guidelines to support building this important community.

7. **Physical environment.** *Discussion teaching should be used in a physical environment that accommodates the interactions necessary in this type of learning.*[11] Creating an environment where participants can easily communicate usually means that the chairs and table, writing boards or flip charts, and media screens are placed in a manner conducive to discussion. U-shaped room settings are popular, as are movable chairs and tables for ease of change for large- or small-group interactions. Arrangements that allow participants easy access to the instructor and other participants will assist in the flow of discussions with this methodology. A circle structure is another popular one for small-group activities and has the characteristics of being easy to arrange and break up, and therefore can be set up in almost any space. The environment should not add to the barriers for communication with this method, and should therefore be set up on a consistent basis to favor exchanges that support the pedagogy.

The Practice of Discussion Teaching

In this section I will describe how one might get started in the practice of discussion teaching. Some of the ideas in the section are adapted from my own experience and resources in discussion teaching, along with Christensen et al. (1991) and Brookfield and Preskill (2005).

1. **Get started/develop a plan.** A teaching plan is a necessary tool that not only gives direction for the instructor and participant, but also can be a resource during discussion. It cannot always be followed as written, but discussion teaching can be disastrous without one. The instructor, as facilitator, is still responsible for what happens, though participants can become coleaders and partners once they understand how to proceed. Bohrer (1995) argues that as discussion teaching proceeds, the teaching plan[12] is one of three things of major importance to instructors. The other two are participant's comments and the group's thinking (p. 7). Christensen et al. (1991) teach that instructors have to prepare twice—once for themselves, and again from the students' perspective. This plan should include setting learning objectives. This is a common planning step for any class but is especially important for those new to managing content and process. Silverman, Welty, and Lyon (1993) encourage using the objectives as a guide to prevent the discussion from turning into a "bull session." Read and reread the course as-

---

11. *Editors' note: Here's a tough one. Which layer of design is this?*
12. *Editors' note: Is this an instructional method? If so, what layer of design is it in? If not, what is it?*

signment, immersing yourself in the details, separating factual information from opinions and other information in the dilemma. Master the facts.

   2. **Develop a concept outline.** Identifying key concepts then sub-issues gives direction to the instructor's analysis and can provide direction for the discussion. Welty (1989) and others recommend that an instructor develop a template and begin to map out discussion of key concepts based on the individual's style of analysis. This resource can be used if discussion lags, or can be a guide for linking with other ideas as they come up in class.[13]

   3. **Add a question outline.** Silverman, Welty, and Lyon (1993) believe the question outline should match the concept outline. Questioning is generally thought of as the critical skill for leading a discussion and must be planned carefully to promote discussion throughout a session as well as the course. Broad questions are necessary to invite students into the conversation, and more detailed questions are important as well, to probe and focus on particular areas for analysis and reflection. Louis Barnes, Harvard Business School faculty, and discussion leader of the Derek Bok Teaching Center seminars which I attended, was a skilled questioner who peppered our group with questions of varying intensity and tone, though he was never offensive. Novices need to write their questions as a resource and as a guide to the sessions as the work unfolds.

   4. **Create a visible outline on a black or white board.**[14] This living outline is based on the first two outlines—concept and question—and is used strategically during the discussion to record relevant comments and ideas from students and leaders as the class progresses. A validating experience for students, the outline on display, whether on the board, computer, or in some other way, also helps visual learners keep up with major ideas, and serves as a reminder of the status of the work for all participants. These visual stimuli are particularly helpful in linking concepts to theories and new questions, and in summarizing at the close of discussions.

Educating Students

Beyond preparation for discussion teaching for instructors, students need to be trained and prepared for the methodology. Students' mindset of the traditional direct instruction model can be challenging for them to put aside, especially if they have had negative experiences when they have expressed their opinions in class, thus reinforcing the inequitable relationship between instructor and

---

13. *Editors' note: What kind of knowledge is this? Are these instructions, "1) develop a plan, 2) develop a concept outline, 3) add a question outline," part of an ID process that is done before the instruction begins (instructional-planning theory)? Or are they something that is done during instruction (instructional-event theory)? Is the concept outline a sequence for the instruction and therefore an instructional method? What if no guidance is given for what the sequence should be like?*

14. *Editors' note: Planning this ahead of time would be part of the ID process (instructional-planning theory). Presenting it during the instruction would be an instructional method (instructional-event theory). It is common to synthesize these different kinds of theory in a single document.*

participant. In preparing a plan for discussion teaching, instructors must keep the student perspective in mind.

Some ideas to assist participants in acclimating to being actively involved in the discussion teaching process are: modeling the process, stating clear expectations, setting ground rules, designing practice sessions, and anticipating obstacles and problems.

Modeling the Process through an Actual Demonstration of a "Live" Discussion The discussion can be stopped for the instructor to comment on what is happening to teach participants the process. Commenting on the process as it unfolds can be an important step in participants' understanding of the discussion teaching process.

Stating Clear Expectations The syllabus can offer specifics about the course content, grading, types of participation, definitions of the facilitator's role, as well as that of the student. With a timetable, instructors can describe expectations of participants' behaviors in discussion teaching as they mature as the class evolves.

Setting Ground Rules for Interaction To insure early buy-in to the discussion teaching process, setting ground rules for all can make all the difference in whether students feel safe enough to become coleaders, actively sharing their insights and opinions. Creating the environment for creative, open, spirited interactions is critical in the beginning to help demonstrate how the discussions take place. Thus greater adherence to ground rules is experienced when all parties are involved in their creation.

Designing Practice Sessions The first couple of classes or sessions can be organized to practice discussion teaching to help participants become accustomed to the discussion teaching methodology, and begin to build their confidence about interacting in these new ways. Practice sessions can also take place throughout the session or course, especially when a new process is introduced.

Figuring Out Obstacles and Problems Ahead of Time Researching the challenges in discussion teaching and anticipating how to address them is simply a smart way to plan. Employing "what if" scenarios can assist in this type of planning, along with asking a colleague to review possible outcomes to the plan.

Brookfield and Preskill (2005) describe a few things not to do with this type of pedagogy: (1) Don't lecture—let the process play out; (2) Don't be vague—ask specific questions and give clear directions to launch discussions; (3) don't fear silence—allow it to happen without rushing to fill it; (4) don't misinterpret silence—fear, boredom, and disengagement are not necessarily the reasons for silence. Sometimes people just need enough time to gather their thoughts or to decide how to respond.

The Discussion

There are many ways to begin the discussion: ask for volunteers to respond to a question; call on a particular student to summarize the main points; place students in small groups to identify major concepts, identify a speaker to share their findings; or ask each person to share one question about the problem.[15] However it starts, the instructor must create a safe climate for students to take risks, and carefully listen as the discussion progresses. Appropriate and constructive feedback and subsequent questioning must encourage their thoughts, while following some logical path toward analyzing the problem. Pace, tone, intensity, wait-time, sensitivity to feelings, clarifying and interpreting, all the while thinking and processing for students and yourself, require enormous energy and concentration.

The challenge of sustaining the momentum of the discussion is a main topic of those who undertake this approach. Lively discussion that raises the topic to new levels of understanding with students and instructor intensely engaged in the process is what is desired. Many discussion instructors fear not only silences, but the slow, low-energy lag in dialogue or conversation. Ideally, the teaching plan can be the best resource, but this depends on the depth of the plan and the circumstances surrounding the lag in energy. Dillon (1994) suggests tapping into a list of responses created in advance to anticipate student reaction to the concepts and other materials of the course. He advocates using such a tool, instead of the instructor generating new questions during a down period. Reviewing or bridging comments from participants will often push the conversation forward, as opposed to introducing a new topic or direction. Comparing or relating major ideas or issues to each other is another way to build the fire of conversation, without introducing new material. Many discussion teaching practitioners agree that pacing, changing roles, and injecting small-group exercises are key ways to kick up discussions once they start to lose energy.[16]

Christensen et al. (1991) remind us that discussion teaching at its best is often messy and chaotic, thus instructors should not be afraid to go with the flow:

> In discussion teaching, tidiness can tyrannize. Messiness can work miracles. To succeed, the enterprise requires active contribution, not just merely cooperation, of the discussion group. Mutual cooperation— reciprocity of effort—is not only engaging and exciting for students, it is also imperative for the discussion leader. However impressive your experience or skills, you will have difficulty questioning, listening, and

---

15. *Editors' note: Any time you see alternative methods to choose from, ask yourself "What are the situationalities that tell me when and when not to use each?" If an instructional theory does not get the level of precision of specifying those situationalities, you need to look for literature that provides greater precision, or you need to figure that out on their own. And that may represent a great opportunity for research to provide the additional precision for the theory.*

16. *Editors' note: Again, this paragraph presents intriguing alternatives that beg for situationalities. Here is an opportunity for you to contribute to the common knowledge base about discussion teaching.*

responding while simultaneously observing, synthesizing, reflecting and evaluating dialogue and planning for the rest of the class. (p. 106)

Therefore, as the process unfolds, choices must be made in the midst of action: Should we continue this pace since the group seems to be fully engaged? Should we probe more on this concept to insure greater understanding by all? When shall I link this topic to the others recently covered? Would a small group activity enliven the discussion? How an instructor answers these questions depends on so many factors; her experience and philosophy of teaching; her level of risk-taking; how well she knows the participants; the participants' knowledge of the material; the timeframe in the course; even the nature of the topic under discussion.[17] There are no single, right answers to these types of questions, as they must be dealt with individually.[18] What is clear is that a variety of tools of the teaching professions are necessary to prepare for discussion teaching, and that use of them will aid in the excitement of giving instructors some sense of managing a process that has spontaneity and the unknown at its heart.

The Closing

There are no single right answers, and no easy answers—you might not even finish the discussion in each class. Summarizing major ideas and drafting learning points—individually, then as a group—to share with all, will influence the participants to reflect on what happened during the period, and will help them to recall the often complex journey traveled during the discussion. Having a visible outline is an asset for this, and offers a starting place for the next session. Closings also present opportunities to list or request resources to support main ideas that evolved from the discussion. And finally, it is a time for all to critique the session, perhaps anonymously at first, but always sharing it with the whole group to facilitate whole-group learning. Though these steps are general, they can be implemented with more detailed plans that are tailored to the style of teaching and personality of the instructor and the goals of the program, seminar or course. One very useful resource for ideas for closing discussions is the facilitator's guide for a casebook for teachers and teacher educators by Mesa-Bains and Shulman (1994).

---

17. *Editors' note: These are important situationalities.*
18. *Editors' note: In any particular situation, one alternative may be better than the others, but there may be so many factors that influence which one is best that it is difficult to know for sure, and impossible to teach to a novice all at once. Furthermore, the advantage of the best alternative over the next best one may be minimal. Experts gradually develop heuristics (often tacit) through trial and error. Even if an expert could make all their tacit knowledge explicit, the level of precision of the theory would likely make it unwieldy to use. However, that precision would be highly useful to program into a computer that could facilitate discussion teaching.*

Situational Guidelines for Discussion Teaching

The guidelines presented in this section are examples of particular instructional situations, or circumstances that require adjustments to the universal principals. Reigeluth describes such situations in Volume 2 of *Instructional Design-Theory and Models* (1999) and updated them with Carr-Chellman in chapter 1 of this volume. They have described two main situations that can impact the use of methods: (1) values, which should be aligned with all stakeholders; and (2) conditions, which can be different depending on the content, the learner, the environment, and the instructional constraints. The following are examples of such variations in conditions for discussion teaching.

1. Age and Learning Experience of Students   Adjustments in the primary principle of sharing responsibility for learning are necessary when working with very young participants, young people with special needs, participants who have language impediments or simply lack fluency in the language of instruction. This situation references different types of learners. An instructor may need to determine the degree of shared responsibility, or degree of collaboration due to a lack of understanding, language fluency, or physical incapacity to communicate. Sharing responsibility in areas where they could participate might include various forms of the higher learning activities described earlier, such as listening, linking ideas, or drafting new questions as discussions ensue, or observing small-group activity to report back to the group. Collaboration can take on many forms and varying degrees: collaborating in small groups, between two people who eventually report to the larger group, collaboration on assignments or projects in and out of class. Given the range of ways to share responsibility and collaborate, an instructor can be creative, even brainstorm with students to find suitable ways to share the load.

2. Distance or Online Classes   Using this approach with online discussions would also require adjustments due to dependence on technology[19] as an additional means of interaction among participants. This situation primarily references a difference in the kind of learning environment, and could pose instructional constraints depending on the technological sophistication of the tools employed. The spontaneity and flow of discussions can be heavily influenced by the communication software tools at the institution where the course is taught as well as by the efficiency of the students' computers, yet this mode presents exciting ways to adjust for collaboration, a mainstay of discussion teaching. Collaboration would be different in these distance courses, shifting to reading and writing as key modes, unlike the on-site courses, but there are now multiple ways to communicate through chat rooms, ways to actually see each other via the Web, and greater time frames in which to communicate since the contact is virtual versus on-site. Communication guidelines and tools would have

---

19. *Editor's note: The internet would require design on the control layer, representation layer, media logic layer, and data management layer. This guideline indicates that decisions on one layer can serve as situationalities for decisions on another layer.*

to be aligned with the appropriate technology, programs, and software to work in the virtual environment, yet the same consensus and cooperative setting of ground rules and other factors for discussion teaching and learning would be employed. Face-to-face interactions may or may not be possible, depending on the sophistication of the technology, thus a rather different type of discussion and a different type of community would be built. An instructor's dual competence would increase with online discussions because the instructor would need to be computer literate, and to be knowledgeable about the programs and software used to facilitate the class. This would necessitate preparation far beyond that of the on-site instructor, and is usually aided by the institution's faculty development center or similar services. And depending on the level and type of technical support available, the knowledge needed to co-lead online discussion might increase significantly for all participants.

3. Student Resistance   Student resistance to making the shift from being a passive learner to being a more active one can bankrupt discussion pedagogy before it can be practiced. Students' past experiences with this approach, distrust of the instructor, or lack of investment in their own learning could all influence their resistance to the approach. This situation of resistance references the kind of learner, and can be revealed in many forms: being closed minded, refusal to take responsibility for sharing leadership roles, lack of participation in small group activity, or refusing to contribute to discussions by being silent. Motivating students to become engaged can be a hurdle to overcome before discussion teaching can begin. An instructor may make adjustments by allowing more practice time for the process and by engaging students in more small groups with tasks that require greater interaction with each other before returning to the larger groups. Students with the greatest resistance can be coached in individual sessions; other tools such as critiquing videos or role playing of others in similar situations could engage discussion and provide new learning opportunities for all. Building in time for students more comfortable with the process to share their experiences in class, with some outside optional experiences, can also be helpful. Garvin (1991), Monahan (2000), and Gangel (2006) offer some good ideas to overcome resistance to students committing to this process. Time and skillful coaching can reduce resistance, but discussions may have to be limited to small-group activity until more engagement is fostered to embrace the approach more fully.

Conclusions

In this chapter I have defined the discussion approach to instruction, more commonly called discussion teaching, citing how it is organized, the values inherent in this type of pedagogy, and when it is most appropriate to use. The universal principles of discussion teaching were also described and their relationship was shown to Merrill's *First Principles of Instruction* (2002). Later in the chapter there was a brief how-to guide to this method that offered a glimpse of the factors that influence the instructor's management of both content and process, and the role of the student in partnership with this approach was also highlighted. Throughout the chapter, resources were cited that amplify what was described herein, for those who choose to study further. Finally, I offered some guidance for different situations in which adjustments can be made to tailor the universal principles, and I demonstrated how these situations can be addressed.

Overall, I have made an attempt to meet the goal of the volume in this chapter—to help build a common knowledge base for teaching using this methodology. Though certainly not exhaustive, the work herein is research-based, encompasses the work of the key architects of the methodology, and presents work that is broadly recognized in the field. The excitement in participating in such an endeavor helped me recognize that this, too, is just the beginning as the knowledge base on instruction is built, using the terminology and definitions cited. Yet I eagerly anticipate the additional work and revisions that others will make in the future.

References

Barnes , L. B., Christensen, C. R., & Hansen, A. J. (1994). *Teaching and the case method*. Cambridge, MA: Harvard Business School.

Berquist, W. H., & Phillips, S. R. (1975). Getting students involved in the classroom. In *The handbook for faculty development* . Washington, D.C.: Council for the Advancement of Small Colleges Association with the College Center of the Finger Lakes.

Boehrer, J. (1995). On teaching a case. *International Studies Notes, 19*(2), 1420.

Brookfield, S. D., & Preskill, S. (2005). *Discussion as a way of teaching*. San Francisco: Wiley.

Bruner, J. S. (1966). *Toward a theory of instruction*. Cambridge, MA: Harvard University Press.

Christensen, C. R., Garvin, D., & Sweet, A. (1991). *Education for judgment: The artistry of discussion leadership*. Cambridge, MA: Harvard Business School.

Dewey, J. (1938). *Experience and education*. New York: Macmillan.

Dillon, J. (1994). *Using discussions in classrooms*. Buckingham, UK: Open University Press.

Freire, P. (1970). *Pedagogy of the oppressed*. New York: Continuum.

Freire, P., & Shor, I. (1987). What is the "dialogical method" of teaching? *Journal of Education, 169*(3), 11–31.

Gangel, K. O. (2006). Teaching by discussion. Page 6 in series of 25 at http://www.bible.org

Garvin, J. (1991). Undue influence: Confessions from an uneasy discussion leader. In C. R. Christensen, D. A. Garvin, & A. Sweet (Eds.), *Education for judgment*. Cambridge, MA: Harvard Business School.

Hansen, A. J. (1991). Establishing a teaching/learning contract. In C. R. Christensen, D. A. Garvin. & A. Sweet (Eds.), *Education for judgment* (123–135). Cambridge. MA: Harvard Business School.

Merrill, M. D. (2002). First principles of instruction. *Educational Technology Research and Development Journal, 50*(3), 43–59.

Mesa-Bains, A., & Shulman, J. H. (1994). *Diversity in the classroom: Facilitator's guide*. Hillsdale, NJ: Erlbaum.

Monahan, G. W. (2000). Everybody talks: Discussion Strategies in the Classroom. *Journal of Methods, 25*(1), 6. Emporia State University.

Paul, R. (1995). *Critical thinking.* Santa Rosa, CA: Foundation of Critical Thinking.

Reigeluth, C. M. (Ed.). (1999). *Instructional design theories and models: Vol. 2. A new paradigm of instructional theory*. Mahwah, NJ: Erlbaum.

Rogers, C., & Freiberg, H. J. (1994). *Freedom to learn*. New York: Macmillan.

Schön, D. A. (1987). *Educating the reflective practitioner.* San Francisco: Jossey-Bass.

Silverman, R., Welty, W., & Lyon, S. (1993). *Case studies for teacher problem-solving*. New York: McGraw-Hill.

Welty, W. (1989, July/August). Discussion method teaching. *Change*, 39–49.

Wilkinson, J., & Dubrow, H. (1991). Encouraging independent thinking. In C. R. Christensen, D. A. Garvin, & A. Sweet (Eds.), *Education for judgment* (249–261). Cambridge, MA: Harvard Business School.

7

Experiential Approach to Instruction

LEE LINDSEY
Genworth Financial

NANCY BERGER
Training for Performance, Inc.

Lee Lindsey is currently the learning technology leader for Genworth Financial, a multinational financial security and insurance company. Lee has a PhD in instructional technology from the University of Virginia, an MBA from the College of William and Mary, and a BA in English and Latin from Duke University. Lee spent the first several years of his career as a Latin teacher, and has conducted research in the areas of instructional design practice and academic entrepreneurship in instructional technology.

Nancy Berger is the president of Training for Performance, Inc., a training and development consulting firm. She has a PhD in human resource development from Virginia Commonwealth University, an MA in French from the University of Virginia, and a BA from Thiel College in French and education. She has 28 years of experience in adult learning work in corporations and government, and is currently an instructor at George Washington University.

EDITORS' FOREWORD

Preconditions

Content
- *Any content that is related to experience*

Learners
- *All learners at all levels*

Learning environments
- *All instructional environments*

Instructional development constraints
- *Classroom management plan must be in place*

Values (opinions about what is important

about ends (learning goals)
- *Experience is an important end, as well as a means for reaching more abstract learning goals*

about priorities (criteria for successful instruction)
- *Effectiveness and appeal are valued over efficiency*

about means (instructional methods)
- *Learners should engage their own experiences in the service of learning goals*
- *Real world feedback is preferable*
- *Social constructivist approaches should be used*
- *Experiences should not be "too neat"*

about power (to make decisions about the previous three)
- *Learners should be active participants who assume much self-direction*

Universal Methods

1. *Frame the experience*
   - *Communicate objectives or goals*
   - *Communicate or negotiate assessment methods and criteria*
   - *Establish relationships (peers, teacher, community, context) and expected behavior of participants*
2. *Activate experience*
   - *Ensure authenticity in practice*
   - *Involve the learner in making decisions that have authentic outcomes*
   - *Focus on a problem*
   - *Challenge the students with experiences of optimal difficulty*
3. *Reflect on Experience*
   - *Facilitate deep reflection by challenging assumptions*
   - *Continue to build community*
   - *Help students to understand what happened, why, what was learned, and how to apply that learning in the future*

Situational Principles

  for framing the experience
  - *In online settings, take special note of building community and negotiation tasks.*
  - *When using pairings (for example, a learner with a real-world counterpart), establish an appropriate social structure.*
  - *In many situations, such as novel experiences or where failure presents ethical issues, experiential learning can and should include some didactic instruction, particularly in framing the experience.*
  - *In games, role plays, simulations, or microworlds, set clear expectations, rules, and climate.*
  - *When using role plays or simulations for building empathy, be careful to attend to ethical concerns.*

  for activating prior experience
  - *When there are multiple learners in a classroom, use classroom discussion to activate prior experience.*
  - *When there are multiple learners (in a classroom or online), use discussion boards.*
  - *When the learners have previous experience that is directly relevant to the topic, they may create stories to activate and reflect on that experience.*
  - *When learners cannot reflect due to linguistic or psychological limitations, digital stories may be used*

  for activating new experience
  - *When time allows for extending the learning to new experiences, it should build on prior learning and experience.*
  - *When skills are not desirable to practice in the field (risky, impractical), games, simulations, or role plays should be chosen.*
  - *When trying to help learners find out about and experience cultures, simulations and role plays are particularly powerful.*
  - *If a desired game or simulation is not available, it should only be used when sufficient development time is available.*
  - *When self-concept and/or interdependence are important outcomes, use outdoor experiential learning.*
  - *When instruction can or must be done at the learner's workplace, use action learning.*
  - *When instruction can or must be done in a workplace, use work-based learning where university resources permit.*
  - *In skills learning, teacher as coach may be a particularly appropriate teacher role for demonstration and practice.*
  - *When instructional time allows and the learners are capable of acting autonomously, use apprenticeships, mentorships, internships, or service-learning. The structure of these methods varies depending on the characteristics of the practice environment and the objectives of the instruction.*

for reflection on experience
- *When a teacher may not be available (such as online learning) and the learner is prepared to engage in self-directed reflection, journals and portfolios may serve as a good means of reflection.*

for additional variable methods
- *When instructional time is limited, address application of new knowledge through discussion.*
- *When time allows, provide another experience that builds on the previous experience as much as possible.*

—*CMR & ACC*

EXPERIENTIAL APPROACH TO INSTRUCTION

The topic of this chapter is how experience should be used within instruction to promote learning. Like the other chapters in this section, it presents a prescriptive rather than a descriptive model of experiential instruction, focusing on offering guidelines as to what instruction should be like. This model of experiential instruction is derived from an examination of experiential learning theory, empirical data, and evidence from actual experience, and ultimately synthesizes current knowledge on effective instructional practices into a common knowledge base that practitioners can use as they employ experiential methods.

Experiential learning theory (as embodied by Kolb, 1984) provides insight into how we learn from experience, and will be used here as the foundation for an instructional model. Moon (1999) notes that the use of a learning theory as an instructional model is a confusion of the concepts of "teaching" and "learning." This chapter assumes that organizing instruction so that it explicitly invokes stages of the experiential learning cycle increases the likelihood that learning will occur. In other words, this model is a pedagogical theory of experiential learning that "assumes that certain experiences can be enhanced in ways that produce outcomes desired by the actors or learners involved" (Fenwick, 2000, p. 245). At the same time, however, we must recognize that like any instructional model, the methods are probabilistic rather than deterministic. That is, the methods only increase the chances of attaining learning and development goals, rather than ensuring the attainment of those goals (Reigeluth, 1999, chapter 1).

There is still a challenge in defining experiential instruction, however, because we must differentiate it from other types of learning. All learning is essentially learning from experience, an observation made some years ago by Dewey (1938). Put another way, all instruction must be experiential, the learner being a participant and therefore experiencing it. What type of experience, then, forms the basis of experiential instruction?

The first way to answer this question is to consider experiential instruction as learner-centered versus teacher-centered. In this case, learners are not passive recipients, but *active negotiators* of their experiences. Experiential methods emphasize the "students' active involvement in negotiating the curriculum and shaping both the process and the outcome of the learning" (Felix, 2004, p. 10). Another characteristic of experiential instruction that differentiates it from other types of instruction is that it, "focuses on *authentic learning experiences* as the necessary basis for meaningful skill acquisition and human development" (Jackson & MacIsaac, 1994). Here, "authentic" means that the activities present the same type of cognitive challenges as those in the real world. In addition, the experiences should allow learners a significant degree of *self-direction* in the sense that the experience should allow them to make decisions. The decisions in turn should offer the opportunity for the *feedback* necessary to learn from the experience. Feedback in the form of failure, contradiction, or other outcomes that ask the learners to question their assumptions or their process are particularly valuable, as they initiate reflection. Schank (1997) calls this "expectation failure," and experiences involving such outcomes figure prominently in goal-based learning (Schank, Berman, & Macpherson, 1999—see volume 2). Some researchers (Hastie, 1984; Wong & Weiner, 1981) have even suggested that unexpected outcomes, especially failures, are the strongest stimulants of a learning process (Zakay, Ellis, & Shevalsky, 2004).

Having covered some of the key characteristics[1] that differentiate the experiences of experiential instruction from those of other forms of instruction, we will turn to the foundational theories that underlie experiential instruction.

Foundational Theories

The roots of contemporary experiential learning theory can be traced to John Dewey (1916/1966), who noted that a child learns how to fly a kite not because external facts are conveyed to his brain, but because of the direct experience of flying the kite. Dewey argued that people learn throughout their lives in a cycle of primary and secondary experience. *Primary experiences* are those such as the act of flying a kite, while *secondary experiences* are the ways that people might process those experiences, such as through feedback from peers or mentors. This idea of a cycle of learning from primary and secondary experiences forms the basis of most models of experiential learning.[2]

In recognizing the need to use experience in education, Dewey noted that the quality of experience is paramount. Experience and education cannot be directly equated, because in fact some experiences are "miseducative" in that they arrest or distort the growth of future experience (Dewey, 1938). For example, an experience could engender narrowness of thought so that the "possibilities of having richer experiences in the future are restricted" (Dewey, 1938, p. 26). Dewey called the self-fulfilling trend of past experiences to define future experi-

---

1. *Editors' note: These key characteristics could also be considered fundamental principles of experiential learning.*
2. *Editors' note: This constitutes a method of instruction on a very imprecise level—a method that is patterned after a natural process.*

ences the "continuity of experience." He also noted, however, that the current environment determines the nature of the experience for the individual as much as the legacy of prior experiences. It is the role of the teacher to be aware of the effect of the environment and to utilize all aspects of it to create as worthwhile an experience as possible.

Another important influence on experiential learning theory was Jean Piaget, the Swiss cognitive psychologist whose research into intelligence and cognitive development led him to explanations of the sources of human knowledge. It was Piaget who noted the twin forces of assimilation and accommodation at work in humans as they interact with their world. From the time of birth, Piaget observed, a person is constantly striving to make sense of the world, either in terms of what he already knows or in new terms that he must define. Interaction with the environment either results in a process of assimilation, in which the experience is integrated into existing knowledge, or results in accommodation, in which the knowledge gleaned from the experience forces a modification of existing knowledge. Recognition of this dual process of assimilation and accommodation has important implications for the types of experiences that should be chosen for use in experiential instruction, particularly with respect to the degree of complexity, problem-orientation, and self-directedness that the experience should provide. We learn through the discovery of variation in the environment (Moon, 1999), and the materials of learning should promote this process by challenging the learner.

An additional influence on experiential learning was David Kolb (1984), who synthesized much prior work in offering a continuous, cyclical model of the experiential learning process. Kolb's model consists of four stages: concrete experience (the experience itself), reflective observation (reflection on the experience), abstract conceptualization (building overarching concepts based on the experience), and active experimentation (testing these concepts).[3] In this way a person continually develops through a cycle of drawing meaning from experience and applying that meaning to new experiences. Kolb's model has been criticized for its being a sequential, cyclical model that universally describes the process of learning from experience, and because it does not adequately address the issues of using experience as the basis for learning. These criticisms are explored next.

Criticisms of a Cyclical Model of Learning

The idea of a cycle has been challenged by those who say that learners may not necessarily engage in the steps sequentially, or that some or all of the steps in the cycle may happen simultaneously (Beard & Wilson, 2002). Fenwick notes that "attempted divisions between human experience and reflection on that experience have proved problematic" (2000, p. 243). Boud and Walker (1993)

---

3. *Editors' note: This also constitutes a method of instruction on a very imprecise level.*

describe 'reflection in action,' a process that recognizes the presence of reflection in experience. In a similar manner, it is difficult to understand how a phase of abstract conceptualization, in which a person develops conceptual explanations for the experience, is separate from the process of reflecting on the experience. Furthermore, not all learners will engage in each of the steps —some may learn nothing from an experience, or they may engage in the steps but not in a manner that promotes learning. Many people have learned to probe the underlying meaning of their experiences, but such cognitive ability is not characteristic of all learners (Burrows, 1995). For this reason it is important for a model of experiential instruction to provide the methods for learners to engage in each activity, and particularly reflective ones, in a meaningful way. We do not just learn from experience. The experience has to be arrested, examined, and analyzed in order to generate truly useful knowledge from it.

Criticisms of Using Experience as a Basis for Learning

The use of experience as a basis for learning presents numerous challenges, a few of which are addressed here. First, not all experiences offer good learning opportunities. Some may not hold meaningful information, or may even hold the wrong information. Dewey made a similar observation by noting that some experiences are miseducative, and Merriam (1994) notes that "not all experience leads to the growth of ever-widening and deeper experiences" (p. 81). Second, even for those experiences that offer the potential to be good learning opportunities, the individual's interpretation of the experience may be misguided. The lessons drawn from it may "turn out to be irrelevant, invalid, or even misleading" (Zakay et al., 2004, p. 151). Part of the problem is that our recollection of experience changes as we think back and reflect on it. This might be due to the inadequacy of our memories, or the fact that the retelling of experience is political—the stories we tell change according to our purpose (Zepke & Leach, 2002). What these and other criticisms like them mean is that experiential learning, like all learning, is inherently fallible.

One answer to this dilemma is found in the area of social constructivism, which proposes that, in order for experience (and our interpretation of it) to be used as the basis for knowledge creation, the learning process should occur within a community of learners who share consideration of the experience. Instructional methods anchored in a social–constructivist approach to learning (Duffy & Jonassen, 1992; Savery & Duffy, 1996) assume that "knowledge is individually constructed and socially coconstructed by learners based on their interpretation of experiences in the world" (Jonassen, 1999, p. 217).

The goal of this chapter is to synthesize current knowledge about the most effective route for learning from experience within instruction, and the perspective of social constructivism is valuable in this respect. Individuals may and do learn from experience without validation within a community through the twin processes of assimilation and accommodation, but a social constructivist interpretation of experiential learning is supported by several authors (e.g., Gold & Holman, 2001; Zepke & Leach, 2002; including Baker, Jensen, & Kolb, 2002). Empirical support is provided in a study by Nespor (1995), who examined the growth of the decision-making capacity of small business owners from an experiential perspective and concluded that the input from learning communities separated effective and ineffective critical decisions.

Universal Principles

We will now address how experiential instruction should be structured in order to overcome the challenges described previously. At the same time, we must draw on a relative paucity of empirical support for *what works* when using experience as the basis for instruction. In the end we have found three universal principles for experiential instruction that should be implemented chronologically, and do not necessarily constitute a continuous cycle. Given the inherent problems of using experience as a basis for learning, the vetting of both experience and the interpretation of that experience in collaboration with one's peers is central to this model. Within each of the three universal methods are universal submethods that should be implemented. There are also variable methods that differ according to the instructional situation, and these will be elaborated upon in the last section. The three universal principles, which bear some resemblance to Merrill's "first principles" (discussed below) are:

- **Principle 1: Framing the experience**—Communicating the instructional objectives, assessment criteria, expected behavior, and social structure do much to determine the learners' behavior as they engage in the experience and thus the experience itself. Variable methods such as didactic instruction may also occur in this phase.
- **Principle 2: Activating experience**—Whether prior experience or a newly initiated experience, activating the experience is necessary. There are multiple variable methods for doing so that range from laboratory practice to simulations.
- **Principle 3: Reflecting on experience**—Experience must be analyzed in order to learn from it, and this principle gives formal service to a process that may or may not be automatically occurring. Reflection should involve the learner in answering "What happened?" "Why did it happen?", "What did I learn?", and "How would I apply this knowledge to future experiences?"

These principles are represented graphically in Figure 7.1. We will now expand on each of the principles outlined above and explore the rationale and empirical support for each.

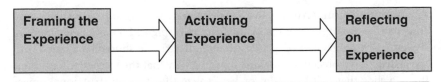

Figure 7.1 A Graphical Representation of the Three Universal Principles of Experiential Instruction

Principle 1: Framing the Experience

In experiential instruction, the learner typically has much greater latitude, so establishing a framework for proceeding during the experience is necessary for making efficient use of the learner's attention both during and after the experience. Doing so tends to increase the subsequent value of the experience as a learning opportunity. This is because how the experience is framed determines the learners' perspectives on the experience and how they engage in it—what they tend to observe or think, what they tend to say or do, and so forth. This, in turn, determines to a great degree how valuable the experience is as a basis for subsequent reflection and learning. Kurt Lewin , for example, a social psychologist who developed experiential methods as part of his research in the 1940s and 1950s, consciously used the word *laboratory* to create an atmosphere of experimentation among the members of his experiential learning groups. In the case of prior experiences that are used as a basis for learning, such framing is equally important in order to focus the attention of the learner on the elements of his or her prior experience that are relevant to the instructional objectives. Guidelines for framing are explored in more detail below.

Defining Instructional Objectives The first element of framing the experience is defining the instructional objectives. The term *instructional objectives* as used here is broader than just *learning objectives*, because they include indication as to the reason for and purpose of engaging in the experience—specifically in relation to the problem or issue that the experience will address. (Problem-orientation is a characteristic of experiences noted below.) Such objectives allow us to differentiate between experiences and activities. Activities involve the learner in doing things, but not all activities are necessarily experiential in nature. For example, interviewing someone as part of an activity designed to teach about a particular subject may not be experiential. Provided with proper instructional objectives and a clearly communicated framework for engaging in the experience, however, it can be experiential. The interview could be part of a larger exercise that is designed to have students learn how to access a variety of primary and secondary resources in researching a subject. Framing the interview as such prior to the experience allows the learner to engage in the interview with an eye toward its value as a method of data collection, and lays the groundwork for a rich analysis of the experience afterwards. As another example, an interview would be a different experience altogether if the learners engaged in it with the purpose of practicing and learning interviewing skills.

Communicating Criteria for Assessment Framing the experience also consists of communicating the criteria for assessment. Like the assessment of student learning in any pedagogical theory, the criteria should be aligned with the instructional objectives, making it more likely that the learner will produce the behavior that will help him or her realize the stated instructional objectives. Here, the concept of assessment should be interpreted in a larger sense than just the formal one in which the teacher is the assessor, however. Bobbit, Inks, Kemp, and Mayo (2000), for example, describe an integrated approach to teaching marketing that involves business students across multiple classes in marketing products for a mock trade show. Besides the motivation of the grade, they suggest that inviting local media, parents, or school officials may "... encourage students to take the project seriously and understand the degree of professionalism necessary..." (p. 23). Communicating the ultimate assessment of students' work from the beginning of the activity can be a significant influence on the nature of their experience.

Formally Defining the Social Structure Another universal element of framing experiential instruction is to formally define the social structure of the participants and their expected behavior—the relationship of the student to the teacher, the student to his peers (if such exist), and the student to the outside world (if the student will venture outside class as part of instruction). For example, teams can be used to promote motivation, and if the students will venture outside class as they would in service learning, they should understand their relationship to those they encounter as part of the instruction.

In summary, the following are universal submethods that are essential elements of framing the experience:

- Communicating the instructional objectives
- Communicating or agreeing on the criteria for assessment
- Establishing the social structure (relationship to peers, to the teacher, and to the environment beyond the class) and the expected behavior of the participants

Principle 2: Activating Experience

Having framed the experience, activating it is the next phase of instruction. The term *activation* is appropriate because this phase can involve the use of prior experience or the creation of new experience. Guidance as to when to use prior experience and new experience as the basis for instruction, as well as the various methods for doing so, are covered in the last section on "Situational Principles." Regardless of method, however, there are universal characteristics of experience that the educator should ensure are present.

Authentic Experience The first universal characteristic is that the experience should be authentic to the real environment. Experiential learning is grounded in the belief that the more authentic the features of the instructional context are, the more the transfer of learning is optimized (Jackson & MacIsaac, 1994). These authentic features might be the qualities of the tasks that the learner should perform or the "ecological setting" (Jackson & MacIsaac, 1994, p. 22) in which instruction occurs. The environment need not be completely authentic—there can be varying degrees of authenticity, as a simulation might reflect the important elements of the real environment but not deliver dangerous consequences. However, increasing the degree of similarity between instructional contexts and relevant application contexts improves transfer of learning from instruction to application (Lee & Caffarella, 1994).

Making Decisions for Authentic Outcomes The second universal characteristic, related to the first, is that the experience should involve the learner in making decisions that have authentic outcomes. In all instruction the learner is a participant, but where experiences are concerned, participation means that the learner is an actor who makes decisions in an authentic environment that provides feedback on the actions in a realistic way. Economic or management simulations are one example. The learner is the chief executive of a start-up, low-cost air carrier, and can choose, among other things, how many planes to buy, how many people to employ, and the price per ticket to charge. The number of planes purchased increases debt, but increases revenue. A greater number of employees decreases profit but improves service, resulting in greater customer satisfaction and therefore greater demand. A lower price per ticket increases demand and therefore revenue, but results in a pricing war with rival airlines. All of the inputs chosen, as a result of their relationship to one another, influence the ultimate barometer of success: the company's stock price. There are consequences of the learner's decisions, and the learner senses those consequences in some way.

Problem Orientation The third universal characteristic is that the experience should be problem-oriented to some degree. Most experiential learning involves a core issue, problem or situation that must be analyzed and then brought to a conclusion or solution. The decisions made during the experience are part of the process of analysis and experimentation that consequently provides the feedback on the problem helpful for learning. A problem-orientation is also important so that the learner, "clearly perceives and accepts the relevance of the specific learning activities in relation to the larger task problem" (Savery & Duffy, 1996, p. 138).

Optimal Difficulty The fourth universal characteristic of experiences, and related to the previous one, is that the experiences should be difficult enough that they challenge the student, but not so difficult that there is not a reasonable expectation of success. In a study of Hungarian English teachers who frequently employed role plays, for example, Halapi and Saunders (2002) found that the quality and difficulty of the problem was important so that learners were engaged and did not lapse into their native language if the task was too ambitious.

In summary, the following are elements of the universal method of activating experience. The experience itself should:

- Be authentic to the practice environment
- Involve the learner in making decisions that have authentic outcomes
- Be problem-oriented to some degree
- Be difficult enough to challenge the student

Principle 3: Reflecting on Experience

Theoretical support for the value of some form of reflection following experience is provided by numerous authors (Boud, Keogh, & Walker, 1985; Dewey, 1938; Kolb, 1984), although the understanding of reflection varies widely among those who write about it. Empirical support is less prevalent in the literature (Mackintosh, 1998; Moon, 2004). One example of empirical support for the benefit of reflection is provided by Ndoye (2003), who examined the farming practices of Senegalese peanut farmers, and found that one of the most significant qualities that separated successful from unsuccessful farmers was that they reflected on the outcomes of new agricultural practices through discussion with other farmers. There is certainly no lack of anecdotal evidence for the value of reflection in learning from experience. The use of portfolios, journals, group discussions, debriefs, and similar reflective methods as a central part of good instruction abounds in the literature. Taken together, such evidence supports Merrill's (chapter 3) analysis that reflection is a universal method for encouraging the integration of new knowledge.

Much of the problem in evaluating reflection is defining it. For example, there are at least two elements—the recollection of "what happened?" and the process of understanding why did it happen?" Hatton and Smith (1995) put forward a four-level framework for reflection, with simple descriptive writing as the lowest level and critical reflection as the highest. The challenge, however, is that not all learners have the innate ability to think critically about experience. Mackintosh (1998), for example, cited studies of nursing students that showed that some nursing students lacked the ability to "think about what they did other than at a superficial level" (p. 556). One way this theory of experiential instruction addresses these challenges is that it calls for a highly social–constructivist learning environment, one in which the learners can be challenged to think critically about their experience. In addition, there are specific methods for stimulating reflection that should be employed.

Teacher Facilitation The first universal submethod for stimulating reflection is the active role of the teacher, who is a facilitator of a social process that involves making meaning from experience. The teacher's role, "includes helping learners to identify their beliefs and working with them to master impediments to understanding," which can be achieved, "by facilitating student-student and student-teacher interaction; using reflective feedback to enhance the nature of discussions; providing critical feedback related to learners' contributions; and challenging learners' naïve conceptions" (Dart, 1997, p. 31). The teacher's role is to encourage and prompt more than a superficial reflection.

Community-Building Establishing a sense of community is critical for such meaningful dialogue to take place, and community-building is the second universal submethod. While community-building is part of the framing of experience, it should also be pursued prior to beginning to reflect. To set the stage for critical reflection, the learners must have a sense that they can comfortably challenge and be challenged by one another and the teacher. A significant element of community building is communicating the equality of the participants and their role in the active critique of others' experience. In situations where there is only one learner, this consists of establishing the teacher as one who can comfortably challenge and be challenged by the student.

Process: What Happened, Why It Happened, What Was Learned, and How to Apply It The third universal submethod is the actual process of reflection, which begins with the learner (or the community of learners) recalling what happened. The U.S. armed services' After Action Review (AAR), a formal institutional process used to learn from operations, establishes precisely what happened before proceeding to discuss why it happened. It is noted in commentaries on the AAR that what should be a straightforward exercise in having different participants agree on what happened is sometimes a difficult one due to differing memories of the experience.

Having established what happened, the second part of the universal process is to have the learners answer why it happened, and the third is to have them explain what they learned. Finally, the learners should explore how they would apply the knowledge in future experiences. This last step, a projection onto future events, creates a framework for applying and evaluating the knowledge so that variance from expectation stimulates learning. Each stage of this process requires a higher degree of cognition. Thus, it becomes increasingly important that the teacher assume the role of facilitator of the process (the first principle).

In summary, the following are elements of the universal principle of reflecting on experience:

- The teacher as a facilitator to prompt reflection by challenging assumptions (either verbally or by prompts within a structured writing exercise)
- Continuing the community-building begun when framing the experience
- Seeing the student answer:
  - *What happened?*
  - *Why did it happen?*
  - *What have I learned?*
  - *How would I apply this knowledge to future experiences?*

Applicability to Merrill's Principles

How applicable are these "universal" principles of experiential instruction to the more general principles of good instruction that Merrill describes in chapter 3? Merrill notes that at the center of many instructional models is a problem that the student must solve (the "Problem" phase). Most experiential activities involve some degree of problem-orientation, for it is a problem that drives the pursuit of the experience. The first experiential principle, framing experience, consequently involves some degree of problem-orientation. Framing the experience appropriately may also involve demonstration of applicable skills (the "Demonstration" phase), and the provision of an organizing framework prior to the use of previous or new experience (the "Activation" phase). The experiential principles of reflection on experience and drawing conclusions from reflection are Merrill's "Integration" phase.

Situational Principles

Having explored the universal, or basic, methods of experiential instruction, this chapter now turns to the situational, or variable (Reigeluth, 1999, chapter 1), methods. The decision about when to use certain variable methods is driven by the nature of the instructional situation. For example, the methods that must be employed at a distance, or in the workplace, differ from those that can be employed in the classroom. Reigeluth (chapter 1, this volume) identifies all of the elements of the instructional situation, but the choice of when to use the variable methods presented here is framed in terms of the nature of the location, of the learner, and of the instructional development constraints. The variable methods are organized according to the larger universal method to which they belong.

Variable Methods for Framing the Experience (Principle 1)

Creating Communities at a Distance (Web-Based) In distance learning, it is difficult to create a sense of community beyond the one-to-one relationship of the student and the instructor. Web technologies, however, have opened the door to viably creating an effective community of learners at a distance. We talk here from the perspective of entirely online experiences, but blended approaches can also take advantage of the anytime/anywhere learning among class members that is possible (and desirable) through Web technologies. Therefore, the following methods are recommended for distance learning and blended learning contexts.

Establishing a sense of one's relationship to others is key to initiating communities in an online environment (Aragon, 2003). Day (2004) recommends beginning with a process of framing the course—establishing the objectives, tone, and expected rules of interaction—through a message on the course home page. Johnson and Aragon (2003) similarly suggested that the instructor create an initial personal connection through an audio-streamed welcome message; where possible, the use of audio among all members of the class is desirable in order to imbue with emotion what text alone cannot do (Aragon, 2003). Also at the beginning of a course, Day (2004) reinforced the sense of community with an introductory e-mail that included a "clue" for an information exchange activity (each student had a different clue, which by itself was not meaningful, but when combined with the others was meaningful). This clue was the lead-in to having learners share their information in an initial online discussion. Another initial part of establishing the sense of face-to-face interaction and personal identity necessary for building the online community was to use an online face book to which each learner submitted his or her picture along with introductory and contact information (Aragon, 2003; Day, 2004).

Establishing the Social Structure Among Students Where the experience involves the participation of more than one learner, formally establishing the social relationships among the students is another opportunity to define the nature of the experience. Cheney (2001), for example, described structured interactions in which a university business student was paired with an international student for direct interaction that could take various forms, including that of live case study, topic discussions, and role plays. In order for such structured interactions to function properly, the professor must ensure that the participants consider themselves to be of equal status, understand their interdependence for the success of the experience, and have ample opportunity to become personally acquainted with each other (Cheney, 2001). Teams are another type of social structure, and when properly formed can promote the desired learning. For more information on effectively structuring teams for use within instruction, see Koppenhaver and Shrader (2003). These methods are not needed in situations where fellow learners are not available.

Providing Didactic Instruction The framing of experience can take the form of providing content-based didactic instruction in order to give the learners the foundational knowledge they require in order successfully to engage in and interpret the experience. Cornelius (2004) described methods that improved the attitudes of nursing students toward the HIV+ population. Presentation of HIV/AIDS didactic content on the physiological basis for the disease preceded a lecture/Question and Answer session with an HIV+ individual and a role play with scenarios that involved HIV+ individuals. Hakeem (2001) provided empirical support for this approach, describing methods in which students in a business statistics course apply the knowledge they have gained in class as they carry out a field-studies project. Macri et al. (2005) showed the effectiveness of an instructional approach in which didactic instruction and a case-based discussion precede a role play in the application of the material. These are specific examples of a more general method—that of in-class didactic instruction followed by an experiential activity—that is common in descriptions of experiential instruction. When should the instructor choose this method? In most situations, in fact, some form of didactic delivery of content will be beneficial. This is especially true in cases where the learner will enter into a novel situation or where student failure presents ethical issues, either for the learner or for others in the environment.

Setting Climate/Rule/Behavior/Expectation Where there is the suspended disbelief of reality, such as in games, simulations, and role plays, it is particularly important to follow a process of climate, rule, behavior, and expectation setting. At the same time that a suspended disbelief of reality affords the learners the opportunity to create situations that might not otherwise be possible, they need to understand their expected roles in order to operate in this alternate environment (Parathian & Taylor, 1993). For example, in a game the motivation of the learners should be to try to win; in a simulation it is to be professional within one's role and situation; and in a role play it is to perform well (Jones, 1998). In like manner, learners should understand the rules in this new environment—are they to collaborate or to compete? These decisions for the operating rules of the new environment do as much to define the experience as the nature of the environment itself.

Establishing an Ethical Environment When experiential methods (particularly role plays and simulations) are employed to build empathy or understanding by placing participants in the shoes of another person, there may be significant ethical considerations (Arthur & Achenbach, 2002). Where participants are asked to assume the role of the disabled or oppressed, anger and resentment (Byrnes & Kiger, 1990), fear and oppression (Zimbardo, 1973), or intimidation (Lexton, Smith, Olufemi, & Poole, 2005) may result. The literature provides several recommendations for establishing an ethically sound environment when such methods are used. Of those, the following might be undertaken during the framing phase of the instruction: making clear that participation is voluntary and that at any time a distressed individual (either participating or observing) has the option to leave (Lexton et al., 2005), and obtaining informed consent from participants. The student should be prepared beforehand to understand the outlet available to grapple with difficult emotions that might emerge from such situations. The instructor should maintain the ethical environment throughout the experience as well (Pedersen & Ivey, 1993), which includes limiting the amount of student self-disclosure (Arthur & Achenbach, 2002).

Variable Methods for the Activation of Experience (Principle 2)

The activation of experience spans a continuum from invoking past experience as a basis for learning, to creating new experience during instruction for the sake of learning. Sutherland refers to these as the long term and short term views of experiential learning (1997), respectively. We will call these the prior experience view and the new experience view, and the variable methods introduced below are accordingly organized. The list is not comprehensive, but considerations are discussed as to when to use each method. For a comprehensive list, see Caffarella and Lee (1994).

The prior experience view takes into account the range of learners' past experience, and methods for activating prior experience should be employed to some extent in all experiential instruction. Support for the activation of prior experience is provided by Caffarella and Barnett (1994), who note that using learners' previous experience in instructional contexts is one of the most important characteristics of experiential instruction for adults. This supports Merrill's (chapter 3) statement that, "Learning is promoted when learners activate relevant cognitive structures by being directed to recall, relate, describe, or demonstrate relevant prior knowledge or experience" (p. 85). The question is not when to use prior experience, for some method should always be employed to invoke previous experience in experiential instruction. The question is how to invoke it, for there are many alternatives.

Methods for activating new experience, such as simulations, role plays, and internships, should be employed in addition to methods that activate prior experience in most situations, particularly where the learners' past experience may be relevant but not directly suitable as a foundation for new learning. Criteria for selecting from among different new methods are noted below.

Activating Prior Experience (The Prior Experience View) There are numerous methods available for activating prior experience, such as class discussion, stories, reflective journals, and critical incident narratives. These are variations, however, on two primary methods for the activation of prior experience that will be discussed here—discussion and stories.

Discussion Classroom discussion should be employed where there are multiple learners. Although suitable for any point in this instructional model, it involves the activation of experience because appropriate discussion should draw on the unique perspectives that come from learners' previous life experiences. As throughout this instructional model, the active role of the teacher is required in order to facilitate such a discussion. Zepke and Leach (2002) describe how their own courses use a diverse range of bibliographic references to bring a diversity of perspectives into class discussion. The authors also recognize the cultural diversity of their learners. For example, the authors describe a situation in which they asked native New Zealanders in the class to engage in a prayer they customarily use before and after learning. Doing so challenged other learners in the class to confront their own personally held assumptions.

Online discussion boards should be used to promote classroom discussion in online learning environments, but are recommended where the instruction is classroom-based as well, for several reasons.[4] First, they are asynchronous, meaning learners have more time to reflect on others' and their own responses. Second, the online medium tends to encourage participation by all members of the class, since some learners may find it difficult to participate in face-to-face discussions due to their personality or learning style. Interactions, or "the reciprocal actions of two or more actors within a given context" (Vrasidas & McIsaac, 1999, p. 25) are important to the success of learning. Furthermore, from a social constructivist perspective, a class cannot strive to create true knowledge unless each learner has a voice. One of the particular values of web-enabled discussions is that they take into account the "heterogeneity of the participating students— both of educational background and work experience, and culture and language" (Booth & Hulten, 2003, p. 66).

Stories When the learners have previous experience that is directly relevant to the topic at hand, they may create stories to activate and reflect on that experience. Here, separating experience from reflection on the experience is difficult to do, as stories tend to be both the documentation and interpretation of events. However, the proper use of stories in experiential instruction sees the story followed by a formal process of reflection.

Gold and Holman (2001) used storytelling in management education to have learners recount a work problem they are currently experiencing. The researchers wrote that such a narrative approach to reflection allows learners to better understand the organization in which they work and the motivations of the actors involved, as well as the assumptions on which they base their decisions. Following the creation of the story, students are provided specific questions to answer in order to spur reflective thinking on what the story represents to them, to their coworkers, and to the organization. Day (2004) described a method in which learners team up to create "story problems," or descriptions of concrete situations from their own experience that illustrate and apply the content covered in the class. A story problem is used as the basis for a topic on the class online discussion board; and different learners are asked to be leaders for the discussion from one assignment to the next.

Digital Stories Using stories in the way just mentioned assumes that learners have the ability to craft such narratives through language. Where such ability is lacking, there should be other means for the retelling of experience. For example, direct reflection on past events may be difficult if the events were painful or traumatic, yet a retelling of the past is needed to treat the psychological effects of the experience. In such cases various methods considered as "art therapy" provide a means for expression of one's experience. Digital stories (movies often created by inserting still images into movie-making software to form a story)

---

4. *Editors' note: This is still situational, because it does not include situations where there are not multiple learners. Furthermore, the discussion boards may be done differently depending on whether or not class discussions are also held.*

are one such example of storytelling methods that have been used in this kind of situation. The benefit of digital stories is that they do not necessarily depend on the ability of the students to express themselves exclusively through writing, instead making the process of personal expression a more visual-symbolic one.

Activating New Experience (The New Experience View) There are numerous methods for the activation of new experience, among them simulations, games, role plays, field studies, field trips, experimentation, action learning projects, and methods that involve experience in authentic environments alongside practitioners (apprenticeships, internships, mentorships, service-learning). A few key variable methods are discussed below: games/simulations/role plays, outdoor-based experiential instruction, work-based instruction, demonstration/practice, and apprenticeships, internships, mentorships, and service learning.

Games/Simulations/Role Plays[5] Games, simulations, or role plays should be chosen where there is the need to learn skills that are not desirable to practice in the field; for example if the relevant context would put the learner or others at risk (e.g., social workers practicing how to respond to child abuse allegations), or the relevant context is impractical to create (e.g., running a company). Although differences exist between the three, games, simulations, and role plays are similar in their suitability for the instructional situations just mentioned. Role plays involve students "getting into character" in practice situations, while games differ from simulations in that games generally feature teams competing against other teams (Saunders, 1997). Empirical evidence supports the value of these methods compared to other methods. Herz and Merz (1998) employed an economic simulation game in a college business class and found increased student engagement in the stages of Kolb's experiential learning cycle compared to traditional lectures. Another study by Steadman et al. (2006) compared training for medical students using mannequin-based simulations to a problem/case based approach in which feedback was provided orally by the instructor. The authors found that the simulations were more effective for improving the ability of doctors to respond to the medical condition being taught.

The use of role plays and simulations is frequently cited in the literature where there is the need to learn about the culture of an individual or a group of individuals, and the interpersonal skills (particularly communication skills) associated with understanding that culture. This is appropriate given the belief that culture must be experienced in order to learn about it (Harrison & Hopkins, 1967; McCaffery, 1986; Pedersen & Ivey, 1993). Nevertheless, evidence on the effectiveness of experiential methods in increasing cross-cultural awareness compared to traditional didactic approaches is mixed (Arthur & Achenbach, 2002; Gannon & Poon, 1997). Overall, role plays and simulations offer a high

---

5. *Editors' note: See also chapter 9.*

degree of instructional effectiveness (where the experience is authentic) at the expense of increased development time (if original activities will be created). Games can also be effective compared to other instructional methods, but should be employed where specific subject matter, especially mathematics, can be targeted (Randel, Morris, Wetzel, & Whitehill, 1992). Where games are original, they can require increased development time as well. These three methods are particularly worthwhile for teaching skills that are not desirable to practice in the field.

Outdoor-Based Experiential Instruction Outdoor-based experiential instruction involves learners in tackling challenging outdoor problems as members of a team, and is used to achieve several outcomes. These outcomes vary, but are rooted in the tendency of learners to gain a greater sense of self-concept, as well as an understanding of their interdependence, through the completion of the activity. Smith, Strand, and Bunting (2002), for example, provide empirical support for a link between college students' participation in a semester-long outdoor challenge course and improved moral reasoning (although the explicit purpose of the course was not to improve moral reasoning).

The term *outdoor-based experiential training* (OBET) refers to one- to two-day programs in which adults tackle group problem-based challenges intended to improve their interpersonal, team, and communication skills in organizational settings. While the degree to which such programs result in transfer of desired behaviors to the job has been questioned, empirical literature supports the capacity of such programs to increase basic measures of interpersonal, team, and communication skills (Mazulewicz, 2002).

Schettler (2002) notes that in order to ensure the success of such outdoor experiential activities, the instructor should ensure that a specific business problem is identified in advance and the activities are tied to this problem. Regardless of the type of learner, outdoor-based experiential methods are best utilized where there is the need to learn intrapersonal and interpersonal skills.

Work-Based Instruction Where the nature of the environment and the learners is such that instruction will (or can) occur while at work, on-the-job experiences can be used within the instructional framework. There are two primary types of work-based instruction described here: action learning exercises and work-based learning.

Action learning is an approach in which groups convene to develop solutions to specific problems, create a plan to carry out their solutions, return to their normal work environment and act on that plan, and reconvene as a group to debrief the entire experience. While action learning is associated with use in business settings, it can be employed in a variety of organizational settings, including business, education, and government.

Work-based learning is a partnership between universities and organizations in which the organizations' employees receive formal credit at the university based on a customized plan of learning that occurs almost exclusively at the workplace (Boud, Solomon, & Symes, 2001). This approach requires the willingness of both parties and university policies and resources to accommodate such. Where work-based learning is concerned, there is a shift in the role of the university instructor from that of expert in a discipline to that of facilitator, a shift in identity that is difficult but necessary where experiential instruction is concerned (Boud & Solomon, 2001).

Demonstration/Practice Instruction in which teacher demonstration is followed by learner practice is a commonly cited method in the literature, and is particularly suited for the acquisition of skills (whether psychomotor ones such as surgical skills or cognitive ones such as critical thinking skills). When this is the case, the teacher should move beyond the role as facilitator to that of coach as well. For example, Qaymi et al. (1999) describe a program on surgical education in which the teacher first demonstrates surgical techniques in a laboratory, then works with individual students to reinforce their skills as they practice. Furthermore, the teacher should reduce the amount of coaching that he or she provides over time.

Apprenticeships/Mentorships/Internships/Service-Learning Apprenticeships, mentorships, internships, and service-learning are methods that offer the opportunity to apply knowledge and skills in authentic, real-world environments, and are appropriate where instructional time allows and where the learners are capable of acting largely or completely autonomously. Of these, service-learning is probably least familiar, and is defined as an experience that includes hands-on volunteer experience in a real-world setting. Apprenticeships, mentorships, internships, and service-learning have been shown to be beneficial for achieving several outcomes, including promoting cultural awareness (Worrell-Carlisle, 2005), preparing learners for careers in the professional practice setting (Saleh, McBride, & Henley, 2006), reducing turnover of new entrants to the practice setting (Newhouse et al., 2007), and allowing learners to identify additional learning needs that had not been provided by experiences prior to the internship (Bullough, 2005).

The structure of these methods varies depending on the characteristics of the practice environment and the objectives of the internship. Bullard and Felder (2003) described a beneficial mentorship program for new college faculty that consisted of a structured process in which the mentor and mentee cotaught a single course, observing each other's classes, and met for a weekly debrief session to reflect on what each had learned in observing the other. Similar approaches are described elsewhere, with differing review intervals (daily, once a month, etc.) depending on the situation, or a differing medium for reflection (e.g., journaling). Overall, apprenticeships, mentorships, internships, and service learning are very effective in helping learners to bridge the gap between theory and practice.

Variable Methods for Reflection on Experience (Principle 3)

The use of journals and portfolios as a means for reflection is discussed in this section. Several methods addressed previously in the section on the activation of experience can be considered both activation of and reflection on experience, such as storytelling and discussion.

Journals and Portfolios Journals and portfolios are reflective vehicles that engage the student in a structured process of documenting and reflecting on their experience. They rely on and attempt to strengthen the reflective capacity of the individual learner, meaning that they are useful in some situations but can present challenges when attempting to implement them in other situations. One situation in which journals and portfolios are particularly useful is where the active presence of a teacher or fellow learners to spur reflection may not be possible, realistic, or desirable. For example, a semester-long internship might use a journal or portfolio as a means for the learner to document and reflect on their experience. In such situations, the journal or portfolio helps achieve what the presence of a teacher or fellow learners would otherwise do. However, the teacher should provide an overall structure, and specific prompts to which the learner should respond.

At the same time that these methods are advantageous, the use of journals and in particular portfolios, when they are used as an assessment of instructional progress, can present challenges. Since the use of portfolios as a means of assessment is a dramatic shift in the role of both the teacher and the learner, they should be used in situations where the teacher and learner are prepared to engage in learner-centered, self-directed reflection. For guidance on portfolios, see Nicholson (2004), and for guidance on journals, see Boud (2001).

While journals and portfolios are internally oriented methods of reflection (versus group or teacher-oriented methods such as discussion), their evaluation may or may not be. Nicholson (2004), following the work of Greene (1994), recommends a "dialogical component" in which the students present their completed course portfolios to the class. This is designed to "engage both students and faculty in a collaborative inquiry that allows all participants to critically examine their own learning" (Nicholson, 2004, p. 334). In like manner, Gold and Holman (2001) suggest that, following the creation of stories to describe work problems, managers present their stories in small groups. With help from the teacher they are encouraged to probe the deeper meanings in dialogue with the others. Both of these examples show that, although initially the documentation or reflection on experience can be an internal process, the validation of experience, reflection on that experience, and the construction of new meaning can ultimately occur within the social community of the classroom.

Additional Variable Methods

Applying Conclusions to a New Experience The application of lessons learned to new experiences is a major variable method that should be implemented as time allows. Where instructional time or instructional development time is limited, the teacher may achieve the application of new knowledge through discussion. In order to do this, the teacher should ask, "How would your new-found knowledge influence the way in which you would have acted during the experience?" or "How will [it] influence the ways in which you engage in similar experiences in the future?"

Where time does allow for the application of new knowledge to another experience, the experience should be implemented with an eye toward building on the previous experience as much as possible. The form this takes could vary. For example, Outward Bound outdoor-based experiential learning programs typically involve repeated cycles of "do-review-plan" with the goal of building self-sufficiency. In this environment, successive experiences should provide the opportunity for added levels of responsibility as participants take on the role of running the program themselves. Neill and Dias (2001) found empirical support that the controlled exposure to challenges of this nature increases participants' psychological resilience, or their capacity to recover after life challenges.

On the other hand, the application of new knowledge in another experience can serve as the culmination of a program of instruction. Long, Larsen, Hussey, and Travis (2001) note that in college gerontology programs, initial service-learning projects can expose students to key issues, while a capstone project at the end of the program can allow them to reflect on their progress and growth over the course of the program. The benefit of this approach according to the authors is that the dual experiences are invaluable in the translation of the students' initial interest in gerontology into the ability to apply their new knowledge and skills in real-world contexts.

The value of applying conclusions to a new experience may vary depending on the particular experiential method, but the outcome is the same in that knowledge is either affirmed or contradicted. This method also represents the opportunity for learners to engage in the application phase that Merrill (chapter 3, this volume) proposes as a universal principle for all good instruction.

Conclusion

This design theory of experiential instruction is derived from an examination of experiential learning theory, empirical data, and evidence from actual experience, and in doing so is based on a social constructivist approach to learning. It is offered as a step in generating a common knowledge base about experiential instruction, with a common terminology. While individuals can and do learn from experience, it is through the shared interpretation of and reflection on experience that learning most effectively occurs in experiential instruction. This chapter provides a synthesis of guidance for the use of universal methods and situational methods for experiential instruction. For more specific guidelines please refer to the citations.

References

Aragon, S. (2003). Creating social presence in online environments. In S. Aragon (Ed.), *Facilitating learning in online environments* (pp. 57–68). San Francisco: Jossey-Bass.

Arthur, N., & Achenbach, K. (2002). Developing multicultural counseling competences through experiential learning. *Counselor Education and Supervision, 42,* 2–15.

Baker, A., Jensen, P., & Kolb, D. (2002). *Conversational learning: An experiential approach to knowledge creation.* Westport, CT: Quorum.

Beard, C. M., & Wilson, J. P. (2002). *The power of experiential learning.* London: Kogan Page.

Bobbitt, L. M., Inks, S., Kemp, K., & Mayo, D. (2000). Integrating marketing courses to enhance team-based experiential learning. *Journal of Marketing Education, 22*(1), 15–24.

Booth, S., & Hulten, M. (2003). Opening dimensions of variation: An empirical study of learning in a Web-based discussion. *Instructional Science, 31,* 65–86.

Boud, D. (2001). Using journal writing to promote reflective practice. In L. English & M. Gillen (Eds.), *Promoting journal writing to enhance reflective practice* (pp. 9–18). New York: Wiley.

Boud, D., Keough, R., & Walker, D. (1985). *Reflection: Turning experience into learning.* London: Kogan Page.

Boud, D., & Solomon, N. (2001). Repositioning universities and work. In D. Boud & N. Solomon (Eds.), *Work-based learning: A new higher education?* (pp. 18–33). Buckingham, UK: Open University Press.

Boud, D., Solomon, N., & Symes, C. (2001). New practices for new times. In D. Boud & N. Solomon (Eds.), *Work-based learning: A new higher education?* (pp. 3–17). Buckingham, UK: Open University Press.

Boud, D., & Walker, D. (1993). Barriers to reflection on experience. In D. Boud, R. Cohen, & D. Walker (Eds.), *Using experience for learning* (pp. 73–86). Bristol, UK: Open University Press.

Bullard, L. G., & Felder, R. M. (2003). Mentoring: a personal perspective. *College Teaching 51*(3), 66–69.

Bullough, R.V. (2005). Teacher vulnerability and teachability: A case study of a mentor and two interns. *Teacher Education Quarterly 32*(2), 23–39.

Burrows, D. (1995). The nurse teacher's role in the promotion of reflective practice. *Nurse Education Today, 15,* 346–350.

Byrnes, D. A., & Kiger, G. (1990). The effect of prejudice-reduction simulation on attitude change. *Journal of Applied Social Psychology, 20,* 341–356.

Caffarella, R. S., & Barnett, B.G. (1994). Characteristics of adult learners and foundations of experiential learning. In L. Jackson & R. S. Caffarella (Eds.), *Experiential learning: A new Approach* (pp. 29–42). San Francisco: Jossey-Bass.

Caffarella, R. S., & Lee, P. (1994). Methods and techniques for engaging learners in experiential activities. In L. Jackson & R. S. Caffarella (Eds.), *Experiential learning: A new approach* (pp. 43–54). San Francisco: Jossey-Bass.

Cheney, R. (2001). Intercultural business communication, international students, and experiential learning. *Business Communication Quarterly, 64*(4), 90–104.

Cornelius, J. (2004). To be touched by AIDS: An HIV-experiential teaching method. *Journal of Nursing Education, 43*(12), 576.

Dart, B. (1997). Adult learners' metacognitive behavior. In P. Sutherland (Ed.), *Adult learning: A reader* (pp. 30–43). Sterling, VA: Stylus.

Day, M. (2004). Enhancing learning communities in cyberspace. In M. Galbraith (Ed.), *Adult learning methods* (pp. 425–450). Malabar, FL: Krieger.

Dewey, J. (1938). *Experience and education.* New York: Touchstone Press.

Dewey, J. (1966). *Democracy and education. An introduction to the philosophy of education .* New York: Free Press. (Original work published 1916)

Duffy, T. M., & Jonassen, D. (Eds.). (1992). *Constructivism and the technology of instruction: A conversation.* Hillsdale, NJ: Erlbaum.

Felix, U. (2004). The web as a vehicle for constructivist approaches in language teaching. *ReCALL, 14*(1), 2–15.

Fenwick, T. J. (2000). Expanding conceptions of experiential learning: a review of the five contemporary perspectives on cognition. *Adult Education Quarterly, 50*(4), 243–273.

Gannon, M. J., & Poon, J. M. (1997). Effects of alternative instructional approaches on cross-cultural training outcomes. *International Journal of Intercultural Relations, 21*(4), 429–466.

Gold, J., & Holman, D. (2001). Let me tell you a story: An evaluation of the use of storytelling and argument analysis in management education. *Career Development International, 6*(7), 384–395.

Greene, M. (1994). Epistemology and educational research: The influence of recent approaches to knowledge. In L. Darling-Hammond (Ed.), *Review of research in education* (Vol. 20, pp. 423–464). Washington, D.C.: American Educational Research Association.

Hakeem, S. A. (2001). Effect of experiential learning in business statistics. *Journal of Education for Business, 77*(2), 95–98.

Halapi, M., & Saunders, D. (2002). Language teaching through role play: A Hungarian view. *Journal of Simulation & Gaming, 33*(2), 169–179.

Harrison, R., & Hopkins, R. L. (1967). The design of cross-cultural training: An alternative to the university model. *Journal of Applied Behavioral Science, 3*, 431–460.

Hastie, R. (1984). Causes and effects of causal attribution. *Journal of Personality and Social Psychology, 46*, 44–56.

Hatton, N., & Smith, D. (1995). Reflection in teacher education—Towards definition and implementation. *Teaching and Teacher Education, 11*(1), 33–49.

Herz, B., & Merz, W. (1998). Experiential learning and the effectiveness of economic simulation games. *Simulation and Gaming, 29*(2), 238–251.

Jackson, L., & MacIsaac, D. (1994). Introduction to a new approach to experiential learning. In L. Jackson & R. Caffarella (Eds.), *Experiential learning: A new approach* (pp. 17–28). San Francisco: Jossey-Bass.

Johnson, S., & Aragon, S. (2003). An instructional strategy framework for online learning environments. In S. Aragon (Ed.), *Facilitating learning in online environments.* San Francisco: Jossey-Bass.

Jonassen, D. (1999). Designing constructivist learning environments. In C. Reigeluth (Ed.), *Instructional-design theories and models: Vol. 2. A new paradigm of instructional theory* (pp. 215–239). Mahwah, NJ: Erlbaum.

Jones, K. (1998). What are we talking about? *Simulation and Gaming, 29*(3), 314–321.

Kolb, D. (1984). *Experiential learning: Experience as the source of learning and development.* Upper Saddle River, NJ: Prentice-Hall.

Koppenhaver, G., & Shrader, C. (2003). Structuring the classroom for performance: Cooperative learning with instructor-assigned teams. *Decision Sciences Journal of Innovative Education, 1*(1), 1–21.

Lee, P., & Caffarella, R.S. (1994). Methods and techniques for engaging learners in experiential learning activities. In L. Jackson & R. Caffarella (Eds.), *Experiential learning: A new approach* (pp. 43–54). San Francisco: Jossey-Bass.

Lexton, A., Smith, M., Olufemi, D., & Poole, G. (2005). Taking a risk and playing it safe: The use of actors in interagency child protection training. *Child Abuse Review, 14*, 195–206.

Long, A., Larsen, P., Hussey, L., & Travis, S. (2001). Organizing, managing and evaluating service-learning projects. *Educational Gerontology, 27*, 3–21.

Mackintosh, C. (1998). Reflection: A flawed strategy for the nursing profession. *Nurse Education Today, 18*, 553–557.

Macri, C. J., Gaba, N., Sitzer, L. M., et al. (2005). Implementation and evaluation of a genetics curriculum to improve obstetrician-gynecologist residents' knowledge and skills in genetic diagnosis and counseling. *American Journal of Obstetrics & Gynecology, 193*(5), 1794–1797.

Mazulewicz, J. (2002). *Facilitating experiential learning based on the primacy of intuitive thinking.* Unpublished doctoral dissertation, University of Virginia, Charlottesville, VA.

McCaffery, J. A. (1986). Independent effectiveness: A reconsideration of cross-cultural orientation and training. *International Journal of Intercultural Relations, 10*, 159–178.

Merriam, S. B. (1994). Learning and life experience: The connection in adulthood. In J. D. Sinot (Ed.), *Interdisciplinary handbook of adult lifespan learning* (pp. 74–89). Westport, CT: Greenwood.

Mezirow, J. (1981). A critical theory of adult learning and education. *Adult Education, 1*, 3–24.

Moon, J. (1999). *Reflection in learning and professional development.* London: Kogan Page.

Moon, J. (2004). *A handbook of reflective and experiential learning.* New York: Routledge Falmer.

Ndoye, A. (2003). Experiential learning, self-beliefs and adult performance in Senegal. *International Journal of Lifelong Education, 22*(4), 353–366.

Neill, J. T., & Dias, K. L. (2001). Adventure education and resilience: The double-edged sword. *Journal of Adventure Education and Outdoor Learning, 1*(2), 35–42.

Nespor, V. N. (1995). Learning processes that contribute to the effective decision-making of small business owners (Doctoral dissertation, Columbia University Teachers College, 1995). *Dissertation Abstracts International, A 55/07*, 1797.

Newhouse, R. P., Hoffman, J. J., Suflito, J., & Hairston, D. P. (2007). Evaluating an innovative program to improve nurse graduate socialization into the acute healthcare setting. *Nursing Administration Quaterly, 31*(1), 50–60.

Nicholson, B. (2004). Course portfolio. In M. W. Galbraith (Ed.), *Adult learning methods* (pp. 321–340). Malabar, FL: Krieger.

Parathian, A. R., & Taylor, F. (1993). Can we insulate trainee nurses from exposure to bad practice? A study of role play in communicating bad news to patients. *Journal of Advanced Nursing, 18*, 801–807.

Pedersen, P., & Ivey, A. (1993). *Culture-centered counseling and interviewing skills: A practical guide.* Westport, CT: Praeger.

Qaymi, A. K., Cheifetz, R. E., Forward, A. D., Baird, R. M., Litherland, H. K., & Koetting, S. E. (1999). Teaching and evaluation of basic surgical techniques: The University of British Columbia experience. *Journal of Investigative Surgery, 12*(6), 341–350.

Randel, J. M., Morris, B. A., Wetzel, C. D., & Whitehill, B. V. (1992). The effectiveness of games for educational purposes: a review of recent research. *Simulation & Gaming, 23*(3), 261–276.

Reigeluth, C. M. (1999). What is instructional-design theory and how is it changing? In C. M. Reigeluth (Ed.), *Instructional-design theories and models: A new paradigm on instructional theory: Vol.2. A new paradigm of instructional theory* (pp. 5–29). Mahwah, NJ: Erlbaum.

Saleh, A., McBride, J., & Henley, J. (2006). Aspiring school leaders reflect on the internship. *Academic Exchange Quarterly, 10*(3), 126–135.

Saunders, P. M. (1997). Experiential learning, cases, and simulations in business communication. *Business Communication Quarterly, 60*(1), 97–115.

Savery, J., & Duffy, T. (1996). Problem based learning: An instructional model and its constructivist framework. In B. Wilson (Ed.), *Constructivist learning environments: Case studies in instructional design* (pp. 135–148). Englewood Cliffs, NJ: Educational Technology.

Schank, R. (1997). *Virtual learning: A revolutionary approach to building a highly skilled workforce.* New York: McGraw-Hill.

Schank, R. C., Berman, T. R., & Macpherson, K. A. (1999). Learning by doing. In C. Reigeluth (Ed.), *Instructional-design theories and models: Vol.2. A new paradigm of instructional theory* (pp. 161–181). Mahwah, NJ: Erlbaum.

Schettler, J. (2002, April). Learning by doing. *Training, 39*(4), 38–43.

Schon, D. (1983). *The reflective practitioner.* New York: Basic.

Smith, C. A., Strand, S. E., & Bunting, C. J. (2002). The influence of challenge course participation on moral and ethical reasoning. *The Journal of Experiential Education, 25*(2), 278–280.

Steadman, R. H., Coates, W., Huang, Y. M., Matevosian, R., Larmon, B. R., McCullough, L., et al. (2006). Simulation-based training is superior to problem-based learning for the acquisition of critical assessment and management skills. *Critical Care Medicine, 34*(1), 151–157.

Sutherland, P. (1997). Experiential learning and constructivism: Potential for a mutually beneficial synthesis. In P. Sutherland (Ed.), *Adult learning: A reader* (pp. 82–93). Sterling, VA: Stylus.

Vrasidas, C., & McIsaac, M. S. (1999). Factors influencing interaction in an online course. *The American Journal of Distance Education, 13*(3), 22–36.

Wong, P. T. P., & Weiner, B. (1981). When people ask "why" questions and the heuristics of attributional search. *Journal of Personality and Social Psychology, 40*, 65–66.

Worrell-Carlisle, P. J. (2005). Service-learning: a tool for developing cultural awareness. *Nurse Educator, 30*(5), 197–202.

Zakay, D., Ellis, S., & Shevalsky, M. (2004). Outcome value and early warning indications as determinants of willingness to learn from experience. *Experimental Psychology, 51*(2), 150–157.

Zepke, N., & Leach, L. (2002). Contextualised meaning making: One way of rethinking experiential learning and self-directed learning? *Studies in Continuing Education, 24*(2), 205–218.

Zimbardo, P. G. (1973). On the ethics of intervention in human psychological research: With special reference to the Stanford prison experiment. *Cognition, 2*, 243–356.

8

Problem-Based Approach to Instruction

JOHN R. SAVERY

University of Akron

John R. Savery is an associate professor in the College of Education at the University of Akron. He received a master's degree from the University of Calgary and a PhD in instructional systems technology from Indiana University. He has worked for over 20 years in the field of instructional technology in both academic and corporate settings. In 2006, he accepted the position of Director of Learning Technologies and Scholar/Learner Services at the University of Akron. As director he provides leadership and vision to support faculty in the design of effective, technology-enriched, online, and hybrid learning environments, the integration of problem-based/inquiry-based learning strategies, and strategies to foster the development of student ownership for learning. His current research projects examine learning opportunities provided by online technologies (Web 2.0 applications/tools), 3D multiuser virtual environments, and ubiquitous computing in a STEM focused middle school.

EDITORS' FOREWORD

Preconditions

Content
- *Complex problems that do not have a single correct answer*

Learners
- *All kinds of learners*
- *Learners must have some prior knowledge gained from real-world experience.*

Learning environments
- *A room with large tables, multiple computers, and access to resources*
- *Instructor and organization must be committed to PBI—the entire approach*

Instructional development constraints
- *Sufficient time and money to develop for find the problems and learning resources*

Values

about ends (learning goals)
- *The development of problem solving and decision-making skills within a content domain*
- *The enhancement of learners' reasoning abilities and self direction*
- *The enhancement of transfer to real-world tasks*

about priorities (criteria for successful instruction)
- *Effectiveness is valued over efficiency*
- *Intrinsic motivation is valued over extrinsic motivation*

about means (instructional methods)
- *The importance of self-direction*
- *The use of complex, authentic problems with no single right answer*
- *The teacher as a tutor, process facilitator, and metacognitive coach*
- *The use of reflection on practice*

about power (to make decisions about the previous three)
- *Student should have more responsibility to direct their own learning*

Universal Methods

1. *Use authentic and meaningful real-world problems that fit within the curriculum for the discipline and encourage cross-discipline thinking. There are four design principles: The problems should be holistic, practice-based, ill-structured, and contemporary.*
2. *The tutor facilitates the development of the learner's metacognitive processing and problem-solving skills.*
   - *Adjust the level of guidance and support to match the needs of the learner.*

- *Provide instructional materials related to the development of anticipated skills along with the preliminary content materials at the start of the problem activity.*
- *Remove the tutor from the role of information provider as much as possible.*

3. *Use authentic assessment practices to validate the learning of content, problem-solving skills, and higher-order thinking skills (including self-direction).*
   - *Each student self-assesses on her or his effectiveness as a researcher and as a contributor to the problem-solving process of the group.*
   - *Students also reflect on process and knowledge gains and the integration of that knowledge with prior knowledge.*
   - *The proposed solution to the problem is assessed on criteria (often developed by the students) such as completeness, accuracy, and viability.*
   - *Learner motivation and collaboration are assessed.*

4. *Use consistent and thorough debriefing activities to consolidate key concepts learned from the experience.*

Situational Principles

- *When students are not familiar with the PBI process, then the teacher must invest considerable effort in managing the learning process for and with the students, as well as providing answers to questions. Use instructional simulations and cases before using a PBI "problem" (to help prepare students to become more self-regulated/independent in their thinking and able to work collaboratively).*
- *The choice of the problem and the level of complexity should always be adjusted to the developmental level (or maturity) of the students.*
- *When a class is large, the instructor should create smaller groups and allow those teams to stay together for multiple problems so they can realize the benefits of collaborative effort.*
- *When a class is large, the instructor should use strategies for forming and managing cooperative groups within a large class.*
- *A large class will need a greater quantity of resources.*

—CMR & ACC

PROBLEM-BASED APPROACH TO INSTRUCTION

This chapter examines the problem-based learning approach to instruction from the perspective of instructional design theory and synthesizes the current knowledge and theory into some universal methods, situational methods, and principles for a theory of problem-based instruction (PBI).[1] The history of public

---

1. *Editors' note: Based on common definitions of the terms, is the difference between PBI and PBL that PBL is the learning that results from PBI?*

education provides many examples of changes in philosophy and shifts in the influences of society on instructional practice. During the transition from the agrarian age to the industrial age, public education adopted a teacher-centered approach to instruction. In the current information age (or knowledge age), in which knowledge work has replaced manual labor as the predominant form of work, methods of instruction that revolved around sorting students are giving way to methods that revolve around helping all learners to reach their potential. One instructional innovation that has persisted and continues to prosper is PBI.

PBI evolved as a pragmatic solution to perceived problems with the traditional approach to medical education during the transition from the industrial age to the information age. During the 1960s, changes in the field of medicine, including new diagnostic tools, new medicines, and new treatments, were entering the knowledge base at an ever-increasing rate, causing a disconnect between knowledge acquired through instruction and application of that knowledge in practice. Howard Barrows, one of the innovators of PBI in medical education at McMaster University in Canada, noted:

> ...studies of the clinical reasoning of students...suggested that the conventional methods of teaching probably inhibit, if not destroy, any clinical reasoning ability (Barrows & Bennett, 1972)...[and] that students had forgotten their freshman [course content] by the time they reached their clinical course as juniors.... [This] led to my design of a method stressing development of the clinical reasoning or problem-solving process. (Barrows, 1996, p. 4)

Simply stated, the process of patient diagnosis (doctor's work) was based on a combination of the hypothetical-deductive process and expert knowledge in multiple domains—the rapidly changing knowledge base was not reflected in the "traditional" lecture approach and thus lacked application. The tutorial process resulting from these insights (Barrows, 1988, 2000) provides a specific instructional method with well-articulated procedures, as well as a philosophy for structuring an entire curriculum to promote student-centered, multidisciplinary education and lifelong learning in professional practice (Wilkerson & Gijselaers, 1996).

In North America and around the world, the use of PBI continues to expand in elementary schools, middle schools, high schools, universities, and professional schools (Torp & Sage, 2002). The Illinois Mathematics and Science Academy (http://www.imsa.edu/center/) has been providing high school students with a complete PBI curriculum since 1985 and has expanded to serve thousands of students and teachers as a center for research on PBI. The Problem-Based Learning Initiative (http://www.pbli.org/) in Springfield, Illinois, has developed curricular materials (i.e., problems) and teacher-training programs in PBI for all core disciplines in high school (Barrows & Kelson, 1993). PBI is widely used in other disciplines within medical education (dentists, nurses, paramedics, radiologists, etc.) and in content domains as diverse as MBA programs (Stinson & Milter, 1996), higher education (leadership education) (Bridges & Hallinger, 1996), chemical engineering (Woods, 1994), economics (Gijselaers, 1996), architecture (Kingsland, 1996), and preservice teacher education (Hmelo-Silver, 2000, 2004). This list is by no means exhaustive, but is illustrative of the multiple contexts in which PBI is being utilized.

As the Information Age continues to impact an ever-increasing number of jobs and disciplines, the skills developed through the PBI approach, such as self-directed, self-regulated, and lifelong learning, assume greater importance and a much larger audience. The significant impact on learning of metacognitive processing, self-monitoring, self-efficacy, volition, and motivation is stressed in the literature on self-regulated learning (Schunk & Zimmerman, 1998; Zimmerman & Schunk, 2001). Schunk (2001) describes self-regulated learning as, "learning that results from students' self-generated thoughts and behaviors that are systematically oriented toward the attainment of their learning goals" (p. 125). The skills necessary to be successful in a broad range of disciplines can be refined through repeated experiences in problem-solving situations and the systematic construction of an integrated knowledge base.

The Wingspread Conference (1994) asked leaders from state and federal governments and experts from corporate, philanthropic, higher education, and accreditation communities for their opinions and visions of undergraduate education. The conference reported the need to address specific problems in complex, real-world settings, and this clearly resonates with the philosophy of problem-based learning and reinforces the importance of explicating a viable design theory for this approach to instruction.

What is PBI?

Problem-based approaches to instruction are rooted in experience-based education (see chapter 7). Research and theory on learning suggest that by having students learn through the experience of solving problems, they can learn both content and thinking strategies. PBI is facilitated problem solving where student learning is organized around a complex problem that does not have a single correct answer. PBI typically starts with the presentation of the problem rather than a lecture or reading assignment intended to impart discipline-specific knowledge to the student. Students engage with the problem, generate ideas and possible solutions, determine what they currently know and do not know, establish learning goals, conduct research to acquire the knowledge and skills needed to develop a viable solution to the problem, reflect on the problem utilizing the new information, and reflect on their problem-solving process (Savery & Duffy, 1995). As the learners work through the hypothetical-deductive reasoning process, the tutor provides support for their learning and their development of metacognitive skills.

For example, first-year medical students meet with their tutor to discuss the patient named Mary, described as a 56-year-old female complaining of recent numbness in her right leg and sporadic blurred vision. The students draw from their prior knowledge and suggest possible explanations for Mary's symptoms. Students must ask for more information, and in response to their specific questions the tutor provides whatever information is available in the case files; for example, current blood pressure, family medical history, any medications. These are the protocols that a physician would follow to diagnose the problem—this is applied practice in the discipline. When the students reach the point where they need more information, they itemize what they need to know, and members of the team take ownership for researching the questions and reporting back to the group. This problem-solving cycle (Barrows' term is *hypothetico-deductive*) continues until the team has agreed upon a diagnosis and course of action for the patient, Mary. The tutor (this role is discussed more fully later) guides the team through a debriefing of the learning experience in which the members assess their team process, their individual process, and the utility/accuracy of the resources used to arrive at their solution. Critical learning outcomes from the problem of Mary are identified, and knowledge gains are consolidated.

PBI is sometimes confused with a case-based approach. While there are several similarities between a problem-based approach and a case-based approach, there are significant differences, as clearly explicated by Williams (1992). The fundamental difference lies in the purpose of the instruction. If the intent is to provide vivid and complex exemplars that assist the learner in forming conceptual relationships with content that may be abstract, then well-written cases are an excellent vehicle. A well-structured case study will include the critical information needed to arrive at a predetermined conclusion. With most case studies there is one right answer (and some close answers) and the learning task for the student is to pick up on all the clues that are important (and avoid the red herrings). Walking this carefully groomed path from situation presentation to solution provides the students with an engaging experience that they can refer back to should they encounter a similar set of circumstances in their future practice. A problem-based approach is different in that the nature of the problem selected is less clearly defined—part of the task for the learner is to refine the general problem into component parts—and the solution or range of solutions is not predetermined. By utilizing current resources, solutions to a problem can change over time.[2]

Although the PBI approach was significantly refined by the work of Barrows and others in the context of medical education, the audiences for PBI are not

---

2. A colleague teaching in the School of Law often clips a news item from the newspaper or video-tapes an item from TV news and uses it as the catalyst for class discussion. These spontaneous problems have multiple possible solutions and provide students with an authentic learning experience—sharpening the skills they will need once they complete their degree.

limited to postgraduate professional education. Torp and Sage (2002), who have done considerable work with high school students at the Illinois Mathematics and Science Academy (http://www.imsa.edu), describe PBI (or PBL) as follows:

> PBL provides authentic experiences that foster active learning, support knowledge construction, and naturally integrate school learning and real life; this curriculum approach also addresses state and national standards and integrates disciplines. The problematic situation offers the center around which curriculum is organized, attracting and sustaining students' interest with its need for resolution while exposing multiple perspectives. Students are engaged problem solvers, identifying the root problem and the conditions needed for a good solution, pursuing meaning and understanding, and becoming self-directed learners. Teachers are problem-solving colleagues who model interest and enthusiasm for learning and are also cognitive coaches who nurture an environment that supports open inquiry. (p. 15)

While individual instructors may use problems to provide a stand-alone learning experience, the greater benefit for the learners occurs when the entire curriculum is problem-based. As is discussed later in this chapter, a problem-based curriculum provides students with a sequence of carefully designed problems (Barrows, 1986) that "crisscross the landscape" (Spiro, Feltovich, Jacobson, & Coulson, 1991) of knowledge and skills determined by a careful review of the domain and the problems/issues identified by expert practitioners (Macdonald, 1997; Stinson & Milter, 1996).

Cognitive theories of learning[3] may be used to further explain the success of the PBI approach. Resnick (1989) suggests three interrelated cognitive theories: (1) learning is a process of knowledge construction, learning occurs not by recording information but by interpreting it; (2) learning is knowledge dependent, people use current knowledge to construct new knowledge; and (3) learning is highly tuned to the situation in which it takes place. Each of these cognitive theories is reflected in the PBI theory.

Learning Is a Process of Knowledge Construction

Duffy and Cunningham (1996) note the importance of active learning, of both understanding and challenging the learner's thinking and the historical use of inquiry-based approaches as a stimulus for learning, including Piaget's term of *disequilibration* and Dewey's term of *perturbation*. They discuss differences between cognitive constructivist theories of individual cognition and social constructivist theories of socially and culturally situated cognition (Katz & Chard, 1989; Moll, 1990; Vygotsky, 1978; Wertsch, 1991). It could be argued that both

---

3. *Editors' note: Note that these are learning theory, not instructional theory.*

aspects of constructivism are necessary components of PBI that contribute to an effective learning experience.

Learning Is Knowledge Dependent

Research by Glaser (as cited by Resnick, 1989) suggests that both reasoning and learning are knowledge driven and, more specifically, that "Those who are knowledge-rich reason more profoundly. They elaborate as they study and thereby learn more effectively. Knowledge thus begets knowledge" (p. 2). Knowledge and experience are supported by research on problem solving as critical elements in effective problem analysis and the development of a viable solution (Jonassen, 2004).

Learning Is Highly Tuned to the Situation

Cognitive flexibility theory (Spiro et al., 1991) suggests that using complex, messy, real-world problems helps students to transfer the knowledge and skills they learn to future complex, real-world problems and learn to apply the knowledge and skills to novel or ill-structured problems (Jonassen, 1997). In a similar vein, Bransford, Brown, and Cocking (2000) identify PBI as a strategy to encourage transfer of learning between school and everyday life (p. 77). Situated cognition theory (Brown, Collins, & Duguid, 1989) identifies the importance to learning of using ill-defined, authentic problems. Thus, these three areas of learning theory collectively underscore the use of a problem-based approach.

PBI has been adopted by different disciplines and, in the process, has been changed in both small and substantial ways to accommodate local conditions. This has led to some misapplications and misconceptions of PBI, and consequently certain practices that are called PBI or PBL do not achieve the anticipated learning outcomes. In the next section, I describe universal principles that must be applied in all uses of the PBI approach.

Universal Principles or Methods for PBI

There is remarkable consistency and convergence among researchers and practitioners concerning guiding principles for the design of effective PBI. The four main clusters of principles that will be unpacked in the following sections are:

1. Select problems that are authentic and fit within the curriculum for the discipline and encourage cross-discipline thinking.
2. The role of the tutor is to support the development of the learner's metacognitive processing skills and the learner's expertise as a problem-solver.
3. Use authentic assessment practices to validate the learning goals.
4. Use consistent and thorough debriefing activities to consolidate key concepts learned from the experience.

Principle 1. Select Problems that Are Authentic and Fit Within the Curriculum for the Discipline and Encourage Cross-Discipline Thinking.[4]

PBI is designed to support the development and refinement of higher-order thinking skills. It is not well suited as an instructional strategy for teaching basic skills. The PBI approach requires the selection of problems for which the learners (even young learners) already have some knowledge, which they have gained from lived experience, so that the application of this prior knowledge with the knowledge acquired through research and problem-solving can generate a deeper understanding.[5] Barrows (1996) explains the use of authentic problems in medical education as,

> [The problem] represents the challenge students face in practice and provides the relevance and motivation for learning. In attempting to understand the problem, students realize what they will need to learn from the basic sciences. The problem thus gives them a focus for integrating information from many disciplines. (p. 6)

Savery and Duffy (1995) proposed eight design principles for PBI, including one for authenticity:

> ***Design an authentic task.*** An authentic learning environment does not mean that the fourth grader should be placed in an authentic physics lab, nor that he or she should grapple with the same problems that an adult physicist deals with. Rather, the learner should engage in scientific activities, which present the same "type" of cognitive challenges. An authentic learning environment is one in which the cognitive demands, i.e., the thinking required, are consistent with the cognitive demands in the environment for which we are preparing the learner (Honebein et al., 1993). Thus we do not want the learner to learn about history but rather to engage in the construction or use of history in ways that a historian or a good citizen would. Similarly, we do not want the learner to study science—memorizing a text on science or executing scientific procedures as dictated—but rather to engage in scientific discourse and problem solving. (p. 33)

Stinson and Milter (1996) implemented their PBI approach with cohorts of MBA students, and the process they used to select problems began with the basic question, "What do we want our students to know, and know how to do, as they leave our program?" To answer that question, they tasked participating faculty with developing a list of the minimum acceptable conceptual knowledge and skills that all MBA graduates should have in their particular discipline area. They

---

4. *Editors' note: Is this instructional theory (how to teach) or curriculum theory (what to teach)? Or some of both? What layer of design is this in?*
5. It is common practice in medical schools using the PBI approach to present first-year medical students with a problem on their first day of class.

asked business people who would be hiring the new graduates what they expected the new graduates to know and be able to do. Finally they conducted a futures analysis to identify short-term and long-term skills and knowledge that graduates would need to be successful. This process resulted in a dozen 'meta-outcomes' and over 150 specific learning outcomes. It could be argued that this exercise to develop clearly defined learning outcomes would be a beneficial activity for any instructional program. To guide the development of problems that would meet the meta-outcomes, they followed these design principles:[6]

1. *Learning outcomes should be holistic, not divided by narrow disciplinary boundaries.* Rationale: to avoid limiting potential learning, and to encourage taking multiple perspectives.
2. *Problems should mirror professional practice.* Rationale: to increase knowledge transfer.
3. *Problems should be ill-structured.* Rationale: real-world problems are messy and learners need to develop the ability to make sense of ambiguous, ill-defined situations.
4. *Problems should be contemporary.* Rationale: learner engagement with the problem is increased when current situations can be drawn into the discussion. (see also Chapman, 2000; Savery, 1999)

In K-12 public education the selection of an instructional problem is influenced by the state mandated curriculum, learning standards, standardized tests, and members of the local community. Teachers should select problems that provide for integration across disciplines and for demonstrations of learning through projects, presentations, or other means that would be appropriate or realistic for the problem situation. The "problem" becomes the focus of the instructional unit. The role or perspective of the student with respect to the problem becomes a variable. For example the "problem" of the endangered spotted owl in old growth forests is viewed differently from the perspective of the lumberman, legislator, environmentalist, and retailer in the local community (Torp & Sage, 2002, pp. 16–18). Also, Wilkerson and Gijselaers (1996) argue that the types of problems selected should represent those that practitioners of the discipline encounter on a regular basis.

In medical education, Macdonald (1997) reported on the process used to select appropriate problems from the large medical education curriculum. Given the huge number of medical conditions or ailments that could be taught, the task was to select problems that had educational importance (defined as clinical logic, prototype value, urgency, treatability, and interdisciplinary input) and also were typical of the medical problems that were prevalent in the general geographic

---

6. *Editors' note: Are these instructional theory (how to teach) or curriculum theory (what to teach), or some of both? What layer of design are these in?*

region. The first step was to obtain and sort the data to identify the major health problems in the area. Macdonald notes that these data are not always available in underdeveloped countries and that countries with advanced health care systems often record the diagnosis but not the health problem (i.e., emphysema was diagnosed, but the cause—smoking—was not identified). These health problems were further filtered based on the criteria of magnitude, fatality rate, quality of life, duration/severity, urgency, preventability, diagnosability, and treatability. Thus, the better problems to include in the curriculum were "common, severe problems, for which effective interventions exist" (p. 98).

Thus, selecting problems for MBA students, K-12 students, and medical students incorporates the same four design principles: holistic (interdisciplinary), practice-based (authentic), ill-structured, and contemporary (see also Schmidt & Moust, 2000, for a taxonomy of problems used in a PBI curriculum).

To summarize, the literature offers the following guidance for instructional designers on the task of PBI problem generation or selection:

1. The problem should be grounded in the knowledge and skills mandated by the curriculum.
2. The problem should engage the learners in a significant aspect of the content within the discipline or across disciplines or domains of knowledge.
3. The problem should be authentic, contemporary, and relevant.
4. The problem should require learners to utilize the same knowledge, skills, and attitudes as would be required in a real-world setting.
5. The problem should be complex enough and large enough to challenge the learners and require contributions from all members of the team.
6. The problem should be ill-structured with missing or contradictory information.
7. Provide instructional materials related to the development of anticipated skills along with the preliminary content materials at the start of the problem activity. Learners will note the existence of the materials and return to them when they have a need and purpose for learning the skill.

Principle 2. The Role of the Tutor is to Support the Development of the Learner's Metacognitive Processing Skills and the Learner's Expertise as a Problem-Solver

Arguably the most critical element in the successful implementation of PBI is the ability of the tutor to function as a facilitator of learning rather than as a provider of content. Barrows (1988) provides extensive detailed guidance on the responsibilities of the tutor and strategies for managing productive group sessions. He summarizes 13 general principles for tutorial teaching that could be applied in most (if not all) tutorial sessions with learners engaged with a PBI experience (pp. 18–20). With respect to managing the PBI sessions Barrows (1988) states that the tutor needs to "keep the learning process moving, to make sure that no phase of the learning process is passed over or neglected and that each phase is taken in the right sequence" (p. 6).[7] The tutor needs to be sure that all students are involved in the group process, that none is allowed to withdraw from the discussions, and that none is allowed to dominate the discussions. The tutor should also be able to modulate the complexity of the problem to avoid extremes of boredom or frustration (p. 10).

With respect to developing knowledge in the domain, Barrows states:

> The tutor must probe the student's knowledge deeply…[and] constantly ask "Why?" What do you mean?" "What does that mean?" "How do you know that's true?"… again and again until the student has gotten down to the depth of understanding and knowledge expected of him and has brought out all he knows (often more than he realizes he knows). The tutor must **never** let ideas, terms, explanations or comments go unchallenged or undefined…. You cannot assume that a student correctly understands a concept or entity because he can use the label correctly. (p. 7)

Therefore, the tutor provides the initial guidance and support with process skills, including metacognitive modeling for individuals and the entire group, while members of the group work cooperatively on the problem. Over time and with experience in PBI, learners take over the tutoring function to support each other by sharing knowledge they have acquired related to understanding and solving the problem (peer tutoring).

The role of the tutor is so critical to the success of the PBI approach that it is worthwhile at this point to distinguish between a tutor and a coach. Collins, Brown, and Newman (1989) describe a cognitive apprenticeship model of teaching in which the teacher serves as a coach who provides the learners with hints, feedback, modeling, reminders, scaffolding, and increasingly challenging tasks with the goal of bringing the performance of the apprentice closer to that of the expert. The teacher/coach models the thinking strategies of an expert in a realistic context, and invites the apprentice to articulate their reasoning, knowledge, or problem solving processes. Thus, a teacher applying a cognitive apprenticeship instructional strategy guides the learner to a level of expert knowledge in the content domain by modeling problem solving strategies within the domain (i.e., watch how "I" do this), coaching the learner on control strategies (i.e., meta-cognitive monitoring) and learning strategies for adding new knowledge and skills, and gradually fading into a minor role as the learner gains confidence and competence. The significant facts, concepts, procedures, principles, rules, and attitudes in the domain are learned in the context of their use (see also situated cognition, Brown et al., 1989).

The tutor in PBI differs from the cognitive apprenticeship coach in the areas of status and ownership of the learning process (Savery, 1996, 1998). The coach,

---

7. *Editors' note: What layer of design are these in?*

being an expert in the content/skill domain, knows how to perform the task better than the learner. The coach's suggestions can be highly directive (didactic show and tell) or highly reflective (what would you do in this situation?). The tutor in PBI may or may not be an expert in the domain. In fact, Barrows (1988) argues the tutor should not be a content expert. In any case the tutor *does not* answer content questions. Rather the tutor operates at the metacognitive level to direct student thinking in the use of productive problem solving strategies. Instead of telling the learners they are missing important facts, the tutor asks the learners if they have all the facts they need to proceed. Group members select areas for further research and report their findings back to the group in an agreed-upon timeframe with an emphasis on how this information is related to the development of a solution to the problem. With younger students in a PBI activity, some limited direct instruction may be necessary (Torp & Sage, 2002)[8] but the focus on cognitive coaching is critical.

To summarize guidance on the role of the tutor in PBI, consider the following:

1. The tutor repeatedly asks questions to probe the depth of the learner's knowledge.
2. The tutor focuses on group process to ensure that *all* learners in the group are involved and articulating their understanding of the problem, the problem-solving process, and the proposed solutions.
3. The tutor prompts learners to think at a metacognitive level and supports the development of self-regulated learning.
4. The tutor avoids the role of information provider as much as possible by making information resources available and promoting collaboration with teammates who may have the necessary skill or knowledge.
5. The tutor senses when the problem is either boring or frustrating the learners and modulates the problem by providing guidance to make the problem more manageable.

Principle 3. Use Authentic Assessment Practices to Validate the Learning Goals[9]

How do we assess individuals working in a group on a problem that is holistic, practice-based, ill-structured, and contemporary? Assuming principle 1 (selection of problems) has been honored, and assuming that the tutor has been effective in facilitating the group problem-solving process, then we should be able to assess (1) content knowledge and skills within a domain; (2) problem-solving skills (process and reflection); and (3) the development of higher-order thinking skills (metacognitive).

---

8. *Editors' note: See chapter 5.*
9. *Editors' note: This is student-assessment theory (see chapter 1), which should often be integrated with instructional theory, especially in the information-age paradigm of education.*

A well-designed problem contains the *criteria* for presentation of the proposed solutions. In a medical context, it could be a formal written report (using standard hospital forms) detailing diagnosis and treatment for the patient that has been decided upon and agreed to by all members of the group. The group members would then explain to the tutor (or an expert panel) the parameters of their solution and their reasoning in arriving at the solution. The proposed solution would then be compared with the opinions of an expert confronted with the same problem or the actual medical case that served as the basis for the problem. Similarities and differences would be discussed to further clarify the understanding of each member of the group to ensure that the critical concepts were understood.

For a problem related to water quality prepared by high school students, the proposed solution could be a report identifying the sources of pollution and strategies for reducing future pollutants. The criteria for the presentation of the proposed solution could include visual aides, graphs, a PowerPoint presentation, or some other media to assist students in developing skills with presentations. A variation on this approach might be a report composed by the learners and sent to either a politician or perhaps a company causing water pollution.

Formative assessment of the viability and utility of information provided by members of the group (obtained through independent research) is an ongoing component of the group problem-solving process. All group members are expected to take responsibility for researching information to bring back to the group and explain how the information they have retrieved contributes to the development of a possible solution. All members of the group are expected to assimilate the content through discussions with their team members and experts (textbooks or humans). Individuals are expected to clearly articulate their understanding of the content addressed by the problem. To assess how individuals within the group are assimilating the collected information, the tutor can ask any student at any time to summarize the collective learning of the group related to the problem. To ensure that both the group and individuals within the group have arrived at the intended learning outcomes, the important learning points are assessed through the debriefing process. There is no "standardized test" to assess the learning outcomes from a given PBI experience.

Torp and Sage (2002) describe multiple assessment strategies that can be used within the PBI approach. They note in particular the use of the "facets of understanding" (Wiggins & McTighe, 1998) approach to assess learner understanding, and the alignment with state and national standards that is an increasingly important element in the accountability of public education. It is beyond the scope of this chapter to provide a review of the six facets of understanding described by Wiggins and McTighe (1998) and their theoretical and practical implications for curriculum, assessment, and teaching. The reader is encouraged to review in detail their conceptual framework and consider its relationship with PBI.

Summative assessments are appropriate with PBI. However, to be authentic, the test should assess students' ability to use reference and resource materials (which experts do in practice) to develop a problem solution, as well as their knowledge of concepts, theories, and terminology within the domain. Summative assessment, such as medical board exams, should be taken after a complete curriculum of problems has been concluded and the content knowledge to be covered by the test has also been covered by the sequence of problems. Summative assessment in the K-12 context is more complicated given the breadth of basic skills that are developed during this time span, the state-specific curriculums that determine the content to be taught, and the various standardized exams used to determine high school completion. Until authentic assessment as described above becomes more widely accepted in public education, it will be challenging to gauge the impact of PBI curricula on student learning.

One of the more challenging aspects of PBI to assess with any certainty is the growth of self-regulation in learning by the students. It is naïve to assume that this growth would be evident after only a few PBI sessions. Rather it is an incremental change over time in the ability of the learners to express their thinking clearly, challenge the thinking of others with insightful comments, conduct effective independent research, and share that with the others in the problem-solving group. During the PBI sessions the tutor is continuously monitoring and assessing the abilities of all the learners in the group. This assessment includes the direct questioning (knowledge probes) by the tutor of all members of the group. This probing reveals the depth of the individual's understanding and also the student's awareness of his or her own thinking and the strategies used to obtain and process information. Similarly, the tutor probes to assess the depth and quality of the independent research presented by individuals.

To summarize guidance on the use of authentic assessment of PBI, consider the following:

1. The instructor/tutor must clearly understand the intended (or anticipated) learning outcomes associated with the problem presented to the learners. The assessment strategies used must align with these intended outcomes.

2. Summative assessment can occur at the end of the problem-solving cycle as student teams present (in whatever format) their proposed solution(s) to the problem. Expert review or comparison with previous/recommended solutions will provide a measure of the accuracy of the group efforts to solve the problem.

3. Formative assessment can occur at any time in the PBI cycle. Barrows (1988) suggests having learners put their name on a page and write about their current understanding of the problem and where the team is in the process of developing a solution. This will help ensure that all students are attending and actively processing information.

Principle 4. Use Consistent and Thorough Debriefing Activities to Consolidate Key Concepts Learned from the Experience

PBI could be considered a form of experiential learning theory (Kolb, 1984; Lindsey & Berger, chapter 7, this volume). Instruction using experiential learning is a cyclic process of setting goals; followed by thinking, planning, experimenting, and decision making; followed by action; followed by observing, reflecting, and reviewing; followed by a bit more thinking, decision making, and sometimes adjusting goals; followed by more action, and so on. This approach utilizes the participants' experience and their reflection about that experience, rather than lecture and theory as the means of generating understanding and transferring skills and knowledge. Most PBI activities involve a similar cyclical process; however, properly implemented there is greater emphasis on the postexperience debriefing activity. Students of all ages will be tempted to skip this reflection step, and unfortunately many teachers will be tempted also to just enjoy the moment of satisfaction that comes from completing the process and arriving at a solution. This would be a mistake, as the debriefing process is critically important to get the learners to recognize, verbalize, and articulate what they have learned, and to integrate the new information with prior knowledge.

Simulations are another form of experiential learning (see next chapter), and the need for debriefing is considered critical to the successful utilization of a simulation for learning. According to Thiagarajan (1993), "People don't learn from experience unless they take time to reflect on that experience, derive useful lessons from it, and identify situations to transfer and apply these lessons" (p. 45). Thiagarajan proposed a sequence for conducting a debriefing that should include: emotional ventilation (let off steam if the experience has been intense); drop roles (return to reality); tell the truth (if deception was part of the simulation); share insights (different perspectives of participants); generate hypotheses (examine cause–effect relationships); transfer to the real world; second thoughts (what to do differently?); and what is (to extrapolate beyond the context of the experience). These elements provide guidance for debriefing in a PBI situation (see also Peters & Vissers, 2004; Steinwachs, 1992 for additional information on debriefing activities).

Barrows (1988) stressed the critical importance of debriefing and evaluation by the learners once the group has finished its work on the problem. He suggests the tutor ask questions such as: "What have we learned with this problem?" "What new facts or concepts?" and, "How has our work with this problem extended our knowledge of [XYZ]?" (p. 40).

To summarize the guidance for instructional designers on the debriefing process, consider the following:

1. The purpose of the debriefing process is to help the learners to recognize, verbalize, and consolidate what they have learned, and to integrate any

---

10. *Editors' note: What layer of design is this in?*

new information with existing knowledge.

2. The job of the tutor/debriefer is to ensure equal voice for all participants, so be careful to listen to all members and to ask all members for their opinions and comments.[10]
3. Follow established debriefing protocols. Know the generic and specific questions to be asked to guide the debriefing session. Prepare question ideas/topics to ensure that you (as debriefer) remember all the learning that has been discussed in the PBI activity.
4. Ask questions that encourage learners to fit the new knowledge into existing schemas.
5. Encourage learners to diagram (or list) what they have learned using concept maps—provide necessary materials.

Situational Principles or Methods for PBI

Given the scope of the adoption of this instructional approach, it is challenging to describe specific situations and methods for implementing PBI. As noted earlier, PBI is widely used in the preparation of professionals in disciplines such as medicine, business, architecture, engineering, law, and in a variety of other disciplines where there is a clear need to integrate theory and practice. There is an established body of research on the effectiveness of PBI with adult learners, and with the growing sophistication of online learning environments studies are underway to adapt PBI for this new delivery format. There is also a growing body of research on implementing PBI with younger learners (high school and elementary school). This section will expand on the principles listed above and examine some situations that may impact on the methods used in PBI.

Situation 1. Learners' Lack of Prior Experience with PBI

Teaching with PBI requires students to verbalize their understanding, work in collaborative teams, and conduct independent research. These skills are articulated in all K-12 and professional curricula in some form or another, but they are often treated as separate skills, rather than integrated with an approach such as PBI. If students are not familiar with the PBI process,[11] the teacher must invest considerable effort in scaffolding their learning experience (White, 2001). If previous educational experiences have "trained" learners to be teacher dependent,[12] most will be uncomfortable and resistant to an instructional environment that asks them to "think" for themselves. Thus, the tutor should determine the level of familiarity with PBI (and the subskills noted above) as part of a learner analysis and adjust the level of guidance and support to match the needs of the audience. This is consistent with the basics of instructional design and the learner analysis phase of the ID process. Learners with minimal PBI experience would

---

11. Editors' note: This is the situationality.
12. Editors' note: This is another situationality.

be taught process skills (how to formulate and articulate ideas and opinions, how to work collaboratively, and how to be an effective researcher) and be directed to problem-specific resources to lead them to the intended learning outcomes. Less support would be necessary as the students grow as self-regulated learners and gain experience with the expectations of the tutor and the PBI approach. Using instructional projects, simulations, or case studies to develop the necessary skills will help prepare students to work effectively on ill-structured problems.

The choice of the problem and the level of complexity should always be adjusted (neither too simplistic nor too predictable) for the age and developmental characteristics of the intended audience.[13] Aligning the problem with curricular goals for the grade level/discipline and empowering the tutor to adjust the level of complexity during the problem-solving process will reduce this potential problem situation. Remember that learning is cumulative, and the same "problem" or a variation can be revisited at a future time. The spiral curriculum approach applies when a PBI approach is followed and a change in problem conditions will challenge the learner to apply previous understandings to new circumstances, thus adding depth to their knowledge base; see also elaboration theory as described by Reigeluth (1999, chapter 18—Volume 2).

Situation 2. Using PBI with Large Class Sizes

Barrows (1988) acknowledges the challenges of large-group tutoring and suggests two strategies. The first strategy, used during both large- and small-group meetings,[14] is to have students sit facing each other and the tutor rather than having the tutor face the whole group. This allows students to interact with each other and removes the instructor from the dominant position. The second strategy, used primarily with large groups, is to have a seating chart (possibly with photographs) and expect that at each session the students will sit in the same place so the tutor can call on them by name. He also suggests with large groups to provide each student with a copy of the case (problem) before the class session with the tutor. At that session the questions from the tutor are more general—"What is going on with this problem?" or "Who wants to start off?" (p. 47). Barrows expects that the tutor will ask probing questions of all students and work to ensure that all are involved, but with a large number of students it may be difficult to engage with every student each session. Over time, as the tutor begins to identify the students who are on target and the ones who are having difficulties, he or she can focus on the students that seem to be in trouble. PBI with large classes is a challenge for even the most experienced tutors and is not recommended as the preferred approach. A small-group format (5–7 members) appears to be the most effective teacher–student ratio.

The small-group format allows every member to be heard in discussions and

---

13. *Editors' note: Age and developmental characteristics are additional situationalities*
14. *Editors' note: If the method is for both large and small groups, is it another situationality?*

to engage with a significant portion of the problem. The instructor will need to create small groups (within the class) and allow those teams to stay together for multiple problems so they can realize the benefits of collaborative effort. Multiple strategies for forming and managing collaborative groups within a large class (balanced by variables such as gender, age, experience with PBI, skills, etc.) have been well documented (Kagan, 1992; Rangachari, 1996) and are applicable in the context of a PBI approach.

Stinson and Milter (1996) taught a single class of 30+ MBA students who worked in small groups on the same problem. These small groups worked in parallel on different aspects of the problem so multiple sets of resources (textbooks, articles, charts, etc.) could be shared between groups. With multiple groups working on the same problem, it may be necessary to duplicate a set of resources for each team to support their initial research efforts. For example, multiple groups working on a problem related to flooding or wetlands pollution or hazardous waste would each receive a packet of articles, reports, and audio/video materials to review and assess prior to refining their specific research questions.

Implementation Issues

Embedded within the situations listed above are some implementation issues worthy of note.[15]

1. Commitment of the instructor and the organization. PBI will not work if the instructor is not committed to its success. If the organization does not believe that significant learning can occur using a learner-centered rather than a teacher-centered instructional format, then PBI will not succeed. Adopting and implementing PBI, particularly in K-12 schools, requires extensive planning, discussion, and communication among teachers, administrators, parents, and students. For a detailed examination of the process of adoption of PBI at the program level, see Anderson (1997), Conway and Little (2000), or Duch, Groh, and Allen (2001).

2. Commitment to the complete PBI process. PBI should not be attempted without a complete understanding of the process and how it works. Boud and Feletti (1997) note that PBI can be confused with simply teaching some problem-solving skills; or adding a problem activity to a teacher-centered instructional environment with the student *product* being rewarded rather than the learning process. To be effective, the problems used in PBI need to be carefully selected and sufficient time and resources need to be provided to students and tutors to ensure that the steps in the learning process from problem introduction to debriefing and evaluation of learning have been thoroughly completed.

3. Shift of teachers' pedagogical beliefs. Relatively few professional educators (classroom teachers, college professors, and practitioners in disciplines) have

---

15. *Editors' note: As you read what follows, try to determine if this is implementation theory or some other kind of knowledge.*

experienced PBI as students. It is axiomatic that we tend to teach as we were taught, so this lack of exposure to a problem-centered instructional methodology will require a sincere effort on the part of tutors to shift their epistemological and pedagogical beliefs to become effective implementers of PBI. Professional development workshops are available for faculty and teachers (e.g., http://www.udel.edu/pbl/ and http://www.imsa.edu/), and there are several excellent how-to books listed in the references.

4. The physical space. The traditional classroom can impose physical constraints on the implementation of PBI. The ideal room for practicing PBI would have large writing surfaces on all four walls, large tables rather than small desks, multiple computers in the room, and a well-stocked library nearby. Most classrooms were designed for the presentation of information rather than the generation of ideas and the resolution of complex, ill-structured problems. Re-design of the learning space to accommodate productive small-group sessions is an important consideration when adopting PBI. Any writing surface will do (flip charts, white boards, black boards), as long as it enables group members to record and view their ideas and share information, and can remain in place for the duration of the problem-solving activity. PBI is not quiet. Students will debate ideas and information (loudly) before they arrive at clarity and consensus. Consider this also when designing the learning space.[16]

Summary

Which professionals are the most respected and rewarded by society? Arguably, doctors, lawyers, scientists, engineers, and architects. What do these professionals do? They diagnose problems and develop solutions. Many of these professions have adopted a PBI approach to educate new members of their profession. If PBI is appropriate for the most complex knowledge domains, would it not also be appropriate for other areas that require diagnostics and the design of solutions? As has been highlighted in the previous sections, the PBI instructional theory is grounded on established theories of learning, and the mechanics of implementing the PBI approach have been well documented in learner populations ranging from elementary school students to medical students. In an effort to describe PBI as an instructional-design theory, the work of many experts in the domain has been presented and synthesized into what I hope will be viewed as a common knowledge base for the PBI approach to instruction. The reader is encouraged to follow the citations to the source articles for greater depth than it was possible to cover in this chapter.

The first two design principles that are keys to the success of a PBI approach are the selection of problems within the content domain—preferably within an entire PBI curriculum—and the ability of teachers to focus on the development

---

16. *Editors' note: Could these be viewed as preconditions for use of the theory? Could they also be viewed as implementation theory? What distinguishes the two?*

of the learners' metacognitive skills and abilities. Since the amount of information (the knowledge base) in every discipline will continue to expand and change over time, teaching facts for students to memorize has marginal value. There is a higher rate of return to facilitating the development of the learner's ability to be a critical thinker who is aware of gaps in his or her own knowledge and is also able to apply strategies to remove those gaps.

The second pair of design principles focuses on assessment and debriefing to ensure the intended learning outcomes are realized. It is critical to complete the experiential learning cycle and debrief on the learning experience, thereby integrating facts and concepts acquired through the problem-solving process with existing knowledge and reflecting on the social, interpersonal, and other metacognitive skills that contributed to the success of the activity.

The design principles outlined in this chapter provide a framework for a host of methods and submethods that will increase the effectiveness of the instruction and the learning experience for the students. In summarizing PBI, Duch (2001) offers this advice:

> Writing PBL problems may be time-consuming, challenging, and sometimes frustrating. However, the process of thinking through the learning priorities of a course and finding, adapting, or writing complex, realistic materials to meet those learning priorities will change how an instructor views his or her course in the future. Any magazine or newspaper article, documentary, news report, book or movie that is seen will become possible material for new problems in the course. Faculty will gain a new appreciation for the concepts and principles that they teach, and the connections that should be made to concepts in other courses and disciplines. (p. 53)

The contextually rich problems that you create will engage learner interest, provide direction and motivation, and because they are messy/ill-structured, they require that the learners filter the important issues and data from the unimportant or un-substantiated. These are some of the life-long learning skills that PBI helps the learner to develop.

References

Anderson, A. S. (1997). Conversion to problem-based learning in 15 months. In D. Boud & G. Feletti, (Eds.), *The challenge of problem-based learning* (2nd ed., pp. 64–72). London: Kogan Page.

Barrows, H. S. (1986). A taxonomy of problem-based learning methods. *Medical Education, 20,* 481–486.

Barrows, H. S. (1988). *The tutorial process.* Springfield: Southern Illinois University School of Medicine.

Barrows, H. S. (1996). Problem-based learning in medicine and beyond: A brief overview. *New Directions in Teaching and Learning, 68,* 3–9.

Barrows, H. S. (2000). *Problem-based learning applied to medical education.* Springfield: Southern Illinois University Press.

Barrows, H. S., & Bennett, K. (1972). The diagnostic (problem-solving) skills of the neurologist. *Archives of Neurology, 26,* 273–277.

Barrows, H. S., & Kelson, A. (1993) *Problem-based learning in secondary education and the problem-*

based learning institute (Monograph). Springfield: Southern Illinois University School of Medicine.

Boud, D., & Feletti, G. (Eds.). (1997). *The challenge of problem-based learning* (2nd ed.). London: Kogan Page.

Bransford, J. D., Brown, A. L., & Cocking, R. R. (Eds.). (2000). *How people learn: Brain, mind, experience, and school.* Washington D.C.: National Academy Press.

Bridges, E. M., & Hallinger, P. (1996). Problem-based learning in leadership education. *New Directions for Teaching and Learning, 68,* 53–61

Brown, J. S., Collins, A., & Duguid, P. (1989). Situated cognition and the culture of learning. *Educational Researcher, 18*(1), 32–42.

Chapman, D. W. (2000). Designing problems for motivation and engagement in the PBL classroom. *Journal on Excellence in College Teaching, 11*(2&3), 73–82.

Collins, A., Brown, J. S., & Newman, S. E. (1989). Cognitive apprenticeship: Teaching the crafts of reading, writing and mathematics. In L. B. Resnick (Ed.), *Knowing, learning and instruction: Essays in honor of Robert Glaser* (pp. 453–494). Hillsdale, NJ: Erlbaum.

Conway, J. F., & Little, P. J. (2000). Adopting PBL as the preferred institutional approach to teaching and learning: Considerations and challenges. *Journal on Excellence in College Teaching, 11*(2&3), 11–26.

Duch, B. J. (2001). Writing problems for deeper understanding. In B. J. Duch, S. E. Groh, & D. E. Allen (Eds.), *The power of problem-based learning* (pp. 47–53). Sterling, VA: Stylus.

Duch, B. J., Groh, S. E., & Allen, D. E. (2001). Why problem-based learning? A case study of institutional change in undergraduate education. In B. J. Duch, S. E. Groh, & D. E. Allen (Eds.), *The power of problem-based learning* (pp. 3–11). Sterling, VA: Stylus.

Duffy, T. M., & Cunningham, D. J. (1996). Constructivism: Implications for the design and delivery of instruction. In D. H. Jonassen, (Ed.), *Handbook of research for eductational communications and technology* (pp. 170–198). New York: Simon and Schuster.

Gijselaers, W. H. (1996). Connecting problem-based practices with educational theory. *New Directions in Teaching and Learning, 68.,*13–21.

Hmelo-Silver, C. E. (2000). Knowledge recycling: Crisscrossing the landscape of educational psychology in a problem-based learning course for pre-service teachers. *Journal on Excellence in College Teaching, 11*(2&3), 41–56.

Hmelo-Silver, C. E. (2004). Problem-based learning: What and how do students learn? *Educational Psychology Review, 16* (3), 235–266,.

Jonassen, D. H. (1997). Instructional design models for well-structured and ill-structured problem-solving learning outcomes. *Educational Technology: Research and Development, 45*(1), 65–94.

Jonassen, D. H. (2004). *Learning to solve problems: An instructional design guide.* San Francisco: Pfeiffer.

Kagan, S. (1992). *Cooperative learning.* San Juan Capistrano, CA: Kagan Cooperative Learning.

Katz, L. G., & Chard, S.C. (1989). *Engaging children's minds: The project approach.* Norwood, NJ: Ablex.

Kingsland, A. J. (1996). Time expenditure, workload, and student satisfaction in problem-based learning. In L. Wilkerson, & W. H. Gijselaers (Eds.), *Bringing problem-based learning to higher education: Theory and practice. New Directions For Teaching and Learning Series, No. 68* (pp. 73–81), San Francisco: Jossey-Bass.

Kolb, D. (1984). *Experiential learning: experience as the source of learning and development.* Englewood Cliffs, NJ: Prentice-Hall.

MacDonald, P. J. (1997). Selection of health problems for a problem based curriculum. In D. Boud, & G. Feletti (Eds.), *The challenge of problem-based learning* (2nd ed., pp. 93–102). London: Kogan Page.

Moll, L. (Ed.). (1990). *Vygotsky and education.* New York: Cambridge University Press.

Peters V. A. M., & Vissers, G. A. N. (2004). A simple classification model for debriefing simulation games. *Simulation & Gaming, 35*(1), 70–84.

Rangachari, P. K. (1996). Twenty-up: Problem-based learning with a large group. In L. Wilkerson, & W. H. Gijselaers (Eds.), *Bringing problem based learning to higher education: theory and practice* (New Directions For Teaching and Learning Series, No. 68, pp. 63–71). San Francisco: Jossey-Bass.

Reigeluth, C. M. (1999). The elaboration theory: Guidance for scope and sequence decisions. In C. M. Reigeluth (Ed.), *Instructional-design theories and models: Vol. 2. A new paradigm of instructional theory* (pp. 425–454). Hillsdale, NJ: Erlbaum.

Resnick, L. B. (1989). Introduction. In L. B. Resnick, (Ed.), *Knowing, learning and instruction: Essays in honor of Robert Glaser* (pp. 1–24). Hillsdale, NJ: Erlbaum.

Savery, J. R. (1996). *Fostering student ownership for learning in a learner centered instructional environment.* Unpublished doctoral dissertation, Indiana University, Bloomington.

Savery, J. R. (1998). Fostering ownership with computer supported collaborative writing in higher education. In C. J. Bonk & K. S. King (Eds.), *Electronic collaborators: Learner-centered technologies for literacy, apprenticeship, and discourse* (pp. 103–127). Mahwah, NJ: Erlbaum.

Savery, J. R. (1999). Enhancing motivation and learning through collaboration and the use of problems. In S. Fellows & K. Ahmet (Eds.), *Inspiring students: case studies in motivating the learner.* (pp. 33–41). London: Kogan Page.

Savery, J. R., & Duffy, T. M. (1995). Problem-based learning: An instructional model and its constructivist framework. In B. Wilson, (Ed.), *Constructivist learning environments: Case studies in instructional design* (pp. 135–148). Englewood Cliffs, NJ: Educational Technology.

Schmidt, H. G., & Moust, J. H. C. (2000). Towards a taxonomy of problems used in problem-based learning curricula. *Journal on Excellence in College Teaching, 11*(2&3), 57–72.

Schunk, D. H. (2001). Social cognitive theory and self-regulated learning. In B. J. Zimmerman, & D. H. Schunk (Eds.), *Self-regulated learning and academic achievement: Theoretical perspectives* (pp. 125–151). Mahwah, NJ: Lawrence Erlbaum.

Schunk, D. H., & Zimmerman, B. J. (Eds.). (1998). *Self-regulated learning: From teaching to self-reflective practice.* New York: Guilford.

Spiro, R. J., Feltovich, P. L., Jacobson, M. J., & Coulson, R. L. (1991). Cognitive flexibility, constructivism, and hypertext: Random access for advanced knowledge acquisition in ill-structured domains. *Educational Technology 31*(5), 24–33.

Steinwachs, B. (1992). How to facilitate a debriefing. *Simulation & Gaming, 23*(2), 186–195.

Stinson, J. E., & Milter, R. G. (1996). Problem-based learning in business education: Curriculum design and implementation issues. In L. Wilkerson & W. H. Gijselaers (Eds.), *Bringing problem-based learning to higher education: Theory and practice* (New Directions For Teaching and Learning Series, No. 68, pp. 32–42). San Francisco: Jossey-Bass.

Thiagarajan, S. (1993). How to maximize transfer from simulation games through systematic debriefing. In F. Percival, S. Lodge, & D. Saunders (Eds.), *The simulation and gaming yearbook* (Vol. 1, pp. 45–52). London: Kogan Page.

Torp, L., & Sage, S. (2002). *Problems as possibilities: Problem-based learning for K-16 education* (2nd ed.). Alexandria, VA: ASCD.

Vygotsky, L. (1978). *Mind in society.* Cambridge, MA: Harvard University Press.

Wertsch, J. (1991). *Voices of the mind: A sociocultural approach to mediated action.* Cambridge, MA: Harvard University Press.

White, H. B. III (2001). A PBL course that uses research articles as problems. In B. J. Duch, S. E. Groh, & D. E. Allen (Eds.), *The power of problem-based learning* (pp. 131–140). Sterling, VA: Stylus.

Wiggins, G., & McTighe, J. (1998). *Understanding by design.* Alexandria, VA: Association for Supervision and Curriculum Development.

Wilkerson, L., & Gijselaers, W. H. (Eds.). (1996). *Bringing problem-based learning to higher education: Theory and practice.* (New Directions for Teaching and Learning Series, No. 68). San Francisco: Jossey-Bass.

Williams, S. M. (1992). Putting case-based instruction into context: Examples from legal and medical education. *Journal of the Learning Sciences, 2,* 367–427.

Wingspread Conference. (1994). *Quality assurance in undergraduate education: What the public expects.* Denver, CO: Education Commission of the States.

Woods, D. R. (1994). *Problem-based learning: How to gain the most from PBL.* Waterdown, Ontario: Author.

Zimmerman, B. J., & Schunk, D. H. (Eds.). (2001). *Self-regulated learning and academic achievement: Theoretical perspectives.* Mahwah, NJ: Erlbaum.

9

Simulation Approach to Instruction

ANDREW S. GIBBONS
Brigham Young University

MARK MCCONKIE
Utah State University

KAY KYEONGJU SEO
University of Cincinnati

DAVID A. WILEY
Utah State University

Andrew S. Gibbons is department chair in instructional psychology and technology at Brigham Young University. Prior to that, he was a faculty member at Utah State University. He led instructional design projects in industry for 18 years at Wicat Systems, Inc. and Courseware Inc. Dr. Gibbons' work has included large-scale training development projects, reengineering of the development (ISD) process, computer-based instruction, military and commercial aviation training development, and research and development on instructional simulations. Dr. Gibbons' current research focuses on the architecture of instructional designs. He has published a design theory of model-centered instruction, proposed a general layering theory of instructional designs, and is currently studying the use of design languages in relation to design layers as a means of creating instructional systems that are adaptive, generative, and scalable.

Mark McConkie is a PhD candidate in the instructional technology program at Utah State University. In both academic and industry settings, his work has involved the design and development of a broad range of instructional simulations incorporating the principles of model-centered instruction. He has worked for 10 years as an instructional systems design specialist for Parker Hannifin Corporation, a large global manufacturing company, and is currently a Training and Development Manager for its Aerospace Group. He has also worked as a research assistant at the Center for Open Sustainable Learning (COSL), and on an NSF-sponsored curriculum reform grant for the department of Biological and Irrigation Engineering at Utah State University.

Kay Kyeongju Seo is assistant professor of instructional design and technology at the University of Cincinnati in Cincinnati, Ohio. Her research interests include computer-mediated communication, technology integration in K-12 and higher education, multimedia-assisted project-based learning, instructional design languages, Web site usability testing, and instructional simulations and microworlds. Prior to joining the University of Cincinnati, she was assistant professor of educational technology at Rockhurst University in Kansas City, Missouri. At Rockhurst, she focused on preparing in-service and preservice teachers to use technology in their classrooms. Seo received her PhD in instructional technology from Utah State University in Logan, Utah.

David A. Wiley is associate professor of instructional technology at Utah State University, director of the Center for Open and Sustainable Learning, and chief openness officer of Flat World Knowledge. He holds a PhD in instructional psychology and technology from Brigham Young University and a BFA in Music from Marshall University. He has previously been a nonresident fellow at the Center for Internet and Society at Stanford Law School, a visiting scholar at the Open University of the Netherlands, and is a recipient of the U.S. National Science Foundation's CAREER grant. His career is dedicated to increasing access to educational opportunity for everyone around the world.

EDITORS' FOREWORD

Preconditions

Content
- *Integrated skills that consist of multiple complex actions in a fluid sequence and changing circumstances*

Learners
- *All learners*

Learning environments
- *Environments that have the appropriate tools (computers or other materials)*
- *Instructional simulations or microworlds must have augmentations*

Instructional development constraints
- *Simulation or microworld cost must not exceed either available resources (money and time) or benefits*

Values

about ends (learning goals)
- *Understand principles and relationships in dynamic systems*
- *Developing skills for dealing with complex systems*

about priorities (criteria for successful instruction)
- *Effectiveness, efficiency, and appeal can all be maximized, as long as the user population is large enough to make it economical.*

about means (instructional methods)
- *The learning experience should be adaptive, generative, and scalable.*
- *The learning experience should involve authentic tasks and contexts.*
- *The learning experience should involve a dynamic model of physical and/or conceptual systems.*
- *Learner interactions with the model should result in state changes.*
- *The learning experience should have at least one designed augmenting instructional function.*

about power (to make decisions about the previous three)
- *Learners are active participants who have some degree of free agency within the simulated environment.*

Universal Methods

1. *for the content function*
   - *Create an abstract model first, then a computerized model.*
   - *Select the "right" model.*
   - *Select the appropriate type(s) of models (environment, cause-effect, or performance model).*
   - *Select the appropriate forms of models (semantic networks, production rules, equations, Bayesian networks, system dynamics, or object models).*

- *Make a limited number of control points available to learners for manipulation of the system.*
- *Align the different kinds of fidelity and resolution of the model with the learning needs, inasmuch as costs allow.*
- *Escalate performance difficulty by supplying progressions of advanced models, advanced problems, or both.*

2. *for the strategy function (instructional augmentations)*
   - *Design the physical setting and siting.*
   - *Design the social settings (participant roles and patterns of initiative-sharing).*
   - *Describe the properties of models and the range of performances that encompass subject-matter goals, problem solving goals, and learning-to-learn goals within each model.*
   - *Assign instructional scopes (goals) to event blocks and arrange them into sequences (progressions).*
   - *Specify event forms and classes.*
   - *Design augmentation types and rules.*
   - *Use a dramatic context.*
   - *Design the means of supplying problem-related information to learners.*

3. *for the control function*
   - *Provide user controls for each main function.*

4. *for the messaging function*
   - *Generate message units that have certain elements of a human tutor.*
   - *Use approaches for structuring messages.*
   - *Use execution-time construction of messages.*

5. *for the representation function*
   - *Generate and assemble representation elements.*
   - *Change model states according to the cycles of the model.*
   - *Consider giving the learner alternative vantage points.*
   - *Decide what representations a single message should be given.*
   - *Design rules for the execution of the continuously changing displays.*
   - *Design rules for manipulating time and space.*
   - *Design traces that represent trends of change.*

6. *for the media-logic function*
   - *Execute representations and computations.*

7. *for the data management function*
   - *Manage data resulting from interactions.*
   - *Design data collection points and variables.*
   - *Decide on interpretation variables and rules.*
   - *Design a data-gathering framework.*
   - *Decide on points at which to give information to the learner.*

—CMR & AAC

SIMULATION APPROACH TO INSTRUCTION

This chapter describes guidelines for the theory-based design of instructional simulations and microworlds. It adds to earlier writing on simulation by Alessi and Trollip (1991), de Jong and van Joolingen (1998), Gredler (2004), Gibbons, Fairweather, Anderson, and Merrill (1997), Munro, Breaux, Paltrey, and Sheldon (2002), and Reigeluth and Schwartz (1989), in an attempt to foster a common knowledge base in this area. Simulation and microworld design comprises many independent sectors of what has become a large and prosperous industry that creates products of great diversity in numerous subject-matter areas and surface forms.

Simulation and microworld designs are more diverse in their surface features than other instructional forms, and it is sometimes not possible to tell from the surface whether a product is a simulation or a look-alike animation. It seems almost impossible to define a set of design principles that apply to the large and varied class of products called instructional simulations unless we identify design-theoretic schemes that show the similarity of product designs under the surface. We have organized this chapter around such a scheme, which is described later. We will attempt to answer the questions:

- What are instructional simulations and microworlds?
- What underlying structural principles relate them together?
- What design principles apply to the entire class of instructional simulations and microworlds?

Defining Instructional Simulation

For the purposes of this chapter, instructional simulations are defined as:

1. One or more dynamic models of physical or conceptual systems...
2. That engage the learner in interactions with the models that result in state changes...
3. According to a nonlinear logic...
4. With supplementation by one or more designed augmenting instructional functions...
5. Employed in the pursuit of one or more instructional goals.

An instructional simulation involves interaction with a dynamic, changing, computable model; new states of the model are determined by the learner's actions toward the model or by its own continuous computations. One can learn from general purpose simulation models, but a general purpose simulation can be considered instructional only if it is augmented with one or more auxiliary instructional functions that assist the learner in some way during learner–model interaction (Gibbons, 2001; Gibbons et al., 1997). An unaugmented model has limited instructional value, can create instructional inefficiencies, and can lead the learner into misinterpretations and misconceptions.

Simulations are used in the training of integrated skills that consist of multiple judgments, decisions, and actions that take place in a fluid sequence in response to changing circumstances.[1] What is learned and practiced with the aid of an instructional simulation is the ability to adapt action to a momentary problem-solving need. Simulations provide practice in carrying out complex tasks and also in selecting which tasks to carry out at a given moment. They can be used to teach learning strategies and to help learners to achieve the capacity for self-directed learning. Instructional simulations do this through augmentation within an environment that includes some degree of scaffolding, coaching, feedback, or on-the-spot instruction tailored to the circumstances and requirements of performance. Because of this dynamism, the order of instructional events, messages, and representations may be decided at the moment of need and constructed at that moment from primitive elements and computed data.

Because simulations represent an adaptive and potentially costly form of instruction, three general criteria apply to the design of instructional simulations (Atkinson & Wilson, 1969):

- *The criterion of adaptivity*—The ability to modify qualities of the instructional experience based on the actions of the learner
- *The criterion of generativity*—The ability to generate some portion of the instructional artifact at the time of use
- *The criterion of scalability*—The ability to produce instructional experiences in greater quantity without corresponding linear increases in cost

Defining Microworld

A microworld is a model-centered environment in which a model *is constructed* by the learner, using parts and tools supplied by the designer (Colella, Klopfer, & Resnick, 2001; Papert, 1993; Rieber, 1996). The model is then used by the learner through guided or self-directed exploration and experimentation to learn principles and relationships regarding the behavior of the model, as constructed, under different experimental conditions. The construction of multiple models and experimentation with each model provides learning about the sometimes complex behavior of simple systems and, ultimately, about how to conduct learning through self-directed experiment—an approach to instruction termed *constructionist* (Kafai, 2006; Papert, 1993).

The microworld can be considered a species of instructional simulation. That is, microworlds possess all of the characteristics of instructional simulations, but the microworld concept has additional, specialized characteristics that not all instructional simulations share:

---

1 *Editors' note: This is a precondition for use of the theory.*

1. The dynamic model is designed and constructed by the learner.
2. A construction environment created by the designer allows a set of primitive model-building elements to be joined together to embody and illustrate cause–effect model relationships.
3. Tools within the construction environment may be provided by the designer to support learning activities.
4. The set of construction elements is often themed. The elements are like characters in multiple stories that the learner can tell.
5. The learner's nonlinear interactions in constructing models and carrying out model interactions are within a specific range constrained by the set of elements supplied by the designer and the operational commands provided by the designer for use by the learner.
6. One or more guided explorations and exploration supports are normally provided.

The value of microworlds as an instructional tool depends on insightful, disciplined design and execution by the designer of the construction environment and the construction elements. Used casually or carelessly, the concept easily deteriorates into a standard, procedural laboratory exercise. The main effect of the microworld method requires the willing—even eager—participation of learners. Through a scaffolded process they learn how to formulate questions that can be answered through manipulations of constructed models, becoming knowledge producers for themselves. In the remainder of this chapter, we will use the term *simulation* to refer to microworlds as well as other kinds of simulations.

Simulation Architecture

The design architecture of an instructional simulation can be viewed as a composite of many subdesigns, including: (1) a core that computes model state changes; (2) a strategic system of model-experience augmentations; (3) a user control system; (4) a message-generation system; (5) a system for creating surface representation; (6) a system for executing the simulation; and (7) a system for data management.[2] A common approach to simulation design is to center the solution on a software architecture, but doing this indicates an implicit decision that other parts of the design will be forced to fit the software architecture if there is a conflict.

We will describe principles for instructional simulation design under the seven functional headings named above:

1. Content function: Supply model content
2. Strategy function: Implement instructional augmentations
3. Control function: Provide user controls

---

2. *Editors' note: Note that these correspond to Gibbons' and Rogers' seven layers of design (see chapter 14).*

4. Messaging function: Generate message units
5. Representation function: Generate and assemble representation elements
6. Media-logic function: Execute representations and computations
7. Data management function: Manage data resulting from interactions.

Gibbons and Rogers (chapter 14, this volume) suggest that these functional categories apply to instructional designs in general.

1. Content Function: Supply Model Content

This section describes principles for organizing the content functional module of an instructional simulation. Simulation content takes the form of a dynamic model. In this chapter the term *model* means an invisible but computable entity capable of responding to operations upon it in an unpredictable order. Models are dynamic *replicas* of real or imagined systems.

Principle: Abstract Models

Models should be documented independently, in the abstract, before they are embodied into computer code or instructions for human enactment, in order to avoid confusing the model in the designer's mind with the computer program or social structures that will enact it.[3]

Principle: The "Right" Model(s)

The selection of model(s) for instructional simulations sometimes requires subtle distinctions on the designer's part. Bransford, Brown, and Cocking (2000) remark that "one is struck by the complexity of selecting appropriate models for particular mathematical ideas and processes" (p. 168). It is important for designers to avoid the common error of selecting models that are the most visible and interesting or the easiest to build.[4] One design team was so fascinated with the surface interactivity and multimedia attractiveness of an equipment model (a medical analysis machine) that they forgot to design the performance model (making judgments based on the equipment's output) that was of real interest.

Principle: Three Kinds of Models

The simulated model may consist of a single model or a suite of models that interact. Models used for instructional simulations are of three kinds: (1) envi-

---

3. *Editors' note: This does not describe what the instruction should be like, rather what the planning process should be like. Therefore, it is instructional-planning theory, not instructional-event theory.*
4. *Editors' note: Again, this is instructional-planning theory, and it is at a very imprecise level of description, because it does not provide guidance for selecting the "right" model.*

ronment models; (2) cause-effect system models; and (3) performance models. The *environment* model provides a context for the cause–effect and human performance models. The environment model is seldom the focus of instruction, but the designer must design it, because it generates events that influence the states of the other two models. *Cause–effect* models mimic cause–effect systems that are natural or human-made. An *expert performance* model observes and interprets these other two models, makes predictions concerning their future states, discovers or explains cause–effect relationships, operates or controls the models, responds to unexpected changes in model state, and influences the models toward a desired future goal state.[5]

Principle: The Form of Models

Models can take the form of:

Semantic networks. These consist of conceptual networks of meaning nodes and the named relationships among them—propositional knowledge.

Production rules. These are "if…then…" rules constituting decision-action subject-matter.

Equations. These include mathematical and logical formulas that describe a system's behaviors without describing the inner workings of the system. Such collections of formulas normally also specify an order in which the formulas are to be applied, with the output of earlier computations being used as input variables to subsequent computations.

Bayesian networks. These networks define probabilistic pathways between system states. Bayesian networks can be used to represent both conceptual and performance-related content.

System dynamics models. System dynamics models (Milrad, Spector, & Davidsen, 2002; Spector, 2000) identify the elements of a system, along with the input and output variables associated with each element. Formulas or rules are associated with element-to-element relationships and allow computations to update system values in response to events and variable value changes. System dynamics models are useful for describing in detail the cause–effect linkages within a complex system.

Object models. Model content can be captured as a collection of objects, each with its own identity, variable set, behaviors, rules for recomputing internal variable values, and rules for communicating information to other objects through interobject messages.[6]

---

5. *Editors' note: Again, this is instructional-planning theory at a very imprecise level.*
6. *Editors' note: This whole section on forms of models is purely descriptive. There is no design theory here. However, it is certainly useful for designers to understand the forms. This shows the value in integrating descriptive theory with design theory.*

Principle: Input/Output Variables for Each Model

A learner learns from model interaction by observing effects (or output states) that are linked to direct and indirect causes (input states and operations of the model). A limited number of model control points must be made accessible to learners through which input variables can be manipulated. The model uses these values to recompute its output states. The simulation should make clear the specific input variables that the learner will be able to influence, as well as variables that can be influenced by the environment model and other models in the simulation. The designer should also identify the recomputed values that are to be shown to the learner as model outputs. Once this list of variables is obtained, it must be continually maintained as the design evolves, because it is the connecting link between model features and learning performance requirements.

Principle: Fidelity and Resolution Levels

Models by definition lack fidelity and resolution when compared with the system that is being modeled. We call this mismatch the level of *denaturing* of the model (Gibbons, 2001; Gibbons et al., 1997). Denaturing is inevitable because media cannot represent reality faithfully, especially reality taken out of context. A representational medium therefore changes either the exactness (fidelity) of the representation or its granularity (resolution). The fidelity and resolution levels of models must match the learning need within the constraints of simulation costs.

Fidelity. Fidelity describes the degree of resemblance between reality and its model. Fidelity is clearly a factor in the transfer of learning from model situations to real situations. There are few clear guidelines on choosing fidelity levels,[7] and there is much street wisdom that is easily discredited by real evidence. There are many dimensions to fidelity, and a designer must prioritize them according to the given design problem:

- Fidelity related to learner action-taking
  - *Task fidelity*—How closely the actions taken by the learner resemble actions taken in real environments
  - *Environmental fidelity*—How closely the sensations in simulated response environments resemble the sensations produced in real environments (smells, spaces, sounds, etc.)
  - *Haptic fidelity—How realistic control actions feel as they are executed*
- Fidelity related to processing of learner actions by the model
  - *Speed/Timeliness*—The resemblance between model speed and response timing and real speed and timing
  - *Accuracy*—The accuracy of model computations compared to real outcomes

---

7. *Editors' note: This is to say that design theory, specifically instructional-event theory, has not yet been developed for this.*

- *Exactness*—The degree to which the operations of the modeling mechanism resemble real mechanisms
- Fidelity related to the external representation of the model's states and actions
  - *Realism*—The degree to which sensory experiences from external representations of the model conform to sensory information available in real settings

Fidelity issues are critical in instructional simulations because much information is conveyed through nonverbal channels: through visual and auditory channels for most simulations, and in the case of virtual reality environments through kinesthetic and haptic sensations. Learner processing of poorly designed, poorly synchronized, nonverbal information can produce tacit misconceptions in the learner. Reigeluth and Schwartz (1989) suggest that several factors should influence the degree of fidelity in instructional simulations: (1) potential for creating a cognitive overload; (2) ability to promote transfer of learning; (3) possible motivational appeal; and (4) cost.[8] Lathan, Tracey, Sebrechts, Clawson, & Higgins (2002) frame fidelity decisions in a way that suggests three approaches a designer might take in varying fidelity: media replacement, filter and threshold, and transformation.

Resolution. The resolution of a model can be defined as the level of detail or granularity at which it represents the reality to the user. The resolution of a model is somewhat analogous to the resolution of the computer screen: the higher the level of resolution, the more the detail can be discriminated and, up to a point, the more the information conveyed. In the case of dynamic models, resolution can be measured in terms of: (1) inputs and outputs of the model and (2) the unit of timing used as the basis for recomputing model values.

Instruction using simulations can be described as the progressive disclosure of a system's complexity (Burton, Brown, & Fischer, 1984; Gibbons et al., 1997; White & Frederiksen, 1990). Resolution that systematically changes as instruction progresses can be used as a means of evolving model complexity over time, disclosing increasing levels of system detail. Lesgold (1999) proposes that designers should incorporate into their models those elements that the learner can use in reasoning and leave alone esoteric and detailed descriptions of technical systems from which learners cannot benefit. In this view, a designer can often select the details of a model on the basis of the inputs and outputs that the learner must observe and act upon.

Principle: Model (and Problem) Growth Patterns

As experience with a set of models accumulates, performance that was once a challenge to the learner becomes easy, and the designer can escalate difficulty by supplying progressions of advanced models, advanced problems, or both.

---

8. *Editors' note: Here is a little bit of guidance— instructional-event theory.*

Progressions of increasingly complex models are described extensively by White and Frederiksen (1990, 1998). Instructional use of increasingly complex practice worlds is described by Burton et al. (1984).

2. Strategy Function: Implement Instructional Augmentations

Strategy design involves describing the context of instructional settings, social arrangements, goals, resource structures, and events supplied by the designer to augment the learner's interaction with the model. This has been referred to as the "environment of instruction." We will refer to these as the *instructional augmentation* of the model and also refer to it as the *learning companion* function.[9] Within the strategy's functional design there are many distinct subfunctions. The designer must specify:[10]

- Physical settings (classrooms, terminals)
- Social settings that include participants, role expectations, initiative rules
- The structure of instructional goals
- The assignment of goals to event blocks and the sequencing of event blocks
- The specification of event forms and classes
- The strategy (augmentation) rules for event classes
- The use of dramatic context
- The means of supplying problem-related information to learners

These constitute a set of designed site, social, goal, time, event, and product structures within which multiple agents, including learners, peers, instructors, and software can carry out a dynamic instructional conversation.

Principle: Setting and Siting of Instruction

Setting refers to the physical instructional environment and its furnishings. Siting involves the design and configuration of virtual places and their connectivity. These represent major commitments for design and infrastructure-building. Settings for the use of instructional simulations today include homes, specially designed and situation-related training suites, PDA-friendly wireless environments, and electronic classrooms and labs (Dede, 2004; Schauble & Glaser, 1996). Because of this, siting raises new issues of speed, responsiveness, presence, context, persona, and immediacy. Designs may need to include the configuration of software architectures for creating temporary networks of learning sites.

---

9. *Editors' note: This approach of identifying terms that other researchers have used is highly recommended for helping to build a common knowledge base.*

10. *Editors' note: In a certain sense, this is guidance (design theory) because it tells the designer what she or he must do. However, it is at an extremely imprecise level of description, for it does not provide any guidance for making those specifications.*

They may also include determining communication channels among sites and the design of shared representational workspaces.

Principle: Social Context

Social context must be an important consideration in designs, because the increasing use of multiuser simulations forces the designer to consider the implications of the societies they automatically create. A social context causes the designer to define the forms and patterns of communication that can take place among learners, instructors, and instructional agents. In some cases, such as the training of team activity, the social context is determined by the nature of the task. In other cases, social context may be tailored by the designer specifically to represent other values, such as the need to overcome cultural barriers (Cole, Engestrom, & Vasquez, 1997), the need to learn cooperation skills, or the need to form or take advantage of an existing community of practice (Lave & Wenger, 1991). An excellent summary of social issues is given by Lehrer and Schauble (2006). Two aspects of the social context are of special importance to simulation design: participant roles and patterns of initiative-sharing.

The learner's role in a simulation-centered activity is dynamic, changing sometimes moment-by-moment. It involves the sharing of initiative with peers, instructors, and instructional agents (Colella et al., 2001; Gibbons et al., 1997; Johnson, Rickel, & Lester, 2000; Resnick, 1997; Rieber, 2004). Roles must shift as instruction progresses, placing increasingly greater responsibility for learning tasks and initiatives on the learner.[11] Instructional support must fade, and learner initiative must increase. Lave and Wenger (1991) suggest that specific role assignments are not as critical as the fact that role expectations come to exist within a community and that they be known to, and accepted by, both learner and instructor. Some details of role assignments, however, do appear to make a difference. Problem-based learning (Barrows, 1998; Barrows & Tamblyn, 1980) and reciprocal teaching (Brown & Palincsar, 1989) depend on learner acceptance and execution of a precisely defined role. Failure to carry out the role can result in failure of the strategy. In both cases, learners participate in modeling expert performance within a context of scaffolding that gradually fades.

Rules for initiative sharing become more important as the role of the learner grows. Instructional simulations can offer the learner opportunities not only for responding, but also for taking the initiative in areas of strategy implementation, nonsequential event control, or spontaneous messaging and conversation. Microworlds in most cases *require* that the learner take the initiative for one or more of them. Space does not allow for detailing of the dimensions of strategy in which initiative can be shared with, negotiated with, or placed on the learner and the different patterns of initiative-taking that can be constructed from these dimensions (Fox, 1993). A simulation designer, however, must deliberately plan

---

11. *Editor's note: This method, helping learners to assume greater responsibility for their own learning, is an important feature of the Information-Age paradigm of education, to prepare learners to be lifelong learners.*

the possible initiative states, their patterns of changing, and the mechanism for negotiation of the change.

Principle: Instructional Goals

Traditional views of instructional objectives are challenged by the nature of simulations, whose instructional goals simultaneously may include subject-matter goals, problem solving goals, and learning-to-learn goals (Collins, Brown, & Newman, 1989). The fragmented, content-centered goals of the past conflict with performance-centered, integrated (skills, attitudes, values) goals required for simulation design.

The scope of action within a simulated environment is so broad and the integration of goals so extensive that to define instructional goals as a list of separate statements is impractical. A more useful method is to describe the properties of the subject model(s) and to define the desired range of performances learners should be able to demonstrate with respect to models (Gibbons, Nelson, & Richards 2000a, 2000b, 2000c).[12] This form of instructional goal can be generally expressed as:

> Within <environment>
> one or more <actor>
> executes <performance>
> using <tool>
> affecting <system or system process>
> to produce <outcome, artifact>
> having <properties, qualities>.

During design this can be used as a beginning point for determining more detailed requirements through deduction for the environment, cause-effect, and expert performance models.

The global objective is formed in terms of the ranges of values that can be used in each of the variable positions in these statements. This creates a bridge between analysis and design processes by identifying goals in terms of the three types of models that must be created, and at the same time it defines a *simulation scope*: the outer bounds of what must be simulated (Gibbons et al., 1997).

Principle: Specific Instructional Event Goals and Goal Progressions

Individual, transient, momentary *instructional scopes*—instructional goals—can be framed against the backdrop of this comprehensive simulation scope and related to specific time-bound instructional events. These consist of statements

---

12. *Editors' note: This is curriculum design-theory, appropriately integrated with instructional-event theory and instructional-planning theory.*

that momentarily restrict the ranges of the variables described above to within particular values. Individual instructional scopes defined in this way can be used to form progressions of models, trajectories of performance expectation, and performance assessment points (White & Frederiksen, 1990). The *work model* concept proposed by Bunderson, Gibbons, Olsen, & Kearsley (1981) and the *elaboration* concept proposed by Reigeluth (1999) give useful terminology, process, and product guidelines to the designer.

Many principles can be used for sequencing the progression of instructional scopes (goals). These can include ordering for rapid coverage, ordering for maximum coverage in minimum time, ordering in step sizes matched to the learner's rate of progress, ordering according to cognitive load, and ordering to maximize exposure to the widest range of problems.[13] A general sequencing principle for instruction in skills is described by van Merriënboer (1997).

Instructional simulations may: (1) make use of a fixed sequence of problems; (2) provide dynamic computation of problem sequences; (3) allow learner selection of problem sequences; or (4) permit the learner to form the instructional goal. Whichever of these is used, the selection of problems and their sequence is critical to maintaining and adjusting levels of engagement and challenge during simulation instruction. Vygotsky's concept of the zone of proximal development (1978) implies a sequencing principle based on learner readiness.

Selection of goal sequences also implies that problems can be scaled with precision along multiple dimensions of difficulty and indexed according to those dimensions. Studies of domain structure by Bunderson, Wiley, and McBride (chapter 15, this volume), Strong-Krause (2001), and McBride (2005) suggest that this kind of indexing may be possible, but the process of scaling is complex at present and requires very large databases.

Principle: Standard Event Forms

Our most common shared design language terms describing event forms include *lesson*, *lab session*, *recitation session*, and so forth. These terms are generic and do not have sufficient precision to guide a simulation design without additional specification. A simulation designer should define a small number of event forms that can be repeated using different specific content. Event forms define the granularity of instructional elements that can be sequenced. Events during an instructional simulation may occur in unpredictable orders, depending on the flow of responses that make up the learner's side of an instructional conversation. Event forms define the patterns this conversation can employ. A simulation experience in this sense is an emergent phenomenon.

---

13. *Editors' note: While this describes several methods for sequencing, to be design theory it would need to indicate when to use each method (situationalities), and it would also be helpful to provide more precision—details about how to use each method.*

Principle: Augmentation Types and Rules

Augmentation in an instructional simulation supplies that part of the instructional experience (including information and interactions) not generated by the model. Augmentations may consist of many different functions, including: providing reminders, suggesting analogical or metaphorical associations, directing attention, performing parts of a difficult task for the learner, giving suggestions or hints, providing explanations, demonstrating, delivering assessments, evaluating or guiding self-evaluation, diagnosing causes, prescribing action, posing questions or challenges, and many other functions. In instructional simulations augmentations work in parallel and in synchronization with model functions, providing information and interaction that is relevant to current learning tasks.

Augmentations support the learner's actions of model observation, model interpretation, decision making, organization and processing of new information, recalling, acting, judging, valuing, and evaluating. The model generates information that can be made available to the learner about model operations; augmentations supply additional information that helps the learner to use model information to learn.

Augmentations chosen for inclusion in a design make up the *learning companion* functions for the simulation, whether they are human or computer administered. The learning companion is especially important in helping the learner to become self-aware and self-directed with respect to learning processes: to realize that deliberate metacognition can improve learning-directed initiatives (Collins et al., 1989; Elen & Clarebout, 2005). The plan for augmentation functions must specify a set of primitives to be used in augmentation events and a set of rules describing the conditions under which augmentation events occur.[14] The augmentation plan should provide for a staged diminishment of augmentation that encourages increasing learner reliance on personal decision-making, judgment, and initiative.[15]

Principle: Dramatic Context

Instructional problems can be posed within the context of hypothetical situations occurring within simulated, fictional, or imaginary performance settings. Scenarios using narrative techniques can create an imaginary world that involves symbolic personas in representative dramatic roles that have goals and encounter and overcome obstacles to reach them (Schank & Berman, 2002). These can be completely realistic or completely imaginary (Barab, Thomas, Dodge, Carteaux, & Tuzun, 2005; CTGV, 1992; Metcalf-Jackson, Krajcik, & Soloway, 2000).

---

14. *Editors' note: This defines a set of situationalities for selecting the different types of augmentations (methods). However, the level of precision is such that specific situationalities for each augmentation are not provided.*
15. *Editors' note: These last two sentences provide some design theory (primarily instructional-event theory), but they are very imprecise and leave much room for further contributions to a common knowledge base.*

The use of a scenario or story setting for the problem implies the need to design the problem solving environment, which may include something as uncomplicated as a simple interface or as complex as a world made up of connected information-providing locations which the learner navigates to obtain critical information (Gibbons et al., 1997). The latter implies the need for the designer to create an integrated information and world-location structure.

Principle: Problem Information Structure

The *information structure* for an individual learning problem includes the set of data or facts required to pose it (the problem statement) and solve it (the solving resources). The information includes data to be used by the model specifying the problem environment, initial problem states, desired terminal states, and important intermediate solution states. The information structure is necessary to stage a problem, judge solutions, and provide augmentations like coaching and feedback. This information can be captured in several forms: as a database, a set of production (if…then) rules, or as a computable mathematical model. It is significant that the activities of problem-based learning "tutors" in dispensing problem information must be clearly specified, as well as the information itself, for the instructional method to work as expected (Barrows, 1988).

3. Control Function: Provide User Controls

The control function of a simulation design describes the means by which a learner can convey messages that influence the unfolding of the content, strategy, or other dynamic elements of the experience. The design of control systems can be challenging because learner actions take place within a dynamic context and must make use of a history of previous information and control exchanges.

Principle: Controls for Each Main Function of the Design

Control systems consist of sets of special-purpose controls that serve needs related to several simulation functions: (1) controls that allow the learner to act upon the model; (2) controls that adjust patterns of augmentation; (3) controls that adjust the representation of the model or the viewpoint from which the learner can observe the model; and (4) controls over personal data reporting for monitoring outcomes, performance, progress, trends, history, and scheduling. Goals for simulation and microworld control design include: maintaining simplicity, keeping controls transparent, determining priorities among controls, and planning conditions under which controls may be made available or withheld.

Regarding controls that act upon the model (#1 above), Crawford (2003) proposes that "the first rule of all interactivity design is to start with the verbs" (p. 62), rather than the more common approach of "designing the interface."

"During this process you are specifying what the user does, *not* what the screen looks like or what the program will do or how it will work" (p. 94, emphasis in the original). The design of multiuser control systems adds complexity, but it is also approachable using Crawford's linguistic metaphor. New actuation devices make available new terms in the language of controls, including body-part movement, gesturing, sounds, balance displacement, spoken words, whole-body displacement (locomotion), eye movement, facial expression, panel touch, and others (see Moggridge, 2007). These devices supply "verbs" with which a learner can communicate control to the model.

Augmentation controls (no. 2) are for expressing the strategic decisions the designer makes accessible to the learner. In microworld design, this includes controls that modify levels of support or request help. In the design of microworlds the design of control systems is especially important because learners are asked to construct models and operate them to conduct experiments. Designing an efficient and intuitive control set for model construction and operation represents an additional challenge. In terms of strategy, Crawford's nouns are augmentation elements that can be acted upon and his verbs express actions that can be applied to them.

Controls over representation (no. 3) must allow the learner to select elements of the representation to be visible or hidden and must allow the learner to select a vantage point for viewing the environment and its contents. They must also allow the learner to navigate the visible and virtual world created by the model, its augmentations, and all of the data-containing locations associated with them. Representations of models must change state as the variable values of the models themselves change. Moreover, models can be viewed from different perspectives or in different manifestation modes (schematic, realistic, surface, inner workings, etc.). Crawford's nouns and verbs in this instance are representational elements or effects that can be operated upon and operations that can be applied to them.

Finally, the designer must make information available that the learner can use in making decisions. The data reporting function can give the learner much information about progress, status, and scheduling. Data reporting controls (no. 4) must be designed that give the learner access to this information. In this case, Crawford's nouns and verbs consist of data elements and operations upon them.

4. Messaging Function: Generate Message Units

Message structures are the basic building blocks of simulation-to-learner communication. An interactive conversation with a model takes place at the level of numerous individual messages that pass between the learner and the simulation. Message structures are also the vehicle by which other functions of the simulation—the augmentations, the controls, and the data management—express themselves to the learner. Message structure is an important design feature regardless of what medium is used. A designer should define the message units that are used by *live* instructors and tutors during the conversational process (Barrows, 1998).

The messaging language created by the designer is the complement of the control language described earlier. Together they define the quality of the inbound (through controls) and outbound (through messages) communications that can take place. They constitute the heart—invisible and abstract—of the design of a learning interface.

Principle: Message Elements

Messaging can be implemented using the fully adaptive conversational capabilities of a human tutor or can be simplified and routinized for implementation on a computer. Computerizing messaging constrains a design according to Fox (1993), and adjustments like the following may be required:

- Interruptions by the learner should be possible
- Thing reference (pointing) and object sharing should be more formalized
- Silences should be flagged with intent
- Communication of backchannel cues (emotional states, body language, attitude) should be facilitated
- Multiple sequential messages should be possible from the same speaker without a break (e.g., musings "aloud")
- Short delays in correction might be deliberately used to signal to the student the need to think and respond again
- Ways should be found to make the learner's process actions (thinking) known to the tutor.

All of these have the effect of replacing in technology-based tutoring some of the subtle cues that are lost from human-human tutoring.

Principle: Approaches for Structuring Messages

Several theorists and researchers have described systems for: (1) structuring conversational instruction or (2) analyzing the message structure of instructional conversations (for instance, see Horn, 1997; Merrill, 1994; Sawyer, 2006; Simon & Boyer, 1974; Smith & Meux, 1970).[16]

Principle: Execution-Time Construction of Messages

Messages can be constructed from a set of primitives at the time of instruction, in response to a momentary strategic need. For example, most designers provide

---

16. *Editors' note: These different approaches should be accompanied by situationalities that indicate when each should be used.*

Table 9.1 Message Elements that might be Included in a Typical Feedback Message Following a Learner Action

Message element	Message intent
\<right/wrong notification>	That was not an appropriate choice at this point.
\<the learner's response>	You increased the temperature to \<value>.
\<expected answer>	You should have decreased the temperature or increased the pressure in the deposition chamber.
\<why correct/expected>	This would lower condensation index below \<value> and initiate deposition.
\<correct principle>	Deposition cannot take place when the condensation index falls in the area above the Critical Value line shown in red on the Condensation Index chart.

some type of feedback during instruction to follow learner responses: either to confirm or to correct. These messages are usually a composite of smaller message elements like those shown in Table 9.1. A designer's personal design philosophy might choose a different set of message elements and a different way of combining them, but the principle of message generativity would still apply. Therefore, the example in Table 9.1 shows only one of many possible combinations.

Drake, Mills, Lawless, Curry, and Merrill (1998) use this method to generate all of the necessary presentation-, demonstration-, and practice-related messages for a simulation that teaches the operation of a canal lock system. One advantage of message generation is that the composition rule can be made context-sensitive, so that messages can strategically increase or decrease the degree of support given. This is a requirement for truly adaptive instruction.

5. Representation Function: Generate and Assemble Representation Elements

New technologies for computer-generated representation are developing rapidly. One of the forces behind this rapid advance has been the need for better visualization systems for simulations. Today the creation of two- and three-dimensional worlds through representation is an important area of innovation.

The representation function of a simulation design is the most visible and tangible. Its design involves all sensory elements of the simulation experience— sights, sounds, tactile sensations, and kinesthetic sensations. The representation function design describes all sensory experiences that will be staged and how they will be integrated and synchronized. All of the structures described to this point for content, strategy, controls, and messages are abstractions and become visible only through representation design. Therefore, representation is the bridge that links abstract design elements with specific symbolic media elements.

The representation of a simulation can be dynamic and can be constantly changing. Simulation representations are driven by and reflect current model, strategy, control, and messaging function states. Microworld designers must provide the visual and other sensory elements of an interesting and intuitive model-building work space as well as a model-running work space.

The representation function is driven by messages. It maps message elements to representation elements. Computer-based simulation representations can be created in two main ways: (1) from static, premade representation elements drawn together to satisfy a momentary need; or (2) through data-generated graphical forms whose position and motion are computed. Some simulations combine these methods.

Modularity of the representation functions can allow the style of representations to be changed without disturbing the workings of other functions. Zen Garden (Mezzoblue.com) for instance, gives an example of how the innovation of cascading style sheets (CSS) allows identical message elements to be given multiple, diverse visual surfaces. CSS is a tool for modularizing some of the functions of representation.

Principle: The Representation Refresh Cycle

The most important task of representation in a simulation is to make the operations of an otherwise invisible model visible (Collins et al., 1989; Gibbons, 2001). The representation of model states must change according to the cycles of the model.

Principle: View Perspectives and Styles

A model can be viewed from different vantage points. Moreover, it can be viewed in different stylized forms. Designers should determine whether there is advantage in giving the learner alternative viewing positions in real or metaphorical space. Adequate model representation may also require multiple styles, such as schematic, conceptual, or realistic representations. Views of a cause–effect model being operated upon may include a realistic view of controls and a symbolic view of the internal effects of control manipulations.

Principle: Message-to-Representation Mapping Rules

Every message that can be formed must be given representation. In some cases, messages and representations are mapped one-to-one, meaning that for a single message element there is a single stored or generated representation. In some cases, however, a designer may specify that a single message be given multiple representations simultaneously, or that multiple messages be combined for representation by a single representation element. For example, single message unit (<correct answer>) giving feedback following a learner's response, may map to multiple simultaneous representation elements: the learner's response turns green, a success tone is heard, a text message appears. The value of thinking in terms of message units and representation elements separately becomes clear in this case: a single rule can be expressed to describe the relation between message units and representation elements. Similarly, a rule can be expressed that causes a particular combination of message units to trigger a single representation.

Principle: Display Assembly and Coordination Rules

The coordination of a simulation display involves synchronization. Mayer (2001) has described the importance of timing in the appearance of media events related to the same message unit. It is significant that some of the most popular development software is based on a timeline structure for the coordination of media representations. Future tool versions may allow the designer to coordinate media events with message units, strategic events, and model events as well. Rules for the execution of the continuously changing displays must also be designed.

Principle: Rules for Manipulating Time and Space

Instructional simulations telescope time and space; they speed up processes that are slow and retard processes that are fast so that they can be observed. Simulations are time machines that interleave learner actions with model actions in warped time. Repeated practice under simulated conditions can concentrate greater amounts of practice into instructional time. Altered time can contribute to the efficiency of learning, but in order to prepare learner performances for the real world, timing must eventually tend toward real-world speeds as the learner's ability permits.

Space is likewise manipulated by simulations. Virtually all simulations create action spaces larger than the simulation itself requires. Simulations compress space by allowing learners to zoom (in and out) and navigate imaginary spaces. A simulation designer should thoughtfully address maximization of time and space.

Principle: Rules for Representation Trace

A simulation's effectiveness depends in part on the ability of the learner to detect changes in represented model states in response to actions on the model. However, information of even greater value lies in visual vectors that we will call *traces* that represent *trends* of change. Using a representation trace, a learner can pose and answer questions using the information history the trace provides. A trace preserves a record of interactions among input variable settings, internal model forces, and output variables.

A simulation designer must consider how to choose traces to make visible, how to allow the learner to construct traces, how to facilitate navigation through the details of a trace, how to present multiple traces in a way that correlation and comparison are facilitated, how to highlight important elements of traces, and how to help students to see patterns within traces and interpret them. Examples of trace are provided by Edward Tufte (1997), Wurman (1997) and Edgerton (MIT-Libraries, n.d.).

6. Media-Logic Function: Execute Representations and Computations

The media-logic function executes representations and carries out the logical operations that allow simulation events to occur. This can also include calculations and data gathering. Not all simulations are computer-based, but all simulations require that the media-logic functions be carried out. The media-logic function of a design enacts the conceptual structures from all of the other functional areas of the design, giving them dynamism and synchronizing their operations. According to Gibbons et al. (2001), "this is the place where the designer's abstract instructional constructs and concrete logic constructs [of] the development tool come together."

The media-logic design must incorporate: (1) instructions for executing the models; (2) instructions for coordinated execution of the augmentations; (3) instructions for accepting learner responses and control actions; (4) instructions for forming messages; (5) instructions for providing representations to the learner; and (6) instructions for collecting, storing, processing, and displaying personal data the learner can use in decision making about learning.

Media-logic for human-based simulations can be challenging, because human tutors require guidelines that are robust to individual differences while preserving the discipline of the design. Computer-based designers must take into account available hardware and software infrastructure; distribution methods; location of processing; processing and networking loads; facilities for delivery; availability of development skills, tools, and processes; availability of expertise in subject-matter; life cycle software plans; and security issues.

Modularization of the media-logic function is an important consideration for long-term maintainability of a simulation. Baldwin and Clark (2000) describe how modularization of computer operating system software designs by IBM set the stage for a revolution in the economics of both computers and software. It has been proposed that the monolithic nature of earlier systems has been an obstacle to integration with other advanced simulation-centered tutoring components. A modular architecture for simulation design can provide advantages from component reuse, improved maintainability, rapid adaptation, and support for a range of tutorial applications as shown by Munro, Surmon, and Pizzini (2006).

7. Data Management Function: Manage Data Resulting from Interactions

The data management function of an instructional simulation supports and makes possible its adaptivity to individual learner actions and requests. It differs from the existing concept of computer-managed instruction (CMI) by adding functions that incorporate recent actions by the learner into decision making in which the learner participates. The data management function supports the learner's negotiation of instructional event sequences; it records large amounts of data at a (potentially) high degree of granularity, it stores the data, analyzes it, interprets it, and provides reports to the learner that can be used to monitor progress and make instructional decisions.

In the principle statements below, the wording suggests that the data collection and analysis functions are assumed to be computerized. However, the principles pertain to noncomputerized simulations as well.

Principle: Sampling Points and Variables

Data collection points are defined in terms of the computational cycle of the models, which will be either event-driven or time-driven. At data collection points, values are recorded for specific variables and stored for analysis and interpretation—some immediate, and some later.

Principle: Interpretation Variables and Rules

Interpretation variables accumulate the values that result from interpretation of raw interaction data. They store interpreted values that are determined by rules and formulas supplied by the designer. Interpretation variables may themselves be subjected to further analysis aimed at reaching conclusions about the state of the learner's knowledge, the attitude of the learner, and the growing skill levels of the learner.

Principle: Data Gathering Framework

The designer must specify the timing of the analysis and interpretation cycle events. These events use interpretation variable values in making instructional decisions. The data gathering framework describes these operations and the storage and reporting of data to the learner for decision making as well.

Principle: Reporting

The simulation designer should specify the points at which information is made available to the learner. These points should at least coincide with decision making points at which the learner is given choices. Learner progress and performance data may be shown to take advantage of the opportunity to teach the learner how to use data reports in making learning decisions.

Conclusion

Simulations are particularly powerful and effective because they enhance student vigilance and scanning skills, enhance student integration of skills in varied performance contexts, adjust to varied learning rates through dynamic performance scopes, and help learners see patterns over time in dynamic systems. We have described a number of specific principles which can guide design, and while space limitations have kept us from including *all* of the possible guidance principles, we believe that this chapter helps identify the current state of knowledge for a common knowledge base for the design of instructional simulations.

References

Alessi, S. M., & Trollip, S. R. (1991). *Multimedia for learning* (3rd ed.). Boston, MA: Allyn & Bacon.

Atkinson, R. C., & Wilson, H. A. (Eds.). (1969). *Computer-assisted instruction: A book of readings.* New York: Academic.

Baldwin, C. Y., & Clark, K. B. (2000). *Design rules: Vol. 1. The power of modularity.* Cambridge, MA: MIT Press.

Barab, S., Thomas, M., Dodge, T., Carteaux, R., & Tuzun, H. (2005). Making learning fun: Quest Atlantis, a game without guns. *Educational Technology Research and Development, 53*(1), 86–107.

Barrows, H. S. (1988). *The tutorial process* (Rev. ed.). Springfield: Southern Illinois University School of Medicine.

Barrows, H. S. (1998). The essentials of problem-based learning. *Journal of Dental Education, 62*(9), 630–633.

Barrows, H. S., & Tamblyn, R. M. (1980). *Problem-based learning: An approach to medical education.* New York: Springer.

Bransford, J. D., Brown, A. L., & Cocking, R. R. (Eds.). (2000). *How people learn: Brain, mind, experience, and school* (Rev. ed.). Washington, D.C.: National Academy Press.

Brown, A. L., & Palincsar, A. S. (1989). Guided, cooperative learning and individual knowledge acquisition. In L. Resnick (Ed.), *Knowing, learning, and instruction: Essays in honor of Robert Glaser.* Hillsdale, NJ: Erlbaum.

Bunderson, C. V., Gibbons, A. S., Olsen, J. B., & Kearsley, G. P. (1981). Work models: Beyond instructional objectives. *Instructional Science, 10*, 205–215.

Burton, R. R., Brown, J. S., & Fischer, G. (1984). Skiing as a model of instruction. In B. Rogoff & J. Lave (Eds.), *Everyday cognition: Its development in social context.* Cambridge, MA: Harvard University Press.

CTGV. (1992). The Jasper experiment: An exploration of issues in learning and instructional design. *Educational Technology Research and Development, 40*(1), 5–34.

Cole, M., Engestrom, Y., & Vasquez, O. (1997). *Mind, culture, activity: The seminal papers from the Laboratory of Comparative Human Cognition.* Cambridge, UK: Cambridge University Press.

Colella, V., Klopfer, E., & Resnick, M. (2001). *Adventures in modeling: Exploring complex, dynamic systems with StarLogo.* New York: Teachers College Press.

Collins, A., Brown, J. S., & Newman, S. E. (1989). Cognitive apprenticeship: Teaching the crafts of reading, writing, and mathematics. In L. Resnick (Ed.), *Knowing, learning, and instruction: Essays in honor of Robert Glaser.* Hillsdale, NJ: Erlbaum.

Crawford, C. (2003). *The art of interactive design.* San Francisco: No Starch.

de Jong, T., & van Joolingen, W. R. (1998). Scientific discovery learning with computer simulations of conceptual domains. *Review of Educational Research, 68*(3), 179–201.

Dede, C. (2004). *Emerging technologies that enable distributed-learning communities.* Paper presented as the Keynote speech to the Conference of the Association for Educational Communications and Technology.

Drake, L., Mills, R., Lawless, K., Curry, J., & Merrill, M. D. (1998). *The role of explanations in learning environments.* Paper presented at the Annual Meeting of the American Educational Research Association, San Diego.

Elen, J., & Clarebout, G. (2005). Support in learning environments: Touching the limits of instructional design. *Educational Technology*, 45(5), 44–47.

Fox, B. A. (1993). *The human tutorial dialogue project: Issues in the design of instructional systems.* Hillsdale, NJ: Erlbaum.

Gibbons, A. (2001). Model-centered instruction. *Journal of Structural Learning and Intelligent Systems*, 14(4), 511–540.

Gibbons, A. S., Fairweather, P. G., Anderson, T., & Merrill, M. D. (1997). Simulation and computer-based instruction: A future view. In C. R. Dills & A. J. Romiszowski (Eds.), *Instructional development paradigms* (pp. 769–805). Englewood Cliffs, NJ: Educational Technology.

Gibbons, A. S., Lawless, K. A., Anderson, T. A., & Duffin, J. R. (2001). The web and model-centered instruction. In B. R. Khan (Ed.), *Web-based training*. Englewood Cliffs, NJ: Educational Technology.

Gibbons, A., Nelson, J., & Richards, R. (2000a). The nature and origin of instructional objects. In D. Wiley (Ed.), *The instructional use of learning objects*. Bloomington, IN: Association for Educational Communications and Technology.

Gibbons, A. S., Nelson, J., & Richards, R. (2000b). *Model-centered analysis process (MCAP): A pre-design analysis methodology* (White Paper). Idaho Falls, ID: Center for Human-Systems Simulation, Idaho National Engineering and Environmental Laboratory (DOE).

Gibbons, A. S., Nelson, J., & Richards, R. (2000c). *Theoretical and practical requirements for a system of pre-design analysis: State of the art of pre-design analysis* (White Paper). Idaho Falls, ID: Center for Human-Systems Simulation, Idaho National Engineering and Environmental Laboratory (DOE).

Gredler, M. E. (2004). Games and simulations and their relation to learning. In D. H. Jonassen (Ed.), *Handbook of research on educational communications and technology* (2nd ed., pp. 571–583). Mahwah, NJ: Erlbaum.

Horn, R. E. (1997). Structured writing as a paradigm. In C. R. Dills, A. Romiszowski, & A. J. (Ed.), *Instructional development paradigms*. Englewood Cliffs, NJ: Educational Technology.

Johnson, W. L., Rickel, J. W., & Lester, J. C. (2000). Animated pedagogical agents: Face-to-face interaction in interactive learning environments. *International Journal of Artificial Intelligence in Education, 11*, 47–78.

Kafai, Y. B. (2006). Constructionism. In R. K. Sawyer (Ed.), *Cambridge handbook of the learning sciences* (pp. 35–46). Cambridge, UK: Cambridge University Press.

Lathan, C. E., Tracey, M. R., Sebrechts, M. M., Clawson, D. M., & Higgins, G. A. (2002). Using virtual environments as training simulators: Measuring transfer. In K. M. Stanney (Ed.), *Handbook of virtual environments: Design, implementation, and applications* (pp. 403–414). Mahwah, NJ: Erlbaum.

Lave, J., & Wenger, E. (1991). *Situated learning: Legitimate peripheral practice*. Cambridge, UK: Cambridge University Press.

Lehrer, R., & Schauble, L. (2006). Cultivating model-based reasoning in science education. In R. K. Sawyer (Ed.), *The Cambridge handbook of the learning sciences*. Cambridge, UK: Cambridge University Press.

Lesgold, A. (1999, July, 1999). *Intelligent learning environments for technical training: Lessons learned.* Paper presented at the Advanced Training Technologies and Learning Environments, Langley Research Center, Hampton, VA.

Mayer, R. E. (2001). *Multimedia learning*. Cambridge, UK: Cambridge University Press.

McBride, R. (2005). *Toward a domain theory of fluent oral reading with expression*. Provo, UT: Brigham Young University.

Merrill, M. D. (1994). The descriptive component display theory. In M. D. Merrill & D. G. Twitchell (Eds.), *Instructional design theory*. Englewood Cliffs, NJ: Educational Technology.

Metcalf-Jackson, S., Krajcik, J. S., & Soloway, E. (2000). Model-It: A design retrospective. In M. Jacobson & R. B. Kozma (Eds.), *Innovations in science and mathematics education: Advanced designs for technologies and learning*. Mahwah, NJ: Erlbaum.

Mezzoblue.com. (2006, December 12). Zen garden. Retrieved from http://www.mezzoblue.com/zengarden/alldesigns/

Milrad, M., Spector, J. M., & Davidsen, P. I. (2002). Model facilitated learning. In S. Naidu (Ed.), *Learning and teaching with technology: Principles and practices*. London: Kogan Page.

MIT-Libraries. (n.d.). Harold Eugene Edgerton, 1903–1990: Papers, 1889–1990; Manuscript Collection—MC 25. from http://libraries.mit.edu/archives/collections-mc/mc25/index.html#collection

Moggridge, B. (2007). *Designing interactions*. Cambridge, MA: MIT Press.

Munro, A., Breaux, R., Paltrey, J., & Sheldon, B. (2002). Cognitive aspects of virtual environment design. In K. M. Stanney (Ed.), *Handbook of virtual environments* (pp. 415–434). Mahwah, NJ: Erlbaum.

Munro, A., Surmon, D. & Pizzini, Q. (2006). Teaching procedural knowledge in distance learning environments. In R. Perez & H. O'Neal (Eds.), *Web-based learning: Theory, research, and practice.* Mahwah, NJ: Erlbaum.

Papert, S. (1993). *Mindstorms: Children, computers, and powerful ideas* (2nd ed.). New York: Basic.

Reigeluth, C. M. (1999). The elaboration theory: Guidance for scope and sequence decisions. In C. M. Reigeluth (Ed.), *Instructional-design theories and models: Vol. 2. A new paradigm of instructional theory* . Mahwah, NJ: Erlbaum.

Reigeluth, C. M., & Schwartz, E. (1989). An instructional theory for the design of computer-based simulations. *Journal of Computer-Based Instruction, 16*(1), 1–10.

Resnick, M. (1997). *Turtles, termites, and traffic jams: Explorations in massively parallel microworlds.* Cambridge, MA: MIT Press.

Rieber, L. P. (1996). Seriously considering play: Designing interactive learning environments based on the blending of microworlds, simulations. and games. *Educational Technology Research and Development, 44*(2), 43–58.

Rieber, L. P. (2004). Microworlds. In D. H. Jonassen (Ed.), *Handbook of research for educational communications and technology* (2nd ed., pp. 583–603). Mahwah, NJ: Erlbaum.

Sawyer, R. K. (2006). Analyzing collaborative discourse. In R. K. Sawyer (Ed.), *The Cambridge handbook of the learning sciences.* Cambridge, UK: Cambridge University Press.

Schank, R. C., & Berman, T. R. (2002). The pervasive role of stories in knowledge and action. In M. C. Green, J. J. Strange, & T. C. Brock (Eds.), *Narrative impact: Social and cognitive foundations.* Mahwah, NJ: Erlbaum.

Schauble, L., & Glaser, R. (1996). *Innovations in learning: New environments for education.* Mahwah, NJ: Erlbaum.

Simon, A., & Boyer, E. G. (1974). *Mirrors for behavior III: An anthology of observation instruments.* Wyncote, PA: Communication Materials Center in Cooperation with Humanizing Learning Program, Research for Better Schools.

Smith, B. O., & Meux, M. O. (1970). *A study of the logic of teaching.* Urbana: University of Illinois Press.

Strong-Krause, D. (2001). English as a second language speaking ability: A study in domain theory development. *Dissertation Abstracts International,* DAI-A 61/12, 4746.

Tufte, E. R. (1997). *Visual explanations: Images, quantities, evidence, and narrative.* Cheshire, CT: Graphics.

van Merrienboer, J. (1997). *Training complex cognitive skills: A four-component instructional design model for technical training.* Englewood Cliffs, NJ: Educational Technology Publications.

Vygotsky, L. S. (1978). *Mind and society: The development of higher mental processes.* Cambridge, MA: Harvard University Press.

White, B. Y., & Frederiksen, J. (1990). Causal model progressions as a foundation for intelligent learning environments. *Artificial Intelligence, 24,* 99–157.

White, B. Y., & Frederiksen, J. (1998). Inquiry, modeling, and metacognition: Making science accessible to all students. *Cognition and Instruction, 16*(1), 3–118.

Wurman, R. S. (1997). *Information architects.* New York: Graphis.

Unit 3
Theories for Different Outcomes
of Instruction

Unit Foreword

In unit 2 we reviewed a number of promising approaches to instruction. This unit addresses different kinds of learning outcomes that have usefulness for deciding what methods to use. It is important to understand that while these different learning outcomes have distinct identities, they are not wholly separate. They can overlap or be used in the service of one another in similar fashion to approaches.

We distinguish this orientation from Bloom's traditional learning outcomes distinctions of affective, psychomotor, and cognitive because we understand most learning outcomes, not just skills, to include all three components, and there is powerful evidence that all learning has a significant affective component (see chapter 12). While each learning outcome has elements of all three of Bloom's domains, each also has its own identity, which calls for a different galaxy of instructional methods.

Chapter 10 addresses skills learning, which was developed, historically, very early. Alex Romiszowski defines skills instruction as the ability to perform a task at a given level of mastery. He clearly differentiates skill from knowledge, saying that knowledge is a go-no go quantity, whereas skills develop gradually with experience. Among the most important messages communicated in this chapter is the notion that skilled performance requires both knowledge and skill. Learning to perform a skill requires very different methods from other kinds of learning, such as developing understandings or emotional development. Skills instruction requires generalizing, and this, in turn, requires a variety of demonstrations and practice in order to generalize sufficiently to diverse situations. Thus, the basic stages in skills learning are first, to acquire knowledge of what should be done; second, to execute the actions; third, to transfer control from the eyes to other senses; fourth, to automate the skill; and finally, to generalize the skill. This leads to specific steps in skills instruction, which: (1) impart basic knowledge, (2) impart basic skill, and (3) develop proficiency. We feel that skills instruction is necessary to include here because skills are essential for almost all tasks. Intellectual skills, metacognitive skills, and physical skills are essential building blocks for reading, writing, and arithmetic. Skills are necessary for higher-order thinking and a variety of job performances. Skills are ultimately what enable us to do almost all things, and as such are among the most important kinds of learning

In chapter 11 Stone Wiske and Brian Beatty distinguish learning for understanding as a performance capability, not merely a possession of some knowledge (our more colloquial idea of understanding). Learning for Understanding is made up of five elements: generative curriculum topics, explicit understanding goals, a rich sequence of performances of understanding, ongoing assessment, and collaborative, reflective communities. We see understanding as a critically important kind of learning that is receiving increased attention, as there is more and more need for deep understandings in the information age, a period of increasing complexity and dynamism. Because learners are encouraged to apply their learning to real situations in creative ways, this outcome is particularly well-suited to the information age. We also agree with Wiske and Beatty that recent advances in information technologies are making the teaching for understanding framework more realistic than it has been in recent past.

In chapter 12, emotional development is defined by Barbara Bichelmeyer, James Marken, Tamara Harris, Melanie Misanchuk, and Emily Hixon as a subtopic of the broader affective domain of learning that is fundamental to all affective learning. We agree with Daniel Goleman's primary argument that emotional intelligence is more important to success in life than is intellectual intelligence. This kind of learning is crucial for addressing social problems such as drug abuse, violence, teen pregnancy, and even international conflicts. In society, emotional development can serve our systems as well by helping us to understand what is fair, equitable, and socially just. There are five universal principles of instruction for emotional intelligence: use stories, teach the language of emotion, model the skills of emotional intelligence, take time to deal with emotions, and provide active and integrated experience to foster emotional competence.

In chapter 13, theme-based instruction is defined by Brian Beatty as thematically unified learning across various domains of learning. We believe that integrated learning replicates real life in which domains are indeed integrated and present themselves as complex mixtures of many domains often centered on a particular theme. Thus, we agree with Beatty that theme-based instruction is a more natural way of learning and is certainly reflective of more natural ways of performing. Skills, understandings, and emotional development are all bundled together in real-life learning; and math, science, English, history, literature, and social studies are all relevant to real-world problems or situations. The whole is more than the sum of its parts and therefore learning each domain individually is not sufficient. Learners also need to understand the relationships between domains, such as math and science. There are five universal principles of thematic instruction: use a unifying theme, focus instruction on primary learning goals, use a variety of instructional activities, provide useful instructional resources, and evaluate achievement through authentic assessment. In the real world things are integrated and thus, they should be taught that way. Beatty also makes the point that theme-based instruction improves learning and is widespread, with a variety of examples at all levels of education.

We have not included psychomotor or physical skills as a separate learning outcome because we found that it has a tremendous amount of overlap with cognitive skills, and therefore there is a great deal of overlap in the methods as well. There certainly are other kinds of learning outcomes that we have not addressed here, such as memorization. Due to space limitations, again, we were unable to include the full variety of learning outcomes that exist, but we do encourage other theorists and researchers to contribute to a common knowledge base for these other outcomes as well.

—CMR & ACC

10
Fostering Skill Development Outcomes

ALEXANDER ROMISZOWSKI

Syracuse University and TTS Global Consulting

Alexander Romiszowski, PhD, currently divides his time between the United States where he teaches in the instructional design and development program at Syracuse University, and Brazil, where as director and chief consultant of TTS Global Consulting, he undertakes a variety of course development, curriculum development, and organizational development projects in both the developed and developing world. Recent projects have included the design and implementation of distance learning systems in Brazil and Mozambique, curriculum development in Azerbaijan, teacher professional development in East Timor, and ICT integration into schools in Romania. Among his many award winning publications are the "trilogy": *Designing Instructional Systems, Producing Instructional Systems*, and *Developing Auto-Instructional Materials*; the chapter on "Message Design for Psychomotor Task Instruction" in Fleming and Levie's *Instructional Message Design*, and *Instructional Development Paradigms*, coedited with Charles Dills.

EDITORS' FOREWORD

Preconditions (when to use the theory)

Content
- All kinds of skills: reproductive skills, productive skills, abilities, competencies

Learners
- All learners, including all k-12, corporate, higher education and others.

Learning environments
- All environments, as long as there is appropriate space and equipment for practicing skills

Instructional development constraints
- All levels of resource availability

Values (opinions about what is important)

about ends (learning goals)
- It is important to ensure that all parts of the skills-cycle have been learned (receive signal, perceive and interpret, decide on action, take action).

about priorities (criteria for successful instruction)
- Effectiveness and efficiency are typically valued most for this kind of instruction, but increasingly appeal is recognized as important.

about means (instructional methods)
- Decisions about methods should be made based on what works (research), rather than on philosophy (ideology).

about power (to make decisions about the previous three)
- The teacher should be in control.

Universal Methods

1. Stages of development of skill (descriptive model of learning)
   a. Acquire knowledge of what should be done
   b. Execute actions step-by-step
   c. Transfer control from eyes to other senses
   d. Automatize the skill
   e. Generalize the skill
2. Basic steps in instructional strategy for skills development (design theory of instruction)
   a. Impart basic knowledge content
   b. Impart basic skill
   c. Develop proficiency

Situational Principles

for imparting essential information
- If the task is simple, with limited background knowledge, demonstrate and explain as illustrated narrative.

- *If the task is simple, with little or no new knowledge, just demonstrate it.*
- *If the task is complex with relationships among components and a lot of new knowledge but little new skill, use exploratory activity with outline notes or a physical model.*
- *If the task is simple and involves a sequence of consecutive steps, allow the student to observe before attempting to execute it.*
- *If the objective is mastery of a procedure, demonstrate it from the viewpoint of the performer.*

for *providing for practice*
- *If the objective is to learn integrated and coordinated activities, use the "whole task" method.*
- *If the task is a sequence of independent actions, use the "progressive parts" method.*
- *If prerequisite subskills are initially below "minimum threshold levels," develop them prior to practice of the whole task.*
- *For highly coordinated and "productive" tasks, provide continuous practice.*
- *For repetitive and high-speed "reproductive" tasks, use spaced practice.*
- *If the task involves heuristically based productive skills, use mental rehearsal strategies and reflection-in-action.*
- *If task is a sequential procedure that mainly involves reproductive skills, supply verbal coding, or cueing, with model demonstration.*
- *For high-speed tasks, use forced pacing for more rapid mastery.*

for *giving feedback*
- *If the objective is to develop simple sensorimotor skills, use "learning feedback" (results information), not "action feedback" (control information).*
- *If the objective is to develop complex skills, feedback should include information about the process as well as the product.*
- *When teaching "productive" skills, supply knowledge of performance through a process of "debriefing" or "reflection-in-action."*

for *promoting transfer*
- *If the task is a productive skill, vary practice.*
- *If the task is reproductive, no need for variety in practice.*
- *When teaching for transfer, practice should define or refine motor concepts and a motor schema in the learner's mind.*
- *If the task is reproductive, use overlearning.*
- *If the task is productive, use debriefing to promote reflection-in/on-action.*

—CMR & ACC

FOSTERING SKILL DEVELOPMENT OUTCOMES

The aim of this chapter is to identify a common knowledge base for the development of skills—not only physical skills as in sports and manual tasks, but any and all types of skills as practiced in any context.

Some Basic Concepts and Definitions

As a first step toward defining the scope and focus of this chapter, let us review some definitions of the terms that we shall be using. These include basic terms such as *knowledge, skill, performance*, and *competence* The intention is not to invent or refine a particular set of personal definitions, but to seek some form of consensus on how the terminology tends to be used in our field, and also to identify critical differences between our use of certain key terms and how they are used in other fields.

Knowledge is most commonly defined as information of which a person, organization, or other entity is aware.

Skill is typically defined as the capacity to perform a given type of task or activity with a given degree of effectiveness, efficiency, speed, or other measure of quantity or quality. Skills are typically classified according to the parts of the executing organism that are predominantly involved in the execution and management of performance: *intellectual or cognitive* skills involve the use and management of the mind; *motor, sensorimotor, or psychomotor* skills involve the use and management of the body; *personal*, also called *reactive* skills, such as self-expression, self-assertion, self-control, or self-discipline, involve the use and management of emotions; and *interactive* or *interpersonal* skills involve the management of relationships and interactions between oneself and others. Although this classification is intuitively elegant and apparently based on a logical analysis of the performer, it is not all that clear-cut. For example, in a *motor skill* there is always a greater or lesser amount of intellectual (*cognitive*) activity involved, and the performance of motor skills, especially in contexts such as sports, is also dependent on the performer's emotional state, and therefore some *personal* self-management skills may be essential to competent performance.

One approach to the classification of skills is in terms of their complexity or sophistication. A useful distinction may be made between:

- *Reproductive skills*—activities that are repetitive and largely automatic, involving the reproduction of the same standard procedure every time they are practiced—these may be considered as the selection and application of an appropriate procedure, or algorithm, for the task in hand;
- *Productive skills*—activities that involve the planning of a procedure appropriate to the specific situation, through the application of theory, general principles, and creativity—the underlying knowledge is heuristic rather than algorithmic.

A given skilled activity may be placed at some point on the reproductive–productive scale according to the amount of cognitive processing that is required in order to plan how best to act. In this context, the word *act* may refer to physical, intellectual, personal, or interpersonal activity. Thus, any skilled activity, whatever its category, may be classified on this scale—the more deep and reflective the *thinking* that is required, the more productive is the skill.

Ability is defined in many different ways: the quality of a person being able to perform a given task; the quality that permits or facilitates achievement or accomplishment; possession of the qualities (especially mental qualities) required to do something or get something done; a talent, such as manual dexterity, visual or spatial acuity, or conceptual thinking; a capacity to perform a physical or mental function; or that which provides the means of performing tasks in a learning, work, or everyday situation. *Ability* seems to be a near-synonym for skill, but the term is often used to describe the basic capabilities, or subskills, that are involved in the execution of specific categories of skilled activity.

Competence (or competency), in the technical sense used in recent educational and corporate human development contexts, is often defined as the cluster of skills, abilities, habits, character traits, and knowledge a person must have in order to perform a specific job well. For instance, management competency includes the traits of systems thinking and emotional intelligence, and skills in influence and negotiation.

The Importance of Differentiating Knowledge and Skill in the ID Process

Given the basic definitions of knowledge and skill presented above, some important implications follow.

1. Knowledge is a "go–no go" quantity. Either you have it or you do not. Or, you may have it but are unable to access and use it due to the way it is currently organized. Partial knowledge is the result of having acquired and integrated some of the information elements or units, and not others. Learning of knowledge involves a combination of (a) the addition of new elements to the store and (b) the reorganizing of the existing, and the new, elements to form new knowledge structures. Furthermore, this learning process can often occur in a one-shot sort of manner—the sudden "eureka" phenomenon of, in an instant, reorganizing one's ideas and acquiring a precious insight. Two people exposed to the same information (experiences) may incorporate different subsets of information elements into their knowledge structures, and even if they acquire exactly the same elements, may integrate them in different ways with previously existing knowledge.[1]

2. Skill, on the other hand, is something that develops with experience and practice. The learning process for skills is seldom if ever one-shot. Repeated and

---

1. *Editors' note: Clearly this category includes both rote and meaningful knowledge as defined by Ausubel (see chapter 4).*

appropriate practice is required to achieve higher degrees of competence. Two people may possess the same skills, but developed to different degrees.

3. Skilled performance, of course, requires the use of knowledge. The more sophisticated and complex the skilled activity, the more it depends on the existence of an adequate knowledge base and its appropriate utilization. The existence of an adequate knowledge base usually implies prior learning, although in some cases the learning of the knowledge may conveniently accompany the practice of the skill (these are the cases where just-in-time-training actually works). In other cases, part of the knowledge-base may be external, as a performance support system to be combined with internally stored knowledge during skilled performance, without ever being formally learnt.

4. The appropriate utilization of the knowledge base (whether internal or external) may involve the use of other supplementary skills (e.g., critical thinking) and knowledge (e.g., problem-solving heuristics) that are necessary for the internal planning or control of the task. These *meta-skills* and *meta-knowledge* elements are internal and not directly observable, but their presence and power may be inferred from the competence with which the skilled activity is performed. Skilled activity can, and indeed should, also be self-evaluated by the performer. This process is called *reflection*. The more knowledge-dependent is the skill, the greater is the importance of reflection for its development.

A Skills-Analysis Approach to Instructional Design

Perhaps one of the weaknesses of much early research that focused principally on the acquisition of motor skills has been the concentration on simple movements or on sequences of simple repetitive steps. However, these are typically performed in real life as components of more complex activity. A distinction was made by Poulton (1957), in the context of sports training, between "closed" and "open" tasks, the former requiring a response to a stable environment (e.g., bowling), and the latter requiring continuous adjustment to an unpredictable, changing environment, as during a football game. Pioneering work in the 1960s at the Perkins factory in the United Kingdom identified the importance in the industrial context of "planning" or "strategy" skills (Wellens, 1974). These have also been referred to as "productive" skills in that they require the performer to produce a situation-specific response. We begin to see the trend toward the integration of instruction across the domains and also the blending, in practice, of ideas on instruction drawn from the apparently opposed camps of behavioral and cognitive psychology.

The Skills Schema

We may conceptualize a continuum of "reproductive to productive" skills as a basic model for the analysis of skills. The position of a given task on this continuum is of great importance to decisions about appropriate instructional

Domain or Category of Skilled Activity	Reproductive Skills	Productive Skills
	Knowledge content: applying standard procedures (algorithms)	Knowledge content: applying principles and strategies (heuristics)
COGNITIVE SKILLS • Decision making • Problem solving • Logical thinking, etc.	Applying a known procedure to a known category of "problem" (e.g., dividing numbers, writing a grammatically correct sentence).	Solving "new" problems or inventing a new procedure (e.g., proving a theorem, writing creatively).
PSYCHOMOTOR SKILLS • Physical action • Perceptual acuity, etc.	Repetitive or automated skills (e.g., typewriting, changing gear, running fast).	"Strategy" or "planning" skills (e.g., painting, defensive driving, playing football).
REACTIVE SKILLS • Dealing with oneself: (attitudes and feelings, habits and self-control)	Conditioned habits and attitudes: attend, respond (Krathwohl et al, 1964); approach and avoidance behaviors (Mager, 1968)	Personal control skills: developing a mental set or value system (Krathwohl, et al, 1964); self-actualization (Rogers, 1969).
INTERACTIVE SKILLS • Dealing with others: (social habits and skills)	Conditioned social responses (e.g., good manners, pleasant tone of voice, socialized behaviors).	Interpersonal control skills (e.g., leadership, supervision, persuasion, salesmanship).

The Skills Continuum

Figure 10.1 The Skills Schema (Romiszowski, 1981)

methods. Figure 10.1 presents a schema that combines a four-domain classification of skills with the reproductive-productive continuum. Whereas the domains may influence certain aspects of instructional decision making (e.g., media selection), the position of a task on the reproduction-production continuum influences instructional decisions in much more fundamental ways; for example, in deciding between expository and experiential instructional methods, or in the extent to which "deep processing" discussions are an essential part of the teaching method (Romiszowski, 1981).

Another point illustrated by Figure 10.1 is the potential for redefinition of the universe of learning objectives into more than the three traditionally accepted domains, adding the fourth domain related to the interpersonal skills area. This gives a model with four content related domains, which refers essentially to the skills of managing your thinking, managing your body, managing your emotions, and managing social situations and other people's reactions. However, we repeat that the position of a given skill on the productive to reproductive dimension may be of greater importance in terms of instructional issues than its position in one or another of the four domains.

The Skills Cycle

Many authors have observed that skilled activity involves a cycle of stages, commencing with the reception of information from the environment and leading to some action on the environment. Wheatcroft (1973), for example, describes the skilled activity cycle as commencing with the formation of an idea or purpose in the mind of the performer. This leads to:

- the reception of relevant information ("S" for *Signal, Stimulus,* or *Situation*);
- its correct perception and interpretation (a variety of skills are involved in this);
- a decision on the appropriate action to take (cognitive processing skills involved);
- and, finally, the action itself ("R" for *Response, Reply, Reaction,* or *Reflection*).[2]

This is then followed by reception of further new information on the results of the action, perception, decision, further action, and so on. By incorporating in this model the aforementioned need to have previously gained knowledge of the procedure to be executed, or of the principles to be used to generate an appropriate procedure, the skill cycle can be represented as shown in Figure 10.2 (Romiszowski, 1981).

This model enables one to distinguish between the automated, *reproductive* (reflexive, closed, etc.) skills and the *productive* (strategy, planning, open, etc.) skills. Indeed, three basic categories of skilled behavior are postulated:

- Totally reflexive and automated skills (like typing), in which the sensory information that is perceived directly triggers a physical action without any significant involvement of conscious cognitive processing. The performance "loop" for such skills may be described as "S - 1 - 4 - R" in Figure 10.2.
- Skills which depend on the recall of a possibly complex, but essentially algorithmic procedure and the execution of a series of linked actions in sequence. Many industrial and sports skills fall into this category. The performance "loop" for these skills can be described as "S - 1 - 2 - 4 - R."
- Skills which depend on the analysis of the incoming sensory information in order to formulate plans of action appropriate to the situation and, possibly, to evaluate alternative plans before deciding on the appropriate action. The performance loop for these skills is "S - 1 - 2 - 3 - 4 - R." Actually, this is a simplification, for a lot of internal looping may take place as well. For example, the internal loop (1 - 2 - 3 - 4) could be repeated, and the 2 - 3 - 2 - 3 - 2 cycle could occur.

The skills cycle draws our attention to the importance of considering such factors as perception, memory, intellectual skills, and cognitive strategies when we engage in the teaching of psychomotor skills. The similarity to the planning

---

2. *Editors' note: This could be considered a part of curriculum theory, for it deals with the nature of what to teach.*

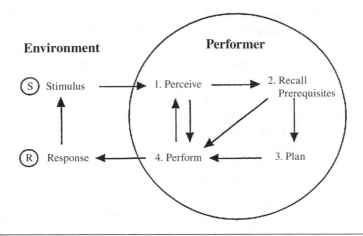

Figure 10.2 A Four-Stage Performance Cycle (Romiszowski, 1981)

issues characteristic of the cognitive domain is quite striking. Also, when viewed in conjunction with the previously presented skills schema, we can see how the basic model may be applied across the whole universe of skilled activities.

Universal Principles and Methods for Teaching Skills

Much has been written on the classification of motor tasks and skills in an attempt to create some form of taxonomy or schema that would assist designers in the psychomotor domain in a way similar to the two well-known taxonomies in the cognitive and affective domains (Bloom, Englehart, Hill, Furst, & Krathwohl, 1956; Krathwohl, Bloom, & Masia, 1964).

A hierarchical model of skill development, based on very detailed experimental observation of industrial skills acquisition and the stages through which the mastery of industrial skills progresses was described by Seymour (1954, 1966). Similar descriptions have appeared more recently in the literature, apparently derived independently in other domains of skilled activity. Examples are Schmidt's (1975) schema-theory model of motor skill learning, the account given by Adler (1981) based on observations in sports activities, and another by Gentner (1984) based on observations of the development of expertise in typing.

The model presented below, of five stages in the development of psychomotor skills, is derived from the above research, particularly that of Seymour. It has been successfully used as the basis for much practical skills training, including in work by the present author (Romiszowski, 1974, 1981, 1993, 1999).[3]

Stage 1: Acquiring knowledge of what should be done, to what purpose, in what sequence, and by what means. Further knowledge is acquired as the learning

---

3. *Editors' note: This model is presented as a descriptive model that describes the natural learning process. While it is not itself an instructional model, it forms the basis for developing one, which is shown in Figure 3.*

process progresses. What is required up-front is the minimum knowledge necessary to start performing the task in a meaningful manner.

Stage 2: Executing the actions in a step-by-step manner for each of the steps of the operation. The characteristics of this stage are: there is a conscious application of the knowledge (i.e., the "what and how" aspects of the operation are controlled by the conscious thinking-out of each step); the perceptual information necessary to initiate and control action—the "when-to-do and how-well-done" aspects—is almost exclusively visual (sometimes auditory). The observable result of these two characteristics is that execution of the task is erratic and jumpy. Time taken on a given step may vary considerably between attempts.

Stage 3: Transferring control from the eyes to other senses or to kinesthetic control through muscular coordination. The release of the sense of vision (at least partially) from the direct control of each movement allows for more efficient "advance planning" of subsequent movements in the sequence. The subsequent actions flow on directly without any apparent break between one movement and the next.

Stage 4: Automatizing the skill via a reduction of the need for conscious attention and "thinking through" of the actions. Performance becomes a set of reflex actions, one triggering the next, without direct conscious effort of the performer. The observable progress in this stage is that the performer may execute the task and at the same time be thinking or talking about other matters, even to some extent attending to other events in the environment, without this having any appreciable effect on the speed or quality of execution of the task.

Stage 5: Generalizing the skill to a continually greater range of application situations. This last stage applies to the productive/strategy/planning end of our skills continuum. In fact, most sports, most crafts, and most design skills are at least in some respects "productive." However well the basic physical skills involved are automated, one can still differentiate football players on the basis of their gamesmanship, motorists on the basis of their "road sense," and lathe operators on the basis of how they strike the balance between speed and quality of work.

The skills-mastery model presented above suggests three basic steps or stages in the overall instructional process (see Figure 10.3).[4] The following paragraphs explain in some more detail the rationale and the alternative instructional methods for each of these stages. It will be seen that, although in some cases the stages may follow one another in a step-by-step sequence, in other cases they may be combined or executed in reverse sequence. These variations in method and sequence are dictated by the nature of the specific skills to be learnt, for example, where they are situated on the reproductive—productive skills continuum.

Step 1: Imparting the basic knowledge content. This refers to the minimum knowledge required to understand why, when, and how to perform the task. It relates to the first stage of skill development as outlined above in the previous section. Generally speaking, this would take place by means of expository

---

4. *Editors' note: Here are the basics of the instructional theory.*

	Reproductive Skills	Productive Skills
Step 1 **Imparting the essential knowledge content**	Expository or experiential methods may be used (dependent on the category of knowledge).	Experiential methods preferred (concept and/or principle learning is always involved).
Step 2 **Imparting the basic psychomotor skills**	Expository methods (demonstration and prompted practice), by either the "whole task" or "progressive parts" methods. Note: Imparting the knowledge and skills content may in some cases be combined in one step.	Expository methods (demonstration and prompted practice), generally by the "whole task" method. Note: This step may sometimes be omitted when the learner starts with well-developed pre-requisite psychomotor skills.
Step 3 **Developing proficiency (speed, stamina and accuracy) and generality (transferability to a range of situations or cases)**	Supervised practice of whole task or special simulation exercises. Continuing corrective feedback (knowledge of results and/or knowledge of performance).	Experiential methods (guided problem solving) across a varying range of cases or examples. Continuing reflective feedback (debriefing; reflection-in-action).

Figure 10.3 Instructional Strategies for Skills Development (Romiszowski, 1981)

methods.[5] However, in the case of productive skills, some or most of the essential knowledge content may be in the form of heuristics—tacit knowledge acquired through experience. Therefore, in line with general principles for instruction in the cognitive domain, it may be desirable to develop this knowledge by means of experiential,[6] or discovery-learning techniques. This would be a knowledge-related outcome of the following two steps. In this case, step 1 would be limited to little more than presentation of the objectives of the learning exercise, defining the importance of this learning in the broader context, and maybe teaching some basic terminology and definitions that will be used to communicate about the learning process.

Step 2: Imparting the basic skill. This refers to the initial demonstration and controlled practice of the task being taught. It relates to the second stage of skill development as outlined in the previous section. The rationale here is that if there is a "best" method of executing the task, it should be demonstrated, or modeled, for the trainee. Unlike the conceptual learning in the previous step, where exposure to "right and wrong" may be beneficial in sharpening the trainee's power of discrimination, there is no benefit for the trainee in practicing an incorrect movement. In cases where the amount of basic knowledge to be imparted is small,[7] it is possible to combine the two steps described above into one. These

---

5. *Editors' note: Here we have a common component method followed by a less common alternative method. The situationality that helps you choose between the two is whether the skill is productive or reproductive.*

6. *Editors' note: See chapter 7.*

7. *Editors' note: This is another situationality.*

cases may include the more simple reproductive skills that do not depend on a great deal of prerequisite knowledge, and also some more complex productive skills that depend principally on tacit knowledge that is best acquired experientially. In this latter case, the acquisition of tacit knowledge may commence in this step, but will continue on through the next step.

Step 3: Developing proficiency. This refers to the provision of appropriate conditions for further practice to mastery. It relates to the remaining three stages of skill development outlined in the previous section—transfer of control, automatization, and generalization. The first two of these are relevant in the case of skills that lie toward the closed, or reproductive, end of our skills continuum.[8] The third relates to skills at the productive end. Typically, however, a complex skilled activity is composed of both reproductive and productive skill elements. Car driving involves the smooth changing of gears, acceleration, automatic glancing in the rearview mirror, and also the road-craft skills of judging safe distances between vehicles, selection of the appropriate gear for each situation, prediction of possible acts by other road users, and the adoption of appropriate defensive-driving strategies. Systematic skills training ought to be based on a detailed task analysis that seeks to identify how these reproductive and productive skill elements may best be taught and in what sequence or combination.[9]

Instructional Tactics for Specific Situations

In this section of the chapter, we shall examine the more specific research-based principles of instruction (listed in *italics*) that underlie the basic model suggested above. We shall group these principles into four categories:

1. Information (explanation, demonstration, and guidance),
2. Practice (frequency, spacing, etc.),
3. Feedback (frequency, form, quality, etc.), and
4. transfer and generalization.

Imparting the Essential Information to the Trainee

> *If the task is simple, with limited background knowledge, then demonstrate and explain simultaneously as an illustrated narrative, BUT .... if the task requires little if any new knowledge to be learnt, apart from the movement pattern of the action, it may be effectively taught without explanations, simply demonstrating a "model performance."*

---

8. *Editors' note: You guessed it! Another situationality!*
9. *Editors' note: This makes it clear how the nature of the analysis you do should be targeted to the situationalities—to informing the decisions you make in selecting among alternatives in an instructional theory. For this reason, it is seldom wise to do all the analysis before doing any design. It is usually better to do some analysis just-in-time for many design decisions (when feasible and cost-effective).*

Experiments on the role of visual demonstration (and feedback) on the mastery of a movement task (Carroll & Bandura, 1982, 1987, 1990) support the importance of a clear and sufficiently repeated visual enactment of the task as the principal factor leading to effective learning. However, in the case of knowledge-based skills, it is important to support the demonstration with appropriate verbal explanation.

If the task is structurally complex, involving relationships among its components and a large amount of new knowledge but little new skill, it is best learned through exploratory activity with outline notes or a physical model to follow.

Retention of a complex task involving procedural knowledge is better if the task is learned through exploratory practice followed by expository review, rather than through expository demonstration followed by practice. Baggett (1983) found that immediate success on a model helicopter assembly task was proportional to the total amount of exploratory practice received and was not dependent on having viewed a film. After an interval of one week, however, the most successful students were those who had the greatest amount of exploratory practice first and then viewed the film last. A possible explanation could be drawn from the general literature on expository versus discovery learning. If there are some "general principles of model assembly" that can help across several phases of the assembly task, then learning is better when they are "discovered". The long-term effect of the film may be due to the promotion of deep processing and organization of the knowledge gained through the practical experience, even though the film script was not specifically designed to promote "reflection-in-action." Those who saw the film before practice had no relevant experience to reflect on; hence no deep processing was possible.

If the task is structurally simple, involving a sequence of consecutive steps or stages, let the student observe the sequential action pattern before attempting to execute it.

Research on tracking skills, springing from wartime gunnery and radar needs, paints a picture that contrasts with the findings just discussed. A series of experiments carried out by Poulton (1957) showed that observation of a pursuit-tracking activity before practicing it significantly improved the accuracy of performance. Similar results have been obtained by other researchers (Carroll & Bandura, 1982). These findings are not necessarily in conflict with those reported by Baggett. They can be seen to support each other at a higher level of generality. The discovery-learning-based explanation of Baggett's findings, proposed above, is based on the hypothesis that instructional methods which involve deeper mental processing of sensory information are more effective. The difference between the two experimental situations lies in the type of task that is being learned. In one case, the critical learning is of visual patterns and relationships among components. In the other, it is the sequence and timing of a single, multistage movement. In the first case, practical exploration presents the visual relationships among parts in a manner that is more conducive to mental representation of the critical information than is a film sequence. In the second case, a film (video) presents the sequence of the task in a manner that is more conducive to its mental representation.

If the objective is to master the execution of a procedure, then always demonstrate it from the viewpoint of the performer. Multiple and varied vantage points, as used in many media presentations, are only useful when the objective is to understand the process.

Often, instructors may demonstrate a sequence of movements while facing a group of students. This is effective for teaching conceptual understanding of the task, but not for its execution. The students must "invert" the demonstration in their minds, which often creates confusion and unnecessary difficulty. It is best to demonstrate exactly what the student will see when performing, as if the learner were peering over the demonstrator's shoulder (Greenwald & Albert, 1968; Roshal, 1961). The use of film and video facilitate this process. However, one has to avoid the temptation to utilize the multi-camera, zoom and other visual capabilities of the media, which tend to work counter to the desired objective.

Providing Opportunities for Practice

If the objective is to learn integrated and coordinated activities, use the "whole task" method.

Several studies suggest that learning is more effective when the task is practiced as a whole, allowing the separate movements to be coordinated in all the practice sessions (Knapp, 1963; McGuigan & MacCaslin, 1955; Naylor & Briggs, 1963). This finding seems to hold true in laboratory experiments, in real-life industrial skills, and in sports.

If the task is composed of a sequence of relatively independent actions, teach it by the "progressive parts" method.

In the "sequential parts" method, a four-step task (e.g., A-B-C-D) would be practiced in four stages, each concentrating on one of the parts; that is, A alone, then B alone, and so on, until all parts have been practiced separately. In the progressive parts method, the stages of practice grow cumulatively; for example, A alone, then B, then A and B, then C alone, then A and B and C, then D, and finally the whole task A-B-C-D. Some research has shown both of these approaches to be equally effective and better than the whole task method for learning simple sequential tasks. However, the bulk of the research supports the superiority of the progressive-parts approach for sequential tasks (Naylor & Briggs, 1963; Seymour, 1954; Welford, 1968).

If prerequisite subskills are initially below "minimum threshold levels," they should be developed prior to the practice of the whole task.

Several examples of such pretraining exercises and their effectiveness in the industrial skills arena are given by Seymour (1954, 1966). Note that the pretraining of specific movement or perceptual subskills before their integration into a more complex pattern of activity is not the same as the practice of the activity itself in separate parts.

For highly coordinated and "productive" tasks, provide continuous practice; BUT for repetitive and high-speed "reproductive" tasks, provide spaced practice.

Some studies suggest that for more complex tasks in which much decision making is involved or where there is a high level of coordination or rhythmic activity, long and continuous practice sessions are more effective than spaced practice (Welford, 1968). Singer (1982) showed that, although spaced practice may show an advantage immediately after a series of trials, this is largely lost over time. Other research suggests that spaced training sessions with short rest stops between every few trials are more effective in the case of repetitive high-speed skills of a "reproductive" nature (Lee & Genovese, 1988).

If the task involves heuristically based productive skills, promote and encourage the mental rehearsal of the task during rest intervals, to enhance its initial learning and long-term retention, by means of a thinking-through, or "reflection in action" activity.

Theoretical justification of mental rehearsal has been provided by many writers (e.g., Luria, 1961; Meichenbaum & Goodman, 1971). Shasby (1984) reviews the research on this technique applied to learning in the psychomotor domain. The use of mental rehearsal as a skills training technique has a long history; for example, in the thinking and talking through of football strategies during a pregame briefing discussion. Often, these "think-through" sessions are taken further, each strategy being given a code name by which it can be evoked during the game. Sometimes the steps or components of the strategy are likewise named, so the players may recall the sequence, pace, or nature of each step by means of an appropriate code word. We may perceive much similarity between the manner of using mental rehearsal for the mastery of productive psychomotor skills, and the "knowing-in-action" and "reflection in action" procedures recommended for the mastery of complex, heuristics-driven, cognitive skills. Schön (1987) contrasts the performance of professionals such as architects, doctors, managers and musicians, when dealing with a problem-situation that is recognized as a familiar example with situations that are unfamiliar and somewhat surprising. The familiar situations elicit the application of known facts, rules, and procedures (knowing in action). The unfamiliar situations lead the professional to enter into an internal conversation in order to reflect on how the current case is different from the norm and how the basic principles and paradigms of the profession may have to be applied, adapted, or extended in order to construct new rules or procedures that are appropriate to the case (reflection in action). He stresses that in both these cases, the process of "coaching" a professional involves the coach in promoting the rehearsal of the problem-solving process, first externally through discussion and demonstration, in order to develop the professional's internal capacities of mental rehearsal.

> *If the task is a sequential procedure that mainly involves reproductive skills, supply verbal coding, or cueing, accompanying a model demonstration, to help the learner to form a mental representation of the action.*

Bandura and Jeffery (1973) found that verbal labels were particularly effective as symbolic codes in terms of long-term retention of a sequential movement skill. The findings suggest that some form of verbal cueing as an aid to the internalization of motor skills should in general be provided. These cues should be meaningful to the learners but as simple and nontechnical as possible. Here we may discern a parallel with the use of mnemonics in the cognitive domain. However, Carroll and Bandura (1990) showed that verbal coding or cueing was not in itself sufficient to overcome the defective instructional design of insufficient demonstration and practice opportunities. One might expect, therefore, that purely verbal instruction would in general be inadequate for the teaching of all but the simplest of physical tasks. Once more, there is a parallel in the cognitive domain, where only very simple memory tasks, such as the recall of factual information, may be successfully taught by purely verbal presentation, but the development of skills in the use of concepts requires, in addition to verbal definitions, the presentation of a carefully selected set of examples and contra-examples, and the development of problem solving skills requires, in addition to all the above, practice opportunities that promote reflection on the problem solving process itself and creation of tacit knowledge in the form of heuristics relevant to a particular class of problems.

> *For high-speed tasks, forced pacing promotes more rapid progress to mastery.*

When forced pacing is applied to the practice of high-speed industrial tasks (Agar, 1962) or to typing skills (Sormunen, 1986) learning rates are very significantly enhanced, and ultimate performance levels achieved may be much higher than under self-paced practice conditions. This principle is often overlooked due to too much emphasis on the principles of self-paced learning. In tasks where speed is a criterion, the principle of allowing a student to progress "at his or her own pace" needs careful interpretation. There is a difference between allowing learners to perform a task at their own pace, and allowing them to progress to more rapid task execution at their own pace. This was well illustrated in such highly effective skills training programs as the Swedish RITT system for training operators of high speed industrial machines (Agar, 1962; Romiszowski, 1986) and Pask's early computer-based SAKI keyboard skills trainer (Pask, 1960; Romiszowski, 1986). The first used audiotaped instructional modules, recorded at different task-execution rates, to provide paced practice somewhat above the trainees' current rate of performance, but allowed the trainees to progress from one task-execution rate to the next at their own pace. The second measured each trainee's response rates for every key on the keyboard and presented practice material at a rate always just a bit higher than an individual's current rate of effective performance; however, the trainees could take as long, and practice as many repetitions, as necessary to elevate their rate of performance. Experimental work with SAKI showed that the typing speeds of most performers could be increased to several times the initial rates, but there was a threshold beyond which further pacing was not only ineffective in further improvement of performance, but actually reduced both speed and accuracy, in some cases most drastically. Pask considered this phenomenon in psychomotor skills training to be analogous to the type of mental breakdown that sometimes is observed in the learning of cognitive skills when overly rapid progress to more complex and difficult problems has led to the phenomenon of information overload. Several approaches have been found to be helpful in avoiding or staving off the onset of information overload (Welford, 1976): devising ways of "chunking" the incoming information so that more can be handled; devising ways of helping the performer be selective in the information attended to; devising better ways of pacing the task so that information overload is avoided; establishing realistic "threshold levels" for the performer and working within them.

Feedback in Skills Instruction

If the objective is to develop simple sensorimotor skills, then "learning feedback" (results information) promotes learning and "action feedback" (control information) does not.

Annett (1959) found that subjects pressing down on a spring balance would not learn to exert a given pressure accurately, despite many trials, when they had the benefit of the scale supplying them with information. When the scale was covered while they made their attempt and then uncovered, they did learn. Thus, continuous knowledge, supplied visually, of the pressure being applied (action feedback) guaranteed error-free practice but did not result in the learning of the "feel" of applying the correct pressure. After-the-fact knowledge (of results) did promote progressively more accurate attempts and led to effective learning of the "feel" of executing the task (hence the term *learning feedback*). The explanation of this is that the continuous action-feedback allows trainees to control their performance during practice by means of visual information, without the need to sense and evaluate the "feel" of the task in the muscles. Thus transfer of control, from the eyes to the arm muscles, does not occur. According to the theory of multiple intelligences (Gardner, 1983; 1993), this would be interpreted as a lack of the necessary transfer from the spatial to the bodily kinesthetic domain.

> *If the objective is to develop more complex skills that involve decisions among alternative actions, or the execution of mutually interdependent tasks, then feedback is more effective in promoting learning when it transmits more complete information about the process as well as the product.*

Knowledge of the results (KOR) of a practice trial and knowledge of performance (KOP—how the results were achieved) highlight two ways in which the instructor may seek to correct the inadequate performance of a task. In the case of more complex physical skills, the supply of KOP was found to be more effective (Wallace & Hagler, 1979). The explanation is that KOR only supplies information about the correctness of a response and possibly the direction and extent of an error, whilst KOP in addition may comment on or correct certain aspects of the process of executing the task. As the more complex skills are more dependent on conceptual knowledge, the role of KOP may be seen (from the perspective of the theory of multiple intelligences) as promoting the transfer of control from the spatial or naturalist to the linguistic or logical-mathematical domain.

> *When teaching "productive" skills, supply knowledge of performance through a process of "debriefing" or "reflection-in-action."*

In the case of skills involving a high level of strategy planning and decision making, the appropriate feedback not only may, but should, take the form of KOP. In these skills, it is not sufficient to compare results with expectations, but it is necessary to engage in an analysis of the causes of an observed discrepancy, reflect on the plans that were implemented, and evaluate the reasons for their shortcomings. All this leads to the synthesis of new plans or strategies for the next practice trial. Such reflective debriefing, either instructor-led or spontaneous, is now recognized as an essential element of the development of productive skills in any domain. In the psychomotor domain, this is exemplified in the sports context by the before-and-after-the-game strategy discussions in the locker room. It is also apparent in the stress laid on the "reflection-in-action" approach to skill development in professions such as surgery (Schön, 1983, 1987). But as Schön so clearly pointed out, the same principles that apply to the development of world-class excellence in a physical-skills domain such as surgery, also apply to intellectual-skills domains such as architecture, management, and teaching.

Teaching for Transfer and Retention

In the case of productive skills, variability of practice exercises enhances transfer and generalization, but in the case of reproductive skills, there is less to be gained through variation of the practice tasks.

According to Gabbard (1984), a major prediction of schema theory is that "increasing the variability of practice on a given task will result in increased transfer to a novel task of the same movement class." However, experience in some sports and in many high-speed, repetitive industrial skills has not supported the variability-of-practice principle. One way to explain this is by means of our "skills continuum." The further an activity is toward the productive end of this continuum, the more important it is to practice across the range of variability in order to ensure effective transfer. The further the activity lies toward the reproductive end, the less permissible is variability in execution, and so the less valuable is variability of practice (indeed it may be harmful).

In the case of teaching for transfer, the variability of the practice exercises should be so designed as to define, or refine, "motor concepts" and "motor schemata" in the learner's mind.

According to Schmidt's (1975) theory, a motor schema is a structure of interrelated "motor concepts" analogous to the structure of a cognitive schema. A concept in the cognitive domain is defined by a series of attributes that define its "boundary" more or less precisely. Just so, a motor concept, such as "throwing a ball accurately," is defined and bounded by certain attributes, such as: distance to throw, force to apply, angle of release of the ball, and arm speed at the moment of release. These attributes are not, of course, defined verbally or mathematically, but are nevertheless "known" and "interrelated" within the player, so that any required distance of throw, as stimulus, produces an appropriate combination of the other attributes as response. The implication for instruction is that practice should be designed to vary in terms of all the critical attributes of the motor concept. Once more we observe a close similarity of the principles of psychomotor skills learning and cognitive skills learning.

Transfer and retention of reproductive skills are improved by "overlearning," and of productive skills by "debriefing" that promotes "reflection-in/on-action."

Both practical observation and experimental evidence suggest that in the case of many skills "the amount of transfer of learning is proportional to the amount of initial practice" (Gagné, 1954). Singer (1982) makes the further point that there is evidence that "overlearning" or "overpractice" is beneficial in terms of long-term retention, although there is a law of diminishing returns in force which may establish limits beyond which formally organized "overpractice" would not be cost-effective. Furthermore, such overlearning is less beneficial in the case of the productive skills components of the task. The explanation is that as productive skills are dependent on the application of conceptual knowledge in order to plan an appropriate strategy of action, and as this knowledge tends to be acquired through insights gained at specific moments in the learning process, often through a "eureka" form of personal discovery, performance improvement is more a function of the insights gained than of the number of repetitions of the task. Therefore, learning for transfer is in this case best promoted through reflection on, and analysis of, the process of successful execution of the task (Romiszowski, 1984).

Linking It All Together

Throughout the preceding sections of this chapter, I have continually referred to the important role of the teaching and learning of knowledge as an integral part of the mastery of new skills. Also, through the distinction made between productive and reproductive skills and their associated needs for the learning of knowledge, I have promoted the use, at appropriate moments, of both expository[10] and experiential[11] approaches to instruction. As the mastery of skills is almost always real-world based in the context of jobs that have to be performed or pastimes that interest and attract the performer,[12] it is almost always based on the execution of authentic and learner-relevant tasks. In the case of productive skills, these authentic tasks generally take the form of problems to be solved: therefore the instructional design takes on most of the characteristics of problem-based learning (PBL).[13] As the mastery of productive skills depends heavily on reflection on the process and the results of execution of a task, the appropriate instructional designs also draw heavily on discussion and dialogue methodologies of instruction.[14] These may sometimes be reality-based and sometimes case-study or simulation-based,[15] but in all cases they implement "Stage 3" of skill development (proficiency) through reflective analysis of experience.[16]

In the case of reproductive skills, on the other hand, PBL and other experiential learning approaches are seldom appropriate: the teaching-learning process takes on most of the characteristics of direct instruction.[17] This may be real-task-based, or for a variety of practical reasons may be simulation-based: our approach thus accommodates both experiential and expositive uses of simulation, and indeed prescribes when each approach is appropriate.

---

10. *Editors' note: See chapter 5.*
11. *Editors' note: See chapter 7.*
12. *Editors' note: Important when the affective priority is high.*
13. *Editors' note: See chapter 8.*
14. *Editors' note: See chapter 6.*
15. *Editors' note: See chapter 9.*
16. *Editors' note: This paragraph illustrates how multiple approaches (Unit 2) can be used to teach a single type of learning outcome (Unit 3).*
17. *Editors' note: This shows the importance of basing instructional decisions on pragmatics (what works best) rather than philosophy.*

Integrating the Performer and the Task: The Extended Skill Cycle

The models and approaches presented in this chapter thus act as a form of integration (and elaboration) of many of the approaches more fully discussed in unit 3 of this book. The process of integration has been developed through the careful distinction of the requirements for learning of different categories of skills, and also the different categories (facts, concepts, procedures, principles, etc.) of the knowledge content that is required as a basis for the execution of these skills. But there is yet another manner in which the analysis of skilled performance may lead to a more complete integration of all the factors that may be relevant in order to ensure the competent execution of skilled activities. In this last section, we return to the concepts defined and analyzed in the opening section of the chapter, and use these concepts as the basis of an extension of our synthesis to include yet other factors that influence human performance in real-world contexts.

We have, so far, considered some aspects of how learners perceive a situation that calls for a skilled response, how they interpret the perceived information and recall prior relevant learning, and how (in the case of productive skills) they use both of these sources of knowledge to plan an appropriate response strategy. We have said less about the final stage of the process, the actual performance of the appropriate response. And we have hardly mentioned the role of personality and affect in this process. It is time to bring these various factors together, in the form of an integrated model of skilled performance: the extended skill cycle.

This model is illustrated in Figure 10.4. It is composed of the cycle of four principal activities involved in the execution of a skilled activity that were already introduced in Figure 10.2. The execution of each of these activities is dependent on the presence of certain abilities or predispositions. The model proposes 12 basic abilities that need to be appropriately developed in order to ensure that a given task category is executed with the desired level of skill. It also suggests that the final level of skilled execution also depends on the "inner self" of the performers: their personality, intellect, feelings, beliefs, and their many past experiences, often stored at a subconscious level, that perhaps are not directly related to the task content but nevertheless may impact the execution of the task.

This model of human performance may be used at different levels of resolution. If all the internal components are ignored, it represents the (behaviorist) "black box" model of a performer receiving certain stimulus information from the environment and responding appropriately. Peeling off one layer, as if it is an onion skin, reveals the array of basic abilities that cognitive research has identified as potentially important in the skillful execution of tasks. Digging yet deeper, reveals the performer's "inner self" that also plays an important part in the process. We close this chapter by considering some examples of how the execution of specific task categories might be influenced by these factors.

The model permits one to apply a special form of task analysis, based on the consideration of the role that each of the 12 abilities may play in the skilled

RECEPTORS　　　　　　　　　　　　　　　**STORE**

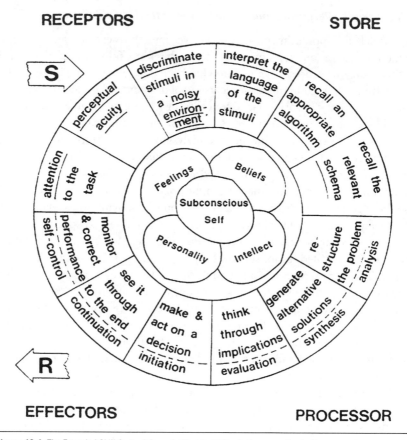

EFFECTORS　　　　　　　　　　　　　　　**PROCESSOR**

Figure 10.4 The Extended Skill Cycle: A Powerful Tool for Skills-Performance Analysis

execution of the task. It is important to emphasize the word *may*, as not all of the abilities are of equal importance for all skills. The goal of this task analysis is to identify the relevant abilities and the way that they influence task execution, assess whether they are present and adequately developed, and so plan an instructional strategy that takes all the relevant factors into consideration.

A Relatively Complex, Productive, Psychomotor Activity

For a start, let us consider the game of tennis.

1. Here is an example of a skilled activity in which the ability to pay attention is of paramount importance. Tennis coaches make a "mantra" out of the admonition to "keep your eye on the ball," though this is a simplification of a more complex process of "paying attention" to the game as a whole.

2. A tennis player's performance will therefore be influenced by the level of perceptual acuity. This is in part nature and in part nurture: a combination of natural abilities and learned habits. The trainer needs to identify the

factors that influence the player's perceptual acuity and plan appropriate exercises to develop it further.

3. However, the trajectory of the ball is but one factor to be perceived. Other relevant factors include the force and style with which the ball was hit by the opponent, the movement of the opponent on the court since the moment of hitting the ball, environmental factors such as wind and light, and so on. The ability to, not only perceive all these factors, but to discriminate which of them are relevant in the specific case, is a vital part of the learning process.

4. All this incoming information is instantaneously interpreted by the player, and leads to:

5. The selection of a particular type of previously learned stroke to return the ball to the opponent's side of the court;

6. The recall of a "motor schema" that best represents the dynamics of this moment in the game;

7, 8, 9. The planning of where to place the ball in the opponent's court and how best to get it there;

10, 11, 12. The initiation of the appropriate sequence of actions, seeing the actions through to the end, and possibly taking some corrective actions during this process as further information about the opponent's movements are perceived, interpreted, and analyzed while the responding stroke is already in process of planning and execution.

One role of the trainer is to analyze all these different aspects of the player's performance, in order to identify exactly what further training will be useful and how that may best be accomplished: this in itself is a highly skilled task, as described so aptly by Gilbert and Gilbert (1988) when analyzing the success of the legendary football coach "Bear" Bryant. But the sports coach (and by analogy, any trainer of complex skilled activities) has another role: to analyze the overall behavior of the player in order to identify other aspects that are influencing performance: the player's attitude, self-belief, level of confidence, assertiveness, and so on. These factors combine to create the psychology of the game: what Gallwey (1974, 1997) originally described as the "inner game of tennis," and later extrapolated to other sporting activities and ultimately other nonsporting areas of skilled activity, in his book *The Inner Game of Work* (Gallwey, 2000).

A Simple, Reproductive Psychomotor Activity

As a contrast to the previous example, let us therefore consider the relatively simple, reproductive, work-related, psychomotor skill of touch-typing on a typewriter or computer keyboard.

1. (2) The ability to attend and concentrate on the task is a relevant factor. Perceptual acuity may sometimes be relevant, for example in the case of copy typing of poorly drafted, handwritten manuscripts.

3, 4. Discrimination and interpretation are hardly involved, but ....

5. the immediate and accurate recall of the appropriate finger movements required to type a given sequence of characters is most relevant.

6, 7, 8, 9. There is no planning involved—the recall of the required finger movement is directly followed by its execution.

10, 11. However, at this stage, accurate work or the ability to maintain a satisfactory typing speed may be influenced by physical factors—insufficient dexterity or muscular control may make certain errors occur with high frequency, and fatigue may creep in as the day progresses to slow down performance and increase the error rate. These factors may be controlled and their influence minimized through appropriate dexterity and stamina training exercises.

12. In a high speed manual task such as typing, there is little opportunity to correct a reaction once it has been initiated—the training program must concentrate on ensuring that the correct response is recalled and initiated.

Finally, however, there may be other sources of error caused by "inner-self" factors; for example, the dyslexic tendency to transpose certain sequences of letters, which may require specialist, even medical, attention; the self-protection tendency to type slower than one is capable of typing in order not to "stand out" in a poorly designed or managed working environment that, instead of rewarding outstanding performance, tends to "punish" it by loading extra work on those who work faster and better. This example illustrates how the extended skill cycle may identify key aspects of the performer's skills and also factors in the work context that influence performance, which often are overlooked in the design of a training program.

A Reproductive Cognitive Activity

It is clearly possible to apply this form of task analysis to any skill category or domain. A simple reproductive cognitive skill, such as the performance of basic arithmetic calculations, may present an analysis that is in some respects similar to, but in other respects quite different from, the typing example:

1. Attention and ability to concentrate on arithmetic tasks is a relevant factor;

2. Perceptual acuity may not be all that relevant, but...

3. the ability to discriminate types of arithmetic tasks and recognize a specific category of task, even when it is presented in "disguised" form as a word problem rather than symbolically, are major sources of learning difficulty...

4. and so is the ability to interpret the symbolic language of mathematics.

5. The ability to recall the appropriate algorithm for the required arithmetical procedure is a critical performance factor, but...

6, 7, 8, 9. are not relevant, given the reproductive nature of the skill.

10, 11. These are not critical factors as the tasks are slow-speed intellectual actions that are not susceptible to fatigue or other physical ailments, but...

12. the ability to control progress and self-correct one's performance during the process of execution of the task is highly critical.

Finally, the "inner-self" factors that often lead to a mental block with respect to mathematics and a belief that such skills are beyond one's capabilities require close analysis and appropriate attention in the instructional design.

Application Across the Entire Spectrum of Skilled Activity

Similar analyses of interpersonal (interactive) skills may reveal why a manager or supervisor who has learned all about people-management, and may indeed perform well in simulation exercises, may nevertheless fail to initiate appropriate action to control some real-life disciplinary problem in the workforce, and analyses of reactive, self-control skills may reveal why people tend to apply different criteria to their own behavior than they do to the behavior of others. These insights are additional to those resulting from traditional content and task analysis methodologies that are used to identify learning objectives and classify them into categories and domains. They offer the instructional designer additional information that is useful for enriching the instructional design and ensuring that all factors that may influence the effectiveness of learning and ultimate performance are addressed in an integrated manner.

References

Adler, J. D. (1981). Stages of skill acquisition: A guide for teachers. *Motor Skills: Theory into Practice, 5*(2), 75–80.

Agar, A. (1962). Instruction of industrial workers by tape recorder. *Affarsekonomi, 10*. (Original in Swedish)

Annett, J. (1959). Learning a pressure under conditions of immediate and delayed knowledge of results. *Quarterly Journal of Experimental Psychology, 11*, 3–15.

Baggett, P. (1983). *Learning a procedure from multimedia instructions: The effects of film and practice.* Boulder: Colorado University, Institute of Cognitive Science. (ERIC Document Reproduction Service No. ED239598)

Bandura, A., & Jeffery, R. W. (1973). Role of symbolic coding and rehearsal processes in observational learning. *Journal of Personality and Social Psychology, 26*, 122–130.

Bloom, B. S., Englehart, M. D., Hill, W. H., Furst, E. J., & Krathwohl, D. R. (1956). *Taxonomy of educational objectives: Handbook 1. The cognitive domain.* New York: McKay.

Carroll, W. R., & Bandura, A. (1982). The role of visual monitoring in observational learning of action patterns: Making the unobservable observable. *Journal of Motor Behavior, 14*(2), 153–167.

Carroll, W. R., & Bandura, A. (1987). Translating cognition into action: The role of visual guidance in observational learning. *Journal of Motor Behavior, 19*(3), 385–398.

Carroll, W. R., & Bandura, A. (1990). Representational guidance of action production in observational learning: A causal analysis. *Journal of Motor Behavior, 22*(1), 85–97.

Gabbard, C. P. (1984). *Motor skill learning in children.* (ERIC Document Reproduction No. ED293645)

Gagné, R. M. (1954). Training devices and simulators: Some research issues. *American Psychologist, 9*(7), 95–107.

Gallwey, W. T. (1974). *The inner game of tennis.* New York: Random House.

Gallwey, W. T. (1997). *The inner game of tennis* (Rev ed.). New York: Random House.

Gallwey, W. T. (2000). *The inner game of work*. New York: Random House.

Gardner, H. (1983). *Frames of mind: The theory of multiple intelligences*. New York: Basic.

Gardner, H. (1993). *Multiple intelligences: The theory in practice*. New York: Basic.

Gentner, D. R. (1984). *Expertise in typewriting*. CHIP Report, 121. La Jolla. University of California, San Diego: Center for Human Information Processing. (ERIC Document Reproduction No. ED248320)

Gilbert, T., & Gilbert, M. (1988, August). The science of winning. *Training*.

Greenwald, A. G., & Albert, S. M. (1968). Observational learning: A technique for elucidating S-R mediation processes. *Journal of Experimental Psychology, 76*, 267–272.

Knapp, B. N. (1963). *Skill in sport: The attainment of proficiency*. London: Routledge & Kegan Paul.

Krathwohl, D. R., Bloom, B. S., & Masia, B. B. (1964). *Taxonomy of educational objectives: Handbook 2. The affective domain*. New York: Longman.

Lee, T. D., & Genovese, E. D. (1988). Distribution of practice in motor skill acquisition: Learning and performance effects reconsidered. *Research Quarterly for Exercise and Sport, 58*(4).

Luria, A. R. (1961). *The role of speech in the regulation of normal and abnormal behavior*. New York: Liveright.

Mager, R. E. (1968). *Developing attitude toward learning*. Belmont, CA: Fearon.

McGuigan, F. J., & MacCaslin, E. F. (1955). Whole and part methods in learning a perceptual motor skill. *American Journal of Psychology, 68*, 658–661.

Meichenbaum, D., & Goodman, J. (1971). Training impulsive children to talk to themselves: A means of developing self control. *Journal of Abnormal Psychology, 77*, 115–126.

Naylor, J. C., & Briggs, G. E. (1963). Effects of task complexity and task organization on the relative efficiency of part and whole training methods. *Journal of Experimental Psychology, 65*, 217–224.

Pask, G.S. (1960). *The teaching machine as a control mechanism*. London: Transactions of the Society of Instrument Technology.

Poulton, E. C. (1957). On prediction in skilled movement. *Psychological Bulletin, 54*, 467–478.

Rogers, C. R. (1969). *Freedom to learn*. New York: Merrill.

Romiszowski, A. J. (1974). *Selection and use of instructional media: A systems approach*. London: Kogan Page.

Romiszowski, A. J. (1981). *Designing instructional systems*. London: Kogan Page.

Romiszowski, A. J. (1984). *Producing instructional systems: Lesson plans for individualized group learning activities*. London: Kagen Page.

Romiszowski, A. J. (1986). *Developing auto-instructional materials*. London: Kogan Page.

Romiszowski, A. J. (1993). Psychomotor principles. In M. Fleming & W. H. Levie (Eds.), *Instructional message design*. Englewood Cliffs, NJ: Educational Technology.

Romiszowski, A. J. (1999). The development of physical skills: Instruction in the psychomotor domain. In C. M. Reigeluth (Ed.), *Instructional-design theories and models: Vol. 2. A new paradigm of instructional theory*. Mahwah, NJ: Erlbaum.

Roshal, S. M. (1961). Film mediated learning with varying representation of the task: Viewing angle portrayal of demonstration, motion and student participation. In A. A. Lumsdaine (Ed.), *Student response in programmed instruction*. Washington, D.C.: National Academy of Sciences, National Research Council.

Schmidt, R. A. (1975). A schema theory of discrete motor skill learning. *Psychological Review, 82*, 225–260.

Schön, D. A. (1983). *The reflective practitioner*. New York: Basic.

Schön, D. A. (1987). *Educating the reflective practitioner*. San Francisco: Jossey-Bass.

Seymour, W. D. (1954). *Industrial training for manual operations*. London: Pitman.

Seymour, W. D. (1966). *Industrial skills*. London: Pitman.

Shasby, G. (1984). Improving movement skills through language. *Motor Skills: Theory into Practice, 7*(1/2), 91–96.

Singer, R. N. (1982). *The learning of motor skills*. New York: Macmillan.

Sormunen, C. (1986). A comparison of two methods for teaching keyboarding on the microcomputer to elementary grade students. *Delta Pi Epsilon Journal, 28*(2), 67–77.

Wallace, S. A., & Hagler, R. W. (1979). Knowledge of performance and the learning of a closed motor skill. *Research Quarterly, 50*, 265–271.

Welford, A. T. (1968). *Fundamentals of skill*. London: Methuen.

Welford, A. T. (1976). *Skilled performance: Perceptual and motor skills*. Glenview, IL: Scott Foresman.

Wellens, J. (1974). *Training in physical skills*. London: Business Books.

Wheatcroft, E. (1973). *Simulators for skill*. London: McGraw-Hill.

11
Fostering Understanding Outcomes

MARTHA STONE WISKE
Harvard University

BRIAN J. BEATTY
San Francisco State University

Martha Stone Wiske is a lecturer at the Harvard Graduate School of Education where she analyzes the integration of new technologies to enhance teaching, learning, and professional development. She is cofounder of Wide World http://wideworld.gse.harvard.edu at Harvard, an interactive, coached online professional development program for teachers, coaches, and school leaders from over 100 countries. Its mission is to improve student performance by strengthening instruction, leadership, and systemic transformation in schools. Dr. Wiske edited *Teaching for Understanding: Linking Research with Practice* (Jossey-Bass, 1998) and is the lead author of *Teaching for Understanding with Technology* (Jossey-Bass, 2005).

Brian J. Beatty is an assistant professor of education in the Instructional Technologies Department at San Francisco State University, California. He teaches graduate courses in instructional systems design, distance education, e-learning development, project management, and technology integration. His research centers on the use of Internet technologies in teaching and learning environments of all sorts, including K-12 classrooms, higher education institutions, and corporate training systems. He is especially interested in the application of Internet-based technologies being used to create virtual, hybrid, and fully networked learning communities; most recently his work has centered on the HyFlex model for hybrid course design. His background includes a decade of K-12 mathematics and science instruction as a classroom teacher and curriculum designer. Brian also has many years of experience in corporate and technical military training design and development.

EDITORS' FOREWORD

Preconditions

Content
- *Many subject areas where application of deep understandings in flexible ways is sought*

Learners
- *All kinds of learners*

Learning environments
- *Best used in open contexts where full frontal teaching or narrowly defined outcome standards are not required*

Instructional development constraints
- *Few resources (development time and money) are needed.*

Values

about ends (learning goals)
- *Deep understandings are important.*
- *Understanding is a performance capability.*

about priorities (criteria for successful instruction)
- *Appeal and effectiveness are paramount; efficiency is less important.*

about means (instructional methods)
- *New technology can support more generative, active learning, and community building, but is not necessary.*

about power (to make decisions about the previous three)
- *Power should ultimately reside with teachers, but they should empower students to some (gradually increasing) extent.*

Universal Methods

1. *Identify **generative topics**.*
   - *They are connected to multiple important ideas within and across academic disciplines, domains, and subject matters.*
   - *They should be framed in ways that are authentic, accessible, and interesting to students.*
   - *They should be fascinating and compelling to the teacher.*
   - *They should be approachable from multiple entry points.*
   - *They should be framed in a way that generates and rewards continuous inquiry.*
   - *They may be enhanced by using networked, multimedia technologies.*
2. *Define and publicize **understanding goals**.*
   - *They should require students to go beyond the information given to construct their own understanding and apply it flexibly.*
   - *They may encompass four dimensions of understanding: knowledge, methods for building knowledge, purposes for learning, and forms of expression.*

- *They should connect coherently across levels of a curriculum plan.*
- *They may be made more accessible and achievable by using networked, multimedia technologies.*

3. Promote **performances** of understanding.
   - *They should require active learning and creative thinking.*
   - *They should constitute a progression of performances that helps students build on what they already know.*
   - *They should be in a cycle of guided inquiry performances in which teachers explain, demonstrate, and guide student investigations, followed by students working more independently in culminating performances that are ideally presented to authentic audiences.*
   - *They may utilize networked, multimedia technologies to enrich the range of ways that learners develop and demonstrate their understanding.*

4. Track, assess, and improve learning through frequent ongoing **assessments**.
   - *They should be based on explicit, public criteria that directly relate to the understanding goals.*
   - *They should generate suggestions for improvement in both the students' work and the teaching.*
   - *They should include informal as well as formal assessment activities.*
   - *They should be conducted by teachers, outsiders, and students themselves (peer and self-assessments).*
   - *Assessment rubrics should be developed jointly with students.*
   - *The "Ladder of Feedback" should be used to provide explicit suggestions for four phases of participating in assessments.*
   - *Technologies may support systematic review and revision.*

5. Engage learners in reflective, **collaborative** communities.
   - *Teachers should engage learners in dialogue and reflection about their understanding.*
   - *Teachers should foster a culture of learning that values respect for diverse perspectives, reciprocity, and collaboration.*
   - *Technologies may be used to support reflection and collaboration.*

Situational Principles

for generative topics
- *In a thematic instruction context, choose generative topics related to the theme.*
- *When dealing with inflexible curricular plans, shift gradually toward framing the required topics in ways that are generative for learners.*

for understanding goals
- *When the context's goals do not align well with understanding goals, begin with areas of alignment.*
- *Where standards and behavioral objectives are required, teachers may*

wish to revise current goal statements to support one or more dimensions of understanding.

for performances of understanding
- *If learners are unfamiliar with Teaching for Understanding principles, begin with easily accessible performances of understanding and gradually progress to more complex ones.*
- *for ongoing assessment*
- *Where standards and standardized tests are the primary measure of accomplishment, teachers should attempt to identify understanding-oriented questions on which to focus ongoing assessment.*
- *When ongoing assessment is unfamiliar, simple forms of feedback aligned with goals may be needed until the culture of analyzing and revising draft work is more familiar and comfortable.*
- *for reflective, collaborative communities*
- *Where competition is the norm, create conditions for collaboration and involve students in the process of defining goals and assessment criteria.*
- *for use of technology*
- *Where technology is basic or limited, begin with simple innovations that address priority goals.*
- *Where technology is available, but teachers are not comfortable with the use of technology, use classroom helpers or guests to model effective practices and assist.*
- *Where technology is readily available, focus on integrating new communication tools to support target understanding goals.*

—CMR & ACC

FOSTERING UNDERSTANDING OUTCOMES

This chapter describes the Teaching for Understanding approach to instruction and ways of using it with new technologies. This framework is compared with other models of instructional design, including Merrill's first principles (chapter 3). Situational variables that affect implementation of this approach are described with recommendations for gradually shifting practice.

Introduction to Teaching for Understanding

The Teaching for Understanding framework synthesizes features of effective strategies for designing lesson plans or curriculum, conducting educational activities with learners, and assessing learners' progress. Researchers at the Harvard Graduate School of Education, working with a range of reflective school teachers, developed the initial framework through multiple rounds of collaborative research over a six-year period. Their purpose was to clarify features of teaching practices that successfully foster students' understanding. They began by clarifying a definition of understanding that highlights understanding as a "performance capability" rather than a mental possession (Perkins, 1998).[1] Students who understand a topic can apply their knowledge of the topic flexibly and creatively in a range of circumstances, including practical situations. The teachers and researchers wrote case studies of curriculum units and teaching practices that seemed particularly successful in developing this kind of understanding, and they analyzed patterns in these cases that correlated with current theories of effective teaching and learning. Synthesizing the empirical and analytic findings led them to formulate a framework designed to provide practical guidance for teachers (Blythe, 1998; Wiske, 1998).

The initial Teaching for Understanding framework consists of four elements along with specific criteria that teachers can use to guide them in designing, conducting, and assessing educational activities. These elements (explained more fully in the next section) are: generative curriculum topics,[2] explicit understanding goals, a rich sequence of performances of understanding, and ongoing assessment of student performances.[3] Recently, educators who have used this framework in conjunction with new educational technologies added a fifth element: collaborative, reflective communities (Wiske, Rennebohm-Franz, & Breit, 2005). This fifth element highlights some features that were implied by the original framework and that are both particularly important and more feasible as networked technologies become widely available to teachers and students.

Educators have found the Teaching for Understanding framework to be widely applicable, across subject matters, grade levels, and contexts. It does not define a particular curriculum, although the framework provides clear guidance to teachers about ways of identifying and defining worthwhile curriculum topics and goals. It does not prescribe highly detailed teaching routines or techniques, but offers specific principles to guide teachers as they sequence educational activities and integrate ongoing assessment of students' work. In short, the framework is roomy yet specific.

The Teaching for Understanding framework provides guidance for teachers whose purpose is to develop learners' understanding in ways that enable the learners to apply what they know flexibly and creatively in the world. This purpose is different from a focus on narrow behavioral objectives, from recall of particular facts or formulas or procedures that might be required to complete structured multiple-choice items on tests, and from conceptual knowledge separated from a capacity to retrieve and fluently apply knowledge in a range of circumstances.

For two synergistic reasons, a reworking of Teaching for Understanding focuses on integrating new educational technologies within the framework (Wiske et al., 2005). First, the Teaching for Understanding framework can guide the

---

1. *Editors' note: This is part of curriculum theory, since it concerns what to teach.*
2. *Editors' note: This also is part of curriculum theory, but it is intimately tied to the instructional method, for without this kind of topic, the method is not possible. This shows the value in addressing multiple kinds of theory in a single document.*
3. *Editors' note: This is part of student assessment theory.*

use of new technologies in ways that specifically foster students' understanding of important goals. Many current analyses of school curriculum and pedagogy advocate integrating new technologies into teaching and learning in schools in order to prepare students for work and citizenship in the 21st century. This era is marked by a transformation of information and communication technologies which alter the kinds of activities that workers will be required to do. As computers are programmed to take over most routine computations and many routine mechanical tasks, human workers are increasingly required to perform "expert thinking" and "complex communication" (Levy & Murnane, 2004). To be responsible and effective citizens in an era when communication and transportation technologies enable collaboration and transfer of goods, information, and services around the globe, students must be able to communicate and collaborate effectively with others, including people quite different from themselves. Being able to use computers and networked technologies fluently is part of the repertoire that workers and citizens will need in the global information economy. All these reasons for integrating new technologies into schools have led to the purchase of hardware and software in many schools. But these acquisitions have not always led to educationally effective applications of the new technologies (Cuban, 2001). The Teaching for Understanding framework guides the selection and use of technologies in ways that directly improve students' understanding of important goals.

A second reason for integrating Teaching for Understanding with new technologies is that many new educational tools offer specific advantages over traditional school materials in fulfilling the criteria of the Teaching for Understanding elements. Interactive, multimedia, networked technologies provide means of making curriculum more generative, making goals accessible through a richer repertoire of learning activities, enabling ongoing assessment, feedback, and revision, and supporting collaboration and reflection among communities of learners. Accordingly, this chapter explicates a form of Teaching for Understanding that systematically integrates new technologies.

Universal Elements of the Teaching for Understanding Framework

The Teaching for Understanding framework is structured by five elements that reinforce and relate to one another coherently. They address fundamental questions that all educators must answer as they design and conduct instruction:

1. What topics are worth studying? *Generative Topics*
2. What exactly should students come to understand about these topics? *Understanding Goals*
3. How will students develop and demonstrate their understanding of these goals? *Performances of Understanding*

4. How will students and teachers track, assess, and improve learning? *Ongoing Assessment*

5. How will students and teachers learn together? *Reflective, Collaborative Communities*

In this section we explain each element, including the criteria that define it more specifically, and describe how new technologies provide particular advantages in fulfilling these criteria.

Generative Topics

When formulating generative curriculum topics, an educator should attempt to fulfill several criteria[4] simultaneously. Generative topics are connected to multiple important ideas within and across academic disciplines, domains, and subject matters. They should be framed in ways that are authentic, accessible, and interesting to students and related to students' experience. Ideally, they are also fascinating and compelling to the teacher, so that the teacher can invest the topic with his or her own passions. Furthermore, generative topics are approachable from what Howard Gardner (1991) calls "multiple entry points." Topics might be investigated through visual arts, music, fundamental or philosophical questions, a narrative story line, with mathematics, or through dance. Selecting topics that provide multiple entry points offers several means by which students can connect their particular interests and strengths to studying the topic. Finally, a generative topic should be one that can be framed in a way that generates and rewards continuous inquiry by revealing new questions as students delve into the topic.

How can new technologies provide significant leverage in making curriculum topics more generative? First, networked technologies may enable teachers to access resources and up-to-date information on the Internet that help students see connections between their lessons and problems or topics of authentic interest in the "real world." Second, multimedia technologies enable teachers and students to work with multiple entry points in ways that may be difficult or inconvenient to orchestrate with traditional technologies.[5] Finally, new technologies may enable teachers to present lessons with multiple pathways, such as WebQuests, that allow students to exercise some choice in the way they pursue their inquiry. In these ways, new technologies can make curriculum topics more generative by relating them to students' varied interests and making them accessible through multiple modes of learning.

---

4. *Editors' note: This method is elaborated to provide more detailed guidance by identifying criteria, rather than parts or kinds.*

5. *Editors' note: This is primarily in the media logic layer of design, but it will likely also require decisions in the message, control, and representation layers and could even involve the data management layer.*

Understanding Goals

To focus students' and teachers' efforts, it is important to define and publicize specific goals about what students should come to understand as they study generative topics. Educators should make the goals public and explicit, to help everyone involved in the learning process concentrate on the larger purposes of their work. The Teaching for Understanding framework emphasizes goals that require students to go beyond "the information given" (Bruner 1990), to construct their own understanding, and to apply their knowledge flexibly and creatively. Learners' understanding is conceived as a capability to perform flexibly and appropriately with what one knows in a range of circumstances.

Although many curriculum guides focus primarily on learning particular content, understanding goals should often encompass other dimensions, too. The Teaching for Understanding project defined four dimensions of understanding goals within and across disciplines: (1) *knowledge* (key theories and concepts or "big ideas"); (2) *methods* used in one or more disciplines to gather, analyze, and validate knowledge; (3) appreciating the *purposes* for learning, including the applications and limitations of particular kinds of understanding and developing the autonomy to formulate one's own purposes for learning; and (4) *forms of expression*, using multiple representations and rhetorical conventions to communicate one's knowledge effectively to different audiences.[6] With these four dimensions of understanding in mind, teachers should review the curriculum mandates and standards that they are required to address. They may be able to combine or relate items to formulate understanding goals that deal with multiple dimensions and focus on a generative topic, thereby accomplishing many parts of their mandated curriculum at once in a way that is meaningful for students.

A final criterion[7] for understanding goals is that they connect coherently across levels of a curriculum plan. For example, specific goals for a curriculum unit relate clearly to more overarching goals or "throughlines" for a semester or year of study. Similarly, understanding goals for a particular lesson or activity clearly connects to unit goals. Of course, students sometimes need to memorize material or practice routine skills or simply absorb information about a topic. These low-level tasks should always be undertaken, however, in pursuit of a higher-level understanding goal. When goals are publicly stated, both learners and teachers are always able to relate the reason for any particular assignment or activity to understanding goals.

How can new technologies help make understanding goals more accessible and achievable? Lesson materials presented in hyperlinked formats can help to make goals clear and explicit by enabling students to link to reminders and supportive information. Computer software can help students make sense of

---

6. *Editors' note: Again, this is part of curriculum theory but is appropriately integrated with instructional theory.*

7. *Editors' note: Again, criteria are used to provide more detail on the method: "present understanding goals."*

difficult, closely related concepts by presenting dynamic, interactive simulations that may illustrate the workings of a key concept in ways that cannot be observed in nature or easily illustrated in a static medium. For example, conceptually enhanced simulations (Snir, Smith, & Grosslight, 1995) help to show how heat and temperature or weight and density are related and illustrate the role of friction in affecting motion. Technology used in this way helps students make sense of conceptually difficult understanding goals.

New technologies can also show multiple linked representations[8] of an entity such as a mathematical function. Graphing calculators that display both the symbolic and graphical representation of a function help students see how to relate these alternative mathematical representations and appreciate the kinds of problems that each representation illuminates most effectively. Of course, such technologies can be used in ways that obscure or undermine understanding instead of promoting it. Identifying and publicizing clear goals and keeping goals visible to learners are ways to gain significant educational leverage from new educational technologies.

Performances of Understanding

By defining understanding as a performance capability, Teaching for Understanding draws attention to active application of knowledge as an essential aspect of learning. In fact, the framework names *Performances of Understanding* as the primary way for students to develop and demonstrate understanding of target goals. Performances of understanding go beyond rehearsing routine skills or recalling information that has been taught. They should require active learning and creative thinking so that students stretch their minds to construct and apply their knowledge of target topics and goals.

The Teaching for Understanding framework recommends that teachers orchestrate a progression of performances[9] that helps students build on what they know initially to develop more complex and sophisticated understanding. An effective sequence of performances enables students to learn and express themselves using a rich range of materials, varied entry points, and "multiple intelligences" (Gardner, 1999). First, introductory or "messing about" (Hawkins, 1965) performances of understanding invite students to relate their prior knowledge and experience to the topic they will study and to pose questions about what they hope to learn. Based on this information, teachers can then present new knowledge connected to what learners already know and care about.

Second, teachers structure a cycle of "guided inquiry" performances. Teachers explain concepts, demonstrate methods, and model effective strategies and

---

8. Editors' note: *This is clearly in the representation layer of design.*

9. Editors' note: *In terms of the categories identified in chapter 2, this method is "content sequencing." Teaching for Understanding is the "instructional approach." And performance of understanding is an "instructional component," while culminating performance (see next paragraph) is one component of this component.*

examples, all with a focus on target goals. In this stage of performances, teachers provide guidance and focus students' attention as students conduct investigations and prepare drafts of products to develop and demonstrate their understanding. Finally, a "culminating performance" should give students an opportunity to work more independently, to synthesize knowledge and skills they have developed, and to apply this understanding by developing and polishing a finished product or performance.

As students progress through this sequence of performances, teachers diminish the coaching they provide as students learn how to exercise more initiative and autonomy in applying their understanding. The culminating performance may be more generative if it allows students to present their knowledge to an authentic audience so that students have an opportunity to explain their ideas in relation to a real-world problem, answer meaningful questions, and practice making their understanding clear to others.

New technologies can enrich the range of ways that learners develop and demonstrate their understanding. Students with different strengths and interests are more likely to engage and learn if performances of understanding include varied tasks and resources with multiple media and formats (Rose & Meyer, 2002). Multimedia technologies allow students to use multiple intelligences: mathematical-symbolic, kinesthetic-movement, verbal, visual, auditory, interpersonal, and intrapersonal-reflective in constructing and expressing their understanding. New tools, including the Internet, enable students to create and synthesize products that combine multiple media and present their work even to distant audiences, using video, music, animated diagrams, and other media that previously required sophisticated professional tools and techniques. Web-Quests and other kinds of inquiry-structuring educational software packages often propose ways for students to conduct inquiry in teams so that students pursue different paths or take on different roles and then collaborate on comparing their findings (Brown & Campione, 1990). The Teaching for Understanding framework provides focused guidance to teachers and students so that their use of these richly engaging tools remains centered on developing understanding of target goals.

Ongoing Assessment

The fourth element identified by the Teaching for Understanding project is ongoing assessment. Both the cases of successful teaching studied by the Teaching for Understanding project and many theories of effective instruction emphasize the value of providing frequent assessments of student performance based on explicit, public criteria that directly relate to target understanding goals. Assessment is most valuable when it is conducted frequently, not just at the end of the process of completing a culminating performance, and when the assessment process generates suggestions for improvement. The suggested improvements may be in the teaching[10] as well as in the students' work. The Teaching for Understanding framework recommends that teachers embed informal assessments into the learning process, such as informal observations of student discussions or casual reviews of written work, as well as more formal assessment activities, such as a structured analysis in relation to a rubric.

Assessments from multiple sources promote understanding. Students often benefit from hearing critiques or feedback from people other than their teachers, such as outside experts, coaches, authentic audiences such as policy makers, and students themselves. Criteria should be made public, so that students can conduct effective assessments of their own and peers' work. Involving students in developing and applying assessment rubrics helps students understand the criteria of high-quality work and see alternative ways for satisfying those criteria.

Students who are not accustomed to shouldering the responsibility and authority for assessing their own work[11] often benefit from specific coaching in strategies for providing effective feedback. Researchers at Harvard's Project Zero recommended a particular protocol called the "Ladder of Feedback" (Perkins, 2003) that provides explicit suggestions for four phases of participating in assessments. These are: ask questions of clarification, value strengths, identify concerns, and offer suggestions for improvement. This protocol structures a process for providing nonthreatening and constructive feedback, couched in relation to a public set of criteria or rubric.

The potential of new technologies to support review and revision is obvious. Capturing student products in digital forms greatly simplifies the process of revision by enabling students to reposition components of their work and change some weak parts while preserving other strong parts. Using a word processor to draft and revise work makes assessment and improvement much easier than writing with the fat red pencils with no erasers that first graders often use. Networked technologies may also help students share their work with diverse audiences and seek feedback from authentic critics outside their classroom.

Reflective, Collaborative Communities

Several people who used the Teaching for Understanding framework with new technologies recognized a fifth element that was implied by the original framework, but not explicitly named. This element is engaging learners in reflective, collaborative communities.[12] Increasing recognition of the importance of social interaction for learning, along with the special opportunities that networked technologies offer for supporting reflection and collaboration, led to the addition of this element to the framework (Wiske et al., 2005).

---

10. *Editors' note: Of course, this is no longer student assessment theory, but instructional evaluation theory. Clearly, the two are highly interrelated and appropriately addressed together here.*
11. *Editors' note: Here we see the values of the theory focusing on student empowerment. This is very important for knowledge works and therefore for an Information-Age educational system.*
12. *Editors' note: This is in the strategy layer of design.*

Teachers should engage learners in dialogue and reflection about their understanding, using shared goals and a common language. Students benefit from learning about diverse perspectives on what they are studying and varied ways of thinking. Peer assessments are valuable in part because they give students an opportunity to use shared criteria to examine multiple responses to a problem or project. Students learn from analyzing and discussing how various examples relate to criteria for high-quality work. This kind of exchange supports learning when it takes place in an atmosphere of respect, reciprocity, and collaboration among members of a community who value their communal accomplishments, as well as individual success.

For this element of Teaching for Understanding, the advantages of using new educational technologies are easily identified. When learners create their work with digital technologies, they can easily combine their components into a collaborative product. Networked technologies allow collaborators who are separated by time or distance to exchange, integrate, and revise work easily. Collaborations mediated by networked communication, such as email or electronic conferencing software, are typically conducted in written language or some other concrete artifact. The process of translating ideas into an artifact promotes a level of analysis and reflection that is not required by oral and nonverbal communication. Such products can then be reviewed and annotated. Thus, online collaboration can be particularly beneficial in promoting reflection.

Teaching for Understanding and Other Educational Frameworks

The Teaching for Understanding framework distills findings from empirical and theoretical research on effective teaching. It is easy, therefore, to correlate elements of this framework with other models and syntheses such as Merrill's first principles of instructional design (chapter 3; Merrill, 2002).

Generative Topics

The element of generative topics is related to several of Merrill's principles. Generative topics may be framed as problems or projects that provide a sustained and meaningful focus of inquiry as students learn and apply a range of understandings. In this respect, the generative topic element may be regarded as similar to project-based learning and the resulting learning experiences should implement Merrill's principle 1—Problem-centered instruction (chapter 3). Generative topics also relate to students' interests and experience and, accordingly, this element addresses Merrill's principle 2—activation of students' prior knowledge. This criterion also recalls the "learner-centered" feature of effective learning environments as characterized by the National Research Council (1999).

Other criteria for generative topics assure that the topic or project also directly relates to important ideas in one or more academic disciplines. Effective investigations of generative topics will also create opportunities for students to apply new knowledge and skills in their lives. So it is likely that Merrill's principle 4—application, and principle 5—integration, are also implemented.

Understanding Goals

According to criteria for the Teaching for Understanding framework, levels of understanding goals relate coherently from lesson goals, to unit goals, to overarching goals for a term or year. This coherent progression responds to Merrill's corollary to principle 1—problem-centered learning: learning is promoted when learners solve a progression of problems that are explicitly compared to one another. Focusing on multiple dimensions of understanding goals provides opportunities for students to solve problems and study topics from multiple perspectives, which addresses Merrill's principle 4—application.

This element of the Teaching for Understanding framework is clearly related to another element of the National Research Council's features of effective designs for learning: that they are "knowledge-centered" (1999). The Teaching for Understanding framework describes a range of dimensions of understanding, however, that broadens conceptions of "knowledge" to encompass more than just subject matter content. As shown in Figure 11.1 (Boix-Mansilla & Gardner, 1998, p. 198), these dimensions include knowledge (concepts and beliefs), methods (attitudes and procedures for building and validating knowledge), purposes (awareness of the uses and limitations of knowledge), and forms (mastery of genres and symbols systems coupled with consideration of audience).

Performances of Understanding

An effective enactment of a sequence of Performances of Understanding, in accord with the Teaching for Understanding framework, addresses each of Merrill's instructional phases as described by his principles 2 through 5: Activation of students' prior knowledge (introductory "messing about" performances); demonstration and application (guided inquiry performances); and integration (culminating performances). The systematic progression of active learning outlined by the criteria for Performances of Understanding is also reminiscent of

Knowledge	Methods	Purposes	Forms
A. Transformed intuitive beliefs	A. Healthy skepticism	A. Awareness of the purposes of knowledge	A. Mastery of performance genres
B. Coherent and rich conceptual webs	B. Building knowledge in the domain or subject matter	B. Uses of knowledge	B. Effective use of symbol systems
		C. Ownership and autonomy	C. Consideration of audience and context

Figure 11.1 Dimensions of Understanding and Their Features

several other theories of learning. Brown, Collins, and Duguid's (1989) theory of situated cognition emphasizes the importance of engaging students in developing understanding by applying knowledge to meaningful tasks. Their conception of cognitive apprenticeship advocates learning through first watching model performances, then attempting similar performances while being coached, and gradually developing expertise as scaffolding is diminished and the learner operates more independently.

A common misperception about the Teaching for Understanding framework is that students should be turned loose for "discovery learning" without any direct instruction from teachers. Of course, students do need to learn some core content and basic skills, and direct instruction methods[13] are sometimes appropriate and valuable. The Teaching for Understanding framework advocates teaching this material as part of the process of studying a generative topic and of developing students' understanding of higher order goals. For example, students can learn proper grammar and spelling and new vocabulary words while preparing a piece of writing for presentation to an audience. Students are more likely to remember and appreciate these basic lessons if they learn them in the process of doing interesting and meaningful work.

Ongoing Assessment

The Teaching for Understanding framework's approach to ongoing assessment is consistent with many other theories of effective learning and teaching that recommend integrated assessments. The National Research Council (1999) framework recommends "assessment-centered" designs for learning. Their criteria correlate well with the Teaching for Understanding framework: public criteria, frequent assessments with feedback, and involving students in assessing their own work. Feedback is widely recognized as one of the most important components of guiding learners (Andre, 1997; Gagné, 1985). Gradually shifting more responsibility to students for tracking and critiquing their own work is consistent with a number of theories that emphasize the importance of developing students' autonomy and confidence in themselves as learners[14] (Collins, Brown, & Holum, 1991; Palincsar & Brown, 1984; Scardamalia & Bereiter, 1985).

The ongoing assessment element of Teaching for Understanding correlates with several of Merrill's principles. Offering frequent and multiple opportunities for students to receive feedback on their performance is part of effectively implementing Merrill's principle 4—application. Ongoing assessment informs teachers about how best to adjust instruction to help students develop and apply their understanding in a range of settings. This process contributes to developing understanding that may prove useful beyond the traditional classroom and

---

13. *Editors' note: See chapter 5 for details. Again, this shows that it is often beneficial to use different approaches in your instruction.*
14. *Editors' note: Again, empowering learners is an important value for an Information-Age educational system.*

implements Merrill's principle 5—integration. The Teaching for Understanding framework's emphasis on the value of assessment from multiple sources, is consistent with Merrill's recommendation that the integration phase include opportunities for students to reflect on their knowledge and discuss or defend it with others.

Reflective, Collaborative Communities

The element of reflective, collaborative communities is consistent with many theories that emphasize the value of dialogue, interaction, modeling, and consideration of principles in relation to practice. Dewey (1916/1966) and Vygotsky (1978) focused on the importance of tools, including language, in mediating learning. Building on their theories, social constructivists highlight the value of both coaches and peers in providing scaffolding that augments the individual's emerging understanding (Burton & Brown, 1979; Collins et al., 1987). The cognitive apprenticeship instructional model (Collins et al., 1991) engages students in working on projects as teams with an instructor who models and coaches desired performances. Lave and Wenger (1990) note that people learn effectively from and with one another when they share common goals and collaborate on defining and developing a joint repertoire of practices. They base this view on their observations of learning in natural rather than formal instructional settings. Reflection (Schön, 1983; Eraut, 1994) is commonly touted as an important part of professional learning, as practitioners analyze practice in relation to principles, but the same processes are beneficial with all learners when the goal is understanding defined as a capability to perform with one's knowledge.

Learning communities developed in keeping with the Teaching for Understanding framework may help implement several of Merrill's first principles. The learning community may be a place for activating student interest and experience (principle 2—activation) as community members share ideas, questions, and emotions about what is being studied. Reflection and collaboration may promote the learning process by providing opportunities for community members to demonstrate new knowledge to each other (principle 3—demonstration) and to apply and reflect on what they are learning (principle 4—application). And when learning communities provide ongoing support to members in creating new expressions of understanding and engage members in reflection about these expressions and the understandings they reveal, the community is implementing the multiple components of Merrill's principle 5—integration.

Section Summary

The relationship between Teaching for Understanding principles and Merrill's first principles is summarized in Figure 11.2. Relationships between related principles are classified as probable—likely to exist; possible—may exist in certain settings; or indirect—indirectly related.

Teaching for Understanding Elements	Merrill's First Principle				
	1: Problem centered	2: Activation	3: Demonstration	4: Application	5: Integration
Generative Topics	Possible	Possible		Indirect	Indirect
Understanding Goals	**Probable**			Enabled	
Performances of Understanding		**Probable**	**Probable**	**Probable**	**Probable**
Ongoing Assessment				**Probable**	Possible
Reflective, Collaborative Communities		Possible	Possible	Possible	Possible

Figure 11.2 Relationship between Teaching for Understanding Elements and Merrill's First Principles

Situational Principles for Teaching for Understanding

As with every instructional theory, situational factors shape how teachers may effectively apply principles of Teaching for Understanding with new technologies. Perhaps the most important situational influences are the teachers and students themselves, including their knowledge, beliefs, skills, and attitudes. Contextual factors are also important, such as key actors (administrators, teaching colleagues, fellow students, and students' families), policies, resources, organizational structures, and cultural characteristics of the educational setting and community. These factors influence how teachers interpret and apply each element of the Teaching for Understanding framework, how they coherently relate these elements, and how they integrate new technologies.

In the following sections, we highlight important situationalities that affect teachers' application of the Teaching for Understanding framework elements in real (and complex) education settings.

Generative Topics

Some schools encourage or require teachers to organize curriculum around a central topic or theme. Others encourage learning through inquiry into engaging problems or by conducting meaningful projects. In these situations, teachers should structure curriculum around generative topics related to these themes or projects, so long as teachers have the flexibility and resources to approach topics in ways that relate to their own passions and students' interests.

In many schools, however, teachers and students are expected to work through a particular textbook or programmed sequence of materials which is not organized around meaningful projects or problems. Under these conditions, teachers may be well advised to shift gradually toward organizing curriculum around a generative topic. For example, the teacher may design a way to introduce a required topic with art work, a poem, music, or a problem that connects the topic to the teacher's own interests or the students' experience, rather than immediately implementing all the principles discussed earlier. The teacher may also formulate an intriguing question about the topic so that students feel invited to pursue continuing inquiry, not just "cover" the required content. By gradually addressing some criteria for generative topics, teachers may make learning somewhat more meaningful for students without being sanctioned for straying too far from the required curriculum. As students demonstrate understanding of required topics taught in generative ways, teachers may be increasingly able to formulate curriculum that more fully fulfills the criteria for generative topics.

One general implication of the Teaching for Understanding framework is that teachers should use their judgment about how to adjust topics and design learning experiences to engage their learners while taking account of norms, materials, and requirements in their setting. Based on their knowledge of their own students' interests and experiences, teachers may modify the formulation and treatment of generative topics to enrich understanding for their particular learners.

Understanding Goals

The extent to which the teachers', students', and context's views of instructional goals align with the goals of Teaching for Understanding will influence the most effective way for teachers to interpret and apply this element of the framework. Initially, the Understanding Goals might reflect areas of agreement between required curriculum content, teachers' own expertise and judgment, and the recommendations of the Teaching for Understanding framework. For example, when teachers are required to address rigidly specified curriculum standards and prepare students for standardized assessments linked to these standards, they might have difficulty identifying items that meet the criteria for understanding goals. A slight shift in wording may transform a low-level goal into one that stimulates more active learning, higher order thinking, and meaningful application. For example, a low-level goal such as "students will learn the steps in the scientific method" suggests that students need only memorize stages in some predefined model of scientific research. In contrast, an understanding goal such as "students will understand how to apply systematic methods of scientific inquiry" incorporates the low-level goal into one that aims for more ambitious, meaningful, and active learning. With the dimensions of understanding in mind, teachers may see ways to integrate standards dealing with content, methods, purposes, and forms to accomplish multiple curriculum goals through inquiry into one generative topic.

Performances of Understanding

The Teaching for Understanding framework emphasizes that learners develop and demonstrate understanding through performances that require them to think with what they know. Accordingly, the framework advocates engaging students in active learning through performances of understanding. However, these pedagogical values and approaches are inconsistent with much of the work that students do in most schools. Goodlad's (1984) characterizations of school activities showed a preponderance of teachers presenting "frontal teaching" and of students engaged in listening or demonstrating simply that they had learned what they were told.

In situations where teachers and students are not accustomed to approaches consistent with Teaching for Understanding principles or the context is not conducive, teachers begin with simple performances of understanding and incorporate more complex performances as students become comfortable with this approach. When a simpler approach is needed, pausing in a lecture to ask a question that does not have a single correct answer may begin to engage students in performances that develop and demonstrate understanding. As students and teachers become more comfortable pursuing open-ended inquiry with rounds of assessment and revision, they may become ready to develop to more complex and challenging performances. Such a gradual refinement and synthesis of students' understanding can lead to a more ambitious culminating performance that may include presenting one's knowledge to an authentic audience. Teachers may help students practice sharing their work effectively with other members of the class before attempting a more public presentation. A public performance works especially well when the content is of interest to the audience and students have created meaningful new understandings to share.

Ongoing Assessment

For several reasons, the ongoing assessment element of the Teaching for Understanding approach may be the most difficult to enact. Implementing this element of the framework requires having successfully addressed the other elements. In order to conduct assessments with explicit, public criteria related to goals, teachers must have clearly defined understanding goals and shared them with their students. In order for students to produce work to assess, they must have been engaged in a series of performances that enabled them to create such products or performances. Finally, meeting the criterion of engaging learners in frequent assessments that generate useful feedback requires teachers to build an atmosphere that encourages sharing "first draft" work, rather than honoring only highly polished products.

The current educational climate in the United States is permeated by a focus on holding schools, teachers, and students accountable through high-stakes standardized tests. In many settings, these tests consist primarily of multiple choice or short-answer items that demonstrate students' ability to recall facts or solve defined problems, but do not require students to demonstrate flexible understanding. In contexts that measure educational achievement in terms of standardized test scores, producing correct answers fast is often more valued than taking time to consider alternative perspectives, puzzle through challenging problems, and revise work through several drafts to develop a more complex and sophisticated understanding.

Recognizing the pressure to succeed on high-stakes tests, teachers in such settings may analyze the tests to look for items that require understanding. They may ask, "What items on these required tests are worth teaching for understanding?" For example, most standardized tests include some tasks that require students to solve complex problems, make sense of extended passages, and produce a paragraph or more of well-reasoned and articulate prose. Teachers may apply the principles of ongoing assessment to such items, for example, by defining with students the criteria of effective responses to these items and using these criteria as the basis for cycles of drafting, reviewing, and revising students' work.

As with other elements of the Teaching for Understanding framework, gradual shifts toward the recommended practices may be appropriate when teachers or students are not familiar with embedded and ongoing assessment. Teachers might start by gradually weaving in some aspects of ongoing assessment, such as publishing assessment criteria well before students must complete their final product. When students are ready, the approach to ongoing assessment can be strengthened by giving students an opportunity to analyze a draft in relation to these criteria, and providing suggestions for revising the work. When the ongoing assessment element requires a fundamentally new approach to assessment, part of the assessment is to teach students specific behaviors and vocabulary for conducting peer and self assessments, such as the Ladder of Feedback approach mentioned earlier. When students and teachers are well-versed in using peer and self-assessment strategies, students become better able to participate in, and realize more educational value from conducting effective assessments of their own and their classmates' performances.

Reflective, Collaborative Communities

Cultivating norms of reflection and collaboration in a community of learners is also subject to situationalities. As we stated earlier, teachers need to establish norms with their students and model through their own behavior the values that such communities practice: respect, reciprocity, and regard for diverse perspectives and for communal efforts. If students are accustomed to competing for high grades or scarce resources, teachers will need to define and create conditions in which other values and strategies lead to success and satisfaction. Making collaboration an explicit part of the learning process and rewarding effective teamwork through assessment and grading practices may motivate students to work with others.

Students may also need practice in analyzing and reflecting on work in relation to specific criteria. Involving students in the process of defining criteria may help them appreciate the meaning of the criteria and the process of using criteria to analyze products or performances. When students are experienced with collaborative learning communities and motivated to participate, the community aspect of the learning environment does not need to be explicitly taught. Rather, reflective, collaborative community is continuously lived out through the daily interactions among teachers, students, and other members of the community.

Technology

Situational factors also affect the way teachers are able to integrate new technologies into their practice. Access to reliable technology is not the only important consideration. Teachers' and students' technical expertise is also relevant, as is their ability to make effective use of this expertise in relation to important learning goals. For example, teachers may be fluent users of a word processing program, but not have a clear plan for teaching students how to improve their writing through effective use of a word processor. In situations where students have access to only a limited number of computers, teachers will need to help students develop effective strategies for taking turns and perhaps working in groups. Teachers who want to integrate complex technology, such as computers linked to the Internet, also need to develop a dependable technical support system, perhaps by working with colleagues, parents, or the technical assistance personnel in their system.

In situations where access to technology, technical expertise, strategies for integrating technology with teaching, or technical assistance is basic or limited, teachers should begin with relatively simple innovations that do not strain their resources. For a simpler approach to using technology, students and teachers might use basic software to create static presentations or communicate outside of class with email. Students who are accustomed to muddling through with unfamiliar technologies in their out-of-school lives are often more willing to proceed through trial and error than teachers who feel responsible for maintaining an orderly and productive classroom atmosphere. When teachers are not comfortable using new technologies, but the technologies are available for use, one strategy that works is to invite helpers into the classroom—parents, older students, technical assistants from the school or community—when the class will be using new tools.

In a context where teachers and students use advanced technologies daily, both in school and out of school, the use of technology is very different. Presentations in class will use multiple media such as video, audio, graphics, and animation. Communication tools may include e-mail, chat, and virtual classroom environments with online collaboration tools. Students in such classes may become expert helpers for other classes. In situations like these, integrated technologies will become embedded in the daily process of teaching and learning, preparing students for future life-long learning in and beyond their formal school years.

Integrating Teaching for Understanding and New Technologies

Teaching for Understanding and integrating new technologies into the classroom are challenging innovations that are best promoted through cycles of taking small steps. Rather than trying to teach with new hardware, new software, and an unfamiliar set of pedagogical strategies, teachers are well advised to introduce new elements incrementally. Teachers' beliefs about students' capabilities and teachers' own expertise often change gradually as they try new strategies and discover that students are able to work more independently, responsibly, and effectively than teachers had imagined (Sandoltz, Ringstaff, & Dwyer, 1997; Wiske et al. 2005).

In attempting to implement new pedagogies and technologies, teachers might apply the principles of Teaching for Understanding to their own process of learning. To make this process generative for themselves, teachers could consider how the framework connects to their own experience, passions, or priority problems. They may identify some elements of the Teaching for Understanding framework that seem particularly promising or valuable and define personal understanding goals. For instance, a teacher might perceive that focusing on generative topics and integrating ongoing assessment were too complex at first. Instead, her initial goal might be learning how to integrate more performances of understanding into her lessons or how to make some understanding goals explicit. Or she might want to understand how to make sure that her uses of technology advance students' mastery of difficult curriculum priorities.

With her own understanding goals clearly in mind, the teacher could plan a sequence of performances to develop this understanding; that is, ways to apply and extend her own understanding through working with students. For example, she might try announcing her understanding goals to students before beginning a unit that integrates new technology. A simple ongoing assessment activity would be reflecting on this experience in relation to the teacher's own understanding goals, guided by the criteria for the relevant elements of the framework. Conducting such an informal assessment may generate ideas for improving the approach next time. Finding one or more colleagues who are interested in collaborating on exploring this framework is an excellent way to share the challenges and satisfactions. Working with colleagues this way is a strategy for developing a collaborative, reflective community to support learning about Teaching for Understanding with new technology.

Teachers who are interested in exploring this approach may want to investigate resources that are available online at a Web site called Education with New Technologies (http:/learnweb.harvard.edu/ent). This Web site includes a gallery of portraits of teachers who use Teaching for Understanding to integrate technology in their classrooms. The Web site also provides a Library of resources and a Workshop with an interactive online tool for developing curriculum structured by this framework. The Education with New Technologies Web site is available at no cost. Educators who want more support or to engage a group, a school, or a district in using the Teaching for Understanding framework or related ideas may want to consider online professional development courses offered through WIDE World (http://wideworld.pz.harvard.edu) at the Harvard Graduate School of Education. WIDE World courses provide personalized coaching on research-based pedagogies including the Teaching for Understanding framework.

Conclusion

We hope that this chapter will help educational practitioners and scholars to build a common knowledge base about how to teach for understanding. In many respects, the elements of the Teaching for Understanding framework are familiar to most thoughtful teachers, school leaders, and analysts of effective pedagogy. Focusing curriculum on generative topics, making understanding goals public, engaging students in meaningful activities to develop target understandings, integrating frequent feedback with suggestions for improvement, and fostering collaborative learning communities are strategies that most educators endorse and believe they practice. Yet they often lack precise language that promotes specific consensus, systematic progress, and reliable assessment focused on these goals. Even superb teachers who work with the Teaching for Understanding framework usually realize that there are at least some small ways in which they can tweak their usual lessons to enact these elements more fully and coherently. Similarly, educational leaders and researchers find that this framework provides specific support for defining, fostering, and measuring improvements in teaching.

Such a framework becomes both more necessary and more feasible with the use of new technologies. It is more necessary to be sure that the new tools actually support better teaching and learning, and more feasible because digital, multimedia, networked tools support active, meaningful learning in richer ways than traditional school texts and chalkboards. Educators who wish to integrate new technologies into their repertoire may want to explicitly apply the principles of the framework as they undertake a process of developing and assessing complex, new practices.

References

Andre, T. (1997). Selected microinstructional methods to facilitate knowledge construction: Implications for instructional design. In R. D. Tennyson, F. Schott, N. Seel, & S. Dijkstra (Eds.), *Instructional design: International perspective* (Vol. 1, pp. 243–267). Mahwah, NJ: Erlbaum.

Blythe, T. (1998). *The teaching for understanding guide.* San Francisco: Jossey-Bass.

Boix-Mansilla, V., & Gardner, H. (1998). What are the qualities of understanding? In M. S. Wiske (Ed.), *Teaching for understanding: Linking research with practice* (pp. 161–196). San Francisco: Jossey-Bass.

Brown, A. L., & Campione, J. C. (1990). Communities of learning and thinking, or a context by any other name. *Contributions to Human Development, 21,* 108–126.

Brown, J. S., Collins, A., & Duguid, P. (1989). Situated cognition and the culture of learning. *Educational Researcher, 18*(1), 32–42.

Bruner, J. (1990). *Acts of meaning.* Cambridge, MA: Harvard University Press.

Burton, R. R., & Brown, J. S. (1979). Toward a natural-language capability for computer assisted instruction. In H. O'Neil (Ed.), *Procedures for instructional systems development.* New York: Academic Press.

Collins, A., Brown, J. S., & Holum, A. (1991). Cognitive apprenticeship: Making thinking visible. *American Educator, 15*(3), 6–46.

Collins, A., Brown, J. S., & Newman, S. E. (1987). *Cognitive apprenticeship: Teaching the craft of reading, writing and mathematics* (Technical Report No. 403). Cambridge, MA: BBN Laboratories, Centre for the Study of Reading, University of Illinois.

Cuban, L. (2001). *Oversold and underused: Computers in the classroom.* Cambridge, MA: Harvard University Press.

Dewey, J. (1966). *Democracy and education.* New York: Free Press. (Original work published 1916)

Eraut, M. (1994). *Developing professional knowledge and competence.* London: Falmer Press.

Gagné, R.M. (1985). *The conditions of learning* (4th ed.). New York: Holt, Rinehart & Winston.

Gardner, H. (1991). *The unschooled mind: How children think and how schools should teach.* New York: Basic Books.

Gardner, H. (1999). *Intelligence reframed: multiple intelligences for the 21st century.* New York: Basic Books.

Goodlad, J. (1984). *A place called school: Prospects for the future.* New York: McGraw-Hill.

Hawkins, D. (1965). Messing about in science. *Science and Children, 2*(5), 5–9.

Lave, J., & Wenger, E. (1990). *Situated learning: Legitimate peripheral participation.* Cambridge, UK: Cambridge University Press.

Levy, F., & Murnane, R. J. (2004). *The new division of labor: How computers are creating the next job market.* Princeton, NJ: Princeton University Press.

Merrill, D. M. (2002). First principles of instruction. *Educational Technology Research and Development, 50*(3), 43–59.

National Research Council. (1999). *How people learn: Brain, mind, experience, and school* (J. D. Bransford, A. L. Brown, & R. R. Cocking, Eds.). Washington, D.C.: National Academy Press.

Palincsar, A. S., & Brown, A. L. (1984). Reciprocal teaching of comprehension-fostering and monitoring activities. *Cognition and Instruction, 1*(2), 117–175.

Perkins, D. (1998). What is understanding? In M. S. Wiske (Ed.), *Teaching for understanding: Linking research with practice* (pp. 39–58). San Francisco: Jossey-Bass.

Perkins, D. (2003). *King Arthur's round table: How collaborative conversations create smart organizations.* Hoboken, NJ: Wiley.

Rose, D. H., & Meyer, A. (2002). *Teaching every student in the digital age: Universal design for learning.* Alexandria, VA: ASCD.

Sandoltz, J. H., Ringstaff, C., & Dwyer, D. C. (1997). *Teaching with technology: Creating student centered classrooms.* New York: Teachers College Press.

Scardamalia, M., & Bereiter, C. (1985). Fostering the development of self-regulation in children's knowledge processing. In S. F. Chipman, J. W. Segal, & R. Glaser (Eds.), *Thinking and learning skills: Research and open questions* (pp. 563–577). Hillsdale, NJ: Erlbaum.

Schön, D. (1983). *The reflective practitioner: How professionals think in action.* London: Temple-Smith.

Snir, J., Smith, C., & Grosslight, L. (1995). Conceptually enhanced simulations: A computer tool for science teaching. In D. Perkins, J. L. Schwartz, M. M. West, & M. S. Wiske (Eds.), *Software goes to school: Teaching for understanding with new technologies.* New York: Oxford University Press.

Vygotsky, L. S. (1978). *Mind in society: The development of higher psychological processes.* Cambridge, MA: Harvard University Press.

Wiske, M. S. (Ed.). (1998). *Teaching for understanding: Linking research with practice.* San Francisco: Jossey-Bass.

Wiske, S., Rennebohm-Franz, K., & Breit, L. (2005). *Teaching for understanding with new technologies.* San Francisco: Jossey-Bass.

12
Fostering Affective Development Outcomes

Emotional Intelligence

BARBARA A. BICHELMEYER
Indiana University

JAMES MARKEN
Old Dominion University

TAMARA HARRIS
IBM Learning Development

MELANIE MISANCHUK
University of Guelph

EMILY HIXON
Purdue University Calumet

Barbara A. Bichelmeyer, PhD, is associate professor of instructional systems technology and associate dean of faculties at Indiana University. As associate professor, Barbara's research, teaching, and service focus on the areas of human performance improvement, interpersonal skill development, instructional design, instructional and program evaluation, adult learning, and technology integration in instructional environments. As associate dean of faculties, Barbara's portfolio of responsibilities includes curriculum development, course transfer, and degree articulation agreements. Barbara has served as consultant for the design, development, and evaluation of educational programs with organizations such as Procter & Gamble, Eli Lilly, and Microsoft. Barbara holds four degrees from the University of Kansas: BS in journalism (1982), BA in English (1986), MS in educational policy and administration (1988), and PhD in educational communications and technology (1991).

James Marken obtained his PhD in instructional systems technology from Indiana University in the summer of 2006; he is currently an assistant professor in the instructional design and technology program in the Darden College of Education at Old Dominion University. Marken's research interests center on the social and structural dynamics in organizations that affect human performance, especially in international contexts. Marken teaches classes in needs analysis, task analysis, human performance technology, knowledge management, and other human performance related areas. He is also active in several professional organizations both at the local and national level, especially AECT and ISPI.

Tamara Harris earned a bachelor of business from Western Illinois University (1992) and an MS in instructional systems technology from Indiana University-Bloomington (2000). Early in her career she worked at The Principal Financial Group in Des Moines, Iowa as a technology trainer and desktop support specialist. Ms. Harris expanded her skills in technology training, instructional design, project management, and network support with Bell Industries Systems Integration Group in Indianapolis, Indiana. After several years in instructional design and delivery, Ms. Harris joined Accenture (formerly Andersen Consulting) and transitioned into human performance consulting where she implemented business process reengineering initiatives for major telecommunications companies in Atlanta. In 2006, Ms. Harris joined IBM Learning Development as a learning specialist/instructional designer.

Melanie Misanchuk is a distance learning program development specialist at the Office of Open Learning at the University of Guelph in Ontario, Canada. She works with university faculty as well as with private sector clients to design courses delivered at a distance. She holds a PhD in instructional systems technology from Indiana University and an MA in French linguistics from the University of Calgary.

Emily Hixon, PhD, is an assistant professor of educational psychology in the Department of Teacher Preparation at Purdue University Calumet. Her degrees are from Indiana University Bloomington in instructional systems technology (MS and PhD) and educational psychology (MS). Prior to joining the faculty at Purdue Calumet in 2006, Dr. Hixon spent five years working in the field of faculty development and enhancement as an instructional designer at university teaching and learning centers. Her research interests involve effective technology integration and professional development and enhancement at both the K-12 and higher education levels. She has also been involved in many distance learning initiatives and is pursuing research in that area as well.

EDITORS' FOREWORD

Preconditions

Content
- *Focus on emotional intelligence as content*

Learners
- *All learners, though formal curriculum has focused on K-12*

Learning environments
- *All settings*

Instructional development constraints
- *No notable resource limitations (time or money)*

Values

about ends (learning goals)
- *Importance of emotional intelligence*
- *Importance of emotional learning to cognitive learning*
- *Importance of emotion and cognition for rational thinking*

about priorities (criteria for successful instruction)
- *[None specified]*

about means (instructional methods)
- *Create an emotionally healthy environment to enhance learning for all students*
- *Cannot be taught in the abstract*

about power (to make decisions about the previous three)
- *Models offered primarily by theorists but adapted by teachers*

Universal Methods

1. *Use stories with a problem orientation.*
   - *Introduce emotion in a non-personal way in stories.*
   - *Purposefully explore the feelings of characters in a story.*
   - *Tie what's happening in a story directly to events that are occurring in the lives of the children in the classroom.*
2. *Teach the language and concepts of emotion.*
3. *Model the skills of emotional intelligence.*
   - *React to the environment in an emotionally healthy way.*
   - *Teach in an emotionally healthy way.*
4. *Take time to deal with emotions.*
   - *Take advantage of varied and multiple practical experiences in the classroom, for application of skills in a variety of situations.*
   - *Introduce activities that foster emotional intelligence into cognitive lessons.*
5. *Provide active, integrated experiences to foster emotional competence.*
   - *Explore stories.*

- *Ask students to reflect on, consider, and name their own emotional responses.*
- *Incorporate instructional activities that foster emotional intelligence into lessons that facilitate cognitive, psychomotor, and social development.*

Situational Principles

- *With very young children (underdeveloped emotional intelligences), explicitly explore how objects can move us into different emotional states.*
- *With older children (more self-regulatory), help them to create their own strategies for display of emotions.*
- *With younger children, empathy can be increased through use of stories and guided discussions.*
- *With older children, lead discussions of how others make us feel and extrapolate to displays of emotion in presence of others.*
- *For extreme emotional problems or inappropriate displays of emotion, use conventional methods from counseling, such as activity reinforcement, activity bouncing, hurdle helping, and signal interference.*
- *With children who are not strong at assimilating emotional experiences and applying that knowledge at later times in other problem situations, diaries, or journaling can be helpful, or discussions of success stories.*
- *Where maladaptive strategies may have been learned at home, use art, stories, or diaries to help learners regulate their emotional responses and teachers understand the students.*

—*CMR & ACC*

FOSTERING AFFECTIVE DEVELOPMENT OUTCOMES: EMOTIONAL INTELLIGENCE

"Bloom's taxonomy" (Bloom, Englehart, Furst, Hill, & Krathwhol, 1956) of educational objectives for the cognitive domain is one of the most well-recognized models among those who work in the field of education. So it may come as a surprise to know that Bloom's taxonomy for the cognitive domain was accompanied by a taxonomy of educational objectives for the affective domain (Krathwohl, Bloom, & Masia, 1956). The authors of the taxonomy noted in the preface that they "found the affective domain much more difficult to structure, and we are much less satisfied with the result. Our hope is, however, that it will represent enough of an advance in the field to call attention to the problems of affective-domain terminology" (p. v).

Introduction to the Affective Domain

Krathwohl's taxonomy is the quintessential example of the broad and unfocused nature of the affective domain.

Definition

As one of the three domains of learning defined by Bloom (the third being the psychomotor domain), affect's place in instruction has long been largely misunderstood. The problems of understanding the role of the affective domain in instruction begin with its very definition. Martin and Briggs (1986) offer this explanation:

> The definition of the domain and the concepts that comprise it are so broad and often unfocused that all aspects of behavior not clearly cognitive or psychomotor are lumped together in a category called the affective domain. For example, all of the following terms can be found associated with affect: self-concept, motivation, interests, attitudes, beliefs, values, self-esteem, morality, ego development, feelings, need achievement, locus of control, curiosity, creativity, independence, mental health, personal growth, group dynamics, mental imagery, and personality...the catch-all phrase has become "the affective domain." (p. 12)

Boundaries of the Chapter

It is interesting that one of the few topical terms that Martin and Briggs's definition excludes is that of emotion. As a basic element of most of the other characteristics in the list, emotion is primordial and fundamental. In the 50 or more years since Krathwohl, Bloom, and Masia constructed a taxonomy for the affective domain, the topic of emotion and how it relates to learning has been the focus of much study. Many researchers have struggled with the general questions of what emotions are and why we have them (Calhoun & Solomon, 1984; Damasio, 1994; 2000; LeDoux, 1996; Plutchik, 1994), while others have concentrated on the role of emotion in intelligence and in learning (Elias et al., 1997; Greenspan & Benderly, 1997; Martin & Briggs, 1986; Salovey & Sluyter, 1997). There is growing acknowledgement that emotion plays a critical role in the learning process (Elias et al., 1997; Kovalik & Olsen, 1998; Vail, 1994).

Because of the important advances that have been made during the recent past in our understandings of emotions and their role in intelligence and learning, the focus of this chapter is on emotion, this one fundamental element of the affective domain. We will explore the role that emotion plays in intelligence, the process of emotional development, and principles of instruction that support the development of learners' emotional intelligence.

We acknowledge the importance of other elements of the affective domain that we will not explicitly be addressing, such as learners' inherent motivation and attitude states (Pintrich & Schunk, 1996), self-efficacy (Bandura, 1997), and interpersonal intelligences (Gardner, 1983). However, we believe that by focusing explicitly and exclusively on emotional intelligence and its development, we will be indirectly addressing the social environment from which emotions are born, as well as the motivations and attitudes that sometimes result from, and sometimes create, the emotions that humans feel (Ekman & Davidson, 1994; Lewis & Haviland, 1993; Plutchik, 1994).

Underlying Theories

Martin and Briggs's explanation of the affective domain exemplifies the long-held view in Western civilization—starting with the Greek philosophers Socrates and Plato, strongly endorsed by Descartes, and continuing through the ages—that emotion and cognition are separate domains (Damasio, 1994; Hunt, 1993), a view which continues to be held by many today. The typical person living in a Western culture views the relationship between cognition and emotion either as one in which emotions do not (and should not) affect the pure rationality of thought and intellect, or if emotions do have an impact, it is a negative sort, a "goad to cognition" (Zimiles, 1981, p. 52).

Recent scholarship from fields such as neurobiology, psychiatry, and research psychology refutes the rational/emotional dualism of Descartes and predecessors, and convincingly demonstrates that the brain/mind is an integrated unit such that thought, emotion, and sensation work together to bring about human experience and understanding of the world (Damasio, 1994; Greenspan & Benderly, 1997; LeDoux, 1996; Plutchik, 1994). It has long been known that "emotional" experiences have cognitive aspects (Izard, 1972; Plutchik, 1962). Recent research has convincingly demonstrated that even the most intellectual of pursuits is rife with emotional overtones (Mayer & Geher, 1996; Mayer & Salovey, 1993, 1997; Salovey & Mayer, 1989–1990; Salovey & Sluyter, 1997). Rather than thinking of cognition and emotion as dualistic, recent research calls us to an integration of these two aspects of learning and being.

Research related to the relationship between cognition and emotion has followed several distinct paths. Working with brain-damaged patients, neurologist Antonio Damasio (1994, 2000) has demonstrated that emotions are essential to rational thinking and that the absence of emotion can have detrimental effects on rationality. From their work with autistic children, Greenspan and Benderly (1997) have found that emotions influence cognitive growth through our abilities to make sense of sensations, to be intentional in our actions, and to understand images, ideas, and symbols. Working as a counseling psychologist, Saarni (1999) identified eight cognitive skills that lead to emotional competence, such as the ability to use vocabulary of emotion and the ability to differentiate experiences, as well as the capacity for self-efficacy.

Mayer and Salovey (1993, 1997) identified the construct of "emotional intelligence"; their work was popularized by journalist Daniel Goleman in the 1995 best-selling book titled after the construct name. Goleman's (1995) conception of emotional intelligence is likely the best known due to the popular success of his book. Hence the five domains of emotional intelligence with which most general readers are familiar are: (1) knowing one's emotions; (2) managing emotions; (3) motivating oneself; (4) recognizing emotions in others; and (5) handling relationships. Goleman asserts that emotional intelligence (EQ) is a better indicator of life success than is cognitive intelligence (IQ). This is a powerful claim and one that has surely caused the concept of emotional intelligence to gain attention in education and corporate training.

Importance of the Area

That emotions impact students' success will come as no surprise to anyone who has spent a measurable amount of time in the classroom. We see the role of emotion at play when students are so anxious about math that they cannot process what is being said, and when students are so excited by an exhibit at the museum that they remember historical dates—the same dates introduced previously by the teacher in the classroom—without successful retention.[1]

Although it comes as no surprise to teachers that emotions affect learning, schools have generally assumed responsibility for the cognitive domain, not the emotional one. Responsibility for emotional development was assumed to lie with parents at home rather than teachers at school. Indeed, one common objection to the integration of emotional elements into formal educational settings comes from those who view it as a sort of brainwashing (Martin & Reigeluth, 1999).

Despite these concerns, recent research showing emotions and cognition are inextricably linked means we can no longer argue about whether or not teachers have a responsibility to address the emotional development of their charges. Noting the simultaneity of affect and cognition, Beane (1990) states that "education *must* be affective and cannot be otherwise, just as it must be cognitive and cannot be noncognitive" (p. 10). Beane argues that "a theory of learning or schooling that ignores or denies affect is incomplete and inhuman" (p. 7).

Goleman's assertion that EQ is more important than IQ may or may not be true, but the researchers cited above have gathered a preponderance of evidence that emotion *is* important to individual success at work, in quality of life, in social experience, in communication, in learning and development, and in basic human cognitive processes and functioning. Because emotion and cognition are so linked in daily life, and because emotional intelligence has historically been ignored in formal education and instruction, the focus on better understanding the role of emotion and cognition has been paralleled by calls for more attention to emotions in formal schooling and instruction.

So, recent advances in research on emotion bring educators to a new point in our practice. The question that we must now address is this: "To what extent can teachers create the sort of environments and engage in instructional approaches that will facilitate the development of emotional intelligence for students in

1. *Editors' note: Addressing emotions in education, both as means for accelerated cognitive learning and as an important kind of learning in its own right, is an important characteristic of the Information-Age paradigm of education.*

their classrooms?" The rest of this chapter will be dedicated to synthesizing the current knowledge about instructional strategies that support the development of emotional intelligence.

General Description of Instructional Models for Emotional Intelligence

A variety of instructional models have been implemented in K-12 settings that address the concept of emotional intelligence. These models may be divided into three categories: (1) models in which the pedagogy or method of instruction requires skills related to emotional intelligence; (2) models that address the interrelationship between emotion and cognition in order to better facilitate cognitive learning; (3) programs that address emotional intelligence as the objective (content) of instruction. The third category is the focus of this chapter; however, instructional models in the first two categories deserve a moment of our attention.

Emotional Skill within a Pedagogical Approach

Notable examples of instructional models in which emotional skills are incorporated into pedagogical approaches come from the many educators who are actively working to make their schools more caring communities. Noddings (1992) has issued "The Challenge to Care in Schools" as an alternative approach to education in which we engage in classroom practices that foster the development of caring as well as competence in our students. Battistich and colleagues (Battistich, Solomon, Watson, & Schaps, 1997) promote the development of "communities" where "members care about and support each other, actively participate in and have influence on the group's activities and decisions, feel a sense of belonging and identification with the group, and have common norms, goals and values" (p. 137). Lewis and colleagues (Lewis, Schaps, & Watson, 1996) define five interdependent principles that must be practiced in order to create a "caring community of learners": warm, supportive, stable relationships; constructive learning; an important, challenging curriculum; intrinsic motivation; and attention to social and ethical dimensions of learning. Such definitions of schools as caring communities assume that students and teachers have certain skills related to emotional intelligence and are actively working toward emotional competence.

The call for emotionally intelligent instructional approaches is certainly warranted and has much merit. However, the focus of this chapter is on emotional intelligence as the goal and content *of* instruction, rather than as the pedagogical approach *to* instruction. Though there is certainly overlap between these two categories (one would hope that teachers model during their instruction the goals they hope their students will attain), the difference between emotional intelligence as a means of instruction and emotional intelligence as the goal of instruction is an important distinction.

Feeling-Thought Integration for Cognitive Development

It should also be noted that there are instructional approaches which address the interconnectedness of thought with feeling in order to foster better learning of cognitive skills. Such models include Caine and Caine's (1994) "brain-based schooling" approach and "integrated thematic instruction" (Kovalik & McGeehan, 1999; Kovalik & Olsen, 1998).These models are clearly distinct from instructional models that address emotional intelligence as the goal of instruction; but such models are relatively new and deserve to be acknowledged for their recognition of the importance of emotion in students' learning and general academic performance.

Programmatic Instruction for Emotional Intelligence

Having given a nod to instructional models that address emotional intelligence by other means, let us now turn our attention to the variety of instructional programs implemented in K-12 settings that focus on the concept of emotional intelligence as the goal of instruction. Many such programs exists, with the most well-known and well-researched being the Promoting Alternative Thinking Strategies (PATHS) program; the Seattle Social Development Project; the Resolving Conflict Creatively Program; Improving Social Awareness-Social Problem Solving Project (ISA/SPSP); the Child Development Project in Oakland, California; the Yale-New Haven Social Competence Promotion Program; Comfort Corner; and the Self-Science program at Nueva School in San Francisco. While all of these programs focus on the development of students' social-emotional learning (SEL), each one has unique features in terms of target audience, curricular material and instructional approaches used. Several programs which target K-12, elementary, gifted, and special needs students are described below.

The Improving Social Awareness-Social Problem Solving Project targets students in kindergarten through 12th grade, with an emphasis on elementary and middle grades. The program was developed by Maurice Elias, a professor of psychology at Rutgers, in collaboration with numerous other associates. The goal of the program is to increase interpersonal effectiveness; social decision making and problem solving activities are integrated throughout the program. The program includes 25 to 30 hours of highly structured classroom activities at each grade level which address three components of emotional intelligence, including stress management and impulse control, social problem solving and information processing, and behavioral social skills. The program generally involves two 40-minute lessons per week, and teachers are trained in specific questioning strategies to facilitate students' decision making and cognitive development. Activities included in each lesson may involve skill modeling, guided practice, role-playing, cooperative group projects, and writing assignments. Results from program assessments indicate that students who completed the program had a better understanding of the consequences of their behavior and were more sensitive to others' feelings than students who did not complete the program. These students also showed signs of better self-control, greater social awareness, and more robust social decision-making skills than students who did not complete the program (Matthews, Zeidner, & Roberts, 2004).

The PATHS program, developed by Mark Greenberg at the University of Washington, was designed for use in grades 1 to 5 with the aim of improving children's abilities to understand, express, and regulate emotion and to improve skills of social problem solving. Greenberg et al. (1995) reported that findings from program assessments indicated that participants improved in the areas of recognizing and understanding emotions, had better self-control as well as better planning skills for solving cognitive tasks, and better abilities to think before acting, along with more effective conflict resolution skills.

The Self-Science program, developed by Karen Stone-McCown and Hal Dillehunt, is currently used in the Nueva School for gifted and talented children in San Francisco. The program emphasizes "social-emotional learning" as well as integrated studies and creative arts (http://www.nuevaschool.org). Its motto is "Learn by doing, learn by caring," and the school aims to "inspire…passion for lifelong learning, foster…social and emotional acuity and develop … the imaginative mind." Haller, Parmer, and Vargo (1999) note that "Nueva's Self-Science program strives to educate the 'intrapersonal and interpersonal' intelligences of each student; to develop a 'cognitive library' for thinking critically about one's behaviors and choices; and to join in the preparation for living a creative, humane and sensitive life" (p. 1).

Some social-emotional learning programs target learners with special needs. One such program is "Comfort Corner," which attempts to provide a caring community for elementary school children who are having difficulties functioning in a classroom. The Comfort Corner is a room in an elementary school where at-risk children can go to participate in such activities as singing, dancing, reading stories, drawing, painting pictures, watching videos, making snacks, playing with puppets, writing letters, playing games, and talking. The goal of the program is to provide a safe, supportive place for children to get a healthy start in school by helping them build friendship skills, communication skills, and self-esteem (Novick, 1998).

Universal Principles of Instruction for Emotional Intelligence

There are two ways to engage in instruction for emotional intelligence: either through school or district-wide programs designed to develop emotional competence (as described in the previous section), or by teachers acting individually within the scope of their own classrooms. Programmatic instruction for emotional intelligence is better at helping students develop good emotional skills and provides more support for individual teachers (Elias et al., 1997). However, to say that programs are more effective than individual efforts is not to say that individual teachers are ineffective. There is much that an individual teacher can do to create an emotionally healthy environment in the classroom, and to support the development of students' emotional intelligence.

In this section of the chapter, we use the framework of Merrill's first principles of instruction (see chapter 3) to identify and discuss instructional strategies that individual teachers may use to help students develop the skills of emotional intelligence, as well as to help create an emotionally positive environment that will help maximize the learning experience of all students. The strategies listed here are grounded in research, but this is by no means an exhaustive discussion of instructional approaches to promote emotional intelligence.

Principle of Problem-Orientation: Use Stories

Merrill's principle of problem-orientation holds that "learning is promoted when learners are engaged in solving real-world problems" (2002, p. 45). Emotion is an experience, and as such, it can never be taught or learned in the abstract. Therefore, teaching affectively or learning about affect always requires a problem-orientation (Bar-On & Parker, 2000; Martin & Briggs, 1986; Salovey & Mayer, 1990). But what is the best way for a teacher to introduce problems of emotion into a classroom? Obviously, using emotional situations that are real to students may create unwanted tension and anxiety, so it is best to find a way to introduce emotion in a nonpersonal way. Stories can provide an excellent starting point for talking about emotional issues arising from circumstances that children may face, for discussing how people might feel in different circumstances, and for speculating on whether those feelings are appropriate, and why.

Mayer and Salovey (1997) have gone so far as to call literature the "...first home of the emotional intelligences" (p. 20). Elementary school teachers and secondary social sciences teachers generally incorporate stories into classroom activities; the challenge presented here is to purposefully explore the feelings of characters in a story, and to tie what's happening in a story directly to events that are occurring in the lives of the children in the classroom. Seeing some connection between their schoolwork and their real life should enhance students' understanding of their emotions, their interest in the lesson, and help them to internalize messages that foster the development of emotional intelligence.

Principle of Activation: Teach the Language of Emotion

Merrill's Principle of Activation states that "learning is promoted when relevant experience is activated." This principle includes a corollary regarding structure, which assumes that "learning is promoted when learners are provided or encouraged to recall a structure that can be used to organize new knowledge" (2002, p. 46). In regard to emotions, students who show the most impulsive and aggressive behavior are often those who lack the labels and conceptual structures to identify their emotional states (Greenberg & Snell, 1997).[2] In such a case, teaching students the language of emotion can be used as an activation technique that provides the necessary structure to help develop basic skills of emotional competence.[3] Students who deal with anger not by lashing out, but by saying "I am angry!" or better yet, "That makes me angry," are developing a key skill of emotional intelligence, and teachers who foster students' ability to recognize their emotions using the principle of activation to teach the language and concepts of emotion help students' develop emotional competence. It is likely that the level of frustration from not being able to label their own feelings may contribute to the disruptive behavior that students often show.[4] To the extent that having a label allows the child to get a hold of the emotions they are experiencing, the emotional behavior can be considered, explored, and understood. Research has shown that there are correlations between children who can verbally express emotion and their teachers' assessments of them as able to cope well (Eisenberg, Fabes, & Losoya, 1997).

Principle of Demonstration: Model the Skills of Emotional Intelligence

Merrill's Principle of Demonstration holds that "learning is promoted when the instruction demonstrates what is to be learned rather than merely telling information about what is to be learned" (2002, p. 47). The best way for teachers to foster the development of emotional intelligence (as with the development of most other cognitive and psychomotor skills) is to demonstrate the skills of emotional intelligence through modeling. In other words, teachers should model appropriate emotional behavior for their students (Elias et al., 1997). By being emotionally positive in their interactions with others, teachers can demonstrate for their students the type of emotional behavior that is expected of them.

For students who follow a typical path of emotional development, the teacher's positive contributions to their emotional environment will help solidify the lessons they learn elsewhere about emotional management, and help them gain control over their emotional reactions.

For students who don't have the sort of home life that provides them with good models for emotional behavior, it becomes all the more important for teachers to provide at least some modeling. The problem is that in such a case, the teacher's influence may be limited. This is not only because the teacher sees the child for a relatively short amount of time, but also because the child may come to the classroom already socialized in emotional behavior that is incompatible with what is expected in the classroom. Physically expressing anger, for instance, may be acceptable in the student's home, and in this case a teacher must be prepared to face a great deal of frustration in getting a student to understand that such

---

2. *Editors' note: Note that this is a descriptive principle.*

3. *Editors' note: This is a design principle.*

4. *Editors' note: This is another descriptive principle.*

expression is inappropriate in the classroom. In such a case, modeling alone will not solve the problem.[5] Nonetheless, it is important that teachers demonstrate that what they believe and how they act are in concert.

Modeling does not merely mean reacting to the environment in an emotionally healthy way; it also means teaching in an emotionally healthy way:[6] "Of particular importance is the manner in which teachers promote cognitive and interpersonal decision making and problem solving in the classroom" (Greenberg & Snell, 1997, p. 113). A teacher should model confidence in addressing potentially negative emotional states, such as the fear of failure during classwork. For example, if a teacher approaches a problem with trepidation, or somehow signals to the class that what they are working on will be difficult for them, students will be less likely to embrace the problem or to believe that they can handle it. This is not to say that the teacher shouldn't sympathetically acknowledge that a particular problem is difficult, but that additionally, the teacher should emphasize that what the students are learning will enable them to solve the problem: "we can do it—you can do it."

The point of modeling positive emotional behaviors is to get students emotionally engaged in the classroom experience. Students who are emotionally involved in their schoolwork demonstrate greater learning of all types (Wolfe & Brandt, 1998). By modeling an emotional involvement with the subject matter, a teacher can inspire students and help them to become emotionally engaged with the material as well. This will not only enhance the students' learning experience, but will make for a healthier classroom environment as well.

Principle of Application: Take Time to Deal with Emotions

Merrill's principle of application is closely related to the principle of problem-orientation. The principle of application is that "learning is promoted when learners are required to use their new knowledge or skill to solve problems" (2002, p. 49). Corollaries to this principle involve recommendations regarding consistency of practice, using varied problems for practice, and diminishing the amount of coaching students receive over time.

As noted earlier in this section, developing emotional intelligence requires a problem-orientation, or the ability to recognize emotions in a given situation and determine how to respond appropriately to those emotions. The appropriateness of emotional responses is situation-specific, and there is not a clear or easy transfer of emotional skills from one situation to another. Therefore, teaching and learning of emotional competence clearly require varied and multiple practical experiences, as well as the application of skills in a variety of contexts so that students learn how to use these skills in new ways and in unique settings (Goleman, 1995). In K-12 classrooms, where issues of affect and emotion have historically been generally ignored and often actively avoided, this means that

---

5. *Editors' note: All of this is descriptive theory. It does not elaborate on the imprecise principle.*

teachers must take time to deal with emotions as they arise in the day-to-day activities of students in class.

One obvious example of the principle of taking time to deal with emotion is when a student's inability to correctly handle his or her emotions interferes with the classroom (whether because they are so deliriously happy that they can't sit still, or because they are upset and disturbing others). It is tempting to see this as a problem which must be addressed; however, in the long run it may be better to think of such a situation as an opportunity. According to Greenberg and Snell (1997), "teaching healthy strategies for coping with, communicating about, and managing emotions assists children in maintaining attention and focus during academic and interpersonal learning contexts" (p. 113). Teachers should take time to deal with the emotion, to see if the student can express what he is feeling that is causing him to behave in such a manner. This doesn't mean making the student the center of attention, but it does mean showing the student that there are good and appropriate ways to handle emotions. Further, teachers should try to avoid the trap of only dealing with disruptive behavior. There may be times when it is appropriate to enhance a student's emotional experience, to help magnify the joy a student feels at an accomplishment, or to encourage the expression of positive emotion at a job well done. Students need to know not only that some emotional behaviors are unacceptable, but that other emotional behaviors are good and should be welcomed. Taking time to encourage these positive emotional experiences would be a good use of class time.

Another, less obvious example of taking time to deal with emotion may involve the introduction of activities that foster emotional intelligence into cognitive lessons such as language classes, history classes, and the social and physical sciences. When discussing historical events or the possible meanings that an author may have intended for a book passage, teachers can take time to help foster the skills of emotional intelligence by asking students to consider what emotions were at play, how emotions motivated the actors, possible strategies for managing those emotions, and how emotions may have impacted relationships among actors in the scenarios being explored.

Principle of Integration: Provide Active, Integrated Experience to Foster Emotional Competence

Merrill's principle of integration states that "learning is promoted when learners are encouraged to integrate the new knowledge or skill into their everyday life" (2002, p. 50) through demonstration, reflection or other creative activity. Emotion is, if nothing else, a sensory experience (LeDoux, 1996). As such, emotions cannot be understood and emotional intelligence cannot be developed, fostered, or otherwise addressed without the active engagement of students in the learning experience. Active and integrated experiences that support the development of emotional intelligence may take many forms,[6] several of which have already been discussed in this section, including exploration of stories; asking students to reflect on, consider, and name their own emotional responses; and incorporating instructional activities that foster emotional intelligence into lessons that also facilitate cognitive, psychomotor, and social development.

The value of integrating lessons for development of emotional intelligence with instructional activities that foster skills development in other domains has its roots in findings from the research of Damasio (1994), Greenspan and Benderly (1997) and others who have demonstrated that emotion never occurs in isolation. Because emotion is integrally linked with cognition and with sensorimotor experience, the development of learners in any domain (cognitive, affective, or sensorimotor) will always be most effective when instructional activities involve the integration of all domains (Elias et al., 1997).

Situational Principles for Development of Emotional Intelligence

Of course, the instructional programs and universal principles cited above provide important guidance for how to foster development of students' emotional intelligence, but as presented in this chapter, these programs and principles are by necessity ideal and abstract. The reality of the classroom is that there are variations in students' developmental levels, as well as factors internal and external to each student that may impact an educator's success in helping children to develop emotional intelligence. In this section, we identify situational principles that educators need to be aware of when attempting to foster emotional development among students in their classrooms.

Situational Principle: Consider Students' Level of Emotional Development

Much research has been conducted regarding children's emotional development over time. Not surprisingly, one consistent finding is that there is a great deal of individual variation. We are, after all, dealing with human beings. Nevertheless, it is also clear that emotional skills follow a developmental order (Mascolo & Griffin, 1998; Saarni, 1999), and there appears to be a pattern that constitutes a typical path of emotional development. Table 12.1 identifies Saarni's (1999) patterns of emotional development in the areas of emotional regulation (coping), expressive behavior, and relationship building. Not surprisingly, these patterns demonstrate that, all other things being equal, older students are better at emotional regulation, expression, and relationship building than younger students. When designing and implementing lessons related to skills of emotional intelligence, teachers must consider whether students have advanced through appropriate developmental levels that are required to master the goals and objectives of the lesson.

In the following sections we introduce several methods that teachers may

---

6. *Editors' note: This is elaborating the precision of the method by identifying kinds of the method.*

Table 12.1 Typical Path of Development of Emotional Competence (adapted from Saarni, 1999)

Developmental level	Behavior
Preschool: 2.5 to 5 years	*Emotional regulation:* Communication with others extends child's evaluation of and awareness of own feelings and of emotion-eliciting events.
	Expressive behavior: Pragmatic awareness that false facial expressions can mislead others about one's feelings.
	Relationship building: Sympathetic and prosocial behavior toward peers.
Early elementary: 5 to 7 years	*Emotional regulation:* Self-conscious emotions (e.g. embarrassment) are targeted for regulation.
	Expressive behavior: Adoption of "cool emotional front" with peers.
	Relationship building: Increasing coordination of social skills with one's own and others' emotions.
Middle childhood: 7 to 10 years	*Emotional regulation:* Perceived level of control dictates whether child uses problem-solving or distancing as coping strategies.
	Expressive behavior: Appreciation of norms for expressive behavior.
	Relationship building: Awareness of multiple emotions toward the same person.
Pre-adolescence: 10 to 13 years	*Emotional regulation:* Capable of generating multiple solutions and differentiated strategies for dealing with stress.
	Expressive behavior: Distinction made between genuine emotional expression with close friends and managed displays with others.
	Relationship building: Increasing social sensitivity and awanress of emotion "scripts" in conjunction with social roles.
Adolescence: 13+ years	*Emotional regulation:* Awareness of one's own emotion cycles (eg., guilt about feeling angry) facilitates insightful coping.
	Expressive behavior: Skillful adoption of self-presentation for impression management.
	Relationship building: Awareness of mutual and reciprocal communication of emotions as affecting quality of relationship.

use to assess the emotional development level of their students,[7] with suggested strategies for helping students progress through a particular stage of emotional development. It should be emphasized that these approaches are to be thought of as suggestions; they are examples of a type of lesson that focuses on a particular level of emotional development, with an eye toward facilitating a student's development to a more advanced level.

---

7. *Editors' note: Such methods are not instructional event theory. If used for deciding what to teach, they are instructional-analysis theory, but if they are used for assessing what a student has learned, they are student-assessment theory.*

Children's Developmental Abilities to Regulate Emotional States and Emotional Display Younger children seem to experience emotion more intensely than older children (Brown, Covell, & Abramovitch, 1991); indeed self-reported intensity of emotion seems to wane over time (Gross et al., 1997). In addition to differences in intensity of emotion, children of different ages have varying abilities to regulate their own emotional reactions. When faced with situations that cause distress, many children suck their thumbs; others use "transitional objects" such as stuffed animals as substitutes for the caring adult they once depended on; while others find unique ways to distract themselves, perhaps by playing with a favorite toy (Kopp, 1989). Children at this stage are clearly aware at some level of their own emotional state, though it is unlikely that they are consciously aware of their feelings in the same manner as adults.[8] This situationality—children's varying abilities to regulate emotional states and display—is based largely on age.

Teachers who hope to help young children improve their ability to regulate emotional states might consider using an instructional method in which they take time during class to explicitly explore how objects can move us into different emotional states.[9] For example, realistic but nonreal objects often associated with different emotions (spiders, flowers, snakes, sports cars, teddy bears, etc.) might be introduced to the class, and the children encouraged to talk about how they feel when they see, touch, hold, or smell these objects. The point of this activity is to help children understand that we can and do react to objects in emotional ways; and not only that, we can use emotions to purposely help us feel certain ways. The use of emotional prompts might lead to a discussion of what other things in our lives affect us emotionally, such as music, art, stories, and physical activities. These discussions could act as a way to segue to other subject matters, such as a music lesson. Alternately, during a music lesson, the teacher might ask students to be aware of and comment on what emotions they are feeling.

As children grow older, they begin to regulate not only their own emotional states, but also the display of those states. Cole (1986) has found that children as young as 3 or 4 years old are capable of controlling the expression of their emotions. Cole presented her subjects with a "disappointing" situation, and found that even the youngest child demonstrated an ability to control the expression of disappointment. Further research has shown that children react differently to emotional situations depending on who they are with, and change their expression of emotion depending on their audience (Zeman & Garber, 1996; Zeman, Penza, Shipman, & Young, 1997).

Teachers should help older students who are more self-regulating to create their own strategies for display of emotions. By providing those children with such strategies, teachers offer students two valuable lessons: (1) that emotions *can* be expressed in numerous ways, and (2) *how* emotions can be appropriately

---

8. *Editors' note: One aspect of an Information-Age educational system is a partnership between the teacher and the parents. Such a partnership would offer the opportunity for a teacher to influence the parents' emotional interactions with their child.*

9. *Editor's note: This is all descriptive theory so far.*

displayed. Teachers who hope to help young children improve their ability to appropriately display emotions may want to adapt Cole's research method as an instructional method. Teachers may use natural circumstances in the classroom, for example, when students receive disappointing test scores or when a student wins a spelling bee, to talk with students about various possibilities for expressing disappointment and pride. Another method that may help give older children practice in regulating their emotional display might be to show them pictures of people in different emotional states and have these children guess what emotion the person is feeling. The students might also share why they made the guesses that they did. Having done this, the students might pair off and model an emotion that another student identifies. A variation might be to do this twice, once using your whole body, and once using just the face, to help students experience variations in intensity of emotional display.

Children's Developmental Abilities to Regulate Others' Emotions As young children learn to control their own emotional expressions and reactions, they begin to understand that others have emotions, too (Saarni, 1997, 1999). With this awareness, a second type of emotional control—attempting to regulate the emotional reactions of others—becomes possible. Looking at 5-, 8- and 12-year-old children, McCoy and Masters (1985) found that even the youngest children were able to nominate strategies for changing the emotional state of a peer, such as cheering them up in the event of a disappointment, though the youngest children took a different approach from the older children. The youngest children nominated strategies which would replace an emotion with its opposite (Brown et al., 1991; McCoy & Masters, 1985), so that if a person is sad, giving them a toy will make them happy. Older children assume that emotion is tied directly to the circumstance that causes the emotion (Brown et al., 1991), so that changing the situation will make the emotion go away.

Teachers should recognize that children have developmentally different abilities to appraise, respond to, and influence the emotions of others. Literature and the use of stories can provide an interesting and ready-made source of material to help students enhance their ability to appraise, respond to, and influence the emotions of others. For example, a teacher might read a story and ask students to nominate strategies for making a character in the story feel differently. Teachers should note whether students use substitution of emotion strategies or strategies to change the situation. When a student clearly displays a particular emotion during the course of a class activity, the teacher might facilitate a discussion with the whole class about what others can do to help the student feel a different emotion, such as happiness, enthusiasm, or calm. With older students, this might lead to discussion of whether we should ever deliberately try and make someone feel a negative emotion.

As children grow older, they develop increased sophistication with language that provides them with more vocabulary to describe and deal with emotion (Brenner & Salovey, 1997; Brown et al., 1991; Greenberg & Snell, 1997; McCoy

& Masters, 1985). Older children have different reasons for choosing to regulate their emotional display than younger children, who see emotion as situation specific (Zeman & Garber, 1996). Older children understand that by displaying certain emotions, they are contributing to the emotional state of another. They may attempt to control their emotional displays not merely to avoid negative consequences for themselves, but to help others feel better about a situation as well. A teacher may ask older children how they feel when they are with people who are happy, sad, or angry to foster discussion of the consequences of displaying our own emotional states.

Situational Principle: Consider Internal Factors that Impact Students' Emotional Development

Two internal factors are critical to consider when choosing methods for the development of a student's ability to manage and regulate emotions: the child's temperament impacts the intensity of emotion that they experience, and brain maturation impacts the child's ability to assimilate the emotional experience.

Temperament and Intensity of Emotion Temperament impacts how children express emotions and how easily emotions are triggered. Some children seem to experience emotion more intensely than others, and these temperamental differences may result in differing ability to manage and regulate emotion in self and others. Klaczynski and Cummings (1989) have found that children high in emotional intensity are more aggressive than other children, while Larsen and Diener (1987) have found that children high in emotional intensity are more arousable than other children. These children have a bigger hurdle to overcome in attempting to manage their own emotional responses, and indeed demonstrate more problem behaviors at home and at school (Eisenberg et al., 1997).

The instructional methods that address emotional regulation which were identified above might be used to help give such children some practice in regulating their own emotions. For students who bring inappropriate or extreme emotional problems to the classroom, the teacher may need to resort to more conventional methods to influence behavior that have been developed through counseling psychology, such as those documented by Ito (1997), including activity reinforcement, activity bouncing, hurdle helping, and signal interference, which are all approaches that may help a teacher to quell the escalation of inappropriate emotional behavior before it reaches a crisis level that impacts negatively on students.

Ability to Assimilate Experiences A child's ability to store experiences—and to tap those experiences later in order to make decisions about how to handle emotional experiences—is another internal factor that impacts emotional regulation. Even the very youngest children experiment with their environment in a variety of ways. "Playing with this toy makes me happy—since I don't want to be sad I'll try playing with this toy—it works, I feel better!" A child who has the ability to assimilate the results of these sorts of interactions with the environment, and to subsequently generalize from them, is better able to manage and regulate their emotions. Rothbart and Bates (1997) have found that children differ in their ability to assimilate emotional experiences, and this difference results in differing ability to handle emotionally charged situations. Additionally, Brenner and Salovey (1997) have found that differences in children's ability to assimilate emotional experiences also result in differences in children's ability to regulate their emotions.

One method teachers may use to help children learn to assimilate experiences might be to have the children keep an Emotion Diary. Students might write about a time when they felt an emotion, then write about how they handled it. Was the student able to name the emotion at the time and enjoy it? If the emotion was negative, what (if anything) did they do to try to moderate it? Were they successful? What other actions might they have taken? The teacher might want to share particularly successful stories of emotional assimilation and regulation, and encourage children to use their past experiences as a springboard to dealing with current or future emotions.

Situational Principle: Consider External Factors that Impact Students' Emotional Development

In addition to the internal factors outlined above, several external factors may influence the choice of methods to develop a child's ability to regulate his or her emotions, such as the child's gender and cultural background. The factor most relevant to teachers is the student's home life. Parents' own temperament characteristics and methods of expressing emotion influence their children's immediate behavior and long-term development. Gottman, Katz, and Hooven (1997) assert that children in emotionally responsive families learn to regulate their feelings so that they are able to attend to other children and appropriately join in rather than becoming overly excited, aggressive, or withdrawn. Conversely, children may learn maladaptive strategies for managing emotion by observing parents who are depressed, angry, or in marital conflict. Greater negative expression at home seems to translate into greater difficulty in expressing positive emotions (Garner & Power, 1996), while greater use of positive facial expressions at home seems to translate into greater prosocial behavior in the child (Zeman et al., 1997). In addition, families that provide children with expectations (such as "You must clean up your toys") and help their children to meet those expectations are providing their children with many opportunities to practice emotion regulation (Kopp, 1989). Schickedanz (1994) contrasts such "authoritative" parents with "authoritarian" ones. Authoritarian parents merely expect obedience and often use forceful or punitive measures to get it, without providing a rationale for their demands or an accepting environment for the child who is still learning the rules. Children raised by authoritarian parents often fail to internalize standards for emotional behavior, and have difficulty handling emotional situations in appropriate ways.

Although home life is important to the emotional development of children, it is an area where teachers have little or no control. Subsequently, it is difficult to suggest methods that can directly address this issue, and teachers would do well (for their own state of mind, if nothing else) to keep in mind that there is only so much they can do. Nonetheless, the teacher may encourage children to use art or stories to describe the emotional state of their home life, which will help the teacher to understand students better, while helping students regulate their own emotional reactions. An emotion diary might be particularly important for students who have a home life that is not ideally conducive to healthy emotional development.

Assessment and Evaluation of Emotional Intelligence

The purpose of this chapter has been to synthesize current knowledge about guidance for teaching students to develop emotional intelligence in the form of universal principles and situational principles, in order to build a common knowledge base regarding the development of emotional intelligence.

In writing this chapter, the authors have assumed that emotional intelligence is a viable psychological construct, one that can be measured, taught, and assessed. However, important philosophical and technical issues regarding emotional intelligence continue to be debated and addressed in the literature. Due to constraints of space, these cannot be treated in this chapter, but readers who would like to learn more about how the key constructs of emotional intelligence are conceptualized, issues and methods related to the assessment of emotional intelligence, and research issues that are impacting our understandings of emotional intelligence are encouraged to access two excellent resources: *The Handbook of Emotional Intelligence* edited by Reuven Bar-On and James Parker (2000) and *Emotional Intelligence: Science and Myth* by Gerald Matthews, Moshe Zeidner, and Richard Roberts (2004).

Conclusion

Collectively, the programs and principles presented in this chapter remind us of what we already know, which is that when we undertake the teaching of emotional skills, we enter into an entirely different realm than when we teach cognitive skills. The complexity and situationality of emotions means that we will not be able to build skills hierarchies, and we will not be able to assess students' abilities based on correct and incorrect answers. Most importantly, there is little certainty of transferability of skills learned from one situation to any other.

Despite these limitations (or perhaps because of them), there is increasing

---

10. *Editor's note: This is a situational principle.*

awareness that teaching the skills of emotional intelligence is critically important at this time in history, when the community of humans is drawn much closer together through communications and transportation technologies. As we more frequently encounter others from cultures, classes, and races different from our own, we face increasing possibilities for misunderstanding, and the consequences of misunderstanding are much more harmful than they have ever been before. For at least this reason, we argue that the idea of intentionally teaching our students to develop the skills of emotional intelligence may be the wisest course of action among all of those proposed by educators who advocate for various approaches to K-12 school reform. We hope this chapter will help scholars to build a common knowledge base for design theory in this important area.

References

Bandura, A. (1997). *Self-efficacy: The exercise of control*. New York: Freeman.

Bar-On, R., & Parker, J. (Eds.). (2000). *The handbook of emotional intelligence: Theory, development, assessment, and application at home, school, and in the workplace*. San Francisco, CA: Jossey-Bass.

Battistich, V., Solomon, D., Watson, M., & Schaps, E. (1997). Caring school communities. *Educational Psychologist, 32*(3), 137–151.

Beane, J. A. (1990). *Affect in the curriculum: Toward democracy, dignity, and diversity*. New York: Teachers College Press.

Bloom, B. S., Englehart, M. B., Furst, E. J., Hill, W. H., & Krathwhol, D. R. (1956). *Taxonomy of educational objectives: The classification of educational goals: Handbook 1. Cognitive domain*. New York: McKay.

Brenner, E. M., & Salovey, P. (1997). Emotion regulation during childhood: Developmental, interpersonal, and individual considerations. In P. Salovey & D. J. Sluyter (Eds), *Emotional development and emotional intelligence: Educational implications* (pp. 168–192). New York: Basic.

Brown, K., Covell, K., & Abramovitch, R. (1991). Time course and control of emotion: Age differences in understanding and recognition. *Merrill-Palmer Quarterly, 37*(2), 273–287.

Caine, R., & Caine, G. (1994). *Making connections: Teaching and the human brain*. San Francisco: Dale Seymour.

Calhoun, C., & Solomon, R. C. (1984). *What is an emotion? Classical readings in philosophical psychology*. New York: Oxford University Press.

Cole, P. M. (1986). Children's spontaneous control of facial expression. *Child Development, 57*(6), 1309–1321.

Damasio, A. R. (1994). *Descartes' error: Emotion, reason, and the human brain*. New York: G. P. Putnam.

Damasio, A. R. (2000). *The feeling of what happens: Body and emotion in the making of consciousness*. New York: Harvest.

Eisenberg, N., Fabes, R. A., & Losoya, S. (1997). Emotional responding: Regulation, social correlates, and socialization. In P. Salovey & D. J. Sluyter (Eds.), *Emotional development and emotional intelligence: Educational implications* (pp. 129–164). New York: Basic.

Ekman, P., & Davidson, R. (1994). *The nature of emotion: Fundamental questions*. New York: Oxford University Press.

Elias, M. J., Zins, J. E., Weissberg, R. P., Frey, K. S., Greenberg, M. T., Haynes, N. M. et al (1997). *Promoting social and emotional learning: Guidelines for educators*. Alexandria, VA: Association for Supervision and Curriculum Development.

Gardner, H. (1983). *Frames of mind: The theory of multiple intelligences*. New York: Basic.

Garner, P. W., & Power, T. G. (1996). Preschoolers' emotional control in the disappointment paradigm and its relation to temperament, emotional knowledge, and family expressiveness. *Child Development, 67*(4), 1406–1419.

Goleman, D. (1995). *Emotional intelligence: Why it can matter more than IQ*. New York: Bantam.

Gottman, J., Katz, L. F., & Hooven, C. (1997). *Meta-emotion*. Hillsdale, NJ: Erlbaum.

Greenberg, M. T., Kusche, C. A., Cook, E. T., Quamma, J. P. (1995). Promoting emotional competence in school-aged children: The effects of the PATHS curriculum. *Development and Psychopathology, 1,* 117–136.

Greenberg, M. T., & Snell, J. L. (1997). Brain development and emotional development: The role teaching in organizing the frontal lobe. In P. Salovey & D. J. Sluyter (Eds.), *Emotional development and emotional intelligence: Educational implications* (pp. 93–119). New York: Basic.

Greenspan, S. I., & Benderly, B.L. (1997). *The growth of the mind and the endangered origins of intelligence.* Reading, MA: Addison-Wesley.

Gross, J. J., Carstensen, L. L., Pasupathi, M., Tsai, J., Skorpen, C. G., & Hsu, A. Y. C. (1997). Emotion and aging: Experience, expression, and control. *Psychology and Aging, 12*(4), 590–599.

Haller Parmer, J., & Vargo, J.-A. (1999). Self-science: Learning to make moral judgments. *The Nueva Journal, 35*(Spring 1993(1), 1–4.

Hunt, M. (1993). *The story of psychology.* New York: Anchor.

Ito, C. (1997). Behavior influence techniques. Retrieved March 26, 2006, from http://www.ttac.odu.edu/Articles/influence_tech.html

Izard, C. E. (1972). *Patterns of emotions: A new analysis of anxiety and depression.* New York: Academic.

Klaczynski, P. A., & Cummings, E. M. (1989). Responding to anger in aggressive and nonaggressive boys. *Journal of Child Psychology and Psychiatry, 30,* 309–314.

Kopp, C. B. (1989). Regulation of distress and negative emotions: A developmental view. *Developmental Psychology, 25*(3), 343–354.

Kovalik, S., & Olsen, K. D. (1998). How emotions run us, our students, and our classrooms. *NASSP Bulletin, 82*(598), 29–37.

Kovalik, S. J. with McGeehan, J. R. (1999). Integrated thematic instruction: From brain research to application. In C. M. Reigeluth (Ed.), *Instructional-design theories and models: Vol. II. A new paradigm of instructional theory* (pp. 371–396). Mahwah, NJ: Erlbaum.

Krathwohl, D., Bloom, B., & Masia, B. (1956). *Taxonomy of educational objectives: The classification of educational goals: Handbook 2. Affective domain.* New York: McKay.

Larsen, R. J., & Diener, E. (1987). Affect intensity as an individual difference characteristic: A review. *Journal of Research in Personality, 21,* 1–39.

LeDoux, J. (1996). *The emotional brain: The mysterious underpinnings of emotional life.* New York: Simon & Schuster.

Lewis, M., & Haviland, J. (1993). *Handbook of emotions.* New York: Guilford.

Lewis, C. C., Schaps, E., & Watson, M. S. (1996). The caring classroom's academic edge. *Educational Leadership, 54*(1), 16–21.

Martin, B. L., & Briggs, L. J. (1986). *The affective and cognitive domains: Integration for instruction and research.* Englewood Cliffs, NJ: Educational Technology.

Martin, B. L., & Reigeluth, C. M. (1999). Affective education and the affective domain: implications for instructional-design theories and models. In C. Reigeluth (Ed.), *Instructional-design theories and models: Vol. 2. A new paradigm of instructional theory* (pp. 371–396). Mahwah, NJ: Erlbaum.

Mascolo, M., & Griffin, S. (Eds.). (1998). *What develops in emotional development? Emotions, personality and psychotherapy.* New York: Springer.

Matthews, G., Zeidner, M., & Roberts; R. (2004). *Emotional intelligence: Science and myth.* Cambridge, MA: MIT Press.

Mayer, J. D., & Geher, G. (1996). Emotional intelligence and the identification of emotion. *Intelligence, 22*(2), 89–113.

Mayer, J. D., & Salovey, P. (1993). The intelligence of emotional intelligence. *Intelligence, 17*(4), 433–442.

Mayer, J. D., & Salovey, P. (1997). What is emotional intelligence? In P. Salovey & D. J. Sluyter (Eds.), *Emotional development and emotional intelligence: Educational implications* (pp. 3–34). New York: Basic.

McCoy, C. L., & Masters, J. C. (1985). The development of children's strategies for the social control of emotion. *Child Development, 56*(5), 1214–1222.

Merrill, M. D. (2002). First principles of instruction. *Educational Technology Research & Development, 50*(3), 43–59.

Noddings, N. (1992). *The challenge to care in schools: An alternative approach to education.* New York: Teachers College Press.

Novick, R. (1998). The Comfort Corner: Fostering resiliency and emotional intelligence. *Childhood Education, 74*(4), 200–204.

Pintrich P., & Schunk, D. (1996). *Motivation in education: Theory, research, and applications.* Englewood Cliffs, NJ: Merrill, Prentice-Hall.

Plutchik, R. (1962). *The emotions: Facts, theories, and a new model.* New York: Random House.

Plutchik, R. (1994). *The psychology and biology of emotion.* New York: HarperCollins.

Rothbart, M., & Bates, J. E. (1997). Temperament. In N. Eisenberg (Ed.), *Handbook of child psychology* (5th ed., Vol. 3). New York: Wiley.

Russell, J. A. (1989). Culture, scripts, and children's understanding of emotion. In C. Saarni & P. L. Harris (Eds.), *Children's understanding of emotion* (pp. 293–318). Cambridge, UK: Cambridge University Press.

Saarni, C. (1997). Emotional competence and self-regulation in childhood. In P. Salovey & D. J. Sluyter (Eds.), *Emotional development and emotional intelligence: educational implications* (pp. 35–66). New York: Basic.

Saarni, C. (1999). *The development of emotional competence.* New York: Guilford.

Salovey, P., & Mayer, J. D. (1989–1990). Emotional intelligence. *Imagination, Cognition & Personality, 9*(3), 185–211.

Salovey, P., & Sluyter, D. J. (1997). *Emotional development and emotional intelligence: Educational implications.* New York: Basic.

Schickedanz, J. A. (1994). Helping children develop self-control. *Childhood Education, 70*(5), 274–278.

Vail, P. L. (1994). *Emotion: The on/off switch for learning.* Rosemont, NJ: Modern Learning.

Wolfe, P., & Brandt, R. (1998). What do we know from brain research? *Educational Leadership, 56*(3), 8–13.

Zeman, J., & Garber, J. (1996). Display rules for anger, sadness, and pain: It depends on who is watching. *Child Development, 67*(3), 957–973.

Zeman, J., Penza, S., Shipman, K., & Young, G. (1997). Preschoolers as functionalists: The impact of social context on emotion regulation. *Child Study Journal, 27*(1), 41–66.

Zimilies, H. (1981). Cognitive-affective interaction: A concept that exceeds the researcher's grasp. In E. K. W. Shapiro (Ed.), *Cognitive and affective growth* (pp. 47–64). Hillsdale, NJ: Erlbaum.

13
Fostering Integrated Learning Outcomes across Domains

BRIAN J. BEATTY

San Francisco State University

Brian J. Beatty is an assistant professor of education in the Instructional Technologies Department at San Francisco State University, California. He teaches graduate courses in instructional systems design, distance education, e-learning development, project management, and technology integration. His research centers on the use of Internet technologies in teaching and learning environments of all sorts, including K-12 classrooms, higher education institutions, and corporate training systems. He is especially interested in the application of Internet-based technologies being used to create virtual, hybrid, and fully networked learning communities; most recently his work has centered on the HyFlex model for hybrid course design. His background includes a decade of K-12 mathematics and science instruction as a classroom teacher and curriculum designer. Brian also has many years of experience in corporate and technical military training design and development.

EDITORS' FOREWORD

Preconditions

Content
- *Must span multiple domains of learning*

Learners
- *All students*

Learning environments
- *All kinds, except the teachers and administrative structure must be supportive.*

Instructional development constraints
- *Requires relatively more development time and unconventional resources, including joint planning time for teachers*

Values

about ends (learning goals)
- *The learning should be relevant to students' lives.*
- *Relationships among domains are important to learn.*
- *Transfer to the "real world" is important.*

about priorities (criteria for successful instruction)
- *Effectiveness and appeal are of great importance.*
- *Efficiency may be relatively less important.*

about means (instructional methods)
- *Goals, activities, resources, and assessments should all be tied directly to a unifying theme.*
- *Rich resources and varied instructional activities are important.*

about power (to make decisions about the previous three)
- *Teachers should be willing to give up some elements of direct control.*
- *Flexibility is needed from rigid administrative demands and state curricular requirements.*

Universal Methods

1. *Use a unifying theme to which all instruction is related.*
   - *Criteria for selection include that the theme: is interesting to students, relates directly to student lives, supports the learning objectives, is age- and experience-appropriate for the learners, and provides a rich setting for learning experiences.*
   - *Select themes with full participation of students when possible.*
   - *One kind of unifying theme is the year-long theme.*
   - *Themes may be problem- or task-oriented, or they may be topic-oriented.*
   - *Themes should be pervasive and integrative.*
2. *Focus instruction on primary learning goals.*

- *Goals may be stated in terms of what students must learn.*
- *Themes may be divided into curricular components, which in turn are divided into specific topics, which in turn are divided into key points (concepts, skills, and knowledge).*
- *Students may play a role in deciding on learning goals.*

3. *Use a variety of instructional activities.*
   - *These typically include introduction, demonstration, opportunity for practice with feedback, and final performance with assessment.*
   - *Learning activities are structured to help learners move from slow to fast, small to large, and simple to complex conceptual understandings.*
   - *Students engage in a cycle of concrete experience, followed by reflective observation, leading to abstract conceptualization, and resulting in active experimentation, which is concrete experience.*
   - *In some cases, students help determine specific activities. In others, teachers are provided with unit plans and lesson plans that spell out every detail of a series of lessons. In most cases, teachers improvise and adapt lessons.*
   - *There should be multiple opportunities for students to apply what they are learning in fun and meaningful ways.*
   - *Many thematic units include a culminating activity that usually results in a meaningful artifact.*

4. *Provide useful instructional resources.*
   - *Use resources from real life, such as content experts, community groups, and technologies, as well as resources in the classroom.*

5. *Evaluate achievement through authentic assessment practices.*
   - *Use portfolios, public presentations, reflection on and revision of work produced, reflective reports, and culminating experiences.*
   - *If possible, this activity should require collaboration among students and other members of the learning community.*
   - *Self-assessment should often be used, especially for adult learners.*

Situational Principles

- *In absence of completely flexible administrative structures, teachers should work within whatever flexibility they do have, such as perhaps combining classes some of the time or swapping teaching responsibilities for short periods of time.*
- *In highly flexible, open entry/open exit systems, modularize units and/or build in frequent interactions across levels.*
- *Instruction should be flexible to adapt to needs of individual learners:*
  - a. *If unable to adapt activities and resources, find alternative ones.*
  - b. *If learning goals are too advanced, new ones may be needed.*
  - c. *If there are great differences among students, offer more multilevel instructional activities.*

     d. *If diversity of learners is valued, activities can be structured to build that*
     appreciation.
- *The amount of integration of disciplines may need to vary on a continuum*
  of five levels:
     a. *For the least administrative flexibility, integration is carried out by teach-*
     ers individually.
     b. *For the most flexibility, a coherent theme is established across several*
     grade levels and subject areas.
- *The amount of integration may vary on a different dimension: multi-*
  disciplinary, interdisciplinary, and transdisciplinary. Selection of these
  alternatives depends on schedule flexibility, staff support, and curriculum
  requirements.

—CMR & ACC

FOSTERING INTEGRATED LEARNING OUTCOMES ACROSS DOMAINS

Definition

Theme-based instruction is an approach to facilitating learning which brings together various domains of learning in order to support a unifying theme. Theme-based instruction is also called integrated thematic instruction (ITI; Kovalik & McGeehan, 1999; Kovalik & Olsen, 2002), integrated theme-based instruction (ITB; Dirkx & Prenger, 1997), integrated or interdisciplinary curriculum (Jacobs, 1989, 1991a; Walker, 1996), and transdisciplinary or holistic learning (Drake, 1991; Miller, Cassie, & Drake, 1990). Common to all of these approaches is the development of instruction for a specified curriculum, with instructional goals, activities, resources, and assessment tied directly to a unifying (or overarching, underlying, foundational, etc.) theme. A unifying theme acts as a lens through which we can view curriculum and learning experiences (Perkins, 1989). This theme is prominently communicated to learners throughout the instructional program.

Importance

Theme-based instruction is important because research has shown that connecting instructional content and student learning activities to a unifying theme can improve student learning (Bergeron & Rudenga, 1993; Haas, 2000; Ritter, 1999; Ross, McCormick, & Krisak, 1986; Swartz, 1991; Yorks & Follo, 1993). Some argue that theme-based instruction represents a more natural way of learning—the way humans might learn best if they were not engaged in a traditional (non-theme-based) program of study.[1] Many school settings have

---

1. *Editors' note: In fact, integrated instruction is an important characteristic of the Information-Age*

adopted theme-based instructional programs and approaches; programs and examples exist at every level of K-12 education. Many programs for adult study have adopted theme-based instruction practices as well, especially in life-skills training programs.

Thematic units, or interdisciplinary thematic units (ITUs), have been used by educators at all levels of education for many years (Roberts & Kellough, 2000; Vars, 1991). Examples of thematic units used in K-12 classrooms include:

- *My Travels with Gulliver* integrates grades 4 through 6 mathematics, literature, writing, and drawing (Kleiman, 1991);
- *Bit by Bit—Building It Together* is a first grade yearlong unit centered on science but integrating all subjects, developed in a school undergoing substantial reconstruction (Greene, 1991);
- *Living in the Future* is a theme selected by eighth grade students which engaged them in planning and developing content and activities across all subjects for an extended length of time (Beane, 1991);
- *Humanitas* is a multiyear, multisubject collection of interdisciplinary thematic units for high school students focused primarily on the humanities. Its primary goal is to develop highly engaged, critically thinking students participating with their teachers in a community of scholars (Aschbacher, 1991).

Volumes have been written listing and describing thematic units for practically every combination of subjects and grade levels. While many of these units are helpful as points of departure for teachers, other programs or guidebooks encourage teacher-developed thematic units because they fit better into local contexts, they can address the specific needs of unique student populations, and their development helps teachers develop professionally.

Next, I provide a brief review of the theoretical foundations of theme-based instructional practice.

Theoretical Foundations

Important theoretical foundations of theme-based instructional theory include brain-based educational research and multiple intelligence theory. Each is briefly reviewed in this section.

Brain-Based Educational Research

Brain research has contributed to our understanding of how people learn from a biological perspective. Using the findings from brain research makes sense as we design environments and develop learning experiences for children and adults. If we can create experiences and environments that work with the brain's

paradigm of education. It is an explicit part of the theories for understanding outcomes (chapter 11) and affective outcomes (chapter 12), as well as for the problem-based approach to instruction (chapter 8), and it is compatible with the rest of the theories in this volume.

Table 13.1 The Five ITI Learning Principles (Kovalik & Olsen, 2002, p. xiv)

1. Intelligence is a function of experience
2. Learning is an inseparable partnership between brain and body
3. There are multiple intelligences or ways of solving problems and/or producing products
4. Learning is a two-step process: 1) Pattern seeking or meaning making through problem solving, and 2) Developing a mental program for using what we understand and wiring it into long term memory
5. Personality impacts learning and performance.

biological systems (chemical, neurological, emotional, etc.), then perhaps the likelihood of meaningful learning will be increased, and our educational system will be improved.[2]

Kovalik and Olsen (2002) base their integrated thematic instruction (ITI) model on five fundamental principles about learning, which have been derived from brain research. These five are listed in Table 13.1.

The most relevant brain research for the discussion in this chapter is that which suggests the importance of pattern making through meaningful problem solving, which is then used to develop a program for using what is known to aid in long-term memory.

Pattern Making through Meaningful Problem Solving The ability of the brain to identify and understand patterns enables humans to recognize people, situations, and instances of abstract concepts, and is key to creating effective learning experiences for both children and adults. Hart (1999) defined learning as a two-step process, starting with detecting and identifying patterns (enabling meaning making) and then developing meaningful mental programs to use and store new understandings. This view of learning fits well with Goldberg's gradiental/distributive model of brain function (Goldberg, 2001). Brain activity tracked at each stage of the learning process shows that different regions of the brain are more active during each phase. When a learner is identifying patterns, the part of the brain which is primarily engaged is the right frontal lobe. This shifts to the left frontal lobe when the learner is making meaning. Primary brain activity shifts toward the back of the brain during the early program-building stage, when a learner is able to use new understandings with external support. Finally, as learning becomes more automatic and new understandings are stored in long-term memory, brain activity shifts further to the back and lower, older regions of the brain. Since there is some evidence that human learning occurs this way, it is important to support this natural learning progression in instructional settings.

Theme-based instruction always centers learning experiences (resources, activities, content) around a comprehensive theme and provides opportunity to

---

2. *Editors' note: This is an important underpinning for the entire Information-Age paradigm of education, due to its focus on learning, as compared to the Industrial-Age focus on sorting students (see chapter 1).*

leverage the human brain's ability and need to identify and understand patterns as learning progresses. Rather than experiencing new information in discrete chunks or separate topics and subjects, a theme-based approach to instruction emphasizes connections among concepts, topics, and subjects; in many cases the theme *becomes* the primary subject, with elements of knowledge from various disciplines introduced to support understanding of the theme. Kovalik and Olsen (2002) explain how specific instructional strategies, applied in the nine Body-Brain Compatible Elements of the ITI model (Kovalik & Olsen, 2002, p. xiv), can be used to enhance pattern making.

Multiple Intelligence Theory

Traditionally, intelligence has been measured by tests that attempt to indicate a person's capacity for learning in educational settings (Daniel, 1997; Sattler, 2002; Sternberg, 1997). A significant limitation of these tests is that they primarily measure a person's abstract reasoning skills and ability, and do not measure other important ways of knowing. In a typical school environment today, the majority of instruction, learning, and assessment focuses on ways of thinking logically (i.e., mathematical or scientific reasoning) or linguistically (i.e., reading and writing). As other ways of knowing have been increasingly identified, discussed, and valued, our understanding of intelligence has become more complex (Gardner, 1999; Lazear, 1994; Perkins, 1998; Wiggins & McTighe, 2005).

Howard Gardner's work in identifying and explaining multiple intelligences is widely known and has been implemented in many educational settings (Gardner, 1983, 1999). Gardner is essentially suggesting that human intelligence is best understood through multiple perspectives, or lenses, on what makes someone intelligent—able to solve problems or create products. Rather than limit our understanding of (and measuring, valuing, seeking to build) intelligence to that which is measured by the classic I.Q. test, there are 10 (or more) types of intelligence for which Gardner sees evidence in human learning. These intelligences are listed in Table 13.2.

Theme-based instructional environments provide meaningful opportunities to support the development and expression of varied types of intelligence, typically

Table 13.2 Multiple Human Intelligences (derived from Gardner, 1999)

1. Logical-mathematical
2. Linguistic
3. Spatial
4. Bodily-kinesthetic
5. Musical
6. Intrapersonal
7. Interpersonal
8. Naturalist
9. Existential
10. Spiritual

including activities that help learners experience and explore content through more than one intelligence. Rather than rely upon activities that allow students to apply only logical-mathematical and linguistic intelligence, well-designed theme-based instructional environments encourage learners to engage in problem solving and create products using a range of intelligences. Each learner has the freedom to develop and express expertise in ways which are most compatible with the way she or he thinks and learns.

An Important Precondition

Advocates of theme-based instruction may emphasize that this approach can be applied in almost any educational setting for just about any content, but there is one important precondition that could preclude the use of theme-based approaches. This is the type and amount of administrative structure present in the educational system. Under certain circumstances the administrative structure can prevent theme-based instruction from working.

Some education systems have centralized, strongly controlling, and rigid administrations which may not allow program flexibility or changes that help make thematic instruction more effective. In some cases, school districts establish curriculum guidelines so detailed that they require all teachers at a certain grade level to teach the same topic at the same time of the year at every school in the district.[3] This rigidity makes thematic instruction impossible unless district-level administration decides to implement thematic instruction across all schools. Yet even when schools are given greater control over curriculum and instructional programs, school-level administration may dictate day-to-day instructional content and practice in classrooms. In this case, also, teachers would likely not be able to implement effective thematic instruction unless the school administrators were directly involved and supportive, specifically allowing the flexibility teachers need to provide rich resources for varied instructional activities and to adapt to individual student needs.

Universal Principles for Theme-Based Instruction

In general, theme-based instructional theories align well with Merrill's first principles of instruction (see chapter 3). Briefly stated, the first principles identified by Merrill include centering instruction around a problem meaningful to the learner, activating a learner's prior knowledge, demonstrating new knowledge to a learner, allowing the learner to apply this knowledge in some authentic way, and then supporting learners as they transfer learning into "real life" outside of the instructional setting. In this section, I present five fundamental principles

---

3. *Editors' note: Such standardization is characteristic of the Industrial-Age paradigm of education and runs counter to the flexible, customized approach of the Information-Age paradigm (see chapter 1).*

found in theme-based instructional theory, and provide a brief discussion of how each aligns with Merrill's first principles.

There is an increasing emphasis on creating and implementing thematic instruction in order to improve teaching and learning, which has led to multiple guides for educators wishing to create their own thematic units (Dirkx & Prenger, 1997; Kovalik & Olsen, 2002; Meinbach, Rothlein, & Fredericks, 1995; Roberts & Kellough, 2000). These guides provide basic methods of integrated thematic instruction, define terms, and explain procedures to create thematic units. Instructional theory does not include the procedures to create instruction[4] (see chapter 1), so guidance for creating thematic units will be addressed only minimally in this chapter.

The fundamental principles of the various theme-based instructional models presented by these guides include: (1) using a unifying theme to which all instruction is related; (2) focusing instruction on primary learning goals; (3) using a variety of instructional activities; (4) providing useful instructional resources for learning; and (5) evaluating achievement through authentic assessment practices. These principles of well-designed and effectively implemented theme-based instruction that implements Merrill's First Principles of instruction are described next.

1. Use a Unifying Theme

The very essence of theme-based instructional models is that instruction (teaching and learning) is conducted in the context of a fundamental theme. This theme provides the problem space, or practice field for learning. The learning environment created is usually directly tied to central features of this theme. Whether the theme is selected with (or perhaps by) students or by teachers or even by curriculum developers,[5] the theme is chosen to be interesting to students, relate directly to student lives, and provide a rich setting for learning experiences.[6] Involving students in the creation of the central theme (Dirkx & Prenger, 1997) provides a powerful opportunity to activate previous student experience, Merrill's second First Principle of instruction.

Yearlong Themes in ITI[7] The ITI Model very clearly describes a comprehensive approach to creating learning environments which implement brain-based research in educational classrooms (Kovalik & Olsen, 2002). An important element of ITI is implementing integrated themes. The purpose for a guiding theme is to "enhance the brain's search for patterns and meaning by creating a giant pat-

---

4. *Editors' note: The knowledge base that addresses this is generally known as ISD process models and primarily includes instructional-analysis theory, instructional-planning theory, and instructional-building theory (see chapter 1).*

5. *Editors' note: Clearly there is flexibility in dealing with values about power.*

6. *Editors' note: Note that this elaboration of this method takes the form of criteria, rather than kinds or parts.*

7. *Editors' note: This is one kind of unifying theme.*

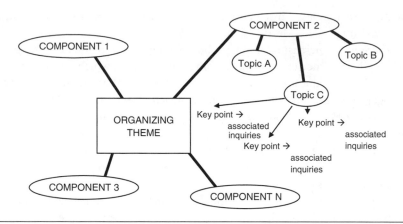

Figure 13.1 Theme Structure in the ITI Model (derived from Kovalik & Olsen, 2002)

tern, a large mental web" (Kovalik & Olsen, 2002, p. 14.1). A comprehensive, yearlong guiding theme is chosen that ties directly to curriculum standards but also engages students in their local, independent, "real" lives. The theme is used to organize major curricular components—interrelated extensions of the conceptual theme (see Figure 13.1).

Adult (Life-Long Learning) Skills An increasingly important goal of education is to help students become life-long learners who pursue new knowledge in order to meet personal goals (Strube, 1993). The field of adult education has been a leader in developing methods for building life-long learning skills in students, and many educators have found that theme-based instruction is an effective approach. Dirkx and Prenger (1997) prepared a guide to help educators of adults use integrated theme-based instruction (ITB) in developmental education programs such as adult literacy, English as a second language (ESL), and family literacy contexts. They chose the ITB approach because they recognized that a strong commonality among the learners in these programs is the relationship between life experiences and their participation in goal-directed adult learning.

Selecting the theme is a major task in ITB, since the theme determines the primary instructional content and activities. This task should involve the adult learners, since their contexts (experiences and goals) will greatly influence their motivation and ultimately their learning. Dirkx and Prenger have found that ITB is most effective when themes are selected with the full (if feasible) participation of students. As mentioned earlier, this may lead to activation of previous experience, Merrill's second principle. In some programs, existing constraints dictate predetermined themes or may not allow for the time needed for full negotiation and teamwork. If this is the case, what is known about the adult learners' experiences and contexts should be considered as themes are developed or instructional programs are selected. Once a theme is selected, it should be evaluated based on meaningfulness to students; interest to students (and the teacher); richness; support for the program objectives; substantive applications to "real life"; and age- and experience-appropriateness for the learners. If the theme does not meet these criteria, it should be revised or replaced.

Themes as Problems Does the theme meet Merrill's problem-centered (now task-centered, see chapter 3) first principle? The answer to this question is "sometimes." Yes, well-chosen themes provide for "a wide range of activities... representative of those the learner will encounter in the world following instruction" (Merrill, 2002, p. 45). Sample themes, such as Growing Up, Becoming a Person, Finding a Job, and Physics in Sports, could certainly include important and interesting problems (or complex tasks) that become the center of learning activities. Some themes may be more topic-driven[8] and might not focus on solving problems or completing projects (or complex tasks). Examples of topic-oriented themes include Seasons of the Year, Time, Temperature, Animals in the Neighborhood, and Patterns of Life. It is important to note that the selection of a theme does not mandate nor preclude the implementation of a problem-centered instructional focus. Some themes may be more naturally accommodating of a problem-centered approach, and may therefore lead to more effective learning, according to Merrill's first principles.

Pervasive and Integrative[9] Suitable integrative themes apply broadly to the major disciplines included in the curriculum; it must not be difficult to find natural connections between curriculum concepts or topics and the theme. A pervasive theme selected for a curriculum which includes physics and geometry, for example, must be naturally applicable to all major topics in both subjects. The theme must disclose fundamental and important patterns in the curriculum and must reveal both similarities and contrasts within and across disciplines (Kovalik & Olsen, 2002; Meinbach et al., 1995; Roberts & Kellough, 2000).

2. Focus Instruction on Primary Learning Goals

Once a theme has been established, primary learning goals should be developed.[10] In some cases, guidance for theme-based instruction strongly recommends student involvement in determining primary learning goals. In other cases, curriculum developers may decide the learning goals instead of teachers and students. These learning goals should reflect learning needs, which include instructional program (curriculum) goals and student interests and expressed learning desires. The overarching goals may be stated in terms of what students must learn in order

---

8. *Editors' note: This is an elaboration on the precision of the method by identifying alternative kinds: problem- or task-oriented versus topic-oriented. This means that a situationality is need to help practitioners decide which alternative to use when.*

9. *Editors' note: These elaborations on the method are criteria.*

10. *Editors' note: Note that this is instructional-planning theory.*

to meet problem-solving or project-based objectives. For example, in a program with the theme "Living in Harmony with our Environment," one learning goal may be "students will learn how to develop an environmental plan" so that they can meet a problem-solving goal of "present a plan to fix one major environmental problem in their neighborhood to a group of local government officials." This goal is a good example of Merrill's problem-centered first principle.

In ITI, the theme is used to organize major curricular components—interrelated extensions of the conceptual theme. Specific topics for study are organized around each component and reflect the primary learning goals in the unit. A topic is one aspect of a component which helps students learn the fundamental concept of the component. For each topic, a list of key points describes the specific concepts, skills, and knowledge that students are expected to learn. Key points align to primary learning goals, curriculum standards, or students' local real-life interests.

3. Use a Variety of Instructional Activities

Once learning goals have been established, specific instructional activities are chosen to help learners achieve the learning goals—Kovalik and Olsen call these "Key Points and Associated Inquiries." Carrying out these activities typically includes the traditional phases of classroom instruction—an introduction, demonstration, opportunity for practice with feedback, and final performance with assessment.[11] For example, a sample instructional activity in a theme-based unit on "Ancient Greek Civilization" is to have students develop small-group presentations about one aspect of Greek civilization, in the presentation format of their choice (Roberts & Kellough, 2000). Some students may choose to create a short drama (play), write a script for a Greek newscast, or carry on a role-playing activity with ancient Greek characters—perhaps debating the wisdom of opening trade with people from northern Europe.

ITB instruction, as described by Dirkx and Prenger, uses a context-based approach to learning (Vella, 1994). Learning activities are structured to help learners move from slow to fast, small to large, and simple to complex conceptual understandings. Kolb (1984) presents a theory of experiential learning as a cycle that typically begins with concrete experience, followed by reflective observation, leading to abstract conceptualization, and resulting in active experimentation. Experimentation leads to new learning, and the cycle begins again at a new level, with more complex, faster, or larger concepts and experiences. When instructional activities are organized around a theme, cycles of experiential learning may be thought of as layers of an onion, with deeper and deeper layers being removed as the cycle repeats, ultimately leading learners to the core—achievement of the primary learning goals and fulfilling the organizing theme.

---

11. *Editors' note: Are these parts or kinds? In a general sense, they are kinds of instructional activities. However, based on the distinctions made in chapter 1, kinds are alternatives from which you choose one for any given situation. However, you would typically use most, if not all, of these instructional activities in any given situation. This makes them parts of this method.*

In theme-based instruction, implementing specific activities is often left to the creativity and energy of the teacher and students. In some cases, students help determine specific activities. In other cases, teachers are provided with unit plans and lesson plans that spell out every detail of a series of lessons. In most cases, teachers improvise and adapt lessons to meet specific demands, needs, and desires of students and contextual factors such as time, weather, etc. At any rate, Merrill's third principle, demonstration, is left up to specific teachers to implement as needed.

Typical guidance for developing instructional activities also focuses on creating multiple opportunities for students to apply what they are learning in fun and meaningful ways. Students might be asked to write a short article describing a recent science experiment they conducted for a local newspaper, or they may be asked to design a science experiment to test a hypothesis they have been noticing in the world around them (e.g., "Why are all the statues downtown green?"). Many thematic units include a culminating activity for students to complete as a way to bring together much of what they have learned in a major project. This major project usually results in a meaningful artifact representing the depth and breadth of student learning.

When classrooms include students with widely varying levels of knowledge, skills, and abilities (such as a classroom that combines two or more grade levels), teachers may choose to use a range of activities to meet the varying needs of students.[12] This is sometimes called "multilevel instruction."

Multilevel Instruction Multilevel instruction refers to instructional environments where different students and groups of students are working on different tasks to meet the same or different learning objectives. Instructional activities and resources help students learn according to their individual preferences and differences—their strengths and weaknesses. Creating a learning environment where multiple tasks are going on at the same time is important for theme-based instructional settings because in most cases teachers create a variety of instructional activities that provide multiple ways for students to meet learning objectives. For example, all students can complete classification tasks, but may do so in very different ways according to their abilities and interests. As well, when students are involved in creating their own learning objectives and resultant activities to meet those objectives, they may end up working on the various components of the established theme at different times, in different ways, and at different levels.[13]

To restate briefly, the opportunities for applying knowledge as part of an instructional activity are many and varied. It seems that Merrill's fourth principle, Application, is likely to be a major part of thematic instruction but is also left up to specific teachers to implement as their creativity, energy, and resources allow.

---

12. *Editors' note: Note that this is a situational principle of instruction.*
13. *Editors' note: This kind of flexibility and customization is a hallmark of the Information-Age paradigm of education.*

4. Provide Useful Instructional Resources

Theme-based instructional units often include lists of specific resources which may be helpful or necessary to conduct suggested instructional activities. Typically, thematic instructional models emphasize the need to use resources from real life, especially nontextbook resources such as newspapers, classical literature, audio and video recordings, experts in various fields (including parents), community organizations and local leaders, regional geographies, cultural events, and more (Meinbach et al., 1995). Kovalik and Olsen (2002) include the creation of an enriched environment—that is rich with experiential resources that immerse students in the learning theme—as part of the fundamental preparation for implementing ITI.[14] Roberts and Kellough (2000) emphasize using both school resources and other resources that are external to the school, such as content experts, community groups, technologies, money, and whatever else is needed to implement the ITU.[15] Using nontextbook resources may help students engage in "hands-on, minds-on" learning activities (Roberts & Kellough, 2000). Immersing students in rich resources and engaging students in instructional activities that require them to use these resources in authentic and useful ways may help activate prior experiences (Merrill's second principle), demonstrate new knowledge in helpful ways (Merrill's third principle), and provide opportunities to apply new knowledge in authentic practices or in creating authentic artifacts (Merrill's fourth principle).

5. Evaluate Achievement through Authentic Assessment Practices

Thematic instruction uses authentic assessment practices to assess student learning.[16] These practices include compiling portfolios of student work throughout a thematic unit, requiring students to prepare public presentations (at the class, school, or community level) of work that shows evidence of learning, encouraging reflection on and revision of work produced, and often involving students in determining specific performances or selecting work samples that will be used for assessment.[17] In some programs, students are asked to write reflective reports about the work chosen for their portfolios. Students may have the opportunity to use an audio or video recording to present work or archive public presentations. Roberts and Kellough (2000) and others emphasize using a culminating experience or final activity to evaluate student learning and close the unit. If possible,

---

14. *Editors' note: The time and money to do this constitute the major instructional development constraint that is a precondition for use of this theory.*
15. *Editors' note: What layer of design do you think this is part of?*
16. *Editors' note: This is student-assessment theory. Again, it is highly appropriate to integrate it with instructional-event theory, primarily because student assessment should be integrated with instruction in an Information-Age educational system.*
17. *Editors' note: Note that these elaborations of the method are alternative kinds that may not all be used in any given situation. Further elaboration of this theory would need to offer guidance as to when and when not to use each.*

Table 13.3 Relationship between Thematic Instruction Principles and Merrill's First Principles

	Merrill's First Principle				
Thematic Instruction Principle	1: Problem-centered	2: Activation	3: Demonstration	4: Application	5: Integration
Use a Unifying Theme	Sometimes	Sometimes			
Focus Instruction on Primary Learning Goals	Sometimes				
Use a Variety of Instructional Activities		Possible	**Likely**	**Likely**	
Provide Useful Instructional Resources		Possible	Possible	Possible	
Evaluate Achievement through Authentic Assessment Practices				**Likely**	**Likely**

this activity should require collaboration among students and other members of the learning community (i.e., parents and community leaders), as appropriate.

In adult thematic instructional programs especially, helping learners assess their own learning is emphasized[18] (Dirkx & Prenger, 1997). ("Can I get a job?" "Can I create a household budget and balance my checkbook?") In some settings, learners assess themselves in actual on-the-job performance, perhaps the ultimate application of authentic assessment. These practices all implement Merrill's fourth and fifth principles, Application and Integration, respectively.

Table 13.3 summarizes the relationship between thematic instruction principles and Merrill's first principles.

Situational Principles for Theme-Based Instruction

Theme-based instruction is implemented in many different ways. The various models of thematic instruction describe several major situational principles, or situationalities, which will help educators decide how to best implement theme-based instruction in their particular context. These situationalities include (1) the nature of *administrative structures* (controlling or supporting); (2) the willingness and ability of those implementing the instructional program to *adapt instruction to individual learners*; and (3) the amount of *disciplinary integration*. In this sec-

---

18. *Editors' note: This is an important situationality.*

tion I describe these important situational principles, which influence how the universal instructional methods are implemented in practice.

1. Administrative Structures

The amount of administrative structure is an important precondition (as described earlier); but even when the structure is flexible enough to allow for theme-based instruction, the amount and nature of administrative structure may also represent situationalities. Are teachers granted the flexibility to change classrooms, students, and subjects from those they were specifically hired to teach? When teachers do not have the flexibility they need to implement the ideal thematic approach, they must consider the flexibility they do have and work within those limits. Perhaps teachers can combine classes some of the time (e.g., twice a week), rather than all of the time. Perhaps teachers can swap content teaching responsibilities for short periods of time (e.g., for a specified week), rather than for a whole unit (which might last for six or eight weeks). Hence, the administration's ability and willingness to provide time, flexibility, and resources impacts the way the thematic unit is designed.

In adult education programs, a different problem may exist if the program administration is too *unstructured*. Many adult education programs allow learners to join at any time and leave at any time (commonly referred to as open entry/open exit) and may even allow a learner to complete course activities on an asynchronous schedule (at their own pace). The highly individualistic nature of many adult-focused programs leads to this flexible enrollment policy. Educators who are trying to implement thematic instruction, however, may find the discontinuity among learners troublesome. Many thematic units rely upon socially interactive learning activities and leverage the growing interrelationships among learners to help everyone learn more effectively. With a constantly changing set of learners entering and exiting the instructional program at irregular times, educators may be hard pressed to maintain a meaningful learning community, which could lessen the overall effectiveness of the instruction. If there is significant learner turnover during the thematic unit, the teacher may be able to modularize the unit so that learners at different stages of learning can still participate (though in different activities). A teacher in this situation might also include activities that allow learners at various levels to interact frequently (e.g., in informal discussion groups, topical roundtables, etc.), which should help strengthen the sense of community.

2. Adaptability and Individualized Instruction

Meaningful differences among learners occur naturally in every instructional setting. Successful theme-based instruction provides opportunities for students to learn within their strengths and to strengthen weaker learning abilities naturally. In order for this to happen, the ideal instruction must be flexibly adaptive to the needs of individual learners. A teacher may be able to determine some of the individual learners' needs before instruction begins, but in most cases will identify more individual needs as instruction progresses. It is at this time the teacher must adapt instruction to fit the learners. Alternate activities (or resources) must be used if a teacher is unable to adapt instructional activities (or resources). If the planned instruction is too advanced or elementary for learners, alternate learning goals may be needed. When this is the case, the teacher should involve students in creating a more appropriate set of goals, activities, resources, and assessments.

At the same time, most instructional programs are implemented in group-based settings, such as schools or community organizations, which require an instructional program that meets external expectations (such as evaluation of student learning) and scales effectively to groups of different sizes. An important consideration for thematic instruction is the range of individual student characteristics (such as ability level, learning preference, and prior experience) and group characteristics (such as size and heterogeneity) that fit within the program. If there are great differences among students, more multilevel instructional activities are needed. If differences among learners are valued, group activities may be used to help students appreciate individual differences and experiences related to the theme.

3. Amount of Disciplinary Integration

In practice, theme-based instruction always involves the integration of disciplines, or curriculum. The amount of integration leads to different requirements for collaboration, scheduling flexibility, and the like. Roberts and Kellough (2000) present a continuum of integration with five levels. Similar to the curriculum integration perspectives of Drake (1991) and Jacobs (1989, 1991a, 1991b) described below, this continuum starts with traditional discipline-based curriculum organization where any integration along themes is carried out by individual teachers working with their own students within the constraints of their particular discipline concentration (such as mathematics or physical science). When topics in separate subjects coincide along a theme, it is accidental or occasional at best.

The continuum describes four other levels; the most integrated level occurs when teachers of several grade levels or subject areas have collaborated with their students to determine a coherent theme with a meaningful content description and learning goals. Each level of integration (from I to V) places increasing emphasis on important aspects of the instructional setting, such as the blurring of subject area content boundaries, collaboration among teachers, and participation of students in developing the thematic unit. An educator's intended level of curriculum integration will require more or less of each of these. Integration at higher levels is more likely to be successful when an educator, and

Table 13.4 The Evolution of Curriculum Integration Approaches (derived from Drake, 1991)

Multidisciplinary →	Interdisciplinary →	Transdisciplinary
Specific subjects connected to one organizing theme	Subjects connected and overlapping each other naturally due to the nature of the organizing theme	Subjects and theme become one entity; a set of common themes, strategies and skills
Teacher as subject-matter expert, finding places for *their* subject to connect to an overall theme	Teacher (subject-matter expert) as collaborator with other teachers	Teacher as connection expert, teaching varied content to support theme-centered goals

an educational system, value thematic integration and the fundamental values described above.

Drake (1991) describes three levels of curriculum integration—multidisciplinary, interdisciplinary, and transdisciplinary—with an increasing level of integration from multidisciplinary to interdisciplinary to transdisciplinary. Table 13.4 provides a brief summary of the type of relationship between subjects and the role of the teacher for each of the levels.

Jacobs (1989, 1991a, 1991b) describes a continuum of instructional program designs that range from traditional discipline-based to completely integrated programs where students' lives and learning experiences are fully integrated. A student interested in motion might spend entire days or weeks exploring the many facets of motion in a wide range of academic disciplines (physics, mathematics, history, social sciences, etc.). While some schools and other instructional settings may be able to support such an intensively integrated and individualized program, most will not. Other options identified by Jacobs include multidisciplinary classes, interdisciplinary units, and integrated day programs (a form of transdisciplinary approach). These approaches typically utilize theme-based instructional practices to organize curriculum and instruction at increasing levels of integration.

The models of Drake (1991) and Jacobs (1989, 1991a, 1991b) suggest the following three major considerations for selecting an overall approach:

1. Schedule flexibility—Will the instructional setting allow time for teacher planning and collaboration? How much will the schedule allow time periods (class periods, days, or weeks) to be reorganized to support learning activities of varying length? More flexibility enables a more integrated approach.
2. Instructional staff support for change—To what extent are teachers and administrators interested and supportive of new ways of structuring teaching and learning? Staff who are new to these ideas may benefit from starting with simple collaborations and a multidisciplinary approach for

small units or clusters of topics before moving on to more integrated approaches.

3. Nature of curriculum requirements—What curriculum constraints exist which may limit or (possibly) enable integration and theme-based approaches? Where are the natural opportunities for thematic integration? What challenges arise from curriculum standards and expectations? Does the curriculum enable special opportunities for thematic integration, such as local festivals, geographies, or cultures? The more a curriculum includes natural connections among content areas, the more integration is possible. And the more teachers and administrators are willing to work to create flexible and interrelated curriculum, the more integration is likely.

Implementing Thematic Instruction

Once a thematic unit is planned or selected, teachers and administrators must decide how to implement the unit:[19] once implemented, specific instructional methods may be revised based on situationalities (as described in the previous section). Major implementation considerations include: (1) the *values and belief systems* about education held by teachers and other key stakeholders of the educational system (administrators, parents, etc.); (2) the timeframe for implementation; (3) teacher preparation; (4) shifting to authentic assessment practices; and (5) working within standardized assessment systems. Each of these considerations is explained next.

1. Values and Belief Systems

The fundamental values about learning that an educator holds form the foundation for the learning environment she or he creates. This is true for entire educational systems as well. For example, an educator (or educational system) who values the development of an interdisciplinary or transdisciplinary learning community will design a learning environment to achieve learning goals and implement instructional methods that are aligned with the value of connectedness among subject areas or the study of subjects situated in a theme-driven context. On the other hand, an educational system that primarily values test scores and rankings in specific subjects will design a system that stresses test achievement, increasing test scores, and winning in peer-level subject-area competition. The various types of theme-based instructional programs are based on common values such as learner-centeredness, interconnectedness of academic disciplines, focus on process rather than *product*, and *multiple and individualized ways of knowing and learning.*[20]

Effective implementation of theme-based instruction requires that key

---

19. *Editors' note: Guidance here represents instructional implementation theory.*
20. *Editors' note: These are values that underlie the Information-Age paradigm of education, and they are important preconditions for use of this theory.*

members of the educational system share and put into practice values such as these. Teachers must be willing to give up important elements of direct control in their classrooms, administrators must be willing to allow flexible (and sometimes messy) scheduling of time and other resources, and parents must be willing to think outside the "subject area box" that may have dominated their own education.[21] If certain teachers or administrators within a system hold these values less strongly than others, they may be less committed to the integrity of the thematic approach, which can be reflected in fewer resources, less flexibility in scheduling activities, more restrictive forms of assessment, and so on. If this is the case, the methods of thematic instruction can still be used, but the expected positive effects on learning are likely to be compromised. Changes in values often take considerable time, and may require several years of paced implementation, complete with regular and frequent time for review, reflection, and revision among the members of the learning community.

Before and during implementation, people in education systems would do well to consider the lessons from change leadership in business and other organizations. Lessons learned about information gathering and sharing, formal and informal discussion of important issues, reaching consensus on fundamental values or beliefs, acknowledging and addressing fears and concerns, and creating long-term plans with short-term goals can be applied in educational organizations to help people adopt the values (stated above) which are important to the ultimate success of thematic instruction.[22] Of course, when the important values are strongly held throughout an education system, much less emphasis on value-changing is needed.

2. Timeframe for Implementation

Thematic instruction usually takes more time to implement than traditional approaches, such as direct instruction. Especially when learners are engaged in deciding upon themes, major instructional goals, and learning activities, some of the time formerly used for instruction is used for exploration and discussion of alternatives.[23] Learner involvement, if valued, must be enabled by allowing time to involve learners as early and as often as possible in the instructional planning process. If an instructional program has the flexibility to increase the length of a course, perhaps that could support a learner-centered planning stage. And it may be the case that the planning and decision-making processes in which learners are engaged help them meet important learning goals. Further, if engaging learners in planning leads to higher motivation levels, this may translate into more active engagement in learning and faster learning, more than making up for the time spent exploring alternatives.

---

21. *Editors' note: These are also important preconditions for use of this theory.*
22. *Editors' note: These are important preconditions for wholesale use of this theory.*
23. *Editors' note: These are the instructional-development constraints that constitute a precondition for use of this theory.*

Even when educators complete most (or all) of the thematic unit planning before learners are part of the instructional process, additional time is needed for planning and developing the components of the instructional unit. When teams of teachers in a district or school join together in this process, it will take time to coordinate schedules and allow normal group process to develop before an effective unit can be implemented. In some cases, schools set aside planning time throughout the school year for the development of thematic units for the following school year. In other cases, groups of teachers schedule regular planning sessions to create thematic units for use later in the same school year. In all cases, "enough" time must be set aside for planning curriculum and developing instructional materials—more time is usually better than less time.

3. Teacher Preparation

Teachers who have never developed a thematic unit may be hard pressed to plan, develop, and implement an effective unit all by themselves. First, teachers must understand and hold the values important to thematic instruction (such as those mentioned above). Teachers who have never learned by using thematic units may be at a disadvantage compared to teachers who have experienced thematic units as students. Traditional education programs, focused on discrete subject areas, tend to create teachers with a similar focus. Many teachers remember what they were good at in school by subject area rather than by a significant theme. "I like history" or "I was always good at math" are more common comments, even among teachers, than "I studied the ocean system" or "I remember searching for patterns in life." Additionally, most courses in teacher preparation programs are typically focused on a specific discipline, such as secondary mathematics, or elementary art, or reading, etc. Teachers may have to unlearn these common perceptions of dissociated content areas before they are able to develop and implement effective thematic units.

Especially when thematic units are developed around the lives and interests of students, teachers must be willing and able to give up privileged control over curriculum and instructional activity. (Conversely, students must be willing to accept responsibility for participation in planning activities.) Some teachers may need time to become comfortable with this reduced classroom structure and control; classrooms using thematic units may appear disorganized and noisy as students engage in varied individual and group activities. When using thematic instruction, many teachers find that a multiage learning community develops, and they become learners with their students. Teachers need time and professional development support to help them understand, accept and thrive in their evolving role. Perhaps theme-based professional development programs that model thematic instruction and engage teachers as learners would prepare teachers to implement their own thematic units more effectively.

An important component related to teacher preparation is the ability to find and use instructional resources. Are teachers given access to the resources they need in order to effectively implement a thematic unit (e.g., instructional material, audiovisual aids, external experts, community groups, etc.)? If resources are lacking, teachers may be able to provide resources themselves or find other teachers willing to share personal resources with them. Perhaps there are members of an online teacher community who can help identify resources. In some communities, businesses are very willing to assist educators if they are asked for help. Teachers who enthusiastically seek out the resources they need often find them in many different places.

4. Authentic Assessment

Authentic assessment occurs when student learning is assessed in ways that are consistent with the content (knowledge, skills, and attitudes) and instructional methods. Assessment activities should also be meaningful and relevant to students (Archbald & Newmann, 1988; Cumming & Maxwell, 1999; Herman, Aschbacher, & Winters, 1992; Wiggins, 1990). In theme-based instruction, student assessment should be accomplished through demonstrations of learning that are directly tied to the overarching theme. Authentic demonstrations of learning may include such elements as research reports, public presentations of research or other information to the local or global community, multimedia presentations delivered online or in local kiosks, artistic (re-)presentations of concepts, or theatrical performances.

The first major key to choosing authentic assessment methods is to align assessment with learning objectives. Does the selected assessment method allow an evaluator (the teacher, in most cases) to judge whether or not student learning has occurred, and to what level learning has occurred? For instance, if an overarching theme of "Animals in Our Ecosystem" is used in a seventh grade writing class, a student assignment to write a short story for a local newspaper or "bedtime" story for a younger child using animal characters found in the local ecosystem, would be an appropriate authentic assessment method. However, an assignment simply requiring students to match pictures of animals to a location on a local map where those animals could be found would not be as authentic. (The reader might consider how this assessment method could be improved to work within an authentic assessment activity.) In thematic units that include the public presentation of reports and other student works, assessment is authentic in the sense that students are communicating what they have chosen to learn about their local environment to the local community.

Another key is to ensure that students are being asked to complete relevant tasks to demonstrate learning. Superficial connection between assessments and overarching themes are simple to create and may be commonly used in practice, but generally do not allow a teacher to effectively evaluate student learning within the theme. Consider the imagined case of the seventh grade writing class again. As part of implementing the writing curriculum, a writing teacher may try to teach students how to write persuasive arguments in essay form. An assignment to write a persuasive essay could be deeply connected to the overarching theme of "Animals in Our Ecosystem" by asking students to write an editorial for a local newspaper urging the protection of the habitat for one or more local animals. An assignment asking students to assume the role of a local animal and write an essay trying to persuade another animal to stop bothering it would be less authentic. In a thematic unit centered on local beaches, a group assignment to research and present an important historical aspect of the beach zone allows student groups to determine a topic of personal group interest, conduct historical research, and create a public presentation of the aspect or event.

If at all possible, evaluations of student learning in theme-based instructional programs should rely upon evidence developed through authentic assessment activities. These activities should assess, in part, how well student learning is tied to the overarching theme naturally, through the assessment itself.

5. Working within Standardized Assessment Systems

In many school settings, educators do not have the luxury or responsibility to determine the most effective method of assessing student learning. Often, authentic assessment methods such as those described above are not considered relevant for summative evaluation of student learning or overall school and teacher performance. In most public school systems, some form of standardized assessment system is used to judge overall student achievement compared to approved national, state, and local standards. How does theme-based instruction fit into an instructional system using standardized assessment?

When standardized assessment systems are used to evaluate student learning, teachers using theme-based instruction must prepare students to demonstrate learning through criterion or norm referenced testing systems. Theme-based instructional methods can prepare students for these tests as long as the instructional program is aligned to state standards with regard to curriculum. It is likely that any curriculum—body of content—can be taught using theme-based instruction. As with many instructional approaches, the creativity, skills, and resources of the teacher control whether or not theme-based instruction can work effectively. Appropriate choices for themes, learning goals, and instructional activities can prepare students to demonstrate learning on standardized tests, and student motivation is likely to be higher.

Conclusions

Proponents of theme-based instruction argue convincingly that this is a powerful instructional strategy to engage students in learning, help students connect new knowledge to their experiences and the real world around them, and create effective learning communities. Though there is little empirical research to support these claims of effectiveness (Ritter, 1999), there is a large amount of anecdotal and descriptive case study research that indicates theme-based instruction can lead to successful student learning.

Theme-based instruction may take many forms, from short and simple interdisciplinary units to fully integrated transdisciplinary multiyear programs. Important factors to consider when designing theme-based instruction include: teacher, student, and administration experience and support for thematic instructional programs, time available for planning, flexibility in schedule, limitations in classroom use and structure, other needed instructional resources, and opportunities to create adaptable individualized instruction.

Successful theme-based instruction should implement all the principles of instruction identified by Merrill. Authentic themes should lead to interesting problems or questions to answer. Effective engagement and interesting instructional activities will lead to activation of prior knowledge and experiences so that new knowledge will become accessible and useful to students. A rich set of diverse instructional resources should provide for many opportunities for new knowledge to be demonstrated from multiple perspectives. Interesting activities (inquiries centered around key points) will allow for student practice of new knowledge. And finally, culminating experiences, such as major project presentations and other authentic assessment methods, should provide natural support for transferring knowledge into real life.

References

Archbald, D., & Newmann, F. (1988). *Beyond standardized testing: Assessing authentic academic achievement in the secondary school.* Reston, VA: National Association of Secondary School Principals.

Aschbacher, P. A. (1991). Humanitas: A thematic curriculum. *Educational Leadership, 49*(2), 16–19.

Beane, J. (1991). The middle school: The natural home of integrated curriculum. *Educational Leadership, 49*(2), 9–13.

Bergeron, B. S., & Rudenga, E. A. (1993). *Delineating and undefining thematic instruction.* Paper presented at the Annual Meeting of the National Reading Conference, Charleston, SC.

Cumming, J. J., & Maxwell, G. S. (1999). *Contextualizing authentic assessment. Assessment in Education: Principles, Policy & Practice, 6*(2), 177–194.

Daniel, M. H. (1997). Intelligence testing: Status and trends. *American Psychologist, 52*(10), 1038–1045.

Dirkx, J. M., & Prenger, S. M. (1997). *Planning and implementing instruction for adults: A theme-based approach.* San Francisco: Jossey-Bass.

Drake, S. (1991). How our team dissolved the boundaries. *Educational Leadership, 49*(2), 20–22.

Gardner, H. (1983). *Frames of mind: Theory of multiple intelligences.* New York: Basic.

Gardner, H. (1999). *Intelligence reframed: Multiple intelligences for the 21st century.* New York: Basic.

Goldberg, E. (2001). *The executive brain: Frontal lobes and the civilized mind.* Oxford: Oxford University Press.

Greene, L. C. (1991). Science-centered curriculum in elementary school. *Educational Leadership, 49*(2), 42–46.

Haas, M. (2000). *Thematic, communicative language teaching in the K-8 classroom..* Washington, D.C.: ERIC Clearinghouse on Languages and Linguistics. (ERIC Digest No. EDO-FL-00-04) Retrieved from http://www.cal.org/ericcll/digest/0004thematic.html).

Hart, L. A. (1999). *Human brain and human learning.* Covington, WA: Books for Educators.

Herman, J. L., Aschbacher, P. R., & Winters, L. (1992). *A practical guide to alternative assessment.* Alexandria, VA: Association for Supervision and Curriculum Development.

Jacobs, H. H. (1989). Design options for an integrated curriculum. In H. H. Jacobs (Ed.), *Integrated curriculum: Design and implementation* (pp. 13–24). Alexandria, VA: Association for Supervision and Curriculum Development (ASCD).Jacobs, H. H. (1991a). On interdisciplinary curriculum: A conversation with Heidi Hayes Jacobs. *Educational Leadership, 49*(2), 24–26.

Jacobs, H. H. (1991b). Planning for curriculum integration. *Educational Leadership, 49*(2), 27–28.

Kleiman, G. M. (1991). Mathematics across the curriculum. *Educational Leadership, 49*(2), 48–51.

Kolb, D. A. (1984). *Experiental learning: Experience as the source of learning and development*. Englewood Cliffs, NJ: Prentice Hall.

Kovalik, S. J., & McGeehan, J. R. (1999). Integrated thematic instruction: From brain research to application. In C. M. Reigeluth (Ed.), *Instructional-design theories and models: Vol. 2. A new paradigm of instructional theory* (pp. 371–396). Mahwah, NJ: Erlbaum.

Kovalik, S. J., & Olsen, K. D. (2002). *Exceeding expectations: A user's guide to implementing brain research in the classroom*. Covington, WA: Kovalik.

Lazear, D. (1994). *Multiple intelligence approaches to assessment: Solving the assessment conundrum*. Tucson, AZ: Zephyr.

Meinbach, A. M., Rothlein, L., & Fredericks, A. D. (1995). *The complete guide to thematic units: Creating the integrated curriculum*. Norwood, MA: Christopher-Gordon.

Merrill, M.D. (2002). First principles of instruction. *Educational Technology Research and Development 50*(3), 43–59.

Miller, J., Cassie, B., & Drake, S. (1990). *Holistic learning: A teacher's guide to integrated studies*. Toronto: OISE Press.

Perkins, D. N. (1989). Selecting fertile themes for integrated learning. In H. H. Jacobs (Ed.), *Integrated curriculum: Design and implementation* (pp. 67–76). Alexandria, VA: Association for Supervision and Curriculum Development (ASCD).

Perkins, D. N. (1998). What is understanding? In M. S. Wiske (Ed.), *Teaching for understanding: Linking research with practice* (pp. 39–58). San Francisco: Jossey-Bass.

Ritter, N. (1999). *Teaching interdisciplinary thematic units in language arts*. Bloomington, IN: ERIC Clearinghouse on Reading English and Communication. (ERIC Digest D142. ED436003)

Roberts, P. L., & Kellough, R. D. (2000). *A guide for developing interdisciplinary thematic units*. Upper Saddle River, NJ: Prentice-Hall.

Ross, S. M., McCormick, D., & Krisak, N. (1986). Adapting the thematic context of mathematical problem solving to student interests: Individualized versus group-based strategies. *Journal of Educational Research, 79*(4), 245–252.

Sattler, J. M. (2002). *Assessment of children: Behavioral and clinical applications* (4th ed.). San Diego, CA: Author.

Sternberg, R. J. (1997). The concept of intelligence and its role in lifelong learning and success. *American Psychologist, 52*(10), 1030–1037.

Strube, P. S. (1993). *Theme studies: A practical guide*. New York: Scholastic Professional.

Swartz, E. (Ed.). (1991). Thematic instruction [Special issue]. *Communicator, 21*(4).

Vars, G. F. (1991). Integrated curriculum in historical perspective. *Educational Leadership, 49*(2), 14–15.

Vella, J. (1994). *Learning to listen, learning to teach: The power of dialogue in educating adults*. San Francisco: Jossey-Bass.

Walker, D. (1996). *Integrative education*. Eugene, OR: ERIC Clearinghouse on Educational Management. (ERIC Digest No. ED 390 112)

Wiggins, G. (1990). The case for authentic assessment. *Practical Assessment, Research & Evaluation, 2*(2). Retrieved August 30, 2005 from http://PAREonline.net/getvn.asp?v=2&n=2 .

Wiggins, G., & McTighe, J. (2005). Understanding understanding. In *understanding by design* (2nd ed., pp. 35–55). Upper Saddle River, NJ: Pearson.

Yorks, P., & Follo, E. (1993). *Engagement rates during thematic and traditional instruction*. (ERIC Document Reproduction Service No. ED 363 412)

Unit 4
Tools for Building a Common Knowledge Base

Unit Foreword

Unit 4 addresses what we feel are some of the more promising conceptual tools for advancing the field of instructional-event theory. The variety of cognitive tools we outline here is, of course, by no means exhaustive of all the tools that may be useful for advancing a common knowledge base, but we find these to be the most compelling, as we outline below.

In chapter 14, Andrew Gibbons and Clint Rogers offer us layers as a tool. Because of its great value in understanding instructional theories (as well as for building them), we briefly summarized this in chapter 1. Layering is a tool that builds more flexibility into improving our instructional designs by making it easier to change one layer without having to change the entire instructional design. Understanding the different layers also helps instructional theorists to not overlook important layers in their theories. We believe that it would be helpful for instructional theories to address each layer, either individually or in congregation. It seems likely that when advice is given for one layer, it would be helpful to address strategies for additional layers that may be impacted. We agree with Gibbons that this is a far more nuanced and complex understanding of instructional design, and this avoids monolithic theoretical constructs. We also agree with Gibbons's point that understanding the architecture of instructional theory will lead to better designs, more consistent and efficient results, clearer mutual understandings among designers, and a stronger ability to effectively communicate among designers. This last point, in particular is very much in our broader service of moving toward a common knowledge base and a common language. Thus, chapter 14 advances a set of tools, language, and methods which we believe have great promise for advancing instructional-event theory.

In chapter 15, C. Victor Bunderson, David A. Wiley, and Reo H. McBride examine domain theory in general, and in particular the methods associated with quantitative domain mapping (QDM). QDM is defined by Bunderson and Wiley as a method by which we describe a specific domain supported by both theory and research data. Domain theory is a particularly powerful tool because it can help us to customize the learning experience for different learners because we can map domains for their diverse competencies and levels of competency.

QDM helps us to figure out what is really happening in the process of learning and helps us to go beyond instinct or inference to have a better measurement of an abstract field. This proposal by Bunderson and Wiley, that there be standard measures, holds out the hope of significant cumulative long-term progress for educators. We believe that this tool, therefore, is a particularly powerful one, being large in scope and specific in method.

In chapter 16 David Wiley addresses the now popular notion of learning objects. The basic idea here, as Wiley shows, is the creation of instruction from existing components. The primary reason that we believe learning objects are an important tool for advancing instructional-event theory is that they hold the promise of more facile reusability. This has the potential to revolutionize the instructional design and development processes. Therefore, instructional-event theories should take into account considerations for reusability. This is related to the notion of layers, and we believe that a keener connection between the components in our designs, be they through learning objects or layers, would help to advance instructional-event theory significantly. Wouldn't it be optimal if we could design learning objects or instructional components in a layered fashion such that they could, at different chronological times, become obsolete and easily replaced? Both layers and learning objects facilitate the notion of melding old and new into single systems. One caution here, however, is that we are not in favor of so isolating components in instruction that they are seen as wholly independent or interchangeable without concern for systemic coherence. We do not believe there will be a time when we can simply walk to a shelf (be it real or virtual) and pull down several bits of instruction and simply plug 'n play them together in a lesson. Rather, the promise of learning objects is the potential for knowledgeable designers to reuse existing proven objects of learning.

In chapter 17, Charles Reigeluth and Yun-Jo An address different approaches to generating theory. They identify distinctions between descriptive and design knowledge and encourage the development of both for the furthering of instructional theory, but focus on design knowledge for the purposes of this book. After Reigeluth and An point to eclectic frameworks for building design research on preferability rather than validity, they recommend an ongoing agenda of design-based research that will formatively inform our common knowledge base. They then turn their attention to four approaches to building design theory, including data-based, values-based, methods-based, and practitioner-driven theory development. These approaches are then explored further through research methods, including grounded theory development, design-based research, and formative research. Chapter 17 closes with a recommendation that is key to this entire volume: the importance of using a common language and knowledge base by linking future research efforts to the general language and common knowledge base. In this way, we very much agree with Reigeluth and An that we will advance the entire field with this disciplined approach to research and development. We feel this is very important as our field continues to evolve and develop new instructional act theories and therefore has a proper place here, near the end of this book.

In chapter 18, Reigeluth extends out from the book's focus on building a common language and common knowledge base to look at how this common language and knowledge base should serve the needs of the broader educational system. Reigeluth describes the systemic nature of schooling, pointing out that instruction must serve the instructional needs of the educational systems, which, in turn, must serve the larger needs of their communities and society. He points to the ways that society's educational needs have been changing and continue to change, and therefore require significantly different things of their educational systems than they did in earlier eras when we were focused on agrarian- or industrial-age educational needs. Reigeluth goes on to draw a vision of an information-age educational system founded on principles of customization and diversity, initiative and self-direction, collaboration and emotional development, and holism and integration that are at the core of information-age educational needs. He lays out the main features of the system as well as the roles technology can play in such a system. And he invites us, as instructional theorists, to engage in the creation of a common knowledge base that will aid development of the new paradigm of education. Understanding the importance of learning experiences and environments to meet the larger needs of schools and societies ties together many of the goals we have shared through the years and weaves in the further development of instructional theory that is the main purpose of this book, calling us to even larger goals of shared knowledge.

—CMR & ACC

14
The Architecture of Instructional Theory

ANDREW S. GIBBONS
Brigham Young University

P. CLINT ROGERS
University of Joensuu

Andrew S. Gibbons is department chair in instructional psychology and technology at Brigham Young University. Prior to that, he was a faculty member at Utah State University. He led instructional design projects in industry for 18 years at Wicat Systems, Inc. and Courseware Inc. Dr. Gibbons' work has included large-scale training development projects, reengineering of the development (ISD) process, computer-based instruction, military and commercial aviation training development, and research and development on instructional simulations. Dr. Gibbons' current research focuses on the architecture of instructional designs. He has published a design theory of model-centered instruction, proposed a general layering theory of instructional designs, and is currently studying the use of design languages in relation to design layers as a means of creating instructional systems that are adaptive, generative, and scalable.

P. Clint Rogers, PhD, teaches, conducts research, and does consulting work primarily regarding IDT, web analytics, and cross-cultural online collaboration and innovation. He has worked with Brigham Young University, and with the University of Joensuu, Finland—coordinating the Cross-Cultural Research Group and supervising dissertations in the IMPDET program (International Multidisciplinary PhD Studies in Educational Technology www.impdet. org). He holds a doctorate in instructional psychology and technology, and has specific research interests in IDT, global virtual teams, fostering human potential, the cultural customization of online collaboration and innovation, the philosophical roots of education and science, and the impact of technological diffusion on international development, business, and social change—and obviously a key interest  in layers and languages in instructional design. For his most recent work and interests, visit: http:// www.clintrogersonline.com/blog.

EDITORS' FOREWORD

Vision

- *To relate instructional theory and instructional design theory*

Kinds of Theory

- *Two Kinds of Theory: Instructional and instructional-design*
- *Design Theory: Applies across all domains of design*
- *Domain Theory: Is particular to a domain of design, e.g. instruction*
- *A basis for the design theory/domain theory distinction: multiple categories of engineering design knowledge*
- *Design instrumentalities and instructional design theory (functional decomposition versus process decomposition)*

Design Layering by Functional Decomposition

- *Employed in numerous design fields, including architecture, computer and software design, multimedia design, and others*
- *Being aware of layers allows us to design for dynamic and changing contexts.*

Design Layering and ID

- *The layering notion for ID includes:*
  - *Content layer*
  - *Strategy layer*
  - *Message layer*
  - *Control layer*
  - *Representation layer*
  - *Media-logic layer*
  - *Data management layer*

Design Languages

- *Design languages and natural languages differ in primitive terms, syntax, and semantics.*
- *A design language is abstracted through patterns from previous designs.*
- *As design languages evolve and we become fluent in using them, the result is advances in design sophistication, effectiveness, productivity, and quality of designs.*

Operational Principles and Instructional Theory

- *Operational principles link design layers and design languages to instructional theory.*

Layers, Languages, Operational Principles, and Instructional Theory

- *ID theory provides a structural framework of layers within which instructional theories can be analyzed and compared.*

- *There is a great deal of work in instructional theory that is related to layers.*

—CMR & ACC

THE ARCHITECTURE OF INSTRUCTIONAL THEORY

This chapter joins a discussion of instructional theory that has been ongoing for nearly a century. It departs in some ways from prior discussions: (1) it considers instructional theory as a species of technological theory rather than as a type of scientific theory,[1] a view expressed more fully elsewhere (Gibbons, 2003a); (2) it adopts the viewpoint articulated in earlier chapters of this book that there are multiple distinct bodies of technological theory that pertain to the work of instructional designers; (3) it attempts to articulate a particular view of the nature of two of those bodies of theory by describing their relationship to each other; and (4) it suggests a direction for the future exploration of additional bodies of theory, based on the writing of Vincenti (1990). Other views of possible theory development are described in Reigeluth and Carr-Chellman (chapter 1, this volume) and Bichelmeyer, Boling, and Gibbons (2006). Each of these views of the future development of theory begins from a different starting point and suggests interesting alternatives for exploration, perhaps leading to a new level of discussion of the role of theory in instructional design.

Most current practitioners of instructional design find it hard to describe in other than very general terms how instructional theories influence their designs. We feel this situation will improve if design theorists can provide a more nuanced view of instructional theory that relates theory more directly to everyday design concepts and practices. In this chapter we describe an architecture of instructional theory that ties the elements of an instructional design in a more detailed way to instructional theory. Rather than tracing the origins of a design back to a single instructional theory, this architecture suggests that different features of a design should be related to different, local, instructional theories. We propose that those local theories work within a larger framework of instructional design theory. These two different bodies of theory—instructional theory and instructional design theory—and their relation to each other are the subject of this chapter.

Distinguishing Two Kinds of Theory

Our discussion highlights a distinction between instructional theory and instructional design theory, consistent with the discussion by Reigeluth and Carr-Chellman (chapter 1, this volume) of *instructional-event* theory and *instructional-planning* theory. However, in this chapter we will adhere to the more familiar terms (*instructional theory* and *instructional design theory*) when

---

1. Editors' note: *This distinction is similar to the one made in chapter 1 between design theory and descriptive theory.*

referring to these two bodies of theory: first, in hopes of clarifying terms already in common use that have been the source of some confusion, and second, to maintain consistency with Vincenti's view of design.[2]

To begin, we should describe the contrast we see. In our view *instructional theory* deals with the structure of instructional conversations, and *instructional design theory* deals with the manner in which the elements of those conversational structures are selected, given dimension, and integrated into a design. This suggests that one body of theory (instructional design theory) provides a framework within which the second body of theory (instructional theory) can be applied. In this perspective, the substance of an instructional theory consists of categories of design building blocks and the rules by which building blocks may be articulated to form different designs. The substance of instructional design theory, on the other hand, consists of methods for analyzing and decomposing design problems, classes of design structure, and principles for deriving design processes appropriate to different types of design problems. If instructional theory reflects a particular theorist's view of effective *instructional* structures and operations during instruction, then instructional design theory reflects a view of effective *design* structures and operations during designing.

This distinction between two types of theory related to instructional design parallels similar views of theory in design fields in general. In virtually all mature design fields there exist multiple domain theories that describe different theorists' views about fundamental building blocks and rules for articulating these building blocks together in workable ways. There exist at the same time in those fields theories that govern the *making* of designs. Both kinds of theory are critical to advances in design practice in those fields. From this point of view we give a more detailed account of instructional theory and its architecture by describing it within a framework of instructional design theory that is expressed in terms of *design layers* and *design languages*. We show how this view of instructional design theory makes possible a more detailed discussion of existing instructional theories and their comparison against a common background. A brief summary of our argument is given below, followed in later sections by a more detailed discussion of key points.

In the past, the most common approach to instructional design theory has been of generic design processes (primarily ADDIE), but we propose that process is only one of many possible approaches to the decomposition of design problems into solvable subproblems. We consider an alternative decomposition scheme that has been used successfully in other design fields—decomposition in terms of artifact functionality—for example, the formation of message structures, the representation of message structures to the senses, and carrying out strategic interactions. Functional design decomposition creates separate design *layers*

---

2. *Editors' note: Our view is that the confusion over the term instructional-design theory is so long-held and deeply engrained that consensus will not be reached on a single meaning for it, and that we are better off to use a different term that is unambiguous. We agree that this distinction is very important; we only disagree on the terms that should be used.*

representing design subproblems that can be addressed somewhat independently. Each layer accounts for the design decisions related to the individual functions that become integrated into a complete design. Design languages, which are collections of abstract structures, supply specific structures and qualities to designed features within these layers. Terms of design languages are supplied by the shared community languages of designers, which include among other things the vocabularies of specific domain theories: instructional theories. Problems within each design layer are solved using layer-related languages. Thus, every design is expressed in the terms of multiple design languages, each having a mixture of theoretical and practical bases.

The specific layers and sublayers involved in a particular design (and therefore the languages used to create the design) evolve and change based on design decisions, constraints, criteria, resources, tools, new technologies, construction (development) methods, and available designer skills and awareness. For instance, commitment to a specific delivery medium (such as videotape) injects certain sublayers and design languages into the design and may remove others (such as those for computers) from consideration. Therefore, each design includes its own unique combination of sublayers. At the most detailed level, layers are created or destroyed according to the decisions and dynamics of a specific project. In this chapter we describe a list of high-level layers that we feel are generic to virtually all instructional designs.

In this view of instructional design theory, an instructional theory can be described as a domain theory—a set of specialized, mutually consistent design languages that consist of defined terms distributed across multiple design layers. That is, an instructional theorist supplies building-block elements that constitute legitimate terms of designing for use within one or more layers. This insight describes the relationship between instructional design theory and instructional theory. Design theory provides the structural framework within which specific instructional theories can be analyzed and compared. Instructional theories work within a framework of functional design layers, however those layers are construed by the theorist.

Design Theory

As we have said, design theory is a body of theory about design making that can be considered independently of the specific fields in which the designs are made. Simon (1999) describes how attention to design architectures, design processes, and design theory have been forced on us by the introduction and widespread use of the computer: the creation of a body of design theory has been motivated mainly by the desire to exploit the power of the computer in making designs. Therefore, Simon argued for the establishment of a general "design science of the artificial" independent of specific application concerns. He challenged design theorists to "discover a science of design, a body of intellectually tough, analytic, partly formalizable, partly empirical, teachable doctrine about the design process" (pp. 131–132). Others (Alexander, 1964, 1979, 1996; Edmondson, 1987; Gross, Ervin, Anderson, & Fleisher, 1987; Newsome, Spillers, & Finger, 1989; Schön, 1987) have taken similar positions on the study of design theory independent of specific fields.

Simon (1999) portrays the controlling logic of design as the formation and exploration of a set of alternative solutions that satisfy a set of constraints and criteria, and then selection of an alternative on the basis of a prioritizing rule. The efficient generation of multiple acceptable ("satisficing," in Simon's terminology) alternative solutions is a key activity of design that should be theory-driven if brute combinatorics and blind search are to be avoided. This is a clue to the nature of design theory: if the essential activity of technology is the creation of alternative structures, then the efficient generation of alternatives that in advance have some promise of being effective is a task that should require theoretical guidance. Design theories are, therefore, theories for use in structuring and synthesis (Gibbons, 2003a). Artifacts begin as conceptual entities, and the function of design theory is to supply the bridge between (1) conceptual entities and (2) workable artifact designs and plans for the construction of artifacts. Design theories compete by being superior in achieving particular ends, measured in terms of one or more dimensions of outcomes. Multiple theories of multiple kinds are required, therefore, because criteria differ from problem to problem and theories are biased in terms of the range of artifacts they can produce, the outcomes they generate, and the side-effects that accompany them.

Domain Theory

Design theory can be contrasted with the domain theories of specific fields of design, such as engineering design, computer and computer chip design, architectural design, manufacturing design, structural design, and others. The most important result of improved domain theories may be the acceleration of advances in the quality and sophistication of designs, particularly in computer-aided design through modeling (Kuehlmann, 2003).

We categorize instructional theories as domain theories, similar in intent to the theories that have led to advances in these other fields. The theory domain of interest in instructional design is the acts that take place during an instructional conversation. Use of the word *theory* was at one time restricted to science, but technologists in general—including instructional technologists—have appropriated the word with increasing frequency and conviction to refer to design domain theory. Bruner (1966), Gage (1964), Gagné (1985), Oswald (1989), Reigeluth (1999), Merrill (Merrill & Twitchell, 1994), Snelbecker (1985), and others have made reference to instructional theory, as differing from learning theory, and have probed the nature and content of instructional theories. Still, many technologists hesitate to speak in terms of theory, being uncertain about what theory means when applied to a design technology rather than a science.

Simon (1999) engages in an extended discussion of the nature of technological (or design) theory and its differences from scientific theory. He explains, "The natural sciences are concerned with how things are.... Design, on the other hand, is concerned with how things ought to be, with devising artifacts to attain goals. We might question whether the forms of reasoning that are appropriate to natural science are suitable also for design" (pp. 114–115).

A Basis for the Design Theory/Domain Theory Distinction

The nature of scientific (or descriptive) theory is described as numerous bounded "local" theories and the hope that scientists might someday find a "theory of everything" (Hawking, 1998). Whether it is appropriate to consider a design "theory of everything" is a point for speculation, but we *can* speak in terms of local design theories and multiple varieties of local design theory. Vincenti (1990) provides insight into the kinds of theory that might be employed by a designer. He describes several categories of organized engineering design knowledge necessary for the solution of technological (or design) problems. They include: operational principles, normal configurations, criteria and specifications, intellectual concepts, mathematical tools, mathematically structured knowledge, device-specific mathematical relationships, phenomenological theories, quantitative assumptions, quantitative data, practical considerations, and design instrumentalities.

All of these categories have importance to the discussion of design theory; each of them is a candidate to evolve in the future a body of synthetic (design-related) theory. Of these categories of design-related knowledge we will concentrate on two to outline their theoretical implications: operational principles, and design instrumentalities. We have selected these two because they deal with core concerns of designs—one with conceptual structures combined into designs, and the other with the processes by which they are brought together. These represent the sides of a gap that is bridged during design: the conceptual world in the designer's mind and the concrete world of designed artifacts. Next we will describe design instrumentality knowledge as it relates to instructional designs. In a later section we will return to the category of operational principle knowledge.

Design Instrumentalities and Instructional Design Theory

An enormous literature exists on design instrumentalities for instructional designers. However, the theoretic roots of current design practices are difficult to trace in that literature. The predominant formalism in the literature on instructional design is a collection of instructional planning methodologies that as a group are referred to as *ADDIE, ISD*, the *systems approach*, or *systematic development model*. These methods are purported to be derived from general systems theory, but the methods are often taught with a high degree of local variation without much reference to the foundational theory. This often includes an admixture of design processes with instructional theory, so that the design process appears to be theory-derived. The result has been a set of loosely specified, nonstandard, highly variable design activities held up professionally more as an ideal than as a criterion, and that conflate the design process with specific domain theories of instruction.

On close examination, the practices of the systems approach appear to be a combination of practical project management considerations, instructional theory, and common sense. Andrews and Goodson (1991) document numerous examples of design and development models that are different combinations and orderings of a common set of design processes. It would not be exaggerating to say that hundreds or even thousands of these exist within training departments in industrial, commercial, government, military, and educational organizations as tailored local versions of a systematic process description.

Systematic instructional design is a process approach to design problem solving analogous to the waterfall process found early on in other design fields but later deemphasized. Such approaches are a way of breaking down large and complex design problems into more easily solved subproblems. Simon (1999) and many others identify problem decomposition as an important step in problem solution and describe different ways in which a problem may be decomposed. Process decomposition is only one of these. The most prominent alternative to process decomposition is functional decomposition (Baldwin & Clark, 2000). Functional decomposition produces layered subproblems that correspond to functions carried out by the designed artifact that enable it to fill its purpose. Brand (1994) describes this type of decomposition with respect to the design of buildings.

Design Layering

Brand (1994) describes the design of a building in terms of several integrated subdesigns, which he calls *layers*. Brand's layers of design represent solutions to design subproblems created by decomposing the original design problem in terms of artifact functions. He therefore characterizes the complete design of a building in terms of multiple coordinated and integrated subdesigns. The layers, according to Brand are "fundamental to understanding how buildings actually behave" (p. 17). Each layer of a design performs one or more functions for the complete design. As the architect proceeds from drawing to drawing through layer after layer, Brand maintains, structures within layers must correspond across layers, and yet the layers are sufficiently independent of each other that changes to the design of one do not destroy the function of another. Baldwin and Clark (2000) refer to this as design modularization and provide an extended case study of how the functional design decomposition used in the design of the IBM 360 operating system revolutionized the design and economics of computers. Brand describes layers present in virtually all modern building designs, as shown in Figure 14.1.

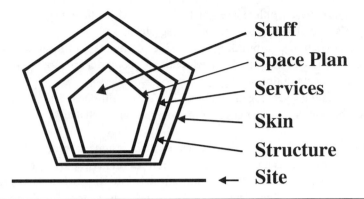

Figure 14.1 Brand's Layers of Building Design (From Brand, 1994)

Brand defines the layers in this way:

- Site —The geographical setting and the legally defined lot, having boundaries and context
- Structure—The foundation and load-bearing elements of the building
- Skin—The exterior surfaces
- Services—The communications wiring, electrical wiring, plumbing, sprinkler system, HVAC (heating, ventilating, air conditioning), and moving parts like elevators and escalators
- Space plan—The interior layout—where walls, ceilings, floors, and doors go
- Stuff—Chairs, desks, phones, pictures, kitchen appliances, lamps, etc.: things that move around inside spaces. (Brand, 1994, p. 13)

These layers have not always been considered part of building designs. The conception of design layers in a professional community may be interpreted as a measure of the maturity of a field of design.

Brand points out several important implications of the influence of layer awareness on designs:

- Layers age and change at different rates, but they can be designed and interfaced in a way that allows relatively independent, nondestructive change to individual layers.
- Layered design can therefore create artifacts that are adaptive and long-lived.
- The sequence of layers from "site" to "stuff" is the general sequence followed in both design and construction; moreover, it is related to the rate of aging of different layers (Note: on this point we disagree with Brand, as we describe below).

- Layers represent different sets of design skills with different agendas, design goals, and problems to solve and integrate.
- The dynamic of a building—the pace of change within and between layers—is dominated by the slowly changing components; rapidly changing components "follow along."
- Embedding layers together looks efficient but ultimately shortens the life of the building as changes become increasingly destructive.

Whether or not designers of buildings see their designs in terms of the layers that Brand describes is an important question. Certainly the trend of modern design standards supports designs that allow below-the-surface layers to be accessed through masking layers, repaired, and even changed with minimal disruption. Standard office building design clearly facilitates the reconfiguration of interior working spaces and the service layers behind them, and this design philosophy has spawned several systems of specialized tools, structural components, and construction methodologies. Examination of early housing designs in America shows that there was a period when simple construction took precedence over adaptability in designs. An innovation called "balloon construction" revolutionized housing design and produced consciously layered designs early in the late 19th and early 20th centuries (Peterson, 2000). This standard set of layers is thrust upon designers in the form of received design practices in which a layering structure that has evolved over many years is implicit: a hint that the development of layers is a cross-generational phenomenon.

The evolution of layer awareness in housing designs seems to have gone through a series of predictable stages. Layering of designs occurs naturally as design criteria become more exacting and as design problems become more complex and demanding. The decisions and plans that could be made originally by an individual, multiskilled person slowly fragment into local designs that involve the assistance of design specialists. Layers become evident in the design itself, which begins to consist of independent subdesigns that are integrated and orchestrated. New and more detailed sublayers of the design come into existence through innovation. Eventually, as criteria continue to arise, a design team composed of specialists and coordinated by a lead designer is required in order to produce complete, consistent, and integrated designs.

Brand's example of building layers is only one of many modern examples that can be provided of the maturation of a design field and the introduction of specialized, layered planning into designs. Additional examples can be found in the recent histories of computer chip design, software design, mechanical engineering of automobiles and aircraft, architecture, computer network design, and others (Baldwin & Clark, 2000; Kuehlmann, 2003; Saabagh, 1996). McCloud (1994) describes a principle of layering in relation to the design of comics. In many cases, rapid developments in a design field are made possible through the creation of design languages within layers that are amenable to computation, and the result is increasingly greater participation of the computer in design activities.

Design Layering and Instructional Design

Gibbons (2004) describes a set of layers derived from the functional properties of virtually all instructional designs. These layers represent specialized design subproblems that result from the decomposition by functionality of whole instructional design problems. A representative set of instructional design problems is named and described by Gibbons (2003b):

- Content layer. A design must specify the structures of the abstract subject-matter to be taught, must identify the units into which the subject-matter will be divided, and must describe how elements of subject-matter will be made available to instructional functions performed by other layers.
- Strategy layer. A design must specify the physical organization of the learning space, social organizations of participants, their roles and responsibilities, instructional goals, allocation of goals to timed event structures, and strategic patterns of interaction between the learner and the instructional experience.
- Message layer. A design must specify the tactical language of message structures through which the instructional experience can communicate content-derived information to the learner in conversational form.
- Control layer. A design must specify the language of control structures through which the learner expresses messages and actions to the source of the learning experience.
- Representation layer. A design must specify the representations that make message elements visible, hearable, and otherwise sense-able: the media representation channels to be used, the rule for assigning message elements to media channels, the form and composition of the representation, the synchronization of messages delivered through the multiple channels, and the representations of content.
- Media-logic layer. A design must specify the mechanism by which representations are caused to occur in their designed or computed sequence.
- Data management layer. A design must specify data to be captured, archived, analyzed, interpreted, and reported.

The concept of design layers constitutes a structuring theory for the creation of instructional designs. Each layer accounts for a certain category of decisions regarding specialized functions that eventually become part of a complete design. The division of layers we present is not scientifically derived, and it is not presented as a "truth." Layers, especially at the more detailed levels of design, evolve and change based on their utility to the designer according to a number of factors that include design constraints, criteria, resources, tools, technology, construction methods, and available designer skills. The list of layers we suggest is generic to virtually all instructional design projects, but one arrangement of specific sublayers may be superior to another and confer advantage on a designer. What is emphasized here is not the power of the particular set of layers we have enumerated, but the power of thinking of instructional designs in terms of layering. We believe that it represents a way to advance thinking about the properties of instructional designs and the relationship between instructional theory and instructional design theory.

Design Languages

Schön (1987) refers to layers as domains of language: "Elements of the language of designing can be grouped into clusters, of which I have identified twelve.... These design domains contain the names of elements, features, relations, and actions and of norms used to evaluate problems, consequences, and implications" (p. 58). He continues: "Aspiring members of the linguistic community of design learn to detect multiple references, distinguish particular meanings in context, and use multiple references as an aid to vision across design domains" (p. 61). Gibbons and Brewer (2005) and Waters and Gibbons (2004) describe in detail design languages and the notation systems that make them public and shareable.

Natural Languages and Design Languages

Natural languages are typified by a set of primitives, a syntax, and a semantic (Berlinski, 2000; Cooke, 2003; Jackendoff, 2002). Table 14.1 highlights differences between natural languages and design languages in these respects. The terms of a natural language tend to evolve from usage, as objects and events are encountered repeatedly in everyday experience, sufficiently to where an abstrac-

Table 14.1 Natural Languages and Design Languages Compared in Terms of Primitives, Syntax, and Semantics

	Natural Language	Design Language
Primitive terms	Centered in everyday things and events; abstractions of experience	Centered in tools, processes, technologies, theories, or best practices of a domain
Syntax	Based on words as a medium of expression in which linear or positional order is critical	Dependent on the medium of problem solving and solution; sometimes time, space, or view-oriented
Semantics	Derived from the world as it is experienced and things that can be, or are desired to be, communicated	Derived from the problem domain, the context of problems in the domain, and available technologies

tion of them is formed and given a name or symbol. General social use of the terms over time brings them into the language. Design languages exist as tools for problem solving and design synthesis. Their expressions have meaning only within the domain of problems for which they were created.

Abstraction of and Naming of Design Concepts

The vast majority of designs employ structures "borrowed" or abstracted from previous designs that can be characterized as the terms of a design language. Alexander (1979) describes the abstraction of architectural patterns—a pattern language—from buildings for the purpose of applying those patterns in later designs. "A pattern describes a problem that occurs over and over again in our environment, and then describes the core solution to that problem, in such a way that you can use this solution a million times over" (Alexander, 1979, p. x). Vincenti (1990) names among his classes of specialized technological knowledge, classes like *Operational Principles, Normal Configurations,* and *Intellectual Concepts* that are closely related to design languages: "Conceiving and analyzing artifacts requires thoughts in people's minds.... Intellectual concepts [and operational principles and normal configurations] provide the language for much of such thinking" (p. 215).

Design Languages and the Advance of Design Practice

Rapid advances in the sophistication, effectiveness, productivity, and quality of designs have been made possible by the cultivation of improved design languages. Most often this accompanies the automation of design processes. For this reason, advances over the past three decades in computer-assisted design (CAD) and computer-assisted manufacturing (CAM) can be attributed to the discovery of specialized languages for problem expression and the representation of solutions whose terms can be translated into languages that are computable (Kalay, 1987; Newsome et al., 1989).

Early CAD/CAM systems did little more than capture data entered into them by a human designer: the software had no ability to recognize higher-order abstractions and no ability to make computations in terms of groupings of lines that might represent a building wall or a hydraulic coupling. As abstractions for such groupings were introduced into the design languages of these programs, the programs could begin to reason about them, making more and more decisions about them as an abstract unit of the design.

The literature documenting the evolution of automated computer chip design systems shows that local problems came under automation or semiautomation as local languages were invented that conveyed to the computer the elements of the problem and the elements of solutions for design subproblems. Today, the great majority of routine design decisions during chip design are made by the computer, and as a result, much more complex and powerful designs have become possible, while design time has been cut significantly.

We have dealt in this section with how Vincenti's *design instrumentalities* category of technological knowledge anticipates a body of theory related to making instructional designs—instructional design theory.[3] We have proposed a layer theory of design structure that is based on an alternative approach to design problem fragmentation that uses artifact function rather than process as the decomposition principle. We have further proposed that layers are defined in terms of multiple design languages used for the solution of layer and sub-layer design problems. In the section that follows we will propose that another of Vincenti's categories, *operational principles*, anticipates a different type of theory that describes how designs work—instructional theory.

Operational Principles and Instructional Theory

Instructional theories are a major source of design languages (other sources being traditional practice, standard-setting, metaphorical extension, popular discourse, and insight and invention).

Design Languages and Operational Principles

Vincenti's category of technological knowledge called *operational principles* is of special importance to linking design layers and design languages to instructional theory. It supplies abstractions that create a semantic context for design language terms and therefore for central structural elements of instructional theory.

An operational principle, according to Polanyi (1958) is part of the "logic of contriving." This logic describes how a human-made artifact works:

> There is a specifiable reason for every step of the procedure and every part of the machine, as well as for the way the several steps and the various parts are linked together to serve their joint purpose. This chain of reasons is set out in the operational principles of the process or of the machine. (p. 332)

Operational principles are abstract descriptions of the oppositions and co-ordinations of dynamic forces that can be incorporated into human-designed artifacts—the essential inner workings of functioning artifacts. They describe those workings—the transmission and transformation of energy and information—independent of specific material form. Operational principles have generative power for the design of artifacts: specific dimensions and materials

---

3. *Editors' note: This is a combination of what we call instructional-planning theory and instructional-building theory (see chapter 1). [Author's note: I have come to see much value in this distinction, but at this late date prior to publication, I will retain my current terminology.]*

are assigned during design to the abstract elements of one or more operational principles.

An operational principle is implemented through substitution:

> Just as the rules of algebra will operate for any set of numbers for which the algebraic constants may stand, so an operational principle applies to any collection of parts which are functioning jointly according to this principle. (Polanyi, 1958, p. 329)

A single operational principle can be used to generate multiple artifact configurations through the substitution of specific mechanisms and materials in place of the abstract elements that make up the principle. Layton (1992) explains that designs are made by assigning specific materials and dimensions to conceptual structures that represent abstract relationships of elements. Layton notes that the design activity of *assigning* dimensions to an abstraction differs from the activity of science, which attempts to discover relationships *as free as possible* of specific dimensions.

Layers, Languages, Operational Principles, and Instructional Theory

We propose that what an instructional theorist expresses in an *instructional theory* is a set of specialized, mutually consistent design languages, consisting of terms the theorist defines, that are distributed across multiple design layers which are defined by an *instructional design theory*. Instructional design theory provides a structural framework of layers within which specific instructional theories can be analyzed and compared. To the extent that different observers can agree upon a common definition of layers, they can jointly and publicly carry out such analyses and comparisons.

The outward form of an instructional theory consists of verbal propositions that relate the design language terms the theorist has chosen to define. Through these propositions we can see a set of operational principles held by the theorist that express the major assumptions—the real fabric—of the instructional theory. The operational principles underlying an instructional theory, and the categories and propositions of the theorist, provide a generative mechanism capable of creating multiple instructional artifact designs which on the surface differ in form but under the surface share a common architecture. Several new-paradigm instructional examples were reviewed by Gibbons and Fairweather (1998) and shown to possess a similar underlying architecture, described by a single operational principle they called "model-centered instruction" (see also Gibbons, 2001).

Table 14.2 presents a layer-by-layer comparison of three well-known instructional theories: John R. Anderson's theory of intelligent tutoring (Anderson, Corbett, Koedinger, & Pelletier, 1995); cognitive apprenticeship (Collins, Brown, &

Table 14.2 Analysis of Some Well-Known Instructional Theories to Show the Relationship of Instructional Theories to the Framework Provided by Layers, Which Have Their Basis in Instructional Design Theory

Theory	Anderson	Cog App	Gagné
Content layer	Content subdivided into two types: "production rules" and semantic units called "working memory elements"	Four content types: -Domain knowledge -Problem solving strategies and heuristics -Control strategies -Learning strategies	Taxonomy divides knowledge into 5 main types; one type, intellectual skills, is subdivided into several sub-categories
Strategy layer	-Production rules learned in prerequisite order -Learning by practice and error correction	6 methods: -Modeling -Coaching -Scaffolding -Reflection -Articulation -Exploration 5 social strategies: -Situated learning -Culture of expert practice -Intrinsic motivation -Exploit competition -Exploit cooperation 3 sequencing strategies: -Increasing complexity -Increasing diversity -Global before local	Conditions to support learning are determined by the type of knowledge to be learned; nine events of instruction provide occasions for those conditions to be expressed
Control layer	Control resides in the system; student responds to problems presented	Implied in apprentice interpersonal relationships, but not enumerated	Implied instructor control; student responds to instruction
Message layer	No formalization of message structuring guidelines	No formalization of message structuring guidelines	Types of message used in illustrations, but no formalization of messaging guidelines
	No formalization of representation terms or guidelines	No formalization of representation terms or guidelines	Types of representation used in illustrations, but no formalization of representation terms or guidelines
Media-Logic layer	No formalization of media-logic guidelines	No formalization of media-logic guidelines	No formalization of media-logic guidelines
Data management layer	Data management specified as use of data from previous responses to influence future selections of the system regarding problems to present	No formalization of data management guidelines	No formalization of data management guidelines

Newman, 1989); and Gagné's theory of the conditions of learning (Gagné, 1985). These theories were chosen because they are clearly expressed, are widely known, and have a history of extensive application. Table 14.2 shows that each theory defines a set of design language terms within one or more design layers.

Anderson's instructional theory contains propositions concerning the organization of the content layer of designs. The theory is based on the assumption of two types of knowledge: production rules and working memory elements. Cognitive apprenticeship defines four categories of knowledge, implying that the result of an analysis of content structures will be expressed in terms of these categories. Though the categories are identified, specific propositions that link categories to strategic patterns are not given. In contrast, Gagné's division of learnable content into five major categories and one of those categories (intellectual skills) into several subcategories is closely linked with the central premise of Gagné's theory—that specific content types can be used to bound instructional strategy design.

Most importantly, all three instructional theories take a position on the nature of content and the appropriate categories into which it is partitioned. A designer who agrees with a theorist's partitioning of content can use the theory—and the content design language of terms it supplies—for analysis purposes. Gibbons and his associates (Gibbons, Nelson, & Richards, 2000a, 2000b) provide a review of the basic principles of predesign analysis that considers in some detail the design issues of the content layer.

The three theorists compared in Table 14.2 differ also with respect to the structures and languages that they propose at the strategy layer of designs. Anderson's theory, as already noted, closely links content structures with interactions, and curriculum tends to be centered on a body of rules practiced in a calculated sequence. Cognitive apprenticeship does not link specific content types with specific instructional methods. However, the theory specifies a great deal more structure at the strategy layer than either Anderson or Gagné. In addition to describing six instructional methods, cognitive apprenticeship describes alternative social organizations (expert practice culture) and employment of social forces (exploit competition, exploit cooperation) for instructional purposes where the other theories are largely silent. The 18 principles of cognitive apprenticeship under four layerlike headings as summarized in Table 1 of Collins et al. (1989) are mostly expressed in a form that reveals the abstract operational principle from which a large family of very different designed surface forms can be generated. In addition to organizations of social forces, cognitive apprenticeship design language terms support the design of instructional sequences.

Gagné's theory links methods of instruction with learning types, as already mentioned. In addition, Gagné describes nine events of instruction that further define those methods. His theory does not give focus to the social dimensions of organization, but a broad outline of assumptions about instructor and learner roles is evident, which is described by Gibbons et al. (in press). The nine events are not described as sequencing constructs, and a caution is given that the structures of the nine events are not meant to correspond with distinct slices of time. However, many of the events described by Gagné have a temporal relationship that is hard to avoid.

The three theorists compared in Table 14.2 say little about the structuring of designs at the remaining layers. We do not feel that this is due to the unimportance of these layers to the theorists but to the immediate purpose of the author in writing and the critical issues the author is trying to bring into focus; the most attention is given to layers the theorists consider most important. We take this as implicit evidence that design involves the use of multiple local theories related to layer-specific concerns rather than single monolithic theories, as is sometimes implied in the instructional design literature.

Table 14.3 shows that other theorists have given attention to different layers. These authors and works are merely suggestive of the layer-relatedness of an enormous body of writing on design principles. Some layers, such as Control, are underrepresented in the design theory literature. However, the control layer has become more central to designers as interest has increased in video games, instructional simulations, and microworlds, in which control systems are necessary for user navigation of complex information, physical, and problem-solving spaces.

The Message layer is also underrepresented in current literature, despite the recent emphasis on social interaction during instruction. However, Sawyer (2006) reviews systems for message structuring and describes the early interest in this area of design language (See also Simon & Boyer, 1967). Messaging in most media is accomplished using precomposed display content (combined graphics and text, animations, or video). However, instructional messages in the future will increasingly be composed at the moment of use from a variety of sources. This trend already supplies the competitive edge for noninstructional marketing Web sites. Seen in this perspective, the deliberate design of messaging patterns that can be filled with specific representation content at the moment of need from diverse sources plays an important intermediary role in assembling the raw elements during the construction of displays. Viewed in this light, Merrill's component display theory (Merrill, 1994), often viewed as a formula for designing instructional strategies, can be seen as a type of message design language for constructing individual messages in the service of a learner- or system-initiated instructional strategy. Message design languages identify message tokens that can be used to carry the intentions of instructional communications, without describing the exact content of the representations.

Representation theories and their associated languages are invisible to most designers because representation technology has for so long been confounded with message and media-logic concerns for precomposing and storing display content. However, recent innovations in representation technologies provide the designer with more options for the display of information, sometimes us-

Table 14.3 Sampling of Work by Theorists or Research Reviewers Attempting to Identify Layer-Specific Principles

Layer	Theorist/Author	Principles
Control	Crawford (2003)	Conversational interaction and the design of interfaces to support rich user communication and conversation with the system
	Gibbons & Fairweather (1998)	Varieties of human-machine communication (learner to system) during instruction and the computer's ability to implement them
Message	Merrill (1994)	Categorization of message elements that make up an instructional strategy; texturing principles that prioritize certain messages and foreground certain information
	Horn (1997)	Categorization and logical grouping of information tableaus; emphasis on underlying relationships within message groupings rather than on their display
	Simon & Boyer (1967)	Compendium of analysis methods for describing student-teacher communications and interpretable actions during classroom instruction
Representation	Mayer (2001)	Principles for the use of synchronized multimedia channels to convey instructional information in a manner that supports learner formation of appropriate mental models
	Tufte (1990, 1997)	Principles for the use of graphical representations to present complex and dynamic bodies of information
	Wurman (1997)	Visual designers explain and illustrate their principles for explaining using visual and textual structure
	Harris (1999)	Varieties of presentation of data in graphical form and principles for constructing data representations
	Fleming (1993)	Message design principles, concentrating on the representation of information
Media-Logic	Gibbons et al. (2001)	Principles of merging media structures with other design structures
	Seels et al. (1996)	Principles related to the design of instruction involving the television medium; extensive glossary of terms, many of which are the terms of a specialized design language
	Hannafin et al. (1996)	Principles related to the design of computer-based instruction as a medium
	Romiszowski & Mason (1996)	Principles related to the design of computer-mediated communication
	Stanney (2002)	Principles related to the design of virtual environments
Data Management	Wenger (1987)	Summary of intelligent computer-based instruction design principles, including use of data to create adaptive instruction
	Stolurow (1969)	Early conception of the principles for the use of data from instructional interactions to determine the future path of instructional events; dated by reference to programmed instruction but relevant in principle

ing data supplied at the moment of need to generate specific display content. As greater amounts of the display are created or arranged at the moment of use, the principled design of representations will take priority over the storing of individual representations.

Media-logic design languages are introduced with each new medium, tool, or technique. Media production is the nexus of the most commonly known instructional design languages, and numerous detailed glossaries and lexicons of such languages are abundant in libraries and on the Web.

Data management layer concerns have become muted as the goals of adaptive and generative instruction have been subordinated over the past three decades to productivity and lowered costs. Stolurow (1969) describes the ideal of adaptive instruction in terms of programmed instructionlike products. Though the fashion in structures manipulated during instruction today has changed, the principle of adaptivity in Stolurow's writing remains unchallenged. Wenger (1987) describes early experiments in adaptive instruction and provides numerous examples of ways in which data resulting from instructional interactions were used to select and sequence future instructional events. As interest in adaptive instruction, adaptive curricula, and adaptive instructional organization increases, the design languages for designing data management systems will become more important.

Conclusion

Our purpose has been to describe a particular view of the architecture of instructional theory, framed within an instructional design theory of function-related design layers. We have related the separation of these bodies of theory to a similar separation that has occurred in other design fields. This more detailed framework for theoretical ideas describes design decision making at a finer granularity and concentrates on the functional characteristics of the designed artifact, rather than on the design process.

We propose that this layered architecture of instructional theory will accomplish the following: it will give designers a tool to create quality designs more consistently, it will facilitate communications about designs and theories, it will allow designers to work efficiently in design teams with a greater degree of mutual understanding, it will suggest functionalities for more advanced and productive design tools, and it will allow experienced designers to communicate design knowledge and judgment to novices more quickly.

References

Alexander, C. (1964). *Notes on the synthesis of form*. Cambridge, MA: Harvard University Press.

Alexander, C. (1979). *The timeless way of building*. New York: Oxford University Press.

Alexander, C. (1996). The origins of pattern theory, the future of the theory, and the generation of a living world. *IEEE Software, 16*(5), 71–82.

Anderson, J. R., Corbett, A. T., Koedinger, K. R., & Pelletier, R. (1995). Cognitive tutors: Lessons learned. *Journal of the Learning Sciences, 14*(2), 167–207.

Andrews, D. H., & Goodson, L. A. (1991). A comparative analysis of models of instructional design. In G. J. Anglin (Ed.), *Instructional technology; Past, present, and future*. Engelwood, CO: Libraries Unlimited.

Baldwin, C. Y., & Clark, K. B. (2000). *Design rules: Vol. 1. The power of modularity*. Cambridge, MA: MIT Press.

Berlinski, D. (2000). *The advent of the algorithm*. New York: Harcourt.

Bernstein, L. (1976). *The unanswered question: Six talks at Harvard* (The Charles Eliot Norton Lectures, 1973). Cambridge, MA: Harvard University Press.

Bichelmeyer, B. A., Boling, E., & Gibbons, A. S. (2006). Instructional design and technology models: Their impact on research and teaching in IDT. In M. Orey, J. McClendon, & R. M. Branch (Eds.), *Educational media and technology and media yearbook, 2006* (Vol. 31). Westport, CT: Libraries Unlimited.

Brand, S. (1994). *How buildings learn: What happens after they're built*. New York: Penguin.

Bruner, J. (1966). *Toward a theory of instruction*. Cambridge, MA: Belknap.

Collins, A., Brown, J. S., & Newman, S. E. (1989). Cognitive apprenticeship: Teaching the crafts of reading, writing, and mathematics. In L. Resnick (Ed.), *Knowing, learning, and instruction: Essays in honor of Robert Glaser*. Hillsdale, NJ: Erlbaum.

Cooke, D. (2003). *A concise introduction to computer languages: Design, experimentation, and paradigms*. Pacific Grove, CA: Brooks/Cole.

Crawford, C. (2003). *The art of interactive design*. San Francisco: No Starch.

Edmondson, A. C. (1987). *A fuller explanation: The synergetic geometry of Buckminster Fuller*. Boston, MA: Barkhauser.

Fleming, M. L. (1993). *Instructional message design: Principles from the behavioral and cognitive sciences* (2nd ed.). Englewood Cliffs, NJ: Educational Technology.

Gage, N. L. (1964). Theories of teaching. In E. R. Hilgard (Ed.), *Theories of learning and instruction: The sixty-third yearbook of the National Society for the Study of Education* (pp. 269–285). Chicago: University of Chicago Press.

Gagné, R. M. (1985). *The conditions of learning* (4th ed.). New York: Holt, Rinehart & Winston.

Gibbons, A. S. (1998). Model-centered instruction. *Journal of Structural Learning and Intelligent Systems, 14*(4), 511–540.

Gibbons, A. S. (2003a). The practice of instructional technology: Science and technology. *Educational Technology, 43*(5), 11–16.

Gibbons, A. S. (2003b). What and how do designers design? A theory of design structure. *Tech Trends, 47*(5), 22–27.

Gibbons, A. S. (2004, June 3–4, 2004). *The interplay of learning objects and design architectures*. Paper presented at the Partnership in Global Learning Workshop on e-Learning Objects and Systems, Orlando, FL.

Gibbons, A. S., & Brewer, E. K. (2005). Elementary principles of design languages and notation systems for instructional design. In J. M. Spector, C. Ohrazda, A. Van Schaack, & D. Wiley (Eds.), *Innovations in instructional technology: Essays in honor of M. David Merrill*. Mahwah, NJ: Erlbaum.

Gibbons, A. S., & Fairweather, P. G. (1998). *Computer-based instruction: Design and development*. Englewood Cliffs, NJ: Educational Technology.

Gibbons, A. S., Lawless, K. A., Anderson, T. A., & Duffin, J. R. (2001). The web and model-centered instruction. In B. R. Khan (Ed.), *Web-based training*. Englewood Cliffs, NJ: Educational Technology.

Gibbons, A. S., Merrill, P. F., Swan, R., Campbell, J. O., Christensen, E., Insalaco, M., & Wilcken, W. (in press). Re-examining the implied role of the designer. *Quarterly Review of Distance Education.*

Gibbons, A. S., Nelson, J., & Richards, R. (2000a). *Theoretical and practical requirements for a system of pre-design analysis: State of the art of pre-design analysis* (White Paper). Idaho Falls, ID: Center for Human-Systems Simulation, Idaho National Engineering and Environmental Laboratory (DOE).

Gibbons, A. S., Nelson, J., & Richards, R. (2000b). *Model-centered analysis process (MCAP): A pre-design analysis methodology* (White Paper). Idaho Falls, ID: Center for Human-Systems Simulation, Idaho National Engineering and Environmental Laboratory (DOE).

Gross, M., Ervin, S., Anderson, J., & Fleisher, A. (1987). Designing with constraints. In Y. E. Kalay (Ed.), *Computability of design*. New York: Wiley.

Hannafin, M. J., Hannafin, K. M., Hooper, S. R., Rieber, L. P., & Kini, A. S. (1996). Research on and research with emerging technologies. In D. H. Jonassen (Ed.), *Handbook of research for educational communications and technology*. New York: Macmillan.

Harris, R. L. (1999). *Information graphics: A comprehensive illustrated reference*. Oxford: Oxford University Press.

Hawking, S. (1998). *A brief history of time*. New York: Bantam.

Horn, R. E. (1997). Structured writing as a paradigm. In C. R. Dills & A. J. Romiszowski, (Eds.), *Instructional development paradigms*. Englewood Cliffs, NJ: Educational Technology.

Jackendoff, R. (2002). *Foundations of language: Brain, meaning, grammar, evolution*. Oxford: Oxford University Press.

Kalay, Y. E. (1987). *Computability of design*. New York: Wiley.

Kuehlmann, A. (Ed.). (2003). *The best of ICCAD: 20 years of excellence in computer-aided design*. New York: Springer.

Layton, E. (1992). Escape from the jail of shape: Dimensionality and engineering science. In P. Kroes & M. Bakker (Eds.), *Technological development in the industrial age*. Dordrecht, The Netherlands: Kluwer Academic.

Mayer, R. E. (2001). *Multimedia learning*. Cambridge, UK: Cambridge University Press.

McCloud, S. (1994). *Understanding comics*. New York: Harper Perennial.

Merrill, M. D. (1994). The descriptive component display theory. In M. D. Merrill & D. G. Twitchell (Eds.), *Instructional design theory*. Englewood Cliffs, NJ: Educational Technology.

Merrill, M. D., & Twitchell, D. G. (Eds.). (1994). *Instructional design theory*. Englewood Cliffs, NJ: Educational Technology.

Newsome, S. L., Spillers, W. R., & Finger, S. (1989). *Design theory '88: Proceedings of the NSF grantee workshop on design theory and methodology*. New York: Springer-Verlag.

Oswald, D. F. (2002). A conversation with Glenn E. Snelbecker. *Educational Technology, 42*(5), 59–62.

Peterson, F. W. (2000). Anglo-American wooden frame farm houses in the Midwest, 1830–1900: Origins of balloon frame construction. In S. A. McMurry (Ed.), *People, power, places*. Knoxville: University of Tennessee Press.

Polanyi, M. (1958). *Personal knowledge: Towards a post-critical philosophy*. New York: Harper Torchbooks.

Reigeluth, C. M. (1999). *Instructional-design theories and models: Vol. 2. A new paradigm of instructional theory*. Mahwah, NJ: Erlbaum.

Romiszowski, A. J., & Mason, R. (1996). Computer-mediated communication. In D. H. Jonassen (Ed.), *Handbook of research for educational communications technology*. New York: Macmillan.

Saabagh, K. (1996). *21st-century jet: The making and marketing of the Boeing 777*. New York: Scribner.

Sawyer, R. K. (2006). Analyzing collaborative discourse. In R. K. Sawyer (Ed.), *The Cambridge handbook of the learning sciences*. Cambridge, UK: Cambridge University Press.

Schön, D. A. (1987). *Educating the reflective practitioner*. San Francisco: Jossey-Bass.

Seels, B., Berry, L. H., & Horn, L. J. (1996). Research on learning from television. In D. H. Jonassen (Ed.), *Handbook of research for educational communications technology*. New York: Macmillan.

Simon, A., & Boyer, E. G. (Eds.). (1967). *Mirrors for behavior: Vol. 3. An anthology of observation instruments*. Wyncote, PA: Communication Materials Center.

Simon, H. A. (1999). *The sciences of the artificial* (3rd ed.). Cambridge, MA: MIT Press.

Snelbecker, G. E. (1985). *Learning theory, instructional theory, and psychoeducational design*. Lanham, MD: University Press of America.

Stanney, K. M. (Ed.). (2002). *Handbook of virtual environments: Design, implementation, and applications*. Mahwah, NJ: Erlbaum.

Stolurow, L. M. (1969). Some factors in the design of systems for computer-assisted instruction. In R. C. Atkinson & H. A. Wilson (Eds.), *Computer-assisted instruction: A book of readings*. New York: Academic.

Tufte, E. R. (1990). *Envisioning information*. Cheshire, CT: Graphics.

Tufte, E. R. (1997). *Visual explanations: Images, quantities, evidence, and narrative*. Cheshire, CT: Graphics.

Vincenti, W. G. (1990). *What engineers know and how they know it: Analytical studies from aeronautical history*. Baltimore, MD: Johns Hopkins University Press.

Waters, S., & Gibbons, A. S. (2004). Design languages, notation systems, and instructional technology: A case study. *Educational Technology Research and Development, 52*(2), 57–69.

Wenger, E. (1987). *Artificial intelligence and tutoring systems: Computational and cognitive approaches to the communication of knowledge*. Los Altos, CA: Morgan Kaufmann.

Wurman, R. S. (1997). *Information architects*. New York: Graphis.

15
Domain Theory for Instruction

*Mapping Attainments to Enable
Learner-Centered Education*

C. VICTOR BUNDERSON
EduMetrics Institute

DAVID A. WILEY
Utah State University

REO H. MCBRIDE
Herzing College Online

C. Victor Bunderson's work centers on the integration of assessment with learning. He has investigated the scientific issues and developed technologies for measuring abilities, learning preferences, and most difficult and important— measuring learning progress as it occurs. His PhD work was completed at Princeton University as psychometric fellow with Educational Testing Service (ETS), and he returned some years later as ETS vice president of research management. He has built technologies that approach the ideal of integration, including the large 1970s TICCIT project (National Science Foundation funded). After TICCIT, he cofounded companies to seek these ideals: WICAT Systems Chief Scientist, Alpine Testing Solutions, and others. He has moved between universities, businesses, and nonprofits. He currently leads the nonprofit EduMetrics Institute. At EduMetrics he and his colleagues have investigated the integration during learning of progress maps displaying valid measurement of learning attainments; also, progress measurement in the context of games. He seeks to recast educational measurement differently from the way in which it is usually practiced and taught.

David A. Wiley is associate professor of instructional technology at Utah State University, director of the Center for Open and Sustainable Learning, and chief openness officer of Flat World Knowledge. He holds a PhD in instructional psychology and technology from Brigham Young University and a BFA in music from Marshall University. He has previously been a nonresident fellow at the Center for Internet and Society at Stanford Law School, a visiting scholar at the Open University of the Netherlands, and is a recipient of the U.S. National Science Foundation's CAREER grant. His career is dedicated to increasing access to educational opportunity for everyone around the world.

Reo H. McBride received both his doctorate in instructional psychology and technology and his BA in elementary education from Brigham Young University; he received his MA degree in education administration from East Carolina University. His research interest is in the area of reading, where he identified and measured the order of difficulty in learning the constructs necessary to attain fluent oral reading with expression. His work in the field of teaching reading has helped both children and adults improve their reading and comprehension abilities, where otherwise they were deficient in such skills. Dr. McBride has served in the military, been a sixth grade teacher, taught at Dubai Women's College in Dubai, United Arab Emirates, worked as the Coordinator of Instructional Technology at Dabney S. Lancaster Community College, Clifton Forge, Virginia, and now serves as a member of the

Curriculum Management Department at Herzing College Online, Milwaukee, Wisconsin.

EDITORS' FOREWORD

Vision

- *Learner-centered, customized instruction that maps student progress*
- *A tool for mapping progressive attainments*

Quantitative Domain Mapping (QDM)

- *Is a subset of domain theory and of validity-centered design*
- *Internal validity assures alignment of assessment and instruction.*
- *The goal is to map (describe pathways graphically for learning in) a domain of knowledge and expertise supported by theory and data.*
  - *A domain map includes:*
  - *Major attainments with boundaries (easiest and hardest versions) of attainments*
  - *Categories of attainments (pathways)*
  - *Sequences of attainments along each pathway*

Method for Quantitative Domain Mapping

1. *Analyze a domain to identify its attainments.*
   - *Hierarchically structured domains with a strong prerequisite structure require different domain analysis methods.*
2. *Synthesize work models as the assessment blueprints.*
   - *Combine performance processes into work models to bring a sense of real-world relevance.*
3. *Create testlets or item bundles.*
   - *They should be linked to each work model and each constituent attainment.*
4. *Identify the dimensionality of the domain.*
   - *Dimensions or pathways are categories of expertise.*
5. *Create a testable theory of progressive attainments (domain story).*
   - *Confirm the hypothesized number of dimensions.*
   - *Hypothesize an order for how the attainments in each dimension are best learned.*
   - *Create a domain map with an interpretive story.*
6. *Confirm or disconfirm and correct the theory of progressive attainments.*
   - *Administer the testlets and revise the domain map and story as indicated by the data.*
7. *Design the next iteration and begin again.*
   - *Additional cycles of tryout and revision are performed as appropriate.*

Implications for Instructional Design and Technology

- *Promises to significantly improve progress in educational research and practice*

- *Impacts instructional design specifically by providing scope and sequence for a domain*
- *Allows for learners to gain progress-sensitive feedback*
- *QDM lays the foundation for a fully articulated descriptive system.*

—*CMR & ACC*

DOMAIN THEORY FOR INSTRUCTION: MAPPING ATTAINMENTS TO ENABLE LEARNER-CENTERED EDUCATION

The Vision

An information-age paradigm of education will be learner centered rather than teacher centered; customized rather than standardized. It will make it possible to keep track of individual learners' attained knowledge and skills within coherent interpretive frameworks. These frameworks—maps of progress within a learning domain—will display how each individual is progressing along each mapped learning pathway. Location on a pathway will show a learner's up-to-date progress in mastering attainments. This interpretive framework will be user centered to enable communication among learners, teachers, and other people who will fill a variety of new roles. These new roles will emerge geared to provide help to individuals and groups who are progressing with the aid of progress maps offering built-in feedback.

Despite the user-centered nature of the interpretive framework, it will be theory-based and empirically connected so that it can be tested and improved. This clear framework for understanding progress will provide an alternative to amorphous course listings with letter grades that serve only to compare a student's performance with that of other students. Knowing where they stand on each of several clearly depicted pathways running through a mapped learning domain will help each student and those who guide learning progress to identify what has been accomplished and what is appropriate to learn next.

There is currently a paucity of tools to address the development of maps of progressive attainment. In this chapter, one such tool, quantitative domain mapping is described. It is based on an understanding of progress measurement and its central role in designing a progress map.

Much Better Measurement Is the Means to Achieve the Vision

Scientific, economic, and societal progress are inseparably connected with measurement (Alder, 2002; Fisher, 2003b). All good measurement is inseparably connected with theory (Kyburg, 1992). If these statements are true, then we may rightly expect progress in education to be highly correlated with advances in both educational measurement and theory. Advances in educational theory about how learners make progress, secluded from progress in educational measurement, is pure fancy. Progress in educational measurement, separated from progress in educational theory, is meaningless data.

Fisher's (2003a, 2003b) analysis of the impact of common metrics on societies indicates that the accumulation of scientific capital, economic capital, and social capital is greatly accelerated by the existence of standard measures. He also makes the point that the acceptance process for these measures is a broadly social one. Alder (2002) recounts the events leading up to the development of the metric system in France, and its later broad acceptance throughout the world. This broad acceptance of standard weights and measures catalyzed enormous progress in science, technology, commerce, and social life. Before the metric system, Alder estimates 250,000 different units of weights and measures were in use throughout France alone in the late 1700s, and showed how this diversity of weights and measures used throughout the country prevented progress in communication, commerce, and the rational administration of the state. Fisher (2003b) comments on the backwardness of measurement in education and health care, noting that this leads to peculiar economies in these areas, such that they both

> fail to transcend the vagaries of local politics because the objects of their conversations are expressed as concrete counts of units that vary in size and order to unknown degrees…. [He further observes that] human capital as currently measured is effectively dead capital, in the sense that the measures are not transferable, being expressed as they are in scale-dependent, non-linear metrics…. (p. 799)

But how can educational research ever arrive at a common set of "weights and measures"? We cannot, as did the French, try to gain worldwide acceptance by measuring the meridian of the earth that everyone shares. (They measured the distance from the equator to the North Pole and divided it by 10 million to arrive at the meter.)

Baker (2000) compares the importance of the task of mapping educational attainments in core areas of schooling to the importance of mapping the human genome. This task:

> requires an understanding of the conceptual and scientific basis of student learning. Rather than continue to patch and accrete more and more incompatible solutions, we need a clear, fully articulated, descriptive system. A major scientific effort is needed to specify the goals, instructional requirements, and potential measured outcomes of learning. (p. 20)

Educational research is in desperate need of common metrics and the scientific and educational capital this will generate. Business, research, and government sectors increasingly focus their activities on information and knowledge, and technology increases the rates at which these knowledge innovations are created and adopted. These changes are chronicled in Friedman's (2005) *The World is*

Flat. Similarly, education must find a standard measurement mechanism that will allow it to keep pace.

In this chapter we propose a method of developing measurements as a seamless part of learning. This method will connect these measures to a theory and map of progressive attainments in each domain, and will commence a process of building a strong validity argument for that evolving description of the learning domain. We believe that these theory-connected measures are candidates to become common metrics that could enable educational research to make cumulative, long-term progress. We will not attempt to deal with the social issue of the acceptance of these measures, nor the diversified staffing that might emerge, but understand that these are steps we must take at a later time.

Quantitative Domain Mapping

The collection of methods we present here, which we refer to as quantitative domain mapping (QDM), is a subset of broader work we are carrying out under the label *domain theory,* or theory of progressive attainments local to a domain. QDM is one of three main parts of a broader design approach called validity-centered design (VCD). QDM performed properly can provide the core element of *internal construct validity* to design. This means we know what is being learned and measured, through empirical evidence internal to the system being developed, and through theoretical rationale. QDM can accomplish this by developing a descriptive theory, and evidence for it, of the dimensions or pathways that learners will progress along, and the sequence of attainments along each pathway. The boundaries (or easiest and hardest challenges to be encountered along each pathway) are also delineated.[1]

Validity centered design also guides the design and the evidence-collection for user-centered aspects of the domain map and measures, such as appeal and usability, and also *external evidence* of validity (in contrast to the internal evidence sought through QDM). External evidence of validity warrants the claims that the assessment and the instruction are correlated with external criteria of success, and generalizes to different kinds of learners. These other two categories of VCD, user-centered and external aspects, are *not* accomplished through QDM. A thorough description of the methods and mathematics of domain theory and of validity-centered design are beyond the scope of this chapter, but we encourage the interested reader to see more complete descriptions published elsewhere (Bunderson, 2006; Bunderson & Newby, 2006; McBride, 2005).

Design theory is contrasted to descriptive theories of science in chapter 1 and in Gibbons and Bunderson (2005), and to exploratory methods. QDM is a design theory—it provides tools and methods for accomplishing a specific goal. Assessing progress continuously provides a strong foundation for instructional

---

1. *Editors' note: We strongly believe that these advances are critical for the Information-Age paradigm of education.*

theories described in chapter 1. It is characterized best by the term *student-assessment design-theory* defined in chapter 1. However, it does not belong to the categories of instructional-event, instructional-planning, or instructional-building design theories.

The specific goal of applying the QDM methods is to arrive at a description of a specific domain of knowledge and expertise, supported by both theory and empirical data. In other words, the goal is the creation of a *descriptive theory* of how learning can progress along one or more separate pathways through a series of increasingly challenging attainments in a specific domain. This descriptive theory is inseparably linked to a measurement instrument that assesses progress in the learning domain. As such, it provides the means to identify what is to be learned, and to tell us when measured learning levels have been attained.[2] To be readily interpreted and used by learners and teachers, a clear interpretive map is needed.

A quantitative domain map includes:

1. The major attainments within a domain that learners should master, with the boundaries identified of easiest and hardest to be encountered within the domain.
2. The categories or groupings of these attainments (dimensions or pathways).
3. The difficulty-based sequences of attainments along each pathway.

Such a map does not provide prescriptions of how to teach, but does provide specific information about groupings of tasks within the domain (i.e., issues of scope that pertain to the domain) and difficulty relationships among these groups of tasks (i.e., issues of sequence that pertain to the domain). This more rigorous understanding of a specific domain can then be joined to an instructional theory that prescribes how to teach and assess so that a learner may achieve each attainment. For example, Wiley's *Learning Object Design and Sequencing Theory* (2000) connects the results of the QDM process to instructional prescriptions given by van Merriënboer (1997) and provides additional guidance in the process of developing learning objects. Connecting the map to an instructional theory not only enables the map to exert an influence on the teaching and learning process, but also generates valuable data that can be fed back into the QDM process in an iterative cycle of design research (Kelley, 2003).

Bunderson and Newby (2006) show how a good domain theory of progressive attainments makes possible a rigorous form of design research when the measurement of learning progress is consistent from one cycle of design-evaluate-improve to the next. As with design research, QDM research should unfold over a series of cycles, each cycle increasing the strength of the argument for validity—that the map accurately represents progress in the domain of interest.

---

2. *Editors' note: These are extremely important in the Information-Age paradigm of education.*

Our approach below will be to explain the component methods of QDM, illustrate each method with one main example (sometimes two), and, finally, discuss the implications and benefits of applying the QDM method.

The example of fluent oral reading used below is drawn from the recent doctoral work of coauthor Dr. Reo McBride in the field of instructional psychology and technology (McBride, 2005b). Because of the simple, nonhierarchical features of the elementary school oral reading domain, another contrasting example is occasionally needed. Therefore, an example from music theory will also be used.

Example: Fluent Oral Reading with Expression (FORE). This example will use Dr. McBride's first name as a story-telling technique. Reo has had a long-standing personal interest in teaching reading to children in the early grades. He has had years of personal experience with methods used by his inventive professor-father for teaching those for whom conventional methods have failed. The methods have strong anecdotal support but lack an empirical and theoretical validity argument. He has narrowed his research study to the domain of fluent oral reading, culminating in expressive oral reading, and has named it FORE.

In his research work (McBride, 2005a, 2005b) Reo called his theory a *local learning theory of progressive attainments* in the domain of FORE. In discussing his example, we will use the term *local theory of attainments*, or simply *domain theory*, to avoid confusion with the global concepts taught in *learning theory* classes. These theories purport to apply across any domain, and are strongly connected to different philosophical stances. A theory of progressive attainments local to a well-delineated domain is fundamental to measuring and tracking progress in that domain, and providing interpretive progress feedback, regardless of the constructivist, instructionist, or other so-called theoretical approach to learning used. By using the term *quantitative*, we are not signaling a narrow philosophical approach rooted in positivism, but an approach that shows the continuity and complementarity of qualitative and quantitative approaches. The reader interested in the philosophical and scientific roots of this position should examine Fisher (2003a, 2003b), Trout (1998), and Bunderson (2006).

Following the statement of each method below, we will describe how Reo uses the QDM method to generate data and theory in support of his validity argument regarding FORE.

The Methods of Quantitative Domain Mapping

1. Analyze Domain/Identify Attainments

The first step in the QDM process is to identify the content, substance, and boundaries of the domain. The content and substance of the domain (the information and skills to be learned) can then be analyzed and their constituent attainments identified. Principled skill decomposition (van Merriënboer, 1997), task analysis, reviews of literature, reflections on successful teaching practice, and other procedures are used to identify the units of expertise within the domain. The specific analysis methodology used should match the features of the domain and what is already known. Methods useful in well-established domains which have accumulated a body of good research are often not possible in brand new domains. Hierarchically structured domains with a strong prerequisite structure require different domain analysis methods than domains like literature or history.

When this step is complete, the designer has created a list of individual attainments a learner must achieve in order to gain expertise in the domain, and has begun to identify the easiest and hardest boundaries to these attainments. The designer has some idea of how many different pathways these attainments fall upon.

Example. Before he narrowed his research program to fluency, Reo worked on a team with two PhD-level instructional technologists to engage in a domain modeling exercise grounded on an existing reading program. This domain modeling procedure produced a map of possible ordered attainments in the sound system and visual reading/writing systems for both beginning reading and beginning writing, culminating in comprehension. Fluent oral reading was a part of this domain model of reading, and the model showed the connection of fluent reading to word knowledge below it, and to comprehension above it. The model showed that at the top level, expression was connected to comprehension.

Later, Reo began an extensive literature review on research in fluency. Combining this literature search with his own experience, he identified oral reading processes he hoped would be important to understanding progress in fluent oral reading. He also sought performance processes which would be explainable and interpretable to teachers and to students, and would be observable. The attainment constructs he synthesized were termed *word knowledge, smoothness, rate, phrasing, confidence,* and *expression.* Subject to ease of understanding by the users, Reo sought to use terminology to name these important processes found in the diverse research literature on fluent reading.

Putting his initial theory of key attainment constructs to a quick test, Reo drafted a set of six rating scales and conducted a pilot study using 30 student readings, which he videotaped. He used four raters who each viewed the videos and rated the students on the six scales in order to see if raters could observe and rate the students, and to get an initial idea of the relative difficulty of the rating scales for students; that is, which attainments were harder to achieve a high rating and which were easier. In the process of this pilot study, he established an understanding of the upper and lower boundaries of his domain, and the conditions for observing the processes of reading.

In thinking about the boundaries of any domain of learning, we must consider conjointly both the proficiency of people and the difficulty of tasks. Reo bounded the domain at the lower end by second graders. Below that level, much of the work was involved in learning new words and in learning to sound out unfamiliar words. He expressed the important principle that the fluency attainments of *smoothness, rate, phrasing, confidence,* and *expression* could not be observed if the student did not know a high percentage of the words automatically (stopping to sound out words defeats fluency). He defined a method for observing word knowledge for a given text: He would point at a number of words to make sure the student knew them to automaticity. If not, he would shift to an easier reading selection. He repeated this until the student was reading at a level where no more than about 2% of the words had to be sounded out.

2. Synthesize Work Models

After performing the domain analysis and gaining an understanding of the specific bits of information and subskills in a domain, these constituent pieces are synthesized (combined back) into *work models*. Gibbons and colleagues (Gibbons, Bunderson, Olsen, & Rogers, 1995) described work model synthesis as "systematically combin[ing] and recombin[ing] tasks and objectives that through task analysis procedures have been fragmented at a low level" (p. 222). One purpose of using work models is to bring a sense of relevance into the instructional experience—human values and expectations. Taking word processing as an example, there is little obvious value in learning to use margin controls. However, there is obvious value in creating a résumé, a task that would combine this and other skills. Thus, work models are collections of individual objectives, or in the case of QDM, groupings of constituent performance processes that must be blended together into a unified act. Work models offer a method of recombining the products of analysis into activities that real people perform in the real world, and therefore have readily apparent value to learners.

When this step has been successful, the designer has examined the analyzed work or performances people with skill and expertise in the domain can do well, synthesized simulationlike models of this work, and created a comprehensive draft list of work models that can be made easier and harder within the boundaries of the domain.

Example. With the help of his advisor, Reo drew up a visual display that used the metaphor of a grove of aspen trees to represent the whole domain of language, of which reading was a part. The trunks were reading, writing, speaking, and listening. He had a separate tree and trunk for reading out loud, positioned between the trees of reading and speaking. He studied the research of another doctoral student who was developing a domain theory of speaking. The work models were clusters of branches, and the social values captured by these work models were illustrated by such visualizable "work" as actors reading scripts, or narrating audio books, with great expression. Other models of valued human work included politicians giving orations from written texts, students presenting papers at conferences, and advanced students reading out loud before the class, with great confidence and commanding positive attention.

Since the boundaries of his domain were children in grades 2 through 6, only the last work model of students reading out loud with commanding expression was actually used. Teachers can be counseled to explain the more advanced professional roles that use oral reading expertise. Every oral reading obtained and videotaped in his later studies used this work model, but the difficulty level had to be selectable. Difficulty of Reo's reading selections therefore ranged from readings at the first grade level to the seventh grade level. He selected texts with different calibrated levels of the Lexile scale (Stenner, 1996). The Lexile scale provides a finer grained measurement of the difficulty of texts, superior to the coarser conventional measurement unit of grade level.

A more hierarchically structured example: It should be noted that other projects may have a more elaborated set of work models than this example from elementary school reading. For example, in an analysis of the domain of music theory as taught in college, a designer may choose to synthesize the constituent skills *identify intervals* and *stack notes in thirds* into a work model, and call it *identify the root, quality, and inversion of chords*, or more simply, *identify chords*. The identification of chords is a valuable skill that composers, arrangers, and musicians who frequently improvise (such as jazz musicians) perform in the real world. Chord identification also plays an important role in performance generally, as coaches or conductors will give instruction such as "always sing on the high side of the third."

The ability to identify chords properly will also allow students to understand how they function (by looking at several chords in sequence, for example), another critical skill for musicians to have. A designer may therefore create another model and call it *identify the harmonic function of chords*.

3. Create Testlets or Item Bundles

Using work models as the assessment blueprints, and considering the attainments subsumed under each work model, the next step is to create small clusters of assessment items requiring responses. These are linked to each work model and to each constituent attainment. Directly linking assessments to the attainment structure of the domain provides a construct-valid way of gathering data regarding both the difficulty of the attainments and of the work models. Creating several items that assess the same attainment within its work model ameliorates problems related to mixing up which attainments are being measured. If carried out thoughtfully, this creation step also will reveal any weaknesses in the items' designs and coverage.

When this step is complete, the designer has developed sets of "testlets" linked to each attainment within each work model. They form a foundation for later work.

Example. Music theory performance processes are hierarchical and differentiated. They can more readily be separated into discrete tasks than can fluent oral reading and would lead to a wider variety of assessment tasks. Because of the integrated nature of the act of reading out loud, Reo did not construct variations in work models that could separately apply to each of the six attainments.

The more general FORE work model analysis did envision the importance of reading out loud to various valuable human roles, but the tasks were all similar: pick a passage to read, then read the passage out loud while being videotaped. Judges later rated this reading using a rating scale instrument. They listened for the substantive processes of fluency during each student's videotaped reading. Because of this, the attainments of word knowledge, smoothness, rate, phrasing, confidence, and expression previously analyzed, and not increasingly complex work models, provided the guidance needed to develop the rating scales.

Reo had already developed version I of his FORE measurement instrument, a set of six rating scales, each with rubrics that yielded the ratings of 1 through 5. A single rating scale does not have the properties of a testlet, which groups together two or more indicators of the same underlying attainment. Therefore, in an iterative process with a group of six raters who were familiar with the approach to teaching FORE that he was studying, he and the raters developed two to four rating scales for each of the six kinds of fluent oral reading attainments. He had three rating scales for Word Knowledge, four for Smoothness, two for Phrasing, two for Confidence, and two for Expression. At this time, he and his experienced judges developed only one rating scale for *Rate*, but he developed a second rating scale for *Rate* during a later cycle of design research.

The benefit of this step in the QDM design process is that each testlet or bundle of two to three items (rating scales) became an empirical object by which Reo could answer the following structural and substantive validity questions in later steps of the QDM process: How many dimensions are required to account for FORE? Is there a developmental learning sequence along any of these dimensions that will enable us to understand the order in which the attainments develop? Most reading theorists in the literature would disagree, claiming that there is no developmental sequence in learning to read fluently. Using the sets of rating scales, his research will provide evidence whether or not the theorists in the literature are right or wrong. Does fluent reading all happen at once, through a type of practice that seemingly cannot be partitioned out, even with the empirical tools of testlets carefully linked by design to the hypothesized attainments? Or, as Reo hypothesized, is there a meaningful developmental order of attainments?

4. Identify the Dimensionality of the Domain.

While we generally think of domains as monolithic regions of related information or skills, it is frequently the case that there are subgroups or categories of expertise within a single domain. For example, in the broad domain of language learning, these categories might be reading, writing, speaking and listening, with oral reading as a combination of reading and speaking. Because QDM data will be visualized as a map, it is helpful to think of these categories of expertise as dimensions in an expertise space, or separate pathways in a learning sequence that must be traversed to attain the expertise.

The process of identifying these dimensions in the first iteration of the QDM process frequently includes the use of qualitative methods, such as reviews and synthesis of existing literature or interviews with subject-matter experts. When testlets have been developed and administered, the resulting data enable the use of quantitative methods such as factor analysis or smallest space analysis in identifying the number and nature of dimensions in a domain. Theory and data should always be equal partners in the exploration of the expertise space of a domain. Overreliance on theory is wishful thinking, and overreliance on data is unprincipled.

Assuming that there is only one type of expertise in a domain when there are actually more—that is to say, assuming that a domain is unidimensional when it is really multidimensional—can be problematic in measuring learning progress as a seamless part of learning.

This step yields a list of the dimension or pathways within the domain.

Example. Reo tried to guess in advance how many separable dimensions would account for the FORE domain, and could then be used to describe separate learning pathways that might have their own developmental sequence. At first he thought that each of the six attainments would be a separate dimension, and bet that there would be six. Later, he came to hope that there would be a smaller number. The ideal would be two dimensions: accuracy (word knowledge) and fluency, with the five fluency attainments all falling along a single fluency dimension. This would be ideal in terms of ease of teaching teachers, tutors, and raters to understand the rating scale instrument, and to use it and interpret it more easily. He found warrant in the literature to believe that accuracy and fluency were two correlated, but separate, dimensions, but wasn't sure that some of the testlets for some of the fluency attainments would not split out into separate dimensions.

Reo obtained ratings from four raters on 202 elementary school students in grades 2 through 6. Using version IV of the rating scale instrument, he found that the interrater reliabilities of each of the 14 rating scales were high enough to use the average ratings in a factor analysis. He used the Promax factor rotation method, which allows the factors to be correlated. He believed that however many factors there were, they would be correlated, because the nature of the oral reading act was unified. He did not use one of the more commonly used rotation methods that give uncorrelated factors or dimensions.

Using various tests of how many factors to keep, including, most importantly, the meaningfulness of the resulting interpretation, Reo decided that the evidence was fairly clear that there were two factors. The three rating scales he had designed for Accuracy all fell on the second factor that accounted for the lesser amount of common variance. All the other rating scales were associated with the Fluency factor that accounted for the most common variance. It had as its highest correlations (loadings) the rating scales for Expression, followed by those for Confidence, then Rate, then Phrasing, then Smoothness.

Reo was not satisfied that the ratings had been conducted with adequate training, nor that the rating scales were yet of the highest quality. Therefore, seven months later, he went through four other short design iterations of rater training. His version V of the rating scale instrument still had 14 scales, but now it had two for Rate instead of one, and the wording changes seemed to make the instrument easier for the raters to use and to interpret in a consistent manner.

After revising the rating scales for this next cycle of design research, 200 students were rated again by four raters. These ratings were factor analyzed. There was evidence of two strong factors, Accuracy and Fluency, as before. There was evidence that the two rating scales in the *Phrasing* testlet could split off into a third weak factor, defined by these two rating scales. It was highly correlated with the Fluency factor but not with the Accuracy factor.

One of the rating scales, *No Repeats,* was found to be a good indicator neither of Accuracy nor of Fluency. Therefore, it was dropped and another factor analysis was run using the remaining 13 rating scales. This time there was no third factor large enough to make an argument for a separate Phrasing factor. The two-dimensional structure now had a strong validity argument, with a correlation of .59 between the two highly related factors.

5. Create a Testable Theory of Progressive Attainments (Domain Story)

This step may start before the dimensionality of the domain is fully established. We must at least have some literature, theoretical rationale, or empirical evidence of the dimensions on which the attainments are ordered. A hypothesis about how many dimensions are in the domain can be confirmed or falsified using data. Once testlets are constructed and empirical data are obtained on all the items, rating scales, or tasks designed to tap each attainment, the hypothesized number of dimensions can be confirmed.

For each dimension, the theory needs next a hypothesized order of difficulty for each of the attainments previously listed. A theory of progressive attainments is really a theory of how learning occurs over a developmental sequence. Is one attainment prerequisite to another one? How does it depend on the earlier one?

The larger goal of QDM is to develop a domain map. The map must be easy to interpret. When looking at a map, we need an interpretive story about a pathway we might take. "First you go here, because you will need to…, then you go here, which will enable you to …" Interpretation is the essence of validity. How we interpret and use assessments in learning systems tells whether what we are doing is valid or not. The system itself is not inherently valid or invalid. Validity lies in interpretations and uses of assessment information (Bunderson, 2006; Messick, 1995). An interpretive story is one means to explain locations and sequences along a learning pathway or dimension.

A *domain story* is simply a way of talking to users—teachers and learners in our case—about progress in a domain, and what depends on what. It should be in a simple language accessible to the users, although in professional publications we can use the jargon of the field. While a domain story gives a brief account of the theory of how progressive attainments are learned, it does not claim that every student must follow exactly the same path in a fixed order, but that on average, one attainment paves the way and makes more accessible the more difficult ones.

At the conclusion of this step the designer has a "domain story" that explains the order in which one learning attainment builds on another as a learner progresses toward expertise. This is a story of the average or composite learner, and allows that individual variations may exist.

Example. Reo had begun development of a tentative "Domain Story" after the instrument development study conducted during the summer of 2004. In the FORE example, often an earlier attainment is a necessary prerequisite for one or more later ones. *Look ahead*, an excellent indicator of smoothness, is also logically and empirically a necessary prerequisite to expressive reading. This is an example of a causal connection in the progression. After the summer study, the domain story could be expressed in a teacher- or tutor-friendly way. What follows is a condensed version of the domain story, leaving out the teaching advice and focusing on the meanings necessary to interpret each attainment:

This is a story of how Fluency develops in the domain of oral reading.

Accuracy: When you want to assess and practice Fluent Oral Reading, you should check a half dozen or so words to eliminate readings where the reader will struggle with words. Pick a lower grade or Lexile level of reading until you find one the student can read without having to sound out unfamiliar words. Picking readings with too many unknown words for a reader makes it almost impossible to observe smoothness, rate, phrasing, and other aspects of Fluency.

Smoothness: When you have succeeded at picking a reading at the right level, you will be able to assess Smoothness by observing whether or not the reader still halts, has false starts, pauses, and so on. The most important smoothness skill is to look ahead while speaking out loud. Looking ahead enables the student to see the next phrase, which helps with the phrasing aspect of Fluent Oral Reading.

Phrasing: You can tell whether the student has seen an entire phrase, and can speak the phrase in a manner that reflects the punctuation and meaning of the phrase by attending to the way the voice communicates each phrase. You should be looking at the same writing to see for yourself what the phrase should be.

Rate: Lack of smoothness slows the rate as well. Adjusting rate to a speed appropriate to the meaning can be accomplished when the reader is able to read smoothly while looking ahead, seeing the phrases, and communicating them well.

Confidence: Readers are aware of how well they are doing. They can hear their own voice and feel their own hesitations. As they observe themselves speaking smoothly, seeing and saying the phrases well, and with an appropriate rate of speed, they begin to feel more confident. Because confidence depends on these self-assessments, ratings on confidence really depend on higher ability in the easier aspects of fluency; rate, phrasing, and smoothness.

Expression: Excellent expression in oral reading is a high skill. Actors have developed it to an exceptional level. To venture to put a lot of expression into an oral reading is a risky undertaking. A student reader has to have enough confidence, and in addition, abilities to interpret the emotional and intentional meaning and convey it with voice and gesture.

This domain story conveys the hypothesis of attainment order, and gives reasons to explain the order of difficulty and the levels of proficiency in the FORE learning theory of progressive attainments.

This domain story was not as well elaborated as is given here before the next two steps were completed. Not all studies will have progressed through the three steps of pilot study, measurement instrument development project, then the final dissertation study. Three cycles in a design research paradigm are very helpful; the theory of progressive attainments keeps evolving over these cycles.

6. Confirm or Disconfirm and Correct the Theory of Progressive Attainments

In this step, the testlets are administered to a group of learners from the target population. These testlets will have been developed with or without the instruction that is eventually to go with them. Analysis of the resulting data is used to confirm or falsify hypotheses of order among the attainments. When hypotheses expressed in the domain story are not confirmed, the theory and the simple story are corrected.

As empirical data become available, various methods can be used to examine difficulty sequence. The simplest method, used in the first pilot study in Reo's example, is to look at the mean difficulties (average ratings over raters) of single items, even before testlets or item bundles are developed. Later, the methods of item response theory can be used to obtain quantitative difficulty estimates for each item, and these may be averaged to obtain an empirical estimate of the difficulty of the specific attainment or work model to which the testlet cluster was linked. As detailed in Newby, Conner, Grant, and Bunderson (2006), using Rasch techniques in the calculation of item difficulties can provide additive units of measurement of difficulty along these dimensions, providing a foundation for the kind of standard measures required for a field to make long-term scientific progress. A variety of programs are available for applying the Rasch model, and it is simpler to use and interpret than other more complex forms of item response theory.

At this point in the QDM process, the dimension really begins to feel like a proper dimension—a number line or a scale—with the difficulty of attainment measures meaningfully increasing as one moves away from the lower boundary of the pathway.

The goal of this step is to obtain data and confirm or falsify the hypotheses of the order of attainments in a representative group of learners. If an order hypothesis is falsified, a better theory of progressive attainments is developed, and the domain story is changed accordingly.

Example. Reo used the data from his two iterations of the design experiment. He created a facets model for the data using the three facets of students, raters, and attainments. He used the Facets program (Linacre, 1995), which calibrates a multifaceted Rasch model for a given data set. The Rasch model assumes unidimensionality, and he had evidence from his factor analysis that the five fluency testlets for *smoothness, rate, phrasing, confidence,* and *expression* were all close enough to being on the same dimension to consider fluency as a single dimension.

The facet for students showed which students were most and least proficient, and gave a normal distribution of student proficiency. The facet for raters showed that the raters differed in severity. Rater D was the most lenient and rater B the most severe. The difficulty facet is the one he was the most interested in to complete this step of the QDM process. It gave the order of attainment difficulty as *phrasing, smoothness, rate, confidence,* and *expression.*

While most of the order dependencies expressed in the domain story were confirmed, there were notable exceptions. *Phrasing* was supposed to depend on *smoothness.* The key rating scale in *smoothness,* called *look ahead,* was thought to be necessary to take in enough of the meaning of the phrase so that the voice intonation and pauses could indicate the rise and fall of the phrase. The data showed that the average location of the two rating scales for *phrasing* was actually easier than the average of the two remaining *smoothness* rating scales, and of these two, *look ahead* was considerably harder than the two *phrasing* items. Clearly the theory was in error in this particular.

On closer examination of the rating scales, it was seen that the idea expressed in the domain story, that phrasing picked up the full meaning of the entire phrase, was not really what the two rating scales were asking the raters to observe. One rating scale asked to rater to observe how well the students voiced the pauses for punctuation marks (the usual best indicator of a phrase). The other rating scales dealt with indications that the student had seen the phrase boundaries. What the theorists had been thinking of as looking ahead to see the entire phrase, including its meaning, was not being assessed by these two rating scales. There was a simple kind of look ahead, to be sure, to see the punctuation marks or other indicators of phrase boundaries, but this fell short of the process rated in the *smoothness* rating scale of *look ahead*. Such a comprehensive meaning of "look ahead" was indeed related to seeing the meaning of phrases, as was prerequisite to the much more difficult attainments of *confidence,* and *expression*.

As a result of these interpretations of the data, the attainment called *phrasing* was renamed *seeing phrase boundaries,* and the domain story was edited to put it in its proper location, easier and prior to *smoothness.* The possibility of creating new rating scales to assess the more meaningful idea of *phrasing* was not acted on, since the attainment of *expression* seemed to capture that idea, and more. Both *confidence* and *expression* were found to fit the hypothesis of following both *smoothness* and *rate,* which fit the domain story.

Other problems were found in a few of the rating scales, which led to corrections in the wording or interpretation of the rating scales in future iterations of this continuing cycle of design research studies.

7. Design the Next Iteration and Begin Again

Finally, a fairly robust map of the domain exists, with an interpretive story to explain how progress happens in the average case. It includes synthesized specifications of the knowledge and skills a learner will need to learn in the domain. It describes a series of simple-to-complex paths of attainments through the expertise space of the domain. The items developed for testlets can be improved based on the last data collected, a broader study designed, and the entire system of instruction integrated with assessment can be administered again. This not only makes it possible to gather empirical evidence regarding the nature of the domain pathways. It also makes it possible to compare different instructional treatments and measure the differences in outcomes accurately. Internal evidence of validity of the dimensions and ordered attainments bolsters the new theory of progressive attainments and can be contrasted to other theories about the nature of the domain.

An argument—a validity argument regarding the nature of the domain itself in terms of the structure of the natural scoping and sequencing of attainments within the domain—now exists to support the domain theory and measurement instrument, and to guide the next steps of using instructional theories to design interventions to speed learners up the maps of progressive attainment. Most importantly (as the social acceptance step is achieved), researchers and practitioners now have the ability to measure progress the same way, on the same commensurable scales from one iteration to another, and from one study to another.

Completion of this step makes it possible to design the next iteration of the design research program, then to gather additional empirical data to be used to investigate instructional designs integrated with ongoing assessment.

Example. Reo wanted to examine the effect of minimal feedback regarding the performance of student readers on how well they would perform a second and third reading. Following the procedures described above to select a reading below the students' ability to read the words, he paused after the first reading and gave a very few comments about smoothness habits and rate, encouraged confidence, and so forth. His feedback depended on the level of progression he felt the individual student had attained. He obtained ratings from the videotapes using the 24 scales of version IV of the FORE instrument. He found a substantial positive effect of the adaptive feedback in the second reading by each student. The substantial impact of such minimal, yet theory-connected, instructional feedback illustrated the potential value to instructional research of having a valid measurement instrument.

He believes that the regular practice of instruction, such as that used in the ordinary sessions of the McBride reading program, can become a continuing series of design research studies once the effort has been made to develop a theory of progressive attainments in a local domain, and once one has a valid measurement system to track progress in a consistent and comparable manner from cycle to cycle.

Implications for Instructional Design and Technology

The QDM process has the potential to impact educational research and practice significantly, providing capabilities frequently employed and enjoyed by business, engineering, and government organizations as they adapt to the emerging "knowledge economy." QDM and validity-centered design also have the potential to provide a solid measurement foundation to educational research and practice, facilitating cumulative progress previously unattainable.

The development and publication of domain maps with interpretive domain stories for a wide variety of domains could have a significant impact on the instructional design process. Because the map provides the designer with empirically validated and theoretically sound scope and sequence information about a given domain, work on the instructional analysis, design, and sequencing can be significantly facilitated. Instructional designers will be empowered to spend more of their time designing instructional messages, practice opportunities, and useful feedback. Professional organizations could become stewards of the map(s) of their given domains, providing individuals with a common interpretive framework and a common measurement framework in which to ground conversations regarding the effectiveness of instruction.

Modeling a domain as a map also provides immediate opportunities to provide learners with progress-sensitive feedback and navigation controls. Consider a simple example from the FORE illustration. There are two learning pathways in this case, one for word knowledge and one for fluent oral reading. Learners and teachers can come to understand that fluent oral reading performance cannot exceed the level of word knowledge. Separate practice for word knowledge can assure that mistakes noted during reading are not because a word is unfamiliar and needs to be sounded out. As students practice and learn, and have their practice efforts assessed, indicators along each pathway can show the student's location—level of attainment. Properly labeled, the location indicator and indicators of lower and higher levels of attainment will provide much more meaningful navigation opportunities than the decontextualized "next" and "previous" of current learning management systems.[3]

Finally, we believe that the QDM method and the larger context of domain theory lay the foundation for what Baker (2000) called "a clear, fully articulated, descriptive system," upon which instructional innovations may be solidly built, enabling the instructional sciences to make the kind of cumulative progress that high standards of measurement have always facilitated in more developed fields.

References

Alder, K. (2002). *The measure of all things*. New York: Free Press.

Baker, E. L. (2000). *Understanding educational quality: Where validity meets technology*. Fifth annual William H. Angoff memorial lecture, Educational Testing Service Policy Information Center, Princeton, NJ.

Bunderson, C. V. (2006). Developing a domain theory: Defining and exemplifying a learning theory of progressive attainments. In M. Garner, G. Engelhard, M. Wilson, & W. Fisher (Eds.), *Advances in Rasch measurement* (Vol. 1). Maple Grove, MN: JAM.

Bunderson, C. V., & Newby, V. A. (2006). The relationships among design experiments, invariant measurement scales, and domain theories. In M. Garner, G. Engelhard, M. Wilson, & W. Fisher (Eds.), *Advances in Rasch measurement* (Vol. 1).Maple Grove, MN: JAM.

Fisher, W. P. Jr. (2003a). Mathematics, measurement, metaphor and metaphysics I. Implications for method in postmodern science. *Theory & Psychology, 13*(6), 753–790.

Fisher, W. P. Jr. (2003b). Mathematics, measurement, metaphor and metaphysics II. Accounting for Galileo's "fateful omission." *Theory & Psychology, 13*(6), 791–828.

Friedman, T. (2005). *The world is flat*. New York: Farrar, Straus & Giroux.

Gibbons, A. S., Bunderson, C. V., Olsen, J. B., & Rogers, J. (1995). Work models: Still beyond instructional objectives. *Machine-Mediated Learning, 5*, 221–236.

Gibbons, A. S., & Bunderson, C. V. (2005). Explore, explain, design. In K. Kempf-Leonard (Ed.), *Encyclopedia of social measurement* (Vol.). Burlington, MA: Academic.

Kelly, A. E. (Ed.). (2003). Theme issue: The role of design in educational research. *Educational Researcher, 32*(1), 3–37.

Kyburg, H. (1992). Measuring errors of measurement. In C. Savage, & P. Ehrlich (Eds.), *Philosophical and foundational issues in measurement theory*. Hillsdale, NJ: Erlbaum.

Linacre, J. M. (1995). Facets Rasch Analysis. [Computer software] Chicago: MESA.

McBride, R. H. (2005a). *The interplay of training materials development and rating scale development in the instruction of raters*. Provo, UT: Author .

McBride, R. H. (2005b). *A domain theory of fluent oral reading*. Unpublished doctoral dissertation, Brigham Young University, Provo, UT.

Messick, S. (1995). Validity of psychological assessment. *American Psychologist, 50*, 741–749.

Newby, V., Conner, G., Grant, C., & Bunderson, V. (2006). The Rasch model and additive conjoint measurement. In M. Garner, G. Engelhard, M. Wilson, & W. Fisher (Eds.), *Advances in Rasch measurement* (Vol. 1). Maple Grove, MN: JAM.

Stenner, A. J. (1996). *The Lexile framework for reading*. Retrieved April 17, 2004, from http://www.lexile.com.

---

3. *Editors' note: This is very important for the Information-Age paradigm of education.*

Trout, J. D. (1998). *Measuring the intentional world, realism, naturalism, and quantitative methods in the behavioral sciences.* New York: Oxford University Press.

van Merriënboer, J. J. G. (1997). *Training complex cognitive skills: A four-component instructional design model for technical training.* Englewood Cliffs, NJ: Educational Technology.

Wiley, D. A. (2000). *Learning object design and sequencing theory.* Unpublished doctoral dissertation, Brigham Young University. Retrieved from http://opencontent.org/docs/dissertation.pdf

16
Learning Objects and Instructional Theory

DAVID A. WILEY
Utah State University

David A. Wiley is associate professor of instructional technology at Utah State University, director of the Center for Open and Sustainable Learning, and chief openness officer of Flat World Knowledge. He holds a PhD in instructional psychology and technology from Brigham Young University and a BFA in music from Marshall University. He has previously been a nonresident fellow at the Center for Internet and Society at Stanford Law School, a visiting scholar at the Open University of the Netherlands, and is a recipient of the U.S. National Science Foundation's CAREER grant. His career is dedicated to increasing access to educational opportunity for everyone around the world.

EDITORS' FOREWORD

Vision

- *To help instructional theorists utilize primitive, reusable components for building instruction.*

Types of Learning Objects

- *Content objects*
- *Strategy objects*
- *Discourse objects*

Issues for Using Learning Objects in Instructional Theories

for content objects

- *Deciding on the degree of content specification*
  - a. *They usually contain strategy as well as content.*
  - b. *Content can be highly structured (automating) or unspecified (anything)*
- *Deciding on the scope of the content object*
  - a. *The larger the scope, the less effective instructionally.*
  - b. *Reusing is easier than repurposing.*
- *Deciding on sequences within and among content objects*
  - a. *Standard instructional sequencing strategies apply.*

for strategy objects

- *Deciding on the degree of specification for strategy objects*
  - a. *Strategy can be highly specified (automating) or unspecified (anything).*
  - b. *At the highly specified end of the continuum, they contain content as well as strategy.*
- *Deciding on the scope of the strategy object*
  - a. *The larger the scope, the less effective instructionally, so strike a balance in scope.*
- *Deciding on the sequence of strategy objects*
  - a. *Use standard micro, meso, and macro sequencing strategies.*

for discourse objects

- *Deciding on the degree of specification for discourse objects*
  - a. *Discourse can be highly specified or unspecified.*
- *Deciding on scope of discourse objects*
  - a. *Decide how many types of discourse to support in the object.*
  - b. *Identify a meaningful unit of interaction in the discourse object.*
- *Deciding on the sequence of discourse objects*
  - a. *Sequence discourse objects with special attention to intra- and interlearning object sequencing, using standard sequencing strategies.*

Learning Objects and New Instructional Theories

- *Learning objects do not change instructional design or instructional theories.*

- *But they do call us to design learning objects, causing increased attention to context-related (situational) problems often ignored in the industrial-age paradigm of education.*
- *Open Educational Resources (OERs) are a type of innovation enabled by learning objects. They create a need for instructional designers to offer guidance for such different activities as localizing, repurposing, and reusing learning objects.*

—CMR & ACC

LEARNING OBJECTS AND INSTRUCTIONAL THEORY

During the mid-1990s "learning objects" became one of the new darlings of instructional design and technology. As an instructional design construct, learning objects are poorly understood. This lack of understanding of the construct itself makes for great difficulties in thinking about learning objects from the standpoint of instructional theory. This chapter will provide instructional designers with a framework for understanding and using learning objects, and conclude by describing the implications of the learning objects paradigm on instructional design and instructional theory.

A Brief History of Learning Objects

The idea of discrete, addressable chunks of information available for use and reuse, as with most innovations in instructional technology, originated outside the field of education. The records in Bush's (1945) Memex system and the hypertext in Nelson's (1974) Xanadu system warrant special mention as intellectual ancestors of this idea. As I write this chapter, innovation in this area continues outside the educational realm under names like *microformats* in Web 2.0 and *microcontent* in the blogosphere.

Building instruction from primitive components has an almost equally long history in instructional technology. The TICCIT system, developed in the late 1960s, exemplified this approach through the use of reusable instructional templates into which content from a variety of areas was added. Similar approaches were taken by PLATO and other systems through the 1970s and 1980s. The idea was repopularized in the early 1990s by Wayne Hodgins, when he named a CEdMa working group "Learning Architectures and Learning Objects." For whatever reason, "learning objects" fired the imagination of instructional technologists everywhere.

The primary interest in learning object-based approaches to instruction relates to the reusability of the learning objects. Reusability across different instructional scenarios makes it possible for instructional development to occur more quickly. Reusability across different delivery technologies, also called interoperability, makes it possible, for example, for learning objects built in

WebCT to also be deployed in Sakai, Blackboard, and other systems. Both types of reusability lower instructional development costs—something just about everyone is interested in.

Several variations on the learning object theme have sprung up, each with its own unique name and each with its own nuances. Hodgins's *learning objects* , Merrill's *knowledge objects* (1997), Downes's *resources*, the Advanced Distributed Learning Initiative's *sharable content objects*, and UNESCO's *open educational resources* all describe a similar approach to designing and building instruction from existing resources. Throughout this chapter I will use the general term *learning objects* to refer to all of these, and *learning object-based instruction* to refer to this entire family of approaches.

Technical specifications for learning objects have proliferated in recent years (e.g., IEEE/LTSC, ADL/SCORM, IMS, and ARIADNE). Each of these specifications or standards details the way learning objects should be described in metadata, the way learning objects should be packaged for transport between two computer systems, and various other noneducational details. The majority of the research resources and effort put into learning objects in the past decade have gone into writing these technical specifications, writing tests to insure that systems conform to the specifications, and developing the conforming software systems. Unfortunately, a proportionally tiny amount of work has gone into addressing learning objects from an instructional perspective. While some have previously attempted to connect learning objects-based approaches with specific instructional design strategies (Merrill, 1999 ; Wiley, 2000), in this chapter I will attempt to provide a higher-level overview not connected specifically to a single instructional approach.

Classes and Characteristics of Learning Objects

The first work done in most descriptive sciences involves observing, collecting, and analyzing specimens in order to enable their classification into various families of related things. In prescriptive or design fields there are no naturally occurring things to observe and analyze, since by definition the articles of interest are all synthetic, designed artifacts. This difference does not, however, reduce the value of taxonomies within design fields. Since at least 1999 educational researchers have worked to describe taxonomies of learning objects and the defining characteristics of learning objects that would cause them to be classified in a specific way (for an early example, see Cisco, 1999). These purpose-driven taxonomies contain different types of learning objects that support design goals like automating assembly (e.g., Cisco, 1999; Dodds, 2001; L'Allier, 1997), maximizing reuse (Wiley, 2000), and enabling semantic web applications (Dingley & Shabajee, 2002).

Learning objects are generally considered to be discrete, addressable chunks of content that can be reused in a variety of instructional scenarios. While this conception is rather blunt, it meets the needs of everyday discourse on the subject. However, when we are engaged in the design, selection, or reuse of learning objects, it is useful to distinguish among at least three types: (1) content objects; (2) strategy objects; and (3) discourse objects. Below I discuss each of these three types of objects and discuss several issues of relevance to instructional designers and developers, specifically:

- issues related to an object's degree of specification— the number of criteria a digital resource must meet to be considered a learning object;
- issues of scope—in other words, how big a learning object should be; and
- issues of intra- and inter-object sequencing—issues related to the sequencing of learning objects and the sequencing of activities and information within a specific learning object.

The discussion of content objects will be the longest, because several of the principles applying to content objects are relevant to strategy and discourse objects.

1. Content Objects

Content objects are generally self-contained chunks of information.[1] This information might be presented as text, visuals, sounds, or audiovisuals. The following is a discussion of issues regarding degree of specification, scope, and sequence of content objects.

Degree of Specification "What is a learning object?" is a question asked frequently by conference attendees, graduate students, and professionals alike. There appear to be nearly as many answers to this question as there are answerers, demarcating a clear continuum of approaches ranging from no specification (e.g., "everything is a learning object") to a high degree of specification (e.g., "only digital content, organized in a specific way, stored in a certain format, and indexed with a certain type of metadata is a learning object"). In a document describing learning object metadata (cataloging) standards, the IEEE/LTSC states:

> Learning Objects are defined here as any entity, digital or non-digital, which can be used, re-used or referenced during technology supported learning…. Examples of Learning Objects include multimedia content, instructional content, learning objectives, instructional software and software tools, and persons, organizations, or events referenced during technology supported learning (IEEE/LTSC, 2000, n.p.).

---

1. *Editors' note: Since content is a matter of what to teach, decisions of this type tend to fall under curriculum design-theory (see chapter 1).*

It would be difficult to imagine a definition that imposes fewer constraints. The old Schoolhouse Rock song comes to mind: "I find it quite interesting, a noun is a person, place, or thing." According to the IEEE definition, all nouns are learning objects. Wiley and Edwards (2002) suggest the only slightly more restrictive, "any digital resource that can be reused to support learning." Imposing still more specification, NETg uses a triangular structure composed of an instructional objective, materials that teach to the objective, and items that assess student mastery of the objective to define their NETg Learning Object. Near the completely structured end of the spectrum is Merrill's work on knowledge objects, which specifies that content be structured as entities, activities, processes, and properties, and stored in a knowledge base (1997).

In the context of the specification of content objects, two points are especially important to consider. The first is that most content objects are not solely content objects; they contain both content and instructional strategy. For example, consider a NETg-style content object. As stated in the description of their model, this content object contains materials that teach a specific objective. If objectives are being taught, we can safely assume that the learning object contains more than inert content—it contains content coupled with instructional strategies by which the designer means to help students achieve the objectives. In practice it is quite difficult to completely separate out instructional strategies from content, and only very highly specified approaches that rely on the completely decontextualized, structural markup of content, like Merrill's knowledge object approach, really achieve this separation. Gibbons's writings on the layered nature of instructional designs (see chapter 14) are worth particular study in this regard.

A second important issue related to the degree of content object specification is the *anything versus automating* conundrum. "Anything" represents the unspecified end of our continuum. On this end, the dozen or more terabytes of content on the publicly accessible Internet are available for use and reuse in instructional scenarios. However, because there is no way of predicting the structure of the content, little can be done to automate the assembly and presentation of the objects. "Automating" represents the other end of the specification spectrum, where content is very highly structured. Knowing the specification of content structure ahead of time allows designers to automate much of the selection, assembly, and presentation of the learning objects. However, because all incoming content must be structured in a certain way, no content objects are usable in this model until they have been specially prepared. As with the issue of breadth versus depth in approaches to searching large information spaces, there is no universally correct answer to the *anything versus automating* question—selecting an appropriate level will always be highly context dependent.

Scope "How big should a learning object be?" is another frequently asked question, and is clearly related to the issue of scope that is so central to instructional design. However, before one can answer questions about the size of a content learning object, the construct *size* must be operationalized. As with the specification of the learning object, there are several opinions on how to interpret the notion of size: the average number of minutes required to complete the instruction, the number of objectives covered, the number of screens shown to the user, the number of steps in a set of procedural instructions, and the size of the digital file in kilobytes or megabytes are examples that have been seen in practice.

The primary principle to consider in designing a content object is the *reusability paradox*. The paradox states "the instructional usefulness of a learning object is inversely proportional to its reusability in instructional scenarios." This principle makes explicit the role of context in how content objects function. A large amount of context within a learning object, or the juxtaposition of several different concepts, examples, images, and other media in a single object, allows that learning object to function instructionally in increasingly meaningful ways. However, this same juxtaposition of multiple concepts and media within the object restricts the number of instructional scenarios in which it can be reused. So, the most instructionally effective learning objects are not very reusable at all, and the most reusable learning objects teach almost nothing at all. These two ends anchor a continuum. My own approach has been to aim for a sweet spot just left of center, as per Figure 16.1. We should make materials work effectively with our target population without sacrificing too much for the sake of hypothetical future reusers.

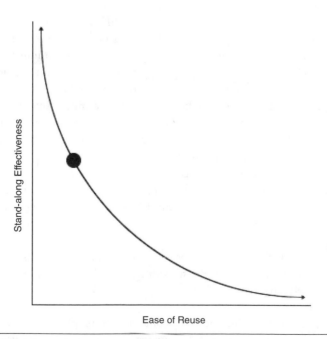

Figure 16.1 The Relationship Between the Stand-Alone Instructional Effectiveness of a Learning Object and the Ease with which an Object May Be Reused

As an example, our O$_2$ approach to using learning objects (Wiley et al., 2004), a problem-centered approach to using them, uses this "left of center" approach:

> O$_2$ is a project-based model of using learning objects which focuses the learning experience on a sequence of increasingly complex projects, following Wiley's Learning Object Design and Sequencing (LODAS) approach (Wiley, 2000) and Gibbons and associates' Work Model Synthesis method (Gibbons et al., 1983). Learning objects are selected and made available to students by the course designers in order to support the accomplishment of project tasks and goals. This use of learning objects follows the "Octopus Method" outlined in previous work, in which a project is placed at the center of the learning experience and learning objects "hang off of the project" like the legs of an octopus (Wiley, 2001). O$_2$ is also strongly influenced by Hannafin and Hill's work in Resource-based Learning Environments or RBLEs (Hannafin & Hill, 2002). (p. 513)

These content objects contain enough content and instructional strategy to teach the specified knowledge, skills, or attitudes, but lack any contextual scaffolds for helping learners see why they should care about the material or how it relates to them. These contextual scaffolds are instead provided outside the content objects via project and scenario descriptions. In this approach, the stand-alone content objects are fairly effective but rather difficult to reuse (as reuse always requires the creation of new project and scenario descriptions).

A momentary digression is justified here to differentiate between reusing and repurposing. Technically, "reusing" refers to using a learning object exactly as one finds it, while "repurposing" refers to making modifications to a learning object before use. Obviously, repurposing is considerably more expensive and time-consuming than reusing. Repurposing costs involve not only the time and talent needed to open and edit a variety of multimedia, but the time, talent, and resources needed to acquire permission from content publishers to make alterations to their materials. Therefore, many approaches (including O$_2$) focus on finding ways to facilitate the *reuse* of learning objects. In general conversation the term reuse is almost always used, regardless of whether or not the speaker is describing an approach in which learning objects are modified prior to use. It is, therefore, always necessary when one hears another speaking about reuse, to determine whether they are really talking about reusing or repurposing learning objects.

The tension between stand-alone effectiveness and ease of reuse is not unique to content objects, but holds true for strategy and discourse objects as well, and we will revisit it below.

Sequence After selecting the right content objects, placing content in them in an instructionally meaningful sequence is the designer's (or system's) most important task. The canonical sequences of instructional design apply without deviation, including the simple-to-complex sequences of Reigeluth's elaboration theory and others, the microlevel randomization of Van Merrienboer's four component instructional design model, and Gagné's prerequisites-first strategy to sequencing content.

In larger content objects that teach multiple concepts or skills, there will be sequencing *internal* to the object (reemphasizing the point that few content objects are comprised solely of content). Because content objects both contain content and are content, there is no difference in considerations of intralearning object and interobject sequencing. Inside and out, a content object is "just another instructional medium," and effective instruction built from learning objects will have the same sequencing characteristics as effective instruction developed from any other media.

2. Strategy Objects

Strategy objects contain no content whatsoever. They are purely logic, containing procedures, processes, and patterns of instruction.[2] They may embody methods for presenting content, providing feedback, or generating practice or assessment items. A useful analogy can be made to data and algorithms in computer programming, in which content objects are analogous to data and strategy objects are analogous to algorithms. Because they operate over content objects in an automated manner, the success of strategy objects depends heavily on the designer's ability to determine the structure of the content objects ahead of time.[3]

Strategy objects are alluring to designers because they will always execute instructional strategies exactly as prescribed. When a designer finds a particularly effective method of teaching a certain type of content, this method can be embodied in a strategy object that will replicate the specific teaching technique faithfully each and every time. This method can then be reused to teach a variety of specific topics or skills, as designers transform content into objects meeting the structural assumptions of algorithms.

Keep in mind the previous comments regarding the relationship between effectiveness and ease of reuse, as they apply to strategy objects just as much as they do to content objects. Just because an instructional strategy is effective in one instructional context doesn't guarantee that it will be effective in another. Of course, the strategy object may in fact be placed in a sequence, it may be "used," but there is no guarantee that the learning object will be equally effective in the new context. The following is a discussion of issues regarding degree of specification, scope, and sequence of strategy learning objects.

Degree of Specification Like their content counterparts, strategy objects can be more or less rigidly specified. At the less specified end of the continuum are

---

2. *Editors' note: Decisions of this nature tend to be in the realm of instructional-event theory.*
3. *Editors' note: This indicates that the nature of the content is a powerful situationality for selecting instructional methods.*

design patterns or templates. For example, designers of online instruction frequently prepare HTML templates that they later fill with content. The templates embody a specific strategy and approach to instruction (whether the designer realizes this or not) and are reusable across a variety of instructional scenarios. Authoring tools like Dreamweaver or Flash also generally contain this kind of template.

Strategy objects at the highly structured end of the continuum are always paired with content objects that are also highly structured. These strategy objects are, in effect, computer algorithms that process content; accordingly, the algorithms depend on the data (content objects) being formatted in a certain way in order to process them properly.

The knowledge objects and instructional transactions of Merrill's instructional transaction theory are examples of this highly specified content object-strategy object pairing. Merrill (1997) describes the types, structures, and interrelations of knowledge objects as follows:

> We have identified four types of knowledge objects: entities, activities, processes, and properties (See Jones & Merrill, 1990). Entities represent objects in the world and can include devices, persons, creatures, places, symbols, etc. Activities represent actions that the learner can take to act on objects in the world. Processes represent the changes that occur in the properties of objects in the world. Processes represent events that occur in the world that change an entity. Processes are triggered by activities or by other processes. Properties represent quantitative or qualitative attributes of entities. (Merrill, 1997, n.p.)

These knowledge objects are the "input data" that will be processed by the instructional transaction "algorithms," of which there are currently about 13 kinds. Merrill next describes a portion of one kind of transaction called "Identify":

> *Presentation.* The presentation mode for the IDENTIFY transaction is as follows: Show the name and portrayal of the referent knowledge object. [In our example the name is in the title bar and the background for the valve including the pipe, the bottom plate of the valve and the switch plate is the portrayal of the referent knowledge object.] Show the portrayal of each part of the referent knowledge object. [In our example the illustration of each part is the portrayal. For example, the valve itself, the flange bolts, the air hose connection, the air hose, etc.] If explore mode is enabled: on mouse enter show the name of each part. On right click show the description of each part. If lecture mode is requested ["Tell me about some of the parts."]: highlight each part in the selected item list, show its name, show its description. For temporal portrayals (video or audio) some graphic portrayal usually accompanies the temporal portrayal to identify the parts in time.

Practice. The practice mode for the IDENTIFY transaction is as follows: If locate parts is selected: present a part name, the student clicks on the part, provide right/wrong with correct answer feedback. If wrong, retain item in the list. If name parts is selected: highlight a part, present a list of part names, the student clicks on the name of the part, provide right/wrong with correct answer feedback. If wrong, retain item in the list. If identify function is selected: present a function description, the student clicks on the part, provide right/wrong with correct answer feedback. If wrong, retain item in the list. (Merrill, 1997, n.p.)

An instructional system's ability to execute these highly specified strategy objects is entirely dependent on the accompanying content objects exhibiting a similarly high degree of structure.

Scope While they may seem exclusive to content objects, issues of scope are also critical for strategy objects. Specifically, how much of the instructional process should a strategy object attempt to address?[4] Gaining student attention? The presentation of information? Practice? Feedback? Assessment? All of these and more? Additionally, how many types of instruction should a strategy object attempt to address?[5] Just paired-associate instruction? Concept instruction? Procedural instruction? All of these and more?

Again we come to the reusability paradox. One giant, integrated learning object that does everything may be compelling in a few instructional scenarios, but an object that provides only paired-associate practice will be reusable in a far greater number of scenarios (usually in combination with other strategy learning objects). The designer should strike a balance between providing enough functionality to be useful, yet not so much functionality as to limit applicability of the object.

Sequence Because sequencing is a key part of what strategy objects do, discussing the sequencing of strategy objects can become bogged down in a "play within a play" sort of confusion. For smaller learning objects, microlevel issues, such as which content or practice item to present first, are of primary consideration. In larger objects that present information and provide practice and feedback, mesolevel issues of sequencing practice and presentation must be determined. How frequently should practice interrupt the presentation of information? How frequently should feedback interrupt the provision of practice opportunities? The greater the variety of strategies embodied in the strategy object, the more complex the intraobject sequencing issues become. The interobject and intraobject sequencing issues are the same here as with content objects. Whether informa-

---

4. *Editors' note: This is the same as the issue of "scope" as described in chapter 1.*
5. *Editors' note: This is the same as the issue of "generality" as described in chapter 1, which deals with the breadth of situations in which the strategy is recommended.*

tion presentation, practice, and assessment are in one object or three, someone must sequence these at some point.

The designer's choice between large and small strategy objects affects reusability as described above. For example, if a designer has selected a strategy sequence of "present a rule statement, present an example of the rule, and present an opportunity for practice with the rule," and she will never vary from this pattern, one large strategy object implementing these three strategies may be appropriate. However, if the designer has a hunch she will sometimes want to present an example without presenting a rule statement before and a practice opportunity after, these three would each need to be developed as individual strategy objects.

3. Discourse Objects

Discourse objects are a special type of strategy object whose content is not created and inserted by instructional designers or automated systems. Their content is created and inserted by *learners*. In other words, discourse objects are a special class of strategy objects that scaffold interactions among learners.[6] Again, issues regarding degree of specification, scope, and sequence are discussed next.

Degree of Specification Similar to content and strategy objects, discourse objects can be specified to greater and lesser degrees. At the less specified end of the spectrum are tools that facilitate interactions while imposing the fewest possible constraints. A wiki is a good example. Wikis are web-based collaboration environments in which anyone can create any content they like and anyone can edit any content in any way they like. Consequently, wikis can be very chaotic. Slightly more structure is frequently given to interactions by codifying and sharing "the way we do things here," such as the netiquette directions frequently found in newsgroups or Wikipedia's *How to Edit a Page*. This Wikipedia document provides instructions like "Use a neutral point of view," "Cite your sources," and "Start your sections as follows...." At the highly specified end of the spectrum are tools that completely constrain and structure interactions. Computer-supported collaborative argumentation tools are good examples of highly specified discourse objects. These tools constrain users to make only statements of certain types (e.g., warrants or claims) and only to make these statements in certain orders or in response to specific types of statements made by others (e.g., claims may only be made after qualifiers have been stated).

Scope How are we to understand "size" in terms of discourse objects? Two issues of scope are relevant to discourse objects: first, deciding how many types of discourse to support in the object, and second, identifying a meaningful unit of interaction in the supported type of discourse. The first consideration is identical

---

6. *Editors' note: These are in the control, representation, and media logic layers of design.*

to the scope issues associated with other strategy objects, so the discussion is not repeated here. The second issue is more interesting ("interesting" as in "difficult"). Functional moves within the grammar can be translated to discrete opportunities for interaction in the discourse object in areas where discourse grammars exist (such as Toulmin's model of argument). For example, presenting an argument, presenting evidence, and presenting a counterargument are all discrete units within the argumentation process. In collaborative, cooperative, and other interaction scenarios for which no model exists, the design of a discourse object must begin with discourse analyses of several successful interactions of the type the designer wishes to support in order to identify these atomic components. Scope decisions then proceed as with other strategy objects, deciding how many of these discrete elements to include in a single discourse object.

Sequence Discourse objects also differ from the others in that there are real differences in their intra- and interlearning object sequences. Intraobject sequencing of learners' anticipated functional moves is driven completely by information from new analyses or existing models of how the desired discourse should progress toward its instructional goal. These sequences are mainly procedural and may have nothing to do with the progressions from simple to complex typical of a novice moving toward expertise. For example, these conversations may spiral toward a shared understanding of a term, or may use a social choice mechanism to iterate toward the selection of a tentative solution to a design problem.

Interobject sequencing of discourse objects resembles interobject sequencing of content and strategy learning objects, including the simple-to-complex and other sequences of elaboration theory, the microlevel randomization of 4CID, and the prerequisites-first approach to sequencing.

4. Learning Objects and New Instructional Theories

The question "How do learning objects change instructional design (and therefore instructional theory)?" is often asked. I believe the answer to this question is simple: they don't. Instructional design is the practice of making those choices best calculated to facilitate learning under whatever constraints the specific participant, physical, political, philosophical, and budgetary environment imposes. Learning-object-based approaches to instructional design do not change this practice of making choices under constraints, and so they do not change the fundamental practice of instructional design at all.

One may argue that learning objects do not even place any new constraints on designers. After all, for over a century now we have located and adapted materials from textbooks, journal articles, newspapers, and other sources as we have designed instruction. Why would adding "the web" and "databases" to this list change things? It does not, and relying on existing learning objects when designing instruction differs little from what we have previously done.

However, as instructional designers we are also charged with designing the learning objects themselves, and this does, in fact, add a novel wrinkle to our practice. The notion of materials designed for reuse in a broad variety of situations brings into sharp relief context-related problems that instructional designers frequently ignore. There is no best approach to designing instruction; there is no technique that works equally well with all content areas or with all people.[7] And when a large training company adopts a single pedagogy and a single system for designing and deploying their instruction, they do so to the detriment of the effectiveness of that instruction (while admittedly realizing obvious financial benefits).

The fields closely related to learning objects have created significant increases and decreases in the constraints designers face. For example, when Requests for Proposals require responders to address and conform to standards related to learning objects, like SCORM. This is a very new, and very significant, constraint placed on the designer. On the other hand, the relatively young area of "open educational resources" (OERs) is an excellent example of the type of innovation enabled by the learning objects approach. OERs are learning objects whose intellectual property status is clearly and intentionally labeled and licensed such that designers are free to adapt, modify, and redistribute them without the need to seek permissions or pay royalties. If you've never seen an OER, look at the 3,000 university courses available from MIT, Utah State University, and hundreds of other universities around the world linked from http://www.ocwconsortium. org/—all the materials in all these courses can be translated, modified, reused, and redistributed without additional permission or payment. Because the legal constraints that have always narrowly confined the ways we could repurpose resources and share them with colleagues and students are so entirely pervasive, most instructional designers don't consciously consider them.

Because OERs are licensed in such a way as to enable legal altering, sampling, translating, and making other changes to instructional materials—and then redistributing those materials—a previously underappreciated form of instructional design is coming to the forefront of the OER movement. *Localization* is the process of adapting instructional materials in ways that make them more appropriate for target users in linguistic, cultural, and other ways. While traditional copyright previously restricted instructional designers to *reusing* learning objects, the existence of OERs opens huge vistas of *repurposing* to instructional designers. In the coming decade we will see the establishment of standard processes and practices involved in the large-scale adaptation of instructional materials. One of the main goals of the OER movement is providing educational opportunities in the developing world, so robust instructional theories must be able to answer questions like "What must be done to instruction that was effective in a specific

---

7. *Editors' note: This is an important principle for the Information-Age paradigm of education. One important implication for instructional theory is the need for it to include more situationalities that help instructional designers to both design and select different learning objects for different kinds of content and learners.*

portion of the English speaking developed world so that it can function effectively in the Chinese speaking developing world?" The area of localization, made newly interesting by the emergence of the open education movement, should be an active area within instructional theory for years to come.

Conclusion

Inasmuch as the primary choices made by instructional designers are decisions of scope and sequence, I have tried to illuminate the impact of learning objects-based approaches on these choices. I have argued that the taxonomies of design fields are different from those of descriptive fields in that our design goals frequently lead to the development of classification schemes first, with the to-be-classified artifacts coming along later. I have also argued that neither learning objects nor the introduction of any other technology or approach to instructional design can change the fundamental practice of instructional design, which is making purposeful choice under constraint. Adding or removing constraints, however, does change the types of choices we are able to make, as the example of open educational resources showed. I hope that, taken together, these thoughts will contribute to the development of better instructional theory, and especially catalyze desperately needed dialogue around the instructional use of learning objects. While I myself developed what might be called an instructional theory for learning objects many years ago, I now believe that learning objects' greatest contribution to the discourse about instructional theory will be the manner in which they bring the issue of localization to the forefront of instructional theory.

References

Barritt, C., Lewis, D., & Wieseler, W. (2005). *Cisco systems reusable information object strategy.* Retrieved September 1, 2006 from http://www.cisco.com/warp/public/779/ibs/solutions/learning/whitepapers/el_cisco_rio.pdf

Dingley, A., & Shabajee, P. (2002). *Today's authoring tools for tomorrow's semantic web.* Retrieved September 1, 2006 from http://www.archimuse.com/mw2002/papers/dingley/dingley.html

Dodds, P. (2001). *Advanced distributed learning sharable content object reference model version 1.2. The SCORM content aggregation model.* Retrieved September 1, 2006 from http://adlnet.org/scorm/history/12/index.cfm

L'Allier, J. J. (1997). *A frame of reference: NETg's map to its products, their structures and core beliefs.* Retrieved September 1, 2006 from http://web.archive.org/web/20030605103751/www.netg.com/research/whitepapers/frameref.asp

Merrill, M. D. (1997). *Instructional transaction theory: An instructional design model based on knowledge objects.* Retrieved September 1, 2006 from http://it.coe.uga.edu/itforum/paper22/paper22a.html

Wiley, D. (2000). *Learning object design and sequencing theory.* Dissertation. Retrieved September 1, 2006 from http://wiley.ed.usu.edu/docs/dissertation.pdf

Wiley, D., & Edwards, E. K. (2002). Online self-organizing social systems: The decentralized future of online learning. *Quarterly Review of Distance Education, 3*(1), 33–46. Retrieved September 1, 2006 from http://wiley.ed.usu.edu/docs/ososs.pdf

Wiley, D., Padron, S., Lambert, B., Dawson, D., Nelson, L., Barclay, & Wade, D. (2004). Overcoming the limitations of learning objects. *Journal of Educational Multimedia and Hypermedia, 13*(4), 507–521.

17
Theory Building

CHARLES M. REIGELUTH

Indiana University

YUN-JO AN

Texas A&M University, Texarkana

Charles M. Reigeluth received a BA in economics from Harvard University. He was a high school teacher for three years before earning his doctorate in instructional psychology at Brigham Young University. He has been a professor in the Instructional Systems Technology Department at Indiana University's School of Education in Bloomington since 1988, and served as chairman of the department from 1990 to 1992. His major area for service, teaching, and research is the process for facilitating district-wide paradigm change in public school systems. His major research goal is to advance knowledge to help school districts successfully navigate transformation to the learner-centered paradigm of education. He has published nine books and over 120 journal articles and chapters. Two of his books received an "outstanding book of the year" award from Association for Educational Communications and Technology (AECT). He also received AECT's Distinguished Service Award and Brigham Young University's Distinguished Alumnus Award.

Yun-Jo An received her PhD in instructional systems technology from Indiana University, Bloomington. She worked for an e-learning company, Option Six, as an instructional designer. She is currently Assistant Professor of Instructional Technology at Texas A&M University, Texarkana. Her research interests include designing digital learning environments, problem-based learning, games and simulations, and instructional theory building.

EDITORS' FOREWORD

Vision

- To provide guidance for developing instructional theory

Basics about Theory and Research

1. *Kinds of knowledge that need to be built*
   - *Both design theory and descriptive theory*
2. *A framework for building instructional theory*
   - *Functional contextualism utilizing multiple perspectives (eclecticism)*
3. *Kinds of research needed to build descriptive and design theory*
   - *Descriptive theory is concerned with validity and truthfulness.*
   - *Design theory is concerned with preferability and usefulness.*
   - *Design theory is advanced by research to prove (confirmatory) and by research to improve (exploratory or developmental).*
4. *When to use research to improve a design theory*
   - *The S curve of theory development*
   - *In early stages of development, use research to improve: formative research and design-based research.*
   - *In later stages of development, use both research to prove and research to improve.*

Approaches to Building Design Theory

1. *Data-based theory development*
   - *Identify boundaries for the instructional theory.*
   - *Observe what methods work and when (situationalities).*
   - *Conduct research to improve the theory.*
2. *Values-based theory development*
   - *Identify boundaries for the instructional theory.*
   - *Identify values you want the instruction to embody.*
   - *Search for imprecise methods that embody the values.*
   - *Elaborate the methods by identifying parts, kinds, and criteria, along with appropriate situationalities.*
   - *Conduct research to improve the theory.*
3. *Methods-based theory development*
   - *Select a general method and describe it on an imprecise level.*
   - *Identify boundaries for the instructional theory.*
   - *Elaborate the methods by identifying parts, kinds, and criteria, along with appropriate situationalities.*
   - *Conduct research to improve the theory.*
4. *Practitioner-driven theory development*
   - *Identify boundaries for the instructional theory.*
   - *Explicate tacit knowledge using case recall.*

- *Elaborate the methods by identifying parts, kinds, and criteria, along with appropriate situationalities, again using case recall.*
- *Identify variations in the methods, and the situationalities that call for each.*
- *Conduct research to improve the theory.*

Approaches to Research on Design Theory

1. *Grounded theory development*
   - *It focuses on inductive processes of theory development without formulating hypotheses in advance.*
   - *Glaser's approach includes: (no preresearch literature review), data collection (qualitative and/or qualitative), open coding, constant comparison, selective coding, theoretical coding, theoretical memoing, and sorting and writing up.*
   - *Strauss and Corbin's approach includes: a preresearch literature review, qualitative data collection only, and different coding processes (open coding, axial coding, and selective coding).*
2. *Design-based research (DBR)*
   - *Characteristics: Driven by theory and prior research, pragmatic, collaborative, contextual, uses multiple dependent variables, is integrative, entails systematic and comprehensive documentation, is iterative, is adaptive/flexible, and seeks generalization.*
   - *Principles: Support design with research, set practical goals and initial plan, do in real-world settings, collaborate closely with participants, do systematically and purposefully, analyze data immediately and continuously, refine designs continually, document contextual influences, and validate generalizability of the design.*
   - *Guidelines: Identify a real-world problem, review literature and set theory development goals, develop a partnership with practitioners, identify dependent and independent variables, develop initial research plan, develop and implement a design, record the design process, collect data, evaluate the design, revise the design, repeat the process, and report the results.*
3. *Formative research*
   - *Purpose: Is intended to improve three things—a particular case, an instructional theory related to that case, and descriptive theory related to the instructional theory.*
   - *Activities: Evaluate the case to identify strengths, weaknesses, and likely improvements for all three; look for variations in methods and their accompanying situationalities; implement and test likely improvements in the case; explore causal dynamics; and suggest potential improvements in the design and descriptive theories.*
   - *It can be used to develop a new design theory or improve an existing design theory and can be used in designed cases, past naturalistic cases,*

and current naturalistic cases. Each of these uses requires variations in the formative research method.

—CMR & ACC

THEORY BUILDING

Building a common knowledge base requires deep understanding of the nature of theories and of the kinds of research that can help us build design theories. In this chapter, we begin by discussing some basics about theory and research. Then we describe four approaches that could be used to build design theory, followed by three approaches that could be used to do research for developing design theory.

Basics about Theory and Research

In this section we discuss: (1) what kinds of knowledge need to be built; (2) what framework is helpful for building instructional theory; (3) what kinds of research are needed to build descriptive and design theories; and (4) when one should use research to improve rather than to prove a design theory.

1. What Kinds of Knowledge Need to Be Built?

Chapter 1 distinguished between design theory and descriptive theory. It explained that *design theory* is a kind of knowledge that identifies the best available methods for accomplishing given goals within given situations. Therefore, it is instrumental knowledge. In contrast, chapter 1 also explained that *descriptive theory* is a kind of knowledge that identifies the causal dynamics that occur within given situations. Therefore, it is descriptive knowledge. Simon (1996) refers to these two types of knowledge as the sciences of the artificial and the natural sciences, respectively. Similar distinctions include applied vs. basic research, engineering vs. science, and technology (broadly defined) vs. science.

However, chapter 1 also explained that these two kinds of knowledge are inextricably interrelated, and most instructional theorists find value in building both kinds of knowledge, often simultaneously. Dewey (1900) described design theory as a "linking science" between learning theory and educational practice. Design theory provides direct guidance for accomplishing one's goals, but descriptive theory provides an understanding or rationale for why that guidance works. Theorists find that developing powerful means to accomplish a goal (design theory) helps them to identify important causal dynamics (descriptive theory) to study, and conversely that discovering important causal dynamics helps them to identify more powerful means to accomplish one's goals.

Therefore, we recommend that those who wish to contribute to knowledge about instruction (including practitioners as well as researchers) attempt to build both kinds of knowledge simultaneously. Since much has been written about how to build descriptive knowledge, we focus in this chapter on how to build design knowledge.

2. What Framework Is Helpful for Building Instructional Theory?

Over the past decade there has been much debate about behaviorism, cognitivism, and constructivism as theoretical frameworks for instructional theory. This debate has generally had a positive impact on the development of the field. However, the radical view that there is one best theoretical perspective has, in our view, had a damaging effect on instructional theory, for it denies the multiple perspectives that are so strongly advocated by constructivists. We have found that all theoretical perspectives make some valuable contributions, or they would not have a following. Holding multiple theoretical perspectives provides a practitioner with a wide variety of instructional "tools" in their toolbox for dealing most effectively with any given instructional situation they encounter.

In essence, we believe that eclecticism, an approach founded in multiple perspectives, is the best approach. This is a *functionalist* view of design theory, a view that advocates using whatever works (functions) best. This is also a *contextual* view of design theory, a view that recognizes that what works best will vary from one situation to another. Therefore, we enthusiastically support the use of *functional contextualism* as a theoretical or even philosophical framework to help in building instructional theory.

Functional contextualism provides "theoretical clarity and philosophical cohesion" (Fox, 2006, p. 6) for understanding instruction and instructional theory, and therefore for building instructional theory. According to Reigeluth and An (2006), it encourages us to focus on producing practical knowledge applicable to similar situations and also provides a philosophical foundation and framework for generating goal-oriented design theories. Functional contextualism is "well suited to the needs of a goal-oriented discipline dedicated to improving the means of fostering human learning and development" (Reigeluth & An, 2006, p. 52).

3. What Kinds of Research Are Needed to Build Each Kind of Knowledge?

Descriptive theory's primary research concern is *validity*: how well do the descriptions (usually of complex causal dynamics) match with reality? In contrast, design theory's primary research concern is *preferability*: which methods are better than the known alternatives for accomplishing given goals under given conditions (see chapter 1). Some students are likely to learn from almost any method of instruction, no matter how poor, so the issue is not whether a method is "valid," but whether it is preferable to other known methods. This is why Richard Snow (1977) characterized design theory as being concerned with *usefulness*, in contrast to descriptive theory's concern with *truthfulness*.

A key point is that design theory's concern with preferability presents different methodological challenges from descriptive theory's concern with validity. Since much has been written about research methods and methodological challenges for building descriptive theory, we will focus here on methods and challenges for building design theory. Here, the research question is not whether a method works, but how well it works and how it can be made to work better. Therefore, for design theory there are two major kinds of research that can be done: research to *prove* and research to *improve*. Research to *improve* focuses on knowledge to advance a given method's ability to achieve given goals under given conditions. In contrast, research to *prove* focuses on knowledge to confirm that a given method is of high quality, which can be assessed in either a relative or absolute way. An absolute assessment of quality measures the method against a standard, whereas a relative assessment measures it against the known alternatives. Research to improve is *exploratory* or *developmental*, whereas research to prove is *confirmatory*. The former is concerned with theory development, while the latter is concerned with theory testing.

4. When Should One Use Research to Improve a Design Theory Rather than Research to Prove a Design Theory?

Every design theory (or system, or technology, broadly defined) undergoes a predictable pattern of development characterized by an "S curve" (Branson, 1987): its effectiveness increases at an accelerating rate for a while, and then it increases at a decelerating rate as it approaches its upper limit (see Figure 17.1). Different theories (or systems) have different upper limits. When a method is in its early stages of development (see Theory 2 at T1 in Figure 17.1), it is premature

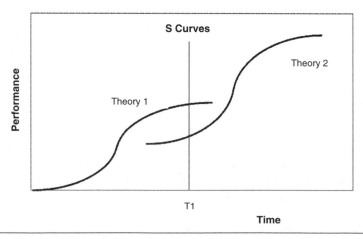

Figure 17.1 The S Curves of Development for Two Instructional Theories

to compare it with alternative methods that are at more advanced stages of development (Theory 1 at T1 in Figure 17.1), because premature comparison can result in abandoning further development that could have resulted in a method superior to the alternatives.

Therefore, research to *prove* that one method is better than another should generally be done only when the methods are at fairly similar, and advanced, stages of development. Experimental designs are highly appropriate for this kind of research. In contrast, research to *improve* a method or design theory is the most productive kind of research when the method or theory is in the earlier stages of its development (e.g., Theory 2 at T1 in Figure 17.1). Evaluation research designs, especially formative research and other kinds of design-based research, are highly appropriate for this kind of research. Therefore, an important need in our field today is not just to work toward development of a common knowledge base with a consistent terminology, but to continually improve that common knowledge base through formative or design-based research.

In the remainder of this chapter we will describe various approaches for developing instructional theories, followed by a description of design-based research and formative research for continually improving such theories. Some guidance for developing descriptive theories is offered by Eisenhardt (1989), Lewis and Grimes (1999), and Weick (1989).

Approaches to Building Design Theory

There is probably an infinite number of ways one can build instructional theory. In this section, we discuss four approaches: data-based (or grounded), values-based, methods-based, and practitioner-led theory construction. Then in the following section, we discuss three research methods that are useful tools for these approaches to theory construction.

1. Data-Based Theory Development

One of the most common approaches to developing design theory is to build it inductively from data, based on what works well. This approach commonly uses a research method called "grounded theory development" (Glaser & Strauss, 1967), which is described in some detail in the next section. However, when the focus of research is to improve rather than to prove, this data-based theory development process should go beyond the grounded theory development guidance to observe, and also try out different methods (or different variations on a method), revise those methods based on formative data, and try them out again. Cycles of trial and revision are key to research that is focused on improving a design theory of any kind. Design-based research and formative research, which are also described in some detail in the next section, are valuable research methods for doing this. We offer the following general guidelines for data-based theory construction, based on our experience with this approach at Indiana University.

Identify Boundaries Start by identifying the boundaries for the instructional theory. For what kinds of conditions is it intended (kinds of content, learners, and learning environments)? For what conditions is it not intended? This restricts the generality of the theory (see chapter 1). The data-based approach typically starts with tight boundaries (a narrow range of conditions), and after achieving a high level of usefulness for that domain, gradually broadens the boundaries and tests and revises the methods and situationalities to accommodate the new conditions.

Observe What Methods Work and When Next, using the grounded theory development method as a guide, you should observe some instruction that is taking place within the boundaries of your theory. The instruction may be designed by someone else for their own purposes or by you for the express purpose of developing your theory. The observations should identify which methods work well (or the best), and if they don't always work well, what situationalities influence when they work well. You should describe the methods in as much detail as a typical practitioner would need to use them well. It may help to interview the teacher afterwards to find out the thinking that guided his or her selection and application of the methods.

Conduct Research to Improve Finally, it is time to look for ways to improve the methods. Using formative research and other kinds of design-based research as a guide, you should use observations and interviews to identify ways that the methods could possibly be improved and to gain greater clarity on when (in what situations) each should and should not be used.

2. Values-Based Theory Development

Values play a central role in design theories (see chapter 1), and they can play the primary role in theory development. Values can guide the selection of learning goals that the instructional theory will address. They can guide the choice of some criteria for judging how good the methods are (effectiveness, efficiency, and appeal), identified as "priorities" in chapter 1. They can guide the choice of other criteria for judging how good the methods are (philosophical point of view). And they can guide the decisions about who will have the power to make either the choices just listed or the choices that take place during the instruction (see chapter 1). We have not been able to find much written about a values-based theory development process, so we again offer some guidelines based on our experience with this approach.

3. Identify Boundaries

Start by identifying the boundaries for the theory. For what kinds of conditions is it intended (kinds of content, learners, and learning environments)? For what conditions is it not intended? This restricts the generality of the theory (see chapter 1).

Identify Values Then identify the values you want the instruction to embody. This should include values about learning goals (e.g., it is important to develop learners' ability to reflect on their learning process), priorities (e.g., it is more important that the instruction be motivating than efficient), methods (e.g., it is important to provide a lot of support and scaffolding for the learner), and power (e.g., it is important to provide learners with some control over both what to learn and how to learn it) (see chapter 1).

Search for Methods Next, you should look for general approaches (called imprecise methods in chapter 1) that embody those values. Don't try to be very detailed or precise at this point about the methods. Think in terms of broad strokes, and try to prioritize the alternative methods based on how well they embody the values and are appropriate for the conditions.

Elaborate the Methods Now the imprecise methods need to be elaborated to greater precision. As described in chapter 1, this is done by identifying (1) parts of each method; (2) kinds of each method or part; or (3) criteria for applying each method. We recommend that this elaboration be done in cycles that span the full range of parts of the method, beginning with relatively imprecise descriptions of the method(s) and progressing to ever greater levels of precision. From a systems thinking perspective, each part of the method must be designed in consideration of the other parts, so that all the parts will work synergistically. So generally it is better if the level of precision for one part of the method does not get too far ahead of that of the other parts. Furthermore, whenever a method is broken into kinds of that method, those kinds are alternatives from which a designer must choose. Therefore, you should identify the situationalities (situational variables) that represent the basis for choosing, so that you can formulate guidelines about when and when not to use each kind.

Conduct Research to Improve Finally, it is time to see how well those methods work and identify ways to improve them. Formative research and other kinds of design-based research are valuable tools for doing this.

4. Methods-Based Theory Development

Instructional methods are the most important part of any instructional theory, because the best selection and use of them is the purpose of an instructional theory (see chapter 1). Therefore, they can play the primary role in theory development. To some extent, the methods-based theory development process can be viewed as a hybrid between the values-based and data-based approaches, because the choice of a method as the starting point for your theory tends to be based heavily of both values and experience. We have not been able to find much written about a methods-based theory development process, so we offer some guidelines based on our experience with this approach.

Select a General Method Start by selecting a general method or methods that you think are likely to be important or useful. As just mentioned, this tends to be strongly influenced by your values and experience. As with the values-based approach, don't try to be very detailed or precise at this point about the methods. Think in terms of broad strokes.

Identify Boundaries Then identify the boundaries for the theory, by trying to imagine the situations (called preconditions) in which you would likely want to use the general method—and trying to imagine the situations in which you would likely not want to use it. The boundaries will later need to be empirically verified.

Elaborate the Method Now the imprecise methods need to be elaborated to greater precision, in the same manner as described for the values-based approach, including the identification of situationalities whenever a method is broken into kinds.

Conduct Research to Improve Finally, it is time to see how well those methods work and identify ways to improve them. Again, formative research and other kinds of design-based research are valuable tools for doing this.

5. Practitioner-Driven Theory Development

Those who use methods of instruction in their work can gain powerful insights into what methods work well and when they work well. They intuitively develop a theory of instruction based on their practice to guide their practice. However, this is often tacit knowledge and is seldom shared with other practitioners or researchers. This is a terrible waste of opportunity to advance our collective knowledge about how to create powerful instruction. Therefore, we strongly encourage all practitioners to contribute to our collective knowledge by using a theory development approach such as the following.

Identify Boundaries Start by identifying the range of situations for which you would like to offer instructional guidance. This may be as narrow as "teaching algebra to ninth graders over the Internet," or as broad as "developing deep understandings in children and adults."

Explicate Tacit Knowledge Next, imagine yourself in a fairly common specific situation—teaching a specific topic or skill to a specific learner or learners in a specific learning environment—within the boundaries of your theory. Go through the process from beginning to end in your mind, and write down the methods at each stage of the process. Also, think if there are general principles that apply more broadly to one particular stage of the process.

Elaborate the Methods Now elaborate those methods to greater precision, in the same manner as described for the values-based approach, including the identification of situationalities whenever a method is broken into kinds, except do so by continuing to imagine yourself in the same specific situation.

Broaden the Methods and Situations Imagine other situations (content, learners, or learning environments) within the boundaries of your theory, and identify ways that the original methods should differ. Describe both the variations in methods and the situations that call for each variation. Elaborate those variations in the same manner as for the initial methods.

Conduct Research to Improve Finally, it is time to test those methods and identify ways to improve them. Again, formative research and other kinds of design-based research are valuable tools for doing this.

6. Section Summary

In summary, there are many different ways to develop an instructional theory. The four described here are the ones we have found most useful, but don't hesitate to experiment and come up with your own approach. These four approaches use many of the same activities, but in different orders or with different emphases. Selection of an approach should depend primarily on personal experiences and preferences. For example, if you feel strongly that a philosophy or set of values should influence your theory, then the values-based approach will likely work best for you. If you like a particular method, then you will probably select the

Table 17.1 Four Approaches for Constructing Instructional Theory

Grounded theory development	Identify boundaries		Observe what works and when		Do research to improve the theory
Values-based theory development	Identify boundaries	Identify values	Search for methods	Elaborate the methods	Do research to improve the theory
Methods-based theory development	Select a general method	Identify boundaries		Elaborate the methods	Do research to improve the theory
Theory development for practitioners	Identify boundaries	Explicate tacit knowledge	Elaborate the methods	Broaden the methods and situations	Do research to improve the theory

methods-based approach. If you have a lot of experience teaching in a certain area, then the practitioner approach should work best. And if you don't have much experience or many preconceptions about what the instruction should be like, the inductive, grounded-theory approach will likely work best for you. Table 17.1 summarizes the main activities for these four approaches.

Approaches to Research on Design Theory

There are many research methods that can help you to build instructional theory. In this section, we discuss three methods: grounded theory development, design-based research, and formative research.

1. Grounded Theory Development

Grounded theory is a research method developed by Barney Glaser and Anselm Strauss that seeks to generate theory from empirical data through both inductive and deductive reasoning processes. In grounded theory, the researcher constantly compares conceptualized data and may also try to verify the hypotheses generated by constant comparisons of data (Glaser & Strauss, 1967). Grounded theory is distinguished from other research methods in that it focuses on inductive processes of theory development without formulating hypotheses in advance (Glaser & Strauss, 1967; Patton, 2002).

With disagreement between Glaser and Strauss on how to do grounded theory (Glaser, 1992; Strauss, 1987; Strauss & Corbin, 1990), two different approaches have emerged.

Glaser's Approach

According to Glaser, grounded theory is not a qualitative research method but a general method that can use any kind of data (Glaser, 2001, 2003). His approach highlights the "emergence" of conceptual hypotheses from empirical data. The following are its major features.

No Preresearch Literature Review Glaser recommends that the researcher refrain from conducting a preresearch literature review that may give preconceptions about the study, and read the literature in the sorting stage treating it as data to code. He insists that "there is a need not to review any of the literature in the substantive area under study" (Glaser, 1992, p. 31).

Data Collection According to Glaser, all is data. The researcher can use any kind of data that he or she encounters (Glaser, 2001). Even television shows or informal chats with people can be used as data in grounded theory. Collected data are recorded in field notes for data coding.

Open Coding At the beginning of the study, the researcher starts with open coding, conceptualizing written data in field notes line by line. The coding is often done in the margin of the field notes. During open coding, substantive codes (categories and properties) are developed ad hoc (Glaser, 1978).

Constant Comparison The researcher constantly compares conceptualized data as he or she codes more data. In this process, coded data may be renamed or merged into new categories (Glaser & Strauss, 1967). The constant comparison of data enables the generation of theory through systematic data analysis.

Selective Coding After identifying the core category, the researcher systematically relates it to other categories. In the selective coding stage, the researcher selectively samples new data with the core category in mind (theoretical sampling), which is a deductive part of grounded theory (Glaser, 1998). For instructional theory, it is likely that the core category will be methods of instruction, and other categories are likely to include the situations in which the methods were used and how well they worked.

Theoretical Coding Theoretical coding is applying a theoretical model to the data. Glaser emphasizes that the theoretical model should not be forced but emerge during the process of constantly comparing the data. Theoretical codes "conceptualize how the substantive codes may relate to each other as hypotheses to be integrated into a theory" (Glaser, 1978, p. 72). For instructional theory, data about how well the methods worked might be used to offer guidelines about which methods to use in which situations.

Theoretical Memoing Theoretical memoing is a continual process conducted in parallel with data collection, coding, and analysis. A memo is a write-up of some hypotheses the researcher has about categories, properties, and their relationships (Glaser, 1998). For instructional theory, this could include hypotheses about which methods should be combined and how they should be combined, unless there are direct data available to guide such syntheses of methods into "package deals."

Sorting and Writing Up Once the researcher has reached theoretical saturation of the categories, he or she starts sorting memos. The sorted memos generate a theoretical outline that is close to the written grounded-theory product (Glaser, 1978). This would be the instructional theory in its full glory.

Strauss and Corbin's Approach

Strauss and Corbin (1990) define grounded theory as "a qualitative research method that uses a systematic set of procedures to develop an inductively derived grounded theory about a phenomenon" (p. 24). This more specific focus is in contrast to Glaser's view that grounded theory is not limited to the realm of qualitative methods (Glaser, 2001, 2003). Strauss and Corbin (1990) also propose conducting a pre-research literature review to identify categories and relate them in meaningful ways, mentioning that "all kinds of literature can be used before a research study is begun" (p. 56). The coding processes they suggest are different from Glaser's approach as well.

Open Coding The researcher identifies categories and their properties by examining field notes and other documents line by line or even word by word.

Axial Coding After open coding, the researcher conducts axial coding by making explicit connections between categories and their properties.

Selective Coding Selective coding involves identifying the core category and relating other categories to that core category. In the case of instructional theory, the core category would likely be methods of instruction.

For axial coding, Strauss and Corbin provide a well-defined coding paradigm which consists of "phenomena," "causal conditions," "context," "intervening conditions,"[1] "action strategies,"[2] and "consequences"[3] (Strauss, 1987, p. 32). The coding paradigm helps the researcher build an "axis" for generating theory and "think systematically about data and to relate them in very complex ways" (Strauss & Corbin, 1990, p. 99).

Glaser (1992) cautions researchers not to "force" categories on the data instead of allowing them to "emerge" by using concepts such as "axial coding" and "coding paradigms." However, the coding paradigm might be most useful to novice researchers who need clear guidance on how to structure data (Kelle, 2005).

These two approaches to grounded theory development (Glaser's and Strauss & Corbin's) are useful tools for data-based theory development, particularly for the "observe what works and when" stage of that process (see Table 17.1).

2. Design-Based Research (DBR)

DBR is "a systematic but flexible methodology aimed to improve educational practices through iterative analysis, design, development, and implementation, based on collaboration among researchers and practitioners in real-world settings, and leading to contextually-sensitive design principles and theories" (Wang & Hannafin, 2005, pp. 6–7). We will describe the characteristics of DBR, principles that underlie it, and guidelines for conducting it.

3. Characteristics

DBR has the following characteristics:

---

1. *Editors' note: Equivalent to instructional situations in instructional theory.*
2. *Editors' note: Equivalent to instructional methods.*
3. *Editors' note: Equivalent to learning outcomes and instructional outcomes.*

- *It is driven by theory and prior research* (Cobb, Confrey, deSessa, Lehrer, & Schauble, 2003; DBRC, 2003; Edelson, 2002; Wang & Hannafin, 2005). DBR researchers seek to revise and refine the theory they selected at the outset, and they draw on prior research.
- *It is pragmatic* (Cobb et al., 2003; Collins, Joseph, & Bielaczyc, 2004; DBRC, 2003; Reigeluth & Frick, 1999; Wang & Hannafin, 2005). It is intended to refine both theory and practice, and the value of theory is appraised by the extent to which principles and concepts of the theory inform and improve practice.
- *It is collaborative* (Barab & Squire, 2004; Cobb et al., 2003; Collins et al., 2004; DBRC, 2003; Wang & Hannafin, 2005). DBR researchers collaborate and interact socially with practitioners in the design, implementation, and analysis aspects of the research.
- *It is contextual* (Collins et al., 2004; DBRC, 2003; Wang & Hannafin, 2005). DBR is conducted in real-world contexts rather than in laboratory settings. Therefore, research results are connected with the authentic setting. Also, guidance for applying generated principles is developed.
- *It uses multiple dependent variables* (Barab & Squire, 2004; Collins et al., 2004). DBR involves multiple dependent variables, including climate variables, outcome variables, and system variables.
- *It is integrative* (Wang & Hannafin, 2005). DBR uses a variety of research methods that "vary as new needs and issues emerge and the focus of the research evolves" (p. 10).
- *It entails systematic and comprehensive documentation* (Cobb et al., 2003; Edelson, 2002; van den Akker, 1999). "To support the retrospective analysis that is an essential element of design research, the design process must be thoroughly and systematically documented" (Edelson, 2002, p. 116).
- *It is iterative* (Cobb et al., 2003; Collins et al., 2004; DBRC, 2003; Wang & Hannafin, 2005). DBR processes are iterative cycles of analysis, design, implementation, and redesign. Formative evaluation is a critical element in DBR (Edelson, 2002; Reigeluth & Frick, 1999; van den Akker, 1999).
- *It is adaptive/flexible* (Barab & Squire, 2004; Cobb et al., 2003; Collins, 2004; DBRC, 2003; Edelson, 2002; Schwartz et al., 1999; Wang & Hannafin, 2005). Initial design plans are revised when necessary, to respond to emergent features of the setting. Although they should be flexibly adaptive, designs should also be consistent with important principles of learning.
- *It seeks generalization* (DBRC, 2003; Edelson, 2002; Wang & Hannafin, 2005). DBR researchers expand their focus beyond the current design context to look for generalization to other contexts. Of course, some methods and some causal relationships are situational—they do not generalize to other contexts. So a key to looking for generalization is to look for situationalities (contextual factors that you think may restrict the generalizability). If none seem important, then you have a case for generalization. If some seem important, then look for other methods (or variations of a

method) or causal relationships that might be appropriate for the other situations to which you might want to generalize, and try to extend your research into those contexts.

4. Principles of DBR

Principles of DBR include the following (Wang & Hannafin, 2005):

1. Support design with research from the outset.
2. Set practical goals for theory development and develop an initial plan.
3. Conduct research in representative real-world settings.
4. Collaborate closely with participants.
5. Implement research methods systematically and purposefully.
6. Analyze data immediately, continuously, and retrospectively.
7. Refine designs continually.
8. Document contextual influences with design principles.
9. Validate the generalizability of the design. (pp. 15–19)

5. Guidelines for Conducting DBR

Guidelines for conducting DBR include the following:

1. Identify a real-world problem (Cobb et al., 2003; Collins et al., 2004; DBRC, 2003; Wang & Hannafin, 2005).
2. Conduct a literature review and set theory development goals (Edelson, 2002; Wang & Hannafin, 2005). Adopt, adapt, or initiate a theory about learning and teaching, and clarify the theoretical intent.
3. Develop a collaborative partnership with practitioners (Barab & Squire, 2004; Cobb et al., 2003; Collins et al., 2004; DBRC, 2003; Wang & Hannafin, 2005).
4. Identify dependent and independent variables (Collins et al., 2004). Try to identify all the variables that affect any dependent variables of interest, rather than controlling them.
5. Develop an initial research plan (Wang & Hannafin, 2005).
6. Design, develop, and implement a design in one or more real-world settings (Collins et al., 2004; DBRC, 2003; Wang & Hannafin, 2005).
7. Generate a comprehensive and systematic record of the design process (Cobb et al., 2003; Edelson, 2002; van den Akker, 1999).
8. Collect data from multiple sources (Cobb et al., 2003; Wang & Hannafin, 2005). Use multiple methods, including observations, interviews, surveys, and document analysis.
9. Analyze data and evaluate the design (Wang & Hannafin, 2005). Conduct data analysis simultaneously with data collection and coding to improve the design and to address theory-generation goals.

10. Revise and refine the design (Collins et al., 2004; DBRC, 2003; Wang & Hannafin, 2005).
11. Iterate the processes of analysis, design, implementation, and redesign (Cobb et al., 2003; Collins et al., 2004; DBRC, 2003; Wang & Hannafin, 2005).
12. Report the results. Collins et al. (2004) suggest that there should be the following five sections:
    a. Goals and elements of the design.
    b. Settings where implemented.
    c. Description of each phase.
    d. Outcomes found.
    e. Lessons learned.

Wang and Hannafin (2005) suggest that DBR reports should generally include:

a. Purpose and goals
b. Design framework
c. Design setting and processes
d. Outcomes
e. Design principles

Design-based research is well suited for the last activity in each of the four approaches for constructing instructional theory shown in Table 17.1.

6. Formative Research

Formative research is a kind of developmental research or design-based research that is intended to improve three things: a particular case (product, event, or combination), an instructional theory related to that case, and descriptive theory related to the instructional theory. Its primary focus is on *improving*, rather than on proving. It can also be used to develop a new design theory instead of improving an existing design theory. It follows a case study approach and uses formative evaluation techniques. It is well suited to functional contextualism, for it explores how to make those three things (case, design theory, and descriptive theory) function better and it explores situational variables that influence how well they work.

The underlying logic of formative research is that if a case is designed using an instructional theory, whatever ways one can find to improve the case may illuminate ways to improve the instructional theory. Furthermore, what one learns about ways to improve the case and theory should illuminate the causal dynamics (descriptive theory) that underlie those improvements.

The major elements of formative research include:

- *observing* the instruction and interviewing the participants (learners and teachers) to identify *strengths* (what should not be changed), *weaknesses* (what should be changed), and *improvements* (what changes should be made) for the instruction,
- *repeating* the observations and interviews for each specific finding to test its trustworthiness and generalizability across different learners and different parts of the instruction (content, teachers, etc.),
- *looking* for variations in how well a method works; and, where there are important variations, exploring what *situationalities* may account for those variations,
- *implementing* potential *improvements* in the case as soon as possible, to test them in a similar manner,
- *asking* "why" questions in the interviews to gain insights into the *causal dynamics* that underlie the effects of different methods in different situations,
- *suggesting* potential improvements for the methods and situationalities in the *instructional theory*, based on your findings in the case, and
- *suggesting* potential improvements for the causal relationships in the *descriptive theories* that are related to the instructional theory.

Reigeluth and Frick (1999, chapter 26—Vol. 2), offer considerable guidance about how to conduct formative research: They report that the methodological procedures vary depending on whether the case is *designed* (based on an instructional theory) or is "*naturalistic*" (not designed based on an instructional theory). Furthermore, for naturalistic cases, the methodology varies depending on whether the observation is conducted *during* or *after* the case. This results in three major types of formative research studies:

1. *Designed cases*, in which the theory is intentionally instantiated for the research.
2. In vivo *naturalistic cases*, in which the formative evaluation of the instantiation is done *during* its application.
3. Post facto *naturalistic cases*, in which the formative evaluation of the instantiation is done *after* its application.

Table 17.2 Kinds of Formative Research Studies

	For an Existing Theory	For a New Theory
Designed Case	Designed case for an existing theory	Designed case for a new theory
In Vivo Naturalistic Case	*In vivo* naturalistic case for an existing theory	*In vivo* naturalistic case for a new theory
Post Facto Naturalistic Case	*Post facto* naturalistic case for an existing theory	*Post facto* naturalistic case for a new theory

Within each of these types of formative research studies, the methodological process also varies depending on whether the study is intended to improve an existing theory or to develop a new theory, resulting in six variations (see Table 17.2). Following is a brief summary of Reigeluth and Frick's methodology for each.

Designed Case to Improve an Existing Theory

1. *Select a design theory.* Begin by selecting an existing design theory that needs improvement.
2. *Design an instance of the theory.* Select a situation that fits within the general class of situations to which that design theory applies, and then design a specific application of the design theory (the case).
3. *Collect and analyze descriptive and formative data on the instance.* Conduct a formative evaluation of the design instance focusing on how to improve the case and on understanding the causal dynamics in it. Three techniques are useful for collecting the descriptive and formative data: observations, documents, and interviews. Conduct data analysis during the data collection process.
4. *Revise the instance.* Make revisions in the instance of the design theory based on the formative data.
5. *Repeat the data collection and revision cycle.* Several additional rounds of data collection, analysis, and revision are recommended. It is important to systematically vary what situationalities you can from round to round, within the boundaries of the theory.
6. *Offer tentative revisions for the theory.* Hypothesize an improved design theory based on your research findings.

Designed Case to Develop a New Theory

1. *Create a case that helps generate the design theory.* Begin by selecting a situation that fits within the general class of situations to which your new design theory is expected to apply. Then design a case for that situation, using experience, intuition, and trial and error. As you develop the case, you should develop a tentative design theory in parallel (methods, plus guidelines for when to use each).
2. *Collect and analyze descriptive and formative data on the instance.* (Same as above)
3. *Revise the instance.* (Same as above)
4. *Repeat the data collection and revision cycle.* (Same as above)
5. *Fully develop your tentative theory.* Revise and elaborate the tentative design theory based on your research findings.

Naturalistic Case to Improve an Existing Theory

1. *Select a design theory.* Begin by selecting an existing design theory that needs to be improved.

2. *Select a case.* Instead of creating an instance or case, select a case that is about to begin (for an in vivo study) or a case that has been completed (for a post facto study). The case should be in a situation that fits within the general class of situations to which the theory applies.

3. *Collect and analyze descriptive and formative data on the case.* There are three major kinds of data to be collected, based on the presence and absence of elements in the theory and in the case: (a) elements that are present in both the theory and the case; (b) elements that are present in the theory but absent in the case; and (c) elements that are absent in the theory but present in the case. These three kinds of data can be collected through observations, interviews, and documents.

4. *Offer tentative revisions for the theory.* Hypothesize an improved design theory based on your research findings.

Naturalistic Case to Develop a New Theory

1. *Select a case.* (Same as above)

2. *Collect and analyze descriptive and formative data on the case.* Use grounded theory techniques (either Glaser's or Straus and Corbin's) to study the case and identify instructional methods—and situationalities when possible. You should rely heavily on intuition, experience, and knowledge of relevant descriptive theory to form categories for methods and situationalities. However, you should go beyond such descriptive data to identify participants' suggestions (through interviews) for ways of improving the methods and their situationalities (if any).

3. *Fully develop your tentative theory.* Revise and elaborate your tentative design theory based on the research findings.

Given that the primary purpose of formative research is to *improve* rather than to *prove*, it is ideally suited for the last activity in each of the four approaches for constructing instructional theory shown in Table 17.1.

Conclusion

In this chapter, we began by discussing what kinds of knowledge need to be built, and we concluded that design theory is most useful to practitioners but descriptive theory is also useful. Second, we described how the "paradigm wars" have been counterproductive for instructional theory and advocated the use of functional contextualism as a helpful framework for building instructional theory. Third, we identified two major kinds of research for design theory: research to prove (confirmatory) and research to improve (exploratory). For both, preferability (usefulness) should replace validity (truthfulness) as the most important research criterion. Fourth, we described the "S curve" of development for instructional theories and argued that research to prove should only be done when a theory has approached its upper limit. Otherwise, research to improve a design theory is far more valuable.

Then we described four approaches that can be used to build design theory: (1) data-based; (2) values-based; (3) methods-based; and (4) practitioner-driven; and we encouraged readers to experiment and develop their own approaches. Finally, we described three research methods for developing design theory: (1) grounded theory development; (2) design-based research; and (3) formative research.

We would like to close by recommending to all who build instructional theory that you place your work in the context of the growing common knowledge base about instruction in an effort to continually improve that common knowledge base. Show where and how it fits and what unique contributions it makes that have not been offered by other theorists. And try to use existing terminology whenever the meaning is the same as yours. This will make life much easier for practitioners, graduate students, and researchers, and it will help our field to advance beyond the early stages of development.

References

Barab, S., & Squire, K. (2004). Design-based research: Putting a stake in the ground. *Journal of the Learning Sciences, 13*(1), 1–14.

Cobb, P., Confrey, J., deSessa, A., Lehrer, R., & Schauble, L. (2003). Design experiments in educational research. *Educational Researcher, 32*(1), 9–13.

Collins, A., Joseph, D., & Bielaczyc, K. (2004). Design Research: Theoretical and Methodological Issues. *Journal of the Learning Sciences, 13*(1), 15–42.

Design-Based Research Collective. (2003). Design-based research: An emerging paradigm for educational inquiry. *Educational Researcher, 32*(1), 5–8.

Edelson, D. C. (2002). Design research: What we learn when we engage in design. *Journal of the Learning Sciences, 11*(1), 105–121.

Eisenhardt, K. M. (1989). Building theories from case study research. *Academy of Management Review, 14*(4), 532–550.

Fox, E. J. (2006). Constructing a pragmatic science of learning and instruction with functional contextualism. *Educational Technology Research & Development, 54*(1), 5–36.

Glaser, B. G. (1978). Theoretical sensitivity: Advances in the methodology of grounded theory. Mill Valley, CA: Sociology Press.

Glaser, B. G. (1992). *Emergence vs. forcing: Basics of grounded theory analysis.* Mill Valley, CA: Sociology Press.

Glaser, B. G. (1998). *Doing grounded theory: Issues and discussions.* Mill Valley, CA: Sociology Press.

Glaser, B. G. (2001). *The grounded theory perspective: Vol.1. Conceptualization contrasted with description.* Mill Valley, CA: Sociology Press.

Glaser, B. G. (2003). *The grounded theory perspective: Vol. 2. Description's remodeling of grounded theory.* Mill Valley, CA: Sociology Press.

Glaser, B. G., & Strauss, A. (1967). *The discovery of grounded theory: Strategies for qualitative research.* Chicago: Aldine.

Kelle, U. (2005). "Emergence" vs. "forcing" of empirical data? A crucial problem of "grounded theory" reconsidered. *Forum: Qualitative Social Research, 6*(2). Retrieved July 11, 2007, from http://www.qualitative-research.org/fqs-texte/2-05/05-2-27-e.pdf.

Lewis, M. W., & Grimes, A. J. (1999). Metatriangulation: Building theory from multiple paradigms. *Academy of Management Review, 24*(4), 672–690.

Patton, M. (2002). *Qualitative research & evaluation methods* (3rd ed.). Thousand Oaks, CA: Sage.

Reigeluth, C. M., & An, Y. J. (2006). Functional contextualism: An ideal framework for theory in IDT. *Educational Technology Research & Development, 54*(1), 46–50.

Reigeluth, C. M., & Frick, T. W. (1999). Formative research: A methodology for creating and improving design theories. In C. M. Reigeluth (Ed.), *Instructional-design theories and models: Vol. 2.
A new paradigm of instructional theory* (pp. 633–651). Mahwah, NJ: Erlbaum.

Strauss, A. (1987). *Qualitative research for social scientists.* Cambridge, UK: Cambridge University
Press.

Strauss, A., & Corbin, J. (1990). *Basics of qualitative research: Grounded theory procedures and techniques.* Newbury Park, CA: Sage.

van den Akker, J. (1999). Principles and methods of development research. In J. van den Akker, N.
Nieveen, R. M. Branch, K. L. Gustafson, & T. Plomp (Eds.), *Design methodology and development
research in education and training* (pp. 1–14). The Netherlands: Kluwer Academic.

Wang, F., & Hannafin, M. (2005). Design-based research and technology-enhanced learning environments. *Educational Technology Research and Development, 53*(4), 5–23.

Weick, K. E. (1989). Theory construction as disciplined imagination. *Academy of Management
review, 14*(4), 516–531.

18
Instructional Theory for Education in the Information Age

CHARLES M. REIGELUTH

Indiana University

Charles M. Reigeluth received a BA in economics from Harvard University. He was a high school teacher for three years before earning his doctorate in instructional psychology at Brigham Young University. He has been a professor in the Instructional Systems Technology Department at Indiana University's School of Education in Bloomington since 1988, and served as chairman of the department from 1990 to 1992. His major area for service, teaching, and research is the process for facilitating district-wide paradigm change in public school systems. His major research goal is to advance knowledge to help school districts successfully navigate transformation to the learner-centered paradigm of education. He has published nine books and over 120 journal articles and chapters. Two of his books received an "outstanding book of the year" award from the Association for Educational Communications and Technology (AECT). He also received AECT's Distinguished Service Award and Brigham Young University's Distinguished Alumnus Award.

EDITORS' FOREWORD

Vision

- *To portray the relationship between instructional theory and the information-age paradigm of education*

Educational systems and their suprasystems' needs

- *Information-age educational needs are substantially different from industrial-age educational needs.*
- *Our educational systems must transform to a customized, learning-focused paradigm of education (from a standardized, sorting-focused paradigm).*

Instructional systems and their suprasystems' needs

- *Information-age educational needs are substantially different from industrial-age educational needs.*
- *Learning experiences must be designed to meet those new educational needs.*
- *Instructional theory must be designed to foster those learning experiences.*

Vision of an information-age educational system

Foundational principles
- *Customization and diversity*
- *Initiative and self-direction*
- *Collaboration and emotional development*
- *Holism and integration*

Main features
- *Attainment-based progress*
- *Personal record of attainments*
- *Criterion-based assessment*
- *Customized, flexible progress*
- *Customized, flexible goals*
- *Customized, flexible methods*
- *Personal learning plan*
- *New teacher roles (e.g., caring mentor, designer of student work, facilitator of the learning process)*
- *New student roles (e.g., worker, self-directed learner, teacher)*
- *Parents as partners in learning*
- *Community-based learning*
- *New roles for technology*

Main roles for technology
- *Record keeping for student learning (standards inventory, personal attainments inventory, personal characteristics inventory)*
- *Planning for student learning (develop a contract that specifies goals, projects, teams, parent and teacher roles, and the deadline for each project)*

- *Instruction for student learning (e.g., simulations, tutorials, drill and practice, research tools, communication tools, and learning objects). Instructional-event theory plays the largest role here.*
- *Assessment for (and of) student learning (integrated with instruction, use authentic tasks, provide immediate formative feedback, certify student attainments—summative assessment)*
- *These four major roles are seamlessly integrated, and such a comprehensive learning management system (LMS) serves other roles, as well.*

How instructional theory can help

- *We need sound guidance for the conduct of all teacher roles: mentor, designer, and facilitator.*
- *We need sound guidance for the design of technology's instructional roles.*
- *This common knowledge base must address systems of methods based on both means (approaches) and ends (outcomes) of instruction.*
- *We need sound guidance for the design of the other three major functions for technology —record-keeping, planning, and assessment systems—all seamlessly integrated with instructional systems.*

—CMR & ACC

INSTRUCTIONAL THEORY FOR EDUCATION IN THE INFORMATION AGE

The primary theme of this book is the need to build a common knowledge base for instruction. Toward that end, it has presented a framework and set of instructional theories and offered some terms for a common language, to initiate a dialogue about that common knowledge base. However, an important principle of systems theory is that a system must meet the needs of its suprasystem.[1] This chapter explores the relationship between this common knowledge base about instructional systems and the larger systems of education that they serve.

Educational Systems and their Suprasystems' Needs

Systems theorists have long shown that social systems must meet the needs of their suprasystem in order for that larger system to sustain them (Banathy, 1996; Checkland & Scholes, 1990). For example, a business must meet a need in its community (however small or large that community may be) in order for the community to be willing to give it resources (money). Similarly, a school system must meet the needs of its community in order for that community to continue to provide the school system with sufficient tax money and students.

The challenge today is that our society and the communities that comprise it have changed in significant, large-scale ways, as we have evolved from the

---

1. A suprasystem is a larger system in which a system is a part (a subsystem).

industrial age to the information age (see Reigeluth, 1999, chapter 1; chapter 1 in this volume). Knowledge work has replaced manual labor as the predominant form of work. There is a much greater need now for lifelong, self-directed learning. There is much greater complexity in our societal systems and technological tools, creating a much stronger need for such types of learning as higher-order thinking skills, problem-solving skills, systems-thinking skills, collaboration skills, emotional development, and character development.

Our educational system was designed for a different era—the industrial age—in which standardization and compliance were needed above all else. The dramatic change in the educational needs of our society is reminiscent of the transformative change in transportation needs that occurred as we evolved from the agrarian age to the industrial age. It became necessary to ship large quantities of raw materials and finished goods to and from factories. To try to improve the horse-and-wagon transportation system to meet these new needs could only provide a slight improvement in meeting those new needs. Turning to a different paradigm, the railroad provided a quantum improvement (an order of magnitude) in meeting the new needs. In a similar way, trying to improve the industrial-age educational system, with its one-size-fits-all, sorting-focused structure (see chapter 1), can at best only provide a slight improvement in meeting the new educational needs of the information age. Transforming it to a customized, learning-focused educational system can provide a quantum improvement in meeting the new educational needs. This has important implications for instructional theory, which I will address shortly.

Instructional Systems and their Suprasystems' Needs

Instructional systems are embedded within educational (or training) systems and therefore must also meet the needs of their suprasystem. Banathy (1991) identified four subsystems that can be viewed as levels of any educational system, and each of those subsystems has a primary process to be performed by a primary agent. The *learning experience system* resides primarily in the student and is focused on the process that a student goes through while learning. The *instructional system* resides primarily in the teaching agent (such as a teacher, textbook, or computer), whose primary process is providing instruction to facilitate the learning experience. The *administrative system* resides primarily in the administrators (such as the principal and the central office personnel), whose primary process is managing the instructional system, among other subsystems (financial, transportation, etc.). And the *governance system* resides primarily in the school board and other policymakers (on the national, state, and district levels), whose primary process is formulating policies to direct the administrative and instructional systems. Banathy proposes that the desired learning experiences should drive the design of the instructional system, which in turn should drive the design of the administrative system, and all of those systems should drive the design of the governance system.

The learning experiences must be designed in such a way as to meet the needs of the larger educational system, which in turn must be designed in such a way as to meet the needs of the information-age society in general and each community and student in particular. Otherwise, there will be continual dissatisfaction with, and turmoil in, our educational systems. And instructional theory must be designed to foster those learning experiences. Next, this chapter proposes a vision of an information-age paradigm of education in the form of (1) some principles that are based on the educational needs of an information-age society and (2) some features that the information-age paradigm of education might possess in order to implement those principles. Finally, it addresses how instructional theory can be most helpful in supporting this customized, information-age paradigm of education.

A Vision of an Information-Age Educational System

Based on the emerging educational needs of the information age, I propose that the new paradigm of education must be grounded in the following "Foundational Principles":

- **Customization and diversity.** First, different students learn at different rates. It is a waste of human potential to make some students wait for the rest of the class after they have learned what was being studied, just as it is a waste to make some students move on before they have learned it. Second, given the far greater complexity of our information-age society, we need citizens who have a much broader range of expertise than during the industrial age. Therefore, we must teach students different attainments from each other, capitalizing on their particular talents and strengths (in addition to a common core of "essential" attainments). Third, different students learn best in different ways. Therefore, we need to offer different instructional methods to different students—methods as different as those presented in unit 2 on different approaches to instruction. In sum, we need our students to be diverse (to learn different things, customized to their talents and interests), and we need our instruction to be diverse (to help students learn in different ways and at different rates, customized to their diverse profiles of strengths and intelligences).
- **Initiative and self-direction.** Given that students today can expect to have over 10 jobs in their lifetimes (http://www.bls.gov/news.release/pdf/nlsoy.pdf), and given the rapid rate at which technology and information change in many knowledge-work jobs, our society needs people who are lifelong learners. This means we need to cultivate in our students both a love of learning and the skills for learning. We need to help students become self-directed learners and develop a mindset of taking initiative in both problem solving and their own learning. This principle has been incorporated into many of the instructional theories in this volume.

- **Collaboration and emotional development.** Given that employers in the information age are increasingly organizing their knowledge workers into teams, and given that research has shown that emotional intelligence is more important than cognitive intelligence to one's success in life (see chapter 12), students need to develop their inter- and intrapersonal skills and knowledge. Just as the values and habits of compliance and conformity were taught in the "hidden curriculum" of the industrial-age paradigm, the values and habits of getting along well with others and understanding one's own emotions, strengths, and weaknesses must be taught in the hidden curriculum of the new paradigm. Learning experiences—and instructional theories—must be conceived in ways that foster the development of these qualities.

- **Holism and integration.** Given the increasing complexity of our systems in the information age, it is ever more important that we develop an understanding of systems thinking—the causal dynamics that underlie the behavior of our systems, such as biological, social, ecological, organizational, physical, and technological systems. All the various school subjects are inextricably interrelated, and it is a serious disservice to students to teach them in isolation from one another. It is also a serious disservice to just address the cognitive development of students, for social, emotional, psychological, physical, and all other aspects of human development are important and are interrelated with each other. Obesity, drug use, bullying, violence, teen pregnancy are but a few of the consequences of not addressing all aspects of human development. Also, research has shown the importance of emotion to successful cognitive learning (Greenspan, 1997). In the information-age paradigm of education, we must treat both the student and the content holistically. Certainly, methods for integrated learning (chapter 13) offer important guidance for implementing this principle.

Main Features for an Information-Age Educational System

Given these foundational principles, what should the instruction be like in the information-age paradigm of education? This is a central concern for instructional theory. The following are some of the main features that I propose, in the spirit of opening an active dialogue.

Attainment-Based Progress Perhaps the most important feature, to change the system from a sorting focus to a learning focus, is to change the student's progress from being time-based to being attainment-based. Rather than moving on to a new topic because it is Monday, students only move to a new topic when they master the current one.

Personal Record of Attainments To have attainment-based progress, it is clearly important to keep track of what each student has learned. In this record of attainments, each attainment is checked off as it is reached (creating an inventory of what the student has learned), and many attainments are accompanied by evidence, such as artifacts of various kinds (creating an electronic portfolio). The personal record of attainments provides an important basis for decisions about what is within reach to learn next (within Vygotsky's "zone of proximal development," 1978).

Criterion-Based Assessment The personal record of attainments also requires a change from norm-based assessment, in which students are compared with each other, to criterion-based assessment—a different paradigm of assessment in which student learning is compared to a standard or set of criteria. This requires setting a standard (and sometimes a progression of standards) for each attainment (see chapter 15), as well as assessment criteria.

Customized, Flexible Progress In attainment-based progress, a student is not forced to move on to a new topic *before* she has mastered it, and she is also allowed to move on to a new topic *as soon as* she has mastered it. In this way, every child succeeds, even those who are severely learning disabled. Some take longer than others and learn less in a year, but each learns to her maximum ability. The major concern that is voiced about this feature is that it is unmanageable or too expensive. I later address how technology makes it possible to manage all students' progress efficiently.

Customized, Flexible Goals As mentioned earlier, there is (1) a societal need for people who have very different kinds of expertise, and (2) a personal need for people to cultivate their individual talents and interests. While there is certainly a core of common knowledge that all students (citizens) should have, the information-age educational system also allows a considerable amount of learning time to be devoted to goals that each student and his parents think are important.

Customized, Flexible Methods Because students learn best in different ways, teachers provide different kinds of learning opportunities (different kinds of instructional methods). Those methods cater to the strengths of each student (see, e.g., Levine, 2002), but some methods are also chosen to cultivate students' strengths in different learning styles and formats, with guidance to support cultivating those new strengths. This is where instructional-event theory (see chapter 1) needs to play the biggest role, and teachers desperately need good guidance about which methods to use when.

Personal Learning Plan To manage customized attainment-based progress, customized goals, and customized methods, each student needs a personal learning plan, somewhat similar to the individualized education plans (IEPs) currently used in special education. This plan takes the form of a contract that is developed every so often (perhaps about two months) by the student, his parents, and a mentor-teacher. They jointly set the goals, but also plan the means and the deadlines, complete with milestones. This helps the student develop expertise in project planning, meeting deadlines, and self-directed learning.

New Teacher Roles To provide this kind of customized instruction, the teacher's role has to change from the "sage on the stage" to the "guide on the side." However, there are several roles involved in being a guide. First, the teacher is a *caring mentor*, a person who is concerned with the full, well-rounded development of the child. A mentor-teacher is responsible for perhaps 25 children of different ages for the span of a developmental stage in the child's life (typically about three or four years). Second, the teacher is a *designer of student work* (Schlechty, 2002). The student work may include project-based learning, experiential learning, discussion-based learning, skill-based tutorials, and all the other "galaxies" of methods described in units 2 and 3 of this book. Third, the teacher is a *facilitator of the learning process*. This includes helping to develop a personal learning plan, coaching or scaffolding the student's learning when appropriate, facilitating discussion and reflection, and arranging availability of various human and material resources. These are only three of the most important new roles that teachers serve, but not all teachers perform all the roles. Different kinds of teachers with different kinds and levels of training and expertise are involved (including students as teachers; see the next section).

New Student Roles First, learning is an active process. The student must exert the effort. The teacher cannot do it for the student. This is why Schlechty (2002) characterizes the new paradigm as one in which *the student is the worker*, not the teacher, and that the teacher is the designer of the student's work. Second, to prepare the student for lifelong learning, the teacher helps each student to become a *self-directed and self-motivated learner*. Students are self-motivated to learn when they first go to school. The industrial-age paradigm systematically destroys that self-motivation by removing all self-direction and giving students boring work that is not relevant to their lives. In contrast, the information-age system is designed to nurture that self-motivation through self-direction and active learning. Student motivation is the key to educational productivity and helping students to realize their potential. It also greatly reduces discipline problems, drug use, and much more. Third, it is often said that the best way to learn something is to teach it. Students are perhaps the most underutilized resource in our school systems. Furthermore, someone who has just learned something is often better at helping someone else learn it than is someone who learned it long ago. In addition to older students teaching slightly younger ones, peers can learn from each other in collaborative projects, and they can also serve as peer tutors. Therefore, new student roles include student as worker, self-directed learner, and teacher.

Parents as Partners in Learning Parents can do much to help their children learn. In some homes they already do; but in all too many they do not, and this creates a handicap for their children that the industrial-age educational system is unable to address. In an information-age educational system, parents are required to meet with the teacher and student to create each new personal learning plan, or contract. The role of the parents in supporting the child's learning is specified in that contract. In some cases, the plan and the work are designed for parents to learn with their child to advance their own education. Since the mentor-teacher is concerned with the whole, well-rounded development of the child, the teacher also supports the parents in their parenting skills. Anyone who has seen the "nanny" shows on TV knows how useful and appreciated this can be for the parents. This certainly requires some special training, and for extreme cases, like those shown on TV, a local social service agency partners with the teachers.

Community-Based Learning The community is involved in many ways. Some projects are designed to address community problems. Some community organizations and individuals serve as volunteers for offering service-learning projects. Some serve as mentors for students in a partnership with the teacher-mentor. Special relationships are developed with such community organizations as museums, zoos, libraries, hospitals, boys and girls clubs, town and county governments, correctional facilities, police and fire departments, and much more.

New Roles for Technology Just as customized learning requires new roles for teachers, students, parents, and the community, it also requires new roles for technology. In fact, the kind of customization described in this vision would be next to impossible for a teacher to carry out without technology. This is such an important feature for the Information-Age paradigm of education that the following section is devoted to describing it.

The Main Roles of Technology in an Information-Age Educational System

I currently see at least four main roles or functions for technology to make the kind of customization and learning focus described above feasible and cost-effective. Each of these is described next.

Record Keeping For Student Learning The personal record of attainments for each student, described earlier, could be a nightmare for teachers to maintain. Here is a role that technology is ideally suited to play, and it saves teachers huge amounts of time. It replaces the current report card, and it has three parts. First, it has a *Standards Inventory* that contains both required educational standards (national, state, and local) and optional educational standards for access by the teacher, student, and parents. Domain theory (see chapter 15) is highly instrumental for designing this technological tool. It presents a list of things that should or can be learned, along with levels or standards or criteria at which they can be learned. Second, it has a *Personal Attainments Inventory* that contains a record of what each student knows. In essence, it maps each student's progress on the attainments listed in the Standards Inventory (and perhaps some that are not yet listed there). It shows when each attainment was reached, which ones are required, what the next required attainments are in each area, and links to evidence of each attainment (in the form of summary data and/or original artifacts). Third, it has a *Personal Characteristics Inventory* that keeps track of each student's characteristics that influence learning, such as learning styles, profile of multiple intelligences, student interests, and major life events.

Planning for Student Learning The personal learning plan, or contract, could also be very difficult for teachers to develop for all of their students. Here, again, is a role that technology is ideally suited to play. It helps the student, parents, and teacher to (1) decide on *long-term goals*; (2) identify the full range of attainments that are presently *within reach* for the student; (3) select from those options the ones that they want to pursue now (*short-term goals*), based on requirements, long-term goals, interests, opportunities, etc.; (4) identify *projects* (or other means) for attaining the short-term goals; (5) identify *other students* who are interested in doing the same projects (if desired); (6) specify the roles that the teacher, parent, and any others might play in supporting the student in learning from the project; and (7) develop a contract that specifies goals, projects, teams, parent and teacher roles, and the deadline for each project.

Instruction for Student Learning Trying to "instruct" 25 students who are all learning different things at any point in time could be very difficult for teachers if they had to be the instructional agent all the time, as is typical in the industrial-age paradigm. However, technology can introduce the project to a student (or small team), provide instructional tools (such as simulations, tutorials, drill & practice, research tools, communication tools, and learning objects) to support learning during the project, provide tools for monitoring and supporting student progress on the project, and even provide tools to help teachers and others develop new projects and instructional tools. Instructional-event theory (see chapter 1) is direly needed here, as are instructional-planning theory and instructional-building theory.

Assessment for (and of) Student Learning Once more, conducting formative and summative assessments of students could be a nightmare for teachers, since students are not all taking a given test at the same time. And once again, technology can offer great relief. First, assessment is *integrated with instruction*. The plentiful performance opportunities that are used to cultivate skills and understandings are used for both formative and summative assessments. Second, the assessments present *authentic tasks* on which the students demonstrate their knowledge, understanding, and skill. Third, whether in a simulation or a tutorial or drill and practice, the technology is designed to evaluate whether or not the criterion was met on each performance and to provide *formative feedback* immediately to the student for the greatest impact. When the criteria for successful performance have been met on x out of the last y performances, the *summative assessment* is complete and the corresponding attainment is automatically checked off in the student's personal inventory of attainments. In the few cases where the technology cannot assess the performance, an observer has a handheld device with a rubric for assessment and personally provides the immediate feedback on student performances. The information from the handheld device is uploaded into the computer system, where it is placed in the student's personal inventory. Finally, technology provides tools to help teachers develop assessments and link them to the standards. Instructional-evaluation theory is critical for technology to reach its potential contribution to this role.

Note that these four roles or functions are seamlessly integrated. The record keeping tool provides information automatically for the planning tool. The planning tool identifies instructional tools that are available. The assessment tool is integrated into the instructional tool. And the assessment tool feeds information automatically into the record keeping tool. The label that comes the closest to describing this kind of comprehensive, integrated tool is *learning management systems* (LMS; Reigeluth et al., 2008; Watson, Lee, & Reigeluth, 2007). Also, please note that there are many other roles or functions for such a learning management system. These secondary functions include communications (e-mail, blogs, Web sites, discussion boards, wikis, whiteboards, instant messaging, podcasts, videocasts, etc.); LMS administration (offering access to information and authority to input information based on role and information type); general student data (student's address, parent/guardian information, mentor-teacher and school, student's location/attendance, health information); school personnel information (address, certifications and awards, location, assigned students, tools authored, student evaluations that they have performed, teacher professional development plan and records, repository of teaching tools, awards their students have received); and more.

It should be apparent that technology will play a crucial role in the success of the information-age paradigm of education. It will enable a quantum improvement in student learning, and likely at a lower cost per student per year than in the current industrial-age paradigm. Just as the electronic spreadsheet made the accountant's job quicker, easier, and less expensive, the kind of LMS described here will make the teacher's job quicker, easier, and less expensive. But instructional theory is sorely needed for technology to realize its potential contribution.

How Instructional Theory Can Help

This is but one speculative vision of the information-age paradigm of education. It is by no means certain that this is what the new paradigm will be like. One thing that is certain, however, is that paradigm change to customized instruction *will* happen in education. It is as inevitable as was the change from the agrarian-age paradigm (the one-room schoolhouse) to the current paradigm at the dawn of the industrial age. Think about how different and more complex our current paradigm is than the one-room schoolhouse. The new paradigm will be even more different, and the difference in complexity will be even greater. It is also likely that there will be far more diversity within this new paradigm than there is in our current paradigm.

While the vision described here is by no means certain, it is grounded firmly in an assessment of the educational needs of the information-age society— educational needs that are vastly different from those of the industrial age. Those needs are represented in the foundational principles described earlier. And the features described herein respond directly to those principles. Of course, other features may also respond to those principles and will likely represent much of the diversity of the new paradigm. I encourage readers to explore other features that might respond better to those principles.

My main reason for asking you to think about a vision for the information-age paradigm of education is that we need instructional theorists to contribute to a common knowledge base for the new paradigm, not for the paradigm of a bygone era. We need sound guidance for the conduct of all teacher roles: mentor, designer, and facilitator. We also need sound guidance for the design of technology's instructional roles. Both of these forms of guidance need to address all of the means and ends of instruction: means like the direct approach (chapter 5), discussion approach (chapter 6), experiential approach (chapter 7), problem-based approach (chapter 8), and simulation approach (chapter 9); and ends like memorization outcomes, skill outcomes (chapter 10), understanding outcomes (chapter 11), affective outcomes (chapter 12), and integrated learning outcomes (chapter 13). We need to move beyond isolated instructional theories to developing a common knowledge base for instruction that will meet the needs of the information-age paradigm.

We also need sound guidance for the design of the other three major functions for technology—record-keeping systems, planning systems, and assessment systems—all seamlessly integrated with instructional systems.

In this third and final volume in the trilogy of *Instructional-Design Theories and Models*, we have offered an understanding of the nature of instructional theory (chapter 1), the nature of instruction (chapter 2), the universal "first principles" of instruction (chapter 3), the situational nature of instruction (chapter 4), the architecture of instructional theory with its layers of design (chapter 14), domain theory for mapping attainments (chapter 15), learning objects (chapter 16), and approaches to theory building (chapter 17). Ali Carr-Chellman and I share the hope that these will help those of you who want to contribute to meeting these pressing needs to make the information-age paradigm of education a reality.

References

Banathy, B. H. (1991). *Systems design of education: A journey to create the future.* Englewood Cliffs, NJ: Educational Technology.

Banathy, B. H. (1996). *Designing social systems in a changing world.* New York: Plenum.

Checkland, P., & Scholes, J. (1990). *Soft systems methodology in action.* New York: Wiley.

Greenspan, S. I. (1997). *The growth of the mind and the endangered origins of intelligence.* Reading, MA: Addison-Wesley.

Levine, M. (2002). *A mind at a time.* New York: Simon & Schuster.

Reigeluth, C. M. (1999). In C. M. Reigeluth (Ed.), *Instructional-design theories and models: Vol. 2. A new paradigm of instructional theory* . Mahwah, NJ: Erlbaum.

Reigeluth, C. M., Watson, S. L., Watson, W. R., Dutta, P., Chen, Z., & Powell, N. (2008). Roles for technology in the information-age paradigm of education: Learning management systems. *Educational Technology, 48*(6).

Schlechty, P. (2002). *Working on the work.* New York: Wiley.

Vygotsky, L. (1978). *Mind in society.* Cambridge, MA: Harvard University Press.

Watson, W. R., Lee, S. K., & Reigeluth, C. M. (2007). Learning management systems: An overview and roadmap of the systemic application of computers to education. In F. M. Neto & F. V. Brasileiro (Eds.), *Advances in computer-supported learning.* Hershey, PA: Information Science.

Author Index

Subject Index

Page numbers in italic refer to Figures or Tables